Internationalizing Multiculturalism

Internationalizing Multiculturalism

Expanding Professional Competencies in a Globalized World

Edited by

Rodney L. Lowman

American Psychological Association

Washington, DC

Published by
American Psychological Association
750 First Street, NE
Washington, DC 20002
www.apa.org

To order
APA Order Department
P.O. Box 92984
Washington, DC 20090-2984
Tel: (800) 374-2721; Direct: (202) 336-5510
Fax: (202) 336-5502; TDD/TTY: (202) 336-6123
Online: www.apa.org/pubs/books
E-mail: order@apa.org

In the U.K., Europe, Africa, and the Middle East, copies may be ordered from
American Psychological Association
3 Henrietta Street
Covent Garden, London
WC2E 8LU England

Typeset in Goudy by Circle Graphics, Inc., Columbia, MD

Printer: Maple-Vail Book Manufacturing Group, York, PA
Cover Designer: Minker Design, Sarasota, FL

The opinions and statements published are the responsibility of the authors, and such opinions and statements do not necessarily represent the policies of the American Psychological Association.

Library of Congress Cataloging-in-Publication Data

Internationalizing multiculturalism : expanding professional competencies in a globalized world / edited by Rodney L. Lowman. — 1st ed.
     p. cm.
   Includes bibliographical references and index.
   ISBN 978-1-4338-1259-0 — ISBN 1-4338-1259-2 1. Multiculturalism. 2. Internationalism.
I. Lowman, Rodney L.

   HM1271.I5945 2013
   305.8—dc23
                                    2012029808

British Library Cataloguing-in-Publication Data
A CIP record is available from the British Library.

Printed in the United States of America
First Edition

DOI: 10.1037/14044-000

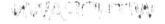

CONTENTS

CONTRIBUTORS

Virginia Floresca Cawagas, EdD, University for Peace, San José, Costa Rica

Wendy Chung, PhD, School of Management, Alliant International University, San Diego, CA

Ayşe Ciftçi, PhD, Purdue University, West Lafayette, IN

Nurcan Ensari, PhD, California School of Professional Psychology, Alliant International University, Los Angeles

Lawrence H. Gerstein, PhD, Ball State University, Muncie, IN

Erica J. Hurley, MA, Ball State University, Muncie, IN

Arpana Inman, PhD, Lehigh University, Bethlehem, PA

Louise Kelly, PhD, School of Management, Alliant International University, San Diego, CA

Sue A. Kuba, PhD, California School of Professional Psychology, Alliant International University, Fresno

Mark M. Leach, PhD, University of Louisville, Louisville, KY

Frederick T. L. Leong, PhD, Michigan State University, East Lansing

Beth Limberg, PhD, California School of Professional Psychology, Alliant International University, Sacramento

Patricia Denise Lopez, PhD, California School of Professional Psychology, Alliant International University, Los Angeles

Rodney L. Lowman, PhD, Organizational Psychology Programs, California School of Professional Psychology, Alliant International University, San Diego

Estela Matriano, EdD, Hufstedler School of Education, Alliant International University, San Diego, CA, and World Council on Curriculum and Instruction

Toh Swee-Hin (S. H. Toh), PhD, University for Peace, San José, Costa Rica

Monique M. Taylor, PhD, New York Institute of Technology, Nanjing, People's Republic of China

Danny Wedding, PhD, MPH, California School of Professional Psychology, Alliant International University, San Francisco

PREFACE

In recent years, it has become almost a cliché to speak of globalization and to say that we live in a borderless world. It is one thing to say it; it is another thing to live it.

It would be naive to suggest that all of our problems of multiculturalism—issues of gender, race and ethnicity, sexual orientation, ageism, religion, national origin, among others—have been resolved even in countries like the United States and those of Europe that have been working on them for a number of decades. Still, in terms of laws prohibiting discrimination and real progress in building a multicultural society, acceptance of differences, and intolerance toward hostile attitudes or behaviors, real progress has been made and continues to be made. We are well positioned to move to the "next big thing," which, this book argues, is the integration of internationalism into multiculturalism.

This book is published by the largest association of psychologists in the world, but it was not written solely for psychologists. Because the volume is intended to address its focal issues with "every professional" in mind and from the perspectives of professionals in any country, the examples intentionally cut across professions to illustrate how the constructs apply in different professional contexts. Necessarily, the book emphasizes some professions (in particular, psychology, business, education) more than others, but the hope is that any professional interested in internationalizing understanding of multiculturalism will also find much in the book that is helpful.

With such a broad intended audience and topic, the book is not intended to be a definitive treatise covering every aspect of its subject matter or the nuances of practice in every profession. Rather, it is written as an invitation to show the need for and potential of internationalizing professional practice. We have not covered every multicultural issue (e.g., there is no chapter on the increasingly important topic of age and ageism), and we have not covered every application. However, we have taken five of the most important major multicultural categories (race, gender, national origin, sexuality and gender identity, and religion and secularism) and tried to show why and how international perspectives matter in each of these areas. Similarly, the book addresses issues related to individuals, groups, organizations, education, mental health, and psychology to exemplify the practical application of these concepts to real-world professional practice.

PERSONAL HISTORY

Each contributor in this book was asked to include some personal information about his or her background and its relevance for writing about his or her respective topic. Indeed, as a psychologist, I am sometimes asked how I became interested in the intersection of multicultural and international issues because, at first glance, there might seem little in my upbringing that would predict the appeal of this subject.

My father was born and raised in Oklahoma. His mother had come to "Indian Territory," as Oklahoma was called before becoming a state, from Kentucky (where she was born) and Tennessee by way of Missouri. As my father's mother described it when she was interviewed in Geary, Oklahoma, in 1937 as part of the Indian-Pioneer History Project,

> I came with my parents in a covered wagon, from Urich, Missouri, to Butte. This place is now known as Oakwood; there was just a store and a post office when we came, and the mail was carried on horseback three times a week from Kingfisher. We had an old white mule and I often would ride this old mule and go to the store [for] what necessities we had money to buy. . . . Many a night and evening all the light we had was a brush fire built on the stove hearth. It kept some one replenishing the fire all the time. Of course, this let the smoke escape into the room and . . . would make our eyes smart and burn . . . [and] turned the ceilings black. We did not have money to keep stove oil all the time. . . .

When I was old enough I worked for $1.50 a week. In this way I helped my folks and bought my clothes for myself and some for my sister. . . . When we went to church and Sunday school we walked about three miles and to save our shoes we carried them and walked barefoot through the blackjacks. The rough paths would have scratched our shoes and worn our soles out but our feet would heal if we snagged or scratched them. We were not the only ones who did this. Most of our neighbors did the same . . . especially if they had to walk.[1]

The major diversity in Oklahoma back then was the coexistence of Native Americans and White settlers, many of whom had come to Indian Territory beginning with the Oklahoma Land Rush of 1889. There were considerable tensions between the White pioneers and the Indians (as they were then called). As my grandmother put it,

Indians were plentiful and [once] an Indian came and put his hand up to his face and looked in the window. I did not know there was anyone near until I saw his shadow on the wall. He was an old Indian and he would come in the house and take hold of you, talking all the time [but] no white people could understand him. Perhaps it was because we women were so scared of him. But he never hurt anyone.[2]

Thus, my father's family were pioneers, but my mother's background was quite different. The two had met in New York when my father, who made his career in the military as a pilot and administrator, returned from fighter pilot service in World War II and from incarceration in a POW camp. My mother, a Latina beauty, was a naturalized U.S. citizen. She had been born in what was then known as Spanish Honduras in Central America. Her mother was originally from Guatemala, and her father was a Canadian engineer who was overseeing the development and management of banana plantations for the United Fruit Company in Central America. An early picture of my mother, her sister, and two brothers shows them smiling and well dressed but standing with my grandmother near a ramshackle building. Spanish Honduras and Guatemala then, as now, were developing countries, quite poor, and my mother's parents carried pistols, used mostly for encounters with snakes and the like. The children grew up speaking both Spanish and English.

My mother was born in 1921 and, to hear her tell it—and as a storyteller, she told it often—life in Central America was idyllic and adventurous. In time, however, a presidential revolution made it necessary for the children

---

[1]Interview with Mrs. Ollie Lowman. (1937, December 14, pp. 1–3). Indian-pioneer history project (Augusta H. Custer, Interviewer). University of Oklahoma Libraries Western History Collections, Volume 56 (Interview ID: 9480). Retrieved from http://digital.libraries.ou.edu/whc/pioneer/papers/9480%20Lowman.pdf

[2]Interview with Mrs. Ollie Lowman, p. 4.

to be sent out of the country to what was then the "go-to" city for Central Americans, New Orleans. Her mother and ultimately her father followed. It was no longer safe for "foreigners" to live in Honduras.

Even in that era, New Orleans was not a typical American city. New Orleans then, like Miami now, was a hub of Latin American culture, and there were many nonstop flights to and from New Orleans and the Central American capital cities—Tegucigalpa, Managua, San Jose—and into the other countries among what were sometimes called then the "banana republics."

Growing up, we usually made annual family trips to both New Orleans and Oklahoma. My older brother and I were not infrequently sent to Oklahoma on our own by air on tiny prop planes for the summer pilgrimage, but we were never independently sent to New Orleans. Trips to Oklahoma were like going back in time.

The major "minorities" in Oklahoma in the years I spent there were Blacks (then called "Negroes" by the polite people and more derisive terms by others) and Native Americans (then called "Indians," rarely politely). The attitudes of my place-bound relatives toward those groups, reflecting the commonly encountered racism of the day, were far from enlightened. Most White people I encountered were unapologetically prejudiced against any groups perceived as being different from them (i.e., anyone from the United States who was not White, as well as those who were "foreign"), and they were not shy, at least with each other, about expressing their opinions. One of my favorite relatives, for example, was an aunt who had earned a university-based nursing degree at a time when few women worked who did not have to, and who had happily lived in the Philippines when her husband had been stationed there. Even she, however, shared the local prejudices and accused me of "trying to make liberals out of us" when I challenged some of the racist comments I heard her and others making. (Even today Oklahoma has one of the smaller percentages in the country of residents who were not born in the United States—5% as of 2008.[3])

In contrast, trips to New Orleans were like going to another country. From the time I could remember, my mother's sister lived with my maternal grandmother in a two-story shotgun-style house on Memphis Street in the Lakeview district in New Orleans. They had a screened-in porch on the second story through which you entered the house and where we spent a lot of time on summer nights trying to escape the dull, pulsing heat and the ubiquitous mosquitoes. Even with relatives there, my aunt and grandmother spoke to each other only in Spanish, and they seemed to argue spiritedly much

---

[3]U.S. Census Bureau. (2011). Table 38. Native and Foreign-Born Population by State: 2008. *U.S. Census Bureau, Statistical Abstract of the United States: 2011* (p. 43). Retrieved from http://www.census.gov/compendia/statab/2011/- tables/11s0019.pdf

of the time. (My correspondence with my mother's mother, *mi abuela*, was also in Spanish.) My aunt's second husband, who had died suddenly of a heart attack before I really knew him, had the last name of deBaroncelli. He was descended from a distinguished French lineage, and at one time he had run the French-language newspaper in New Orleans. Trips to the French quarter or occasional visits with my grandmother's network of Central American friends spoke to a culture that was complex and diverse—lively and engaged but not quite fitting in with their new country. Despite its being an international city, New Orleans was then, and remains today, a Southern American city in the most racist sense, and the Black–White tensions were as palpable as the thick humidity.

Growing up in a military family taught me to expect continual change, at least of place; to quickly adapt to a new culture; and to long for the next move and adventure, knowing the impermanence of the present one. It also caused me to feel like I did not belong in any particular place. My family's mixed origins, from both rural Oklahoma and sophisticated, if racist, New Orleans via Central America and Canada, diffused my identification with any one culture as a primary identity and, I suppose, predisposed me to be interested in international and multicultural issues. However, my upbringing, like those of many from such backgrounds, was a complex mix of cultural contradictions and compartmentalization. In my family, we never discussed or talked explicitly about issues related to race, gender equality, sexual orientation, or anything else concerning the topics of this book. Multicultural and international issues were all around us, but these issues were mostly invisible. As with many such families, the goal was a new and better life, putting the past behind them. Someday, it would be time to put these pieces together more coherently.

ABOUT THIS BOOK

Like me, each contributor to this book has his or her own story to tell related to internationalizing multicultural issues. The authors herein are well qualified, both personally and professionally, to write about their respective topics. As noted earlier, most have included something about their own personal background and how and why these issues apply to them personally. Some have woven their personal experiences intricately into their chapters, enriching the reader's understanding.

In addition to thanking the authors for their fine work, I acknowledge Leadership Worth Following and the International Multicultural Education Research Intervention and Training (I-MERIT) initiative at Alliant International University for their contributions to funding an initial meeting of

Alliant faculty, many of whom contributed chapters to this book. This meeting helped identify many of the issues that this book emphasizes.

Since its inception, Alliant has had a major commitment to multiculturalism long before it became fashionable. Its legacy institutions, the California School of Professional Psychology and U.S. International University, were present at the birth of the multicultural and international movements, respectively. Today, the merged institution of Alliant International University and its I-MERIT initiative strive to integrate across multicultural and international issues in students, faculty, and staff. This book has benefitted from the context of an institution that really cares about such issues.

Leadership Worth Following, another sponsor of the inaugural meeting, is a private consulting firm based in Dallas (and on whose advisory board I serve). It has dedicated itself to changing the world "one organization at a time." Unusual among consulting firms, it sets aside 10% of its pretax revenues for worthy causes.

Finally, I acknowledge the contributions of my family, Dr. Linda Richardson Lowman and Marissa Richardson Lowman. Both inspire all that I do and suffer my time spent on projects such as this with unusual support and good humor.

Internationalizing Multiculturalism

1

MULTICULTURAL AND INTERNATIONAL: WHY AND HOW BOTH SHOULD MATTER IN PROFESSIONAL PRACTICE

RODNEY L. LOWMAN

When people think of San Diego, California, where I currently reside, most know of its famous zoo, world-class beaches and water animal park, idyllic climate, and pervasive natural beauty. Yet the city of San Diego is only one part of San Diego County, the southwestern-most county in the 48 contiguous U.S. states and geographically one of the largest. Its borders extend 65 miles north to south and 86 miles from the Pacific Ocean eastward to include a number of smaller cities in the mountains and rural desert areas that collectively make a county roughly the size of the states of Rhode Island and Delaware combined. The county is bordered to the south by Mexico and is home to the busiest border crossing in the world. San Diego County has the second largest population in California after Los Angeles County. Its population is larger than that of 20 states in the United States.

Once known for being a majority White and conservative geographic area, the city of San Diego and its surrounding metropolitan areas now constitute a

DOI: 10.1037/14044-001
Internationalizing Multiculturalism: Expanding Professional Competencies in a Globalized World,
R. L. Lowman (Editor)

major urban area situated in an otherwise largely rural county. As of the 2010 census, San Diego was a majority minority city and county. The percentage of Whites in the county dropped from 55% in 2000 to 49% in 2010. In contrast, the percentage of Latinos during the same period grew by 32%, the Asian population by 34%, and the population of Pacific Islanders by 11% (Jimenez, 2011). Not all minorities grew in percentage during the first decade of the 21st century. The African American population declined during the decade by 5% and Native Americans by 7% (Jimenez, 2011), although there are still 18 Native American reservations in the county.

From 2006 to 2010, 23.1% of the population in San Diego County was foreign born, which was only slightly lower than the 27.2% for the state of California during the same period. (U.S. Census Bureau, 2012). In San Diego, there are large populations of naturalized citizens and expatriates who came to the area from China, Iraq, Iran, Israel, Japan, Mexico, the Philippines, Saudi Arabia, Vietnam, and many other countries.

Variations of this same story can be found everywhere in the United States and increasingly around the world—and not just in the urban coastal centers. Clearly, professionals can no longer be competently trained if they learn to work primarily with one race, one age group, or one gender. Professionals must know about multiculturalism in all its variations, including the international context, which is the focus of this book. Indeed, in the 2010 U.S. Census, 12.9% of the U.S. population was foreign born (U.S. Census Bureau, 2012; see also Grieco et al., 2012). The United States is now an international, multicultural nation, and professionals ignore this fact at their own peril.

The purpose of this book is to explain how having both multicultural and international skills can enhance professional competence in any field. The book broadens the concept of multiculturalism to encompass internationalism—in other words, it internationalizes multiculturalism. The contributing authors approach this task in two ways. First, they show how major multicultural categories (e.g., race, gender) can be understood from an international perspective. Second, they apply these concepts to real-world professional practice in several specific areas (e.g., business, mental health). The contributing authors review the relevant research and suggest practical recommendations for expanding the modern professional's multicultural and international competence. Additionally, they present their own personal stories about integrating multiculturalism and internationalism (as I have done in the book's preface).

To contextualize the issues in this book, this introductory chapter explores the intersecting and distinct aspects of internationalism, arguing that in today's increasingly boundary-free world, international issues are as compelling as those associated with "domestic multiculturalism." The chapter concludes with an explanation of how the rest of the book is organized.

PROGRESS IN U.S. MULTICULTURALISM: CHALLENGES REMAIN

Appreciation for progress made can be obscured by the injustices that remain to be corrected (see, e.g., Eibach & Keegan, 2006). It might be imagined that the emplacement of legal mechanisms against discrimination would have a snowball effect such that remaining barriers to a truly integrated and accepting society would disappear. Alas, reality proves otherwise. Multicultural progress is closer to a graph that shows the day-to-day ups and downs of a sputtering economy that is ever so slowly inching upward despite the quotidian setbacks. Slow, steady progress is not dramatic but incremental, better appreciated retrospectively.

Yet real progress has been made in the past half century. In my lifetime, social revolutions have fought for—and in many cases won—legal recognition of equal rights among citizens of all races in many parts of the world; likewise, women are treated more equitably, and baby steps have been made toward equality for people of all sexual orientations. Those changes have often come at a steep price, one painful step at a time, and there is unquestionably more work to be done as new plateaus are reached and tested and new, unanticipated challenges come to society's attention, usually through the persistent voices of the oppressed and their advocates.

Advances have also been made in the training of professionals in multicultural issues. Not so long ago, such issues were largely absent from training programs, and professional disciplines proceeded with little concern about the effects of race, gender, sexual orientation, or national origin on their respective specialties (see Heppner et al., 2009). Today, most professional training programs in fields that involve direct interaction with people (e.g., the mental health professions, education) include multicultural training as a standard part of their curricula and practicums.

However, our next major opportunity to increase our multicultural acuity, even if it is somewhat forced on us by economic circumstances, has broadened and made more complex what were once domestic multicultural issues, expanding them into the international arena. If the roots of multiculturalism are in the context of discrimination and mistreatment of specific categories of people (e.g., women; gay, lesbian, bisexual, and transsexual individuals; older people; African Americans; Asian Americans; Native Americans), the new world order forces us to contend with diversity in the context of a decentralized world that is increasingly without boundaries. Of course, international issues do not have to detract from the battles remaining to be fought domestically in the traditional concerns of multiculturalism that, like a whistling teapot, continue to demand our attention. Nonetheless, I believe we make a mistake when we fail to contextualize our country-specific "isms" (e.g., racism, sexism, heterosexism) in a broader, world-relevant context. This book therefore aims to address this perspective. Specifically, the authors demonstrate how the traditional categories of multiculturalism (e.g., race, gender, sexual orientation) can incorporate international perspectives. Today's major missing element in professional training, we argue, is the extension of multiculturalism to an internationalized context (see Belkin & Fricchione, 2005; Bourgeois, 2011; Burke, 2009).

Although everyone's professional competence can be advanced through international multiculturalism, this book will especially appeal to professionals in health and human services (e.g., mental health practitioners), managers and business professionals, and educators. Mental health professionals have always been well positioned to have an impact on the health and well-being of clients, who today are more multicultural and international than ever. Because of the expansion of traditional businesses into multinational markets, business professionals are now also well positioned to have such an impact on their multicultural–international employees and customers. Additionally, educators all over the world and at every level—from kindergarten through college or university—increasingly must address multicultural and international issues in their curriculum content (e.g., addressing immigration and other important issues of the day) and in meeting students' needs. All three of these groups— health and human services professionals, businesspeople, and educators— increasingly require the ability to understand other people's cultural contexts (see, e.g., Leong, Pickren, Leach, & Marsella, 2012; Murdoch-Eaton, Redmond, & Bax, 2011). Thus, the chapters and case examples in this book focus on international multicultural competencies geared toward these three groups. However, the main principle of expanding awareness to consider others' international and multicultural context is relevant to all professionals—engineers, veterinarians, scientists, customer service staff—the list goes on and on.

LIMITATIONS OF MULTICULTURALISM IN INTERNATIONALISM

Multiculturalism has limitations as a starting point for considering internationalism. As Shome (2012) put it:

Multiculturalism . . . came about in Western nations as a nation-based policy or framework for managing and redressing inequalities within a national polity. It came about as a response to racial inequalities produced by North Atlantic slavery, the annihilation of indigenous populations, and postcolonial migrations into the West. But today, the challenge is to consider whether this problem space of multiculturalism is the same as the problem space(s) produced by new forms and disjunctures of transnational relations, as well as by new assertions of modernities that go beyond nation-bound limits of multiculturalism. (p. 149)

This suggests that the process of integrating multiculturalism and internationalism will need to be carefully developed so that it does not simply export U.S.- or Western-centric multicultural constructs to the international context. At the same time, there is much to be learned from the expansive multicultural literature and experiences that may, in a variety of ways, inform internationalism. Additionally, this book argues that those who care about multiculturalism cannot ignore the internationalization process that has infused so much of civilization around the world.

THE "NEW" INTERNATIONAL MULTICULTURALISM

Today's world is multicultural in ways far beyond the traditional American categories of the concept, and thus professionals can make errors of omission and commission if they simply try to apply domestic multicultural models to our new cultural realities. They may categorize persons born in other countries as "just another minority" and fail to recognize, for example, that people who have emigrated from their native country to escape political oppression may have experienced great loss in prestige and income because they are unable to resume their profession. They may also underestimate the prevalence of posttraumatic stress disorder (PTSD) in such individuals. Regarding mental health disorders more generally, American professionals may not contextualize the role of what seeking services might mean in individuals' countries of origin, or they may not understand the grieving and loss associated with having left one's home to be able to earn money in a wealthier country to send back to one's family. For business professionals, internationalism is the new reality of day-to-day work, and the ability to manage teams whose members are located all over the world can be a standard competency expected of employees. As a final example of why internationalism matters, services in a variety of areas (e.g., coaching and business consultation, medical and psychotherapeutic services) can increasingly be delivered electronically all over the world. Knowing the cultures of the professional's clients becomes as important as if one were working with the dominant minority cultures represented in one's own geographic area.

This book therefore aims to help professionals from a variety of backgrounds begin or extend the process of becoming more internationally competent in their professional work. This international focus is relevant even to those whose practices are limited to one geographic area. Featuring contributions from a variety of experts, each chapter demonstrates ways in which the traditional categories of multiculturalism can be expanded and enriched by internationalism.

How Hate Persists

Current challenges of multiculturalism are not confined to any one country or region. From the perspective of the negative aspects of multicultural internationalism, discrimination on the basis of nonchosen human characteristics (e.g., race, age, sexual orientation, gender) is a near-universal societal phenomenon. We also know a good deal more than we once did about the mechanisms through which people discriminate on the basis of stereotypes (see, e.g., Wright & Taylor, 2007).

Prejudice against those who are "different" is neither new nor a social problem that has been solved once and for all. It extends back to early tribalism, when it may have had survival value. To paraphrase Rodgers and Hammerstein's famous lyrics in *South Pacific*, you've got to be carefully taught to hate and fear (Oscar Hammerstein II, cited in Etier, 2012; see also Most, 2000).

Why Hate Persists

Social psychologists (e.g., Devine, 1995), among others, have tried to better understand why negative views of others who are ostensibly not like oneself or one's group persist in modern, supposedly more enlightened times. They differentiate between *stereotyping,* which occurs when characteristics of some members of a group are automatically attributed to all such group members, and *prejudice,* which occurs when negative characteristics are attributed to members of a group different from one's own. Individual difference variables (e.g., the need for structure and authoritarianism) can contribute differentially to each of these dynamics (see Newheiser & Dovidio, 2012; Reynolds, Leavitt, & DeCelles, 2010).

Pettigrew (1979) extended Gordon Allport's classic study on prejudice and racism to consider the *fundamental attribution error*. Through this mechanism, people with negative views of people from certain groups can, in effect, overattribute bad things to specific traits of group members, underestimating the role of situational factors in causing or influencing problematic behavior. Conversely, positive things that happen to individuals can be attributed to chance or deferential treatment rather than to effort. Such views can result in there being little contact with people in the negatively perceived group and thus little interaction to provide evidence to counter the rigidly held views.

Lack of contact can also help explain the persistence of stereotypes and prejudice despite considerable efforts to create more ecumenical societies. The *contact hypothesis*, formulated by Allport (1954), holds that prejudice and stereotyping can be decreased by increasing the contact individuals have with those in their respective outgroups. Indeed, Binder et al.'s (2009) important longitudinal study demonstrated that prejudice may decrease with increased contact, and decreased (or low) contact can increase prejudice. Refining the social contact hypothesis, it is not enough, research suggests, simply to put outgroups together. This must be done carefully and thoughtfully to ensure positive outcomes (see Gaertner & Dovidio, 2005).

Increasingly, however, research also points to the role of automatic (some would say unconscious) cognitive–affective processes through which views that may conflict with a person's explicitly held beliefs remain influential (see Amodio & Devine, 2006). As a person ages, the mechanisms that temper automatic responses through conscious ones may decline, resulting in more, rather than less, explicit prejudice (Gonsalkorale, Sherman, & Klauer, 2009). Automatic responses, however, can be positive as well as negative and can activate egalitarian rather than prejudicial motivation (Johns, Cullum, Smith, & Freng, 2008).

Even when society's or subgroups' customs and norms make it inappropriate to espouse discrimination toward outgroups, there can be unconscious and automatic fear-driven reactions to those who are different. Withdrawal can invoke protective mechanisms that are not consistent with explicit beliefs. Our tribal instincts (e.g., van Vugt, 2011) can cause us to put our own group's needs above those of people who are perceived to be different from us. Furthermore, it may seem as if there is so much diversity in Westernized countries that we cannot make the effort to worry about diversity in other countries.

THE NEED TO REVISE THE CONCEPT OF MULTICULTURALISM

Yet our old conceptualization of multiculturalism is limiting. Today's multicultural issues stretch across national boundaries and force us to confront a new and rapidly changing world order, one much too complex to be confined by constructs that to date have (often appropriately) focused our multicultural attention internally, within our own country. It does not matter if you are a psychologist, a teacher, a lawyer, a nurse, or a physician; chances are, whatever your profession, you will be dealing with an assortment of international issues in working with your clients over the course of your professional life. Perhaps you are a mental health practitioner who will address the needs of a refugee in Los Angeles, or the manager of a corporate team with members located all over the world. Or perhaps you are an educator teaching a diverse group of students new to this country who need not only educational but also legal and professional assistance. Regardless of the field in which you work, knowing about the multicultural–international issues of your clients is not just a "nice" or "enlightened" thing to do. The contributors to this book argue that it is part of the required competency domain of any 21st-century professional.

Today's professionals to some extent—and tomorrow's almost certainly—will need to work not just with the indigenous multiculturalism of their own country but also with the multiculturalism that comes from engaging with diverse people from all over the world—and with people from other countries living in one's own. A few basic templates, at the least, are needed to ensure international multicultural competence. Furthermore, our understanding of traditional multicultural areas, this book argues, will need to be reconceptualized, incorporating both international and local perspectives. Examples include the following: How does one work with people from a transplanted culture in the context of a country to which they have immigrated? When business teams consist of people all over the world, do our current theories for assessment creating change still apply? Do our extant theories of multiculturalism help us understand the values and beliefs of persons who come to a classroom with histories of abuse and trauma in another country?

DEFINITIONS

There are no single, absolute definitions of *multicultural* or *international*, the foci of this book. Still, working definitions will be useful to orient the reader. The American Psychological Association's (APA's) *Guidelines for Multicultural Education, Training, Research, Practice, and Organizational Change for Psychologists* (2003) provides the following definitions:

> The terms *multiculturalism* and *diversity* have been used interchangeably to include aspects of identity stemming from gender, sexual orientation, disability, socioeconomic status, or age. Multiculturalism, in an absolute sense, recognizes the broad scope of dimensions of race, ethnicity, language, sexual orientation, gender, age, disability, class status, education, religious/spiritual orientation, and other cultural dimensions. (p. 380)

What this definition is saying, essentially, is that multiculturalism concerns the categories of personal identity that we traditionally use to group individuals. Although the definition is neutral on the ways such categorization can be used, in practice, minorities placed within such categories have experienced discrimination and prejudice. And multicultural backgrounds interact with international backgrounds to create even more categories of diversity. We therefore need to reduce some of this complexity and to provide a framework for learning and application, which is the primary purpose of this book. As a working definition for *multicultural*, I would adapt the APA definition on page 10 slightly by suggesting that multiculturalism addresses concerns within a single culture or nation, with particular focus on race and ethnicity, gender, sexual orientation, age, religion, and national origin.

A working definition of *international* is more complex (see Scholte, 2004) because it has not been limited to a few domains and because concern with internationalism has to date been driven more by economic factors (see, e.g., Held, McGrew, Goldblatt, & Perraton, 1999) than by social justice concerns. There is little basis for disagreeing with what has now become an almost cliché notion that societies have "gone global" and those who would be left behind do so at their own peril. Yet understanding the idea conceptually does little to integrate it into existing knowledge or professional practice. As Held, McGrew, Goldblatt, and Perraton (1999) noted,

> [Globalization] lacks precise definition. Indeed, globalization is in danger of becoming, if it has not already become, the cliché of our times: the big idea which encompasses everything from global financial markets to the Internet but which delivers little substantive insight into the contemporary human condition. Clichés, nevertheless, often capture elements of the lived experience of an epoch. In this respect, globalization reflects a widespread perception that the world is rapidly being moulded into a shared social space by economic and technological forces and that developments in one region of the world can have profound consequences for the life chances of individuals or communities on the other side of the globe. (p. 1)

In this book, we aim to move beyond the cliché to demonstrate how traditional constructs of multiculturalism will benefit from adding international perspectives to the discourse, emphasizing the need to understand and change how we interact with others. For the purposes of providing a working definition for this volume, I define *international* simply as the approach to multiculturalism that involves both what happens in one's own culture and in at least one other—that is, in the context of two or more countries. Here, an international approach considers how multicultural issues cross international boundaries, addresses the needs of immigrants, and struggles with the tension between the universal (racism in all countries) and the particular (discrimination among individuals on the basis of their national origin). This definition intentionally reflects not so much a precise definition as a working one intended to help orient the reader.

INTERNATIONALISM AS THE NEW NORMAL

We could, of course, discuss the concept of internationalism from a starting point of any one country; however, the major, but by no means exclusive, focus in this book is internationalism in the U.S. context. The United States is often regarded as being somewhat internationally insular, but with its population of more than 307 million, it is now the third largest country in the world after China (1.3 billion) and India (1.1 billion; Central Intelligence Agency [CIA], 2011c). Furthermore, with its periodic influx of immigrants, it is certainly one of the most diverse.

The changing world economic order, like it or not, also thrusts internationalism on the United States. The idea of America as the unrivaled economic world leader is rapidly changing (see, e.g., Subacchi, 2008), and this alone has greatly increased the need for the United States to become more engaged around the world, especially in new, nonmilitary ways. Its economic competitors are rapidly rising in both power and stature—and in democracy, with all its messy complications. Many other countries threaten to burst out of their historic status (in the past century, at least) as Third World countries, changing the United States' role in the international arena. Beyond the obvious current examples (China and India), there are a number of once-poor countries that are increasingly major economic players. Brazil, for example, has a current per capita income of $10,800, and Mexico's per capita income has risen to $13,900. Both are still low compared with the current U.S. per capita income of $47,200, but as the two countries have developed, a middle class has emerged (CIA, 2011a). These are only two examples of countries that are experiencing huge economic growth and are rapidly creating a new world order in which income is differentially perhaps (at the country level at least) more evenly distributed. Demand for goods and services in formerly poor countries is rapidly rising because of this economic growth, and with this has come an increased demand for professional services and increased geographic mobility.

WHAT ARE INTERNATIONAL COMPETENCIES?

Becoming *internationally competent* is in many ways more complex than mastering the domestic multicultural competencies that enable professionals to work successfully with persons of different races, genders, ages, and sexual orientations. As with multicultural competencies, there is more to international competencies than ticking off a list of "now mastered" skills. It is not possible, of course, for professionals to master the complexities and nuances of working with people from each and every international background. Furthermore, so-called domestic multicultural competencies interact with international ones to create even more possible types of clients (e.g., an aging lesbian from Afghanistan). We therefore need to reduce some of that complexity and to provide a framework for learning and application, which is the primary purpose of this book.

From the perspective of professionals working with clients, we can break down the major types of issues for which international competence may be relevant into two categories: (a) working with internationals in one's own country and (b) working with internationals in their country.

Working With Internationals in One's Own Country

Professionals in the United States and other countries today will likely work with a wide range of clients representing multiple cultures and will also likely have occasion to work with immigrants to the culture from other countries. For example, a physician might have clients who are African American and Latino but also clients who are first-generation Vietnamese or Chaldean immigrants. Similarly, mental health professionals increasingly must address the particular mental health needs of immigrants (see, e.g., Beiser, Feng, Hyman, & Tousignant, 2002).

Immigration to the United States

Nations can be divided into those that are net-out migrators or net-in migrators. For some time, the United States has been a major importer of persons from other countries (see, e.g., Migration Policy Institute Data Hub, 2009), although it now has greater competition for importing talent. In 2008, the United States ranked 31st out of 282 nations in terms of net migration rate; 76 countries were net importers of people, 146 were net exporters, and 59 were neutral as to importation (i.e., migration in was matched by migration out; see http://www.nationmaster.com/graph/imm_net_mig_rat-immigration-net-migration-rate).

Migration continues to increase in many parts of the world. As with a number of (mostly wealthy) countries, the United States is a major importer of people from other countries, but it does not lead the net immigration pack. The United Arab Emirates (UAE), for example, has a net migration in rate of 19 migrants per 1,000 population (CIA, 2011b); only approximately 19% of the UAE's population are UAE nationals (Kapiszewski, 2006).

Immigration occurs for many reasons, including joining family members already in another country, escaping political oppression, and seeking out opportunities for economic advancement. Most but not all of the countries that are net exporters of people are poorer (e.g., the Philippines, Guatemala, Mexico), politically repressed (e.g., Iran), or both (e.g., Afghanistan).

The Philippines provides a good example of a country that is a net exporter of people. There, it is common for young adults to be trained in college in English in highly marketable professions (e.g., nursing, engineering) with the expectation that they will work abroad and send money home.

According to the U.S. Census Bureau (2010), 36.7 million (12% of the population) were foreign born, and 33 million (11%) were native-born with at least one foreign-born parent in 2009, which means that approximately 23% of Americans are either first- or second-generation U.S. residents. These figures on foreign-born residents likely underestimate the size of the relevant population, however, because immigrant children, although often native born, may experience many of the same issues as their parents. Overall, the likelihood of professionals in any U.S. region finding themselves in the position of working with persons born outside of the United States or with first-generation clients is increasing.

In the United States, those who were foreign born are more likely to come from Latin America in general and Mexico in particular. The U.S.-born children of these immigrants generally exceed national averages for education and income (U.S. Census Bureau, 2011).

The distribution of immigrants is uneven across the states (see Malone, Baluja, Costanzo, & Davis, 2003). Immigrants to the United States are more likely to settle in the most populous states. Within the states with the largest immigration populations, the percentage of the population that is not native born is large: California, 26.8%; New York, 21.7%; New Jersey, 19.8%; Florida, 18.5%; and Texas, 16%. States with the highest percentages of immigrants are mostly the larger ones, but other, smaller states (e.g., Hawaii, 17.8%; Nevada, 18.9%; Massachusetts, 14.4%) are included. From the perspective of professional practice, in states such as California and New Jersey, for example, if these figures projected from the general population to client populations, professionals would have a one in four or one in five chance that any particular client would be foreign born. Such individuals may seek assistance for similar reasons to native-born clients, but assuredly they come to the professional with complex cultural contextual issues.

Although the foreign-born U.S. population is modally found in the larger states and cities, the national distribution is actually somewhat diffuse and growing everywhere, particularly in the southern states. Indeed, in every state in the United States as well as the District of Columbia, the percentage of foreign-born residents increased from the 1990 to the 2000 census (Malone et al., 2003). Some of the increases were dramatic. With the exception of Maine, every state experienced double- to triple-digit expansion of its foreign-born population in the 1990s with the highest percentage increases occurring in North Carolina (273.7%), Georgia (233.4%), Nevada (202%), and Arkansas (196.3%). These relative changes to some degree reflect a baseline rate that for some states was small, but these figures also point to a major increase in non-U.S.-born residents throughout most of the country.

Of course, no professional can be equally competent in working with individuals from each and every country, but neither are all countries equally represented among immigrants to the United States. In 2009, for example, the most foreign-born persons in the country came, in order, from Mexico (the largest home country by far at 29.8%), the Philippines (4.5%), India (4.3%), China (3.7%), Vietnam (3.0%), El Salvador (3.0%), Korea (2.6%), Cuba (2.6%), Canada (2.1%), and the Dominican Republic (2.1%; Batalova & Terrazas, 2010). Collectively, these countries accounted for almost 60% of the immigration to the United States in 2009.

Knowing about the major international cultures represented in one's geographic area and having a generic template of how international issues affect clients' worldview in ways relevant for the particular work at hand is a helpful start. Institutions (e.g., hospitals, schools, universities) also need to identify the most common immigrants in their client population and communities to ensure that, at the institutional level, their staff are competent to work with them.

Working With Immigrants and First-Generation Families

Having established that the odds are high that many, if not most, professionals will encounter people born in other countries in their professional work, what competencies are needed to work with them?

Specific competencies of course depend on the type of professional work one does. Some good practical guides have been published (e.g., Tarver, & Harden, 2011). Of general importance is understanding the client's culture of origin as it relates to being able to establish a professional relationship with the client and the particular professional work to be done. Thus, a medical doctor or nurse practitioner providing a medical procedure may need little knowledge about the client's culture of origin except as it relates to the complexities of establishing a trusting relationship with any diverse patient, helping to ensure that there is compliance with the self-directed care that often follows assessment and intervention and the ability to understand and relate to the patient's family. However, the meaning of symptoms in a culture, the use of somatization to express psychological stressors, and the role of the family in supporting the patient can also be important factors to be taken into account even when working with a narrowly physical problem.

For a psychologist or counselor working with a client, for a high school teacher, or for an attorney, to name only a few fields, knowledge of the culture of origin, the client's (or client's family's) reasons for leaving their homeland, and the way in which the transition to the new country was made and whether it has been successful are considerations that may help bring many concerns to the surface. When addressing refugee client's needs, it is essential to be sensitive to his or her reasons for coming to the new country. When torture or abuse were part of the reasons for relocation, consideration of posttraumatic stress disorder may need to be taken into account, whatever the specific reasons for which help was sought.

Language issues are also relevant. The professional will never know all languages represented in a diverse international–multicultural population. Access to competent translators may be needed, but with the understanding that translators sometimes may not capture important nuances. When it is immigrants' own children translating for their parents or relatives, there needs to be sensitivity to the context into which this places the child, in some respects reversing traditional roles and, on occasion, creating conflicts of interest, such as when the translation concerns misdeeds at school.

Professionals also need to be aware that no matter what the motivators were to come to the United States or however horrific were the circumstances in the home country, migration to a new country is inherently stressful for many. Both immigrants and their children are at risk for increased mental health and other health difficulties (Kennedy & McDonald, 2006; Lamberg, 2008), but resilience and susceptibility to problems vary by group (see Lee, 2011). Although for many the stress and adverse impact lessen with time in the United States, this is not true for all immigrant groups (see Takeuchi, Alegría, Jackson, & Willams, 2007).

Reasons for the increased rates of distress are numerous and include unemployment, status changes, poverty, lack of linguistic fluency in the new country, cultural assimilation stress, and even reactions to the new physical environment (Callister, Beckstrand, & Corbett, 2011; Dealberto, 2007). Symptoms or beliefs may vary by culture (e.g., Caplan et al., 2011) and may include attributions made to spiritual or behavioral factors affecting likelihood of, or comfort with, help seeking. Although professional sensitivity to mental and physical health issues associated with immigration status is always desirable, professionals also need to understand that differences among various groups of immigrants are common (e.g., Chaumba, 2011), and generalizations across all such groups are therefore risky.

In short, the immigrant or second-generation person in the professional's consultation room is not just another client. Understanding the client's contextual concerns (which may include, among others, health problems, depression, anxiety, family disorders, and bullying) will be an important part of the assessment process. Reaching out to understand the client's life history in another culture and reasons for emigrating will help establish the all-important therapist— or consultant–client relationship. Taking the time to understand, at least at a basic level, the client's cultural beliefs and values both in the parent country and in their new home will help the professional be more effective in delivering services.

Working With Internationals in Their Own Countries

Disappearing boundaries are the norm now, but this is only one part of the story for most professionals as technology increasingly trumps geography. In the area of executive and personal coaching, for example, it is common to provide services across the world by Internet or teleconferencing. The technology—and the demand—is such that one could easily have a practice composed mostly (or entirely) of those residing in other countries. There are also an increasing number of professional services being delivered in delivery systems other than traditional face-to-face encounters in areas as diverse as coaching (e.g., Ghods, 2010; Rankin, 2010), education (Youngman, 2011), health (e.g., "Military health system pursues telehealth options," 2011; Nieves, Briscoe, Edwards, & Flores-Carrera, 2011), and mental health (e.g., Boisvert, Lang, Andrianopoulos, & Boscardin, 2010).

In delivering professional services internationally, professionals must do more than just beam their services electronically around the world. They must understand the meaning of behavior in the context of the cultures in which it occurs, and they must learn the cultural significance of behavior and symptoms in another culture—engaging with the client in the client's context, not simply bringing expertise from on high. Many of the chapters in this book elaborate how international contexts matter for professional work internationally. For example, prevalence rates for various mental health disorders have been demonstrated to vary around the world (Hurley & Gerstein, Chapter 9, this volume; Merikangas et al., 2011).

There are also an increasing number of professionals who provide professional services while traveling abroad. Examples include health and mental health care professionals who go abroad during disasters or emergencies. These duties are often far more complex than anticipated, and increasingly professional associations rightfully suggest the need for special training to provide such care (see, e.g., Mattar, 2011; Schafer, Snider, & van Ommeren, 2010; Schininà, Aboul Hosn, Ataya, Dieuveut, & Salem, 2010). Additionally, medical tourism (see, e.g., Turner, 2011) has become a growth market, as patients cross boundaries in search of less expensive or better services. Such international work is not limited to health and mental health but also includes technological services (Bernovich & Tin, 2009).

The increased numbers of military professionals deployed internationally, particularly in war zones, suggest an expanded need for multicultural–international training (see, e.g., Scannell-Desch, & Doherty, 2010). Such professionals need to understand not just the military culture in which services are provided but also the cultures of the countries in which they have been deployed.

Finally, there are many professions (e.g., nursing; see Habermann & Stagge, 2010) in which international migration is common. Such professionals will inevitably have to deal with both multicultural and international issues.

PROFESSIONAL ASSOCIATION GUIDELINES AND ETHICS CODES AND MULTICULTURAL GUIDELINES

There is no shortage of ethical codes (e.g., APA, 2010; British Psychological Society, 2009; Canadian Psychological Association, 2000) and guidelines (e.g., APA, 2003) relevant to professional work with multicultural groups. The APA has been a leader in this area both in terms of guidelines being issued and in terms of an extensive literature on the topic. An important milestone was passed when the APA (2003) promulgated as official policy its *Guidelines for Multicultural Education, Training, Research, Practice, and Organizational Change for Psychologists*. The guidelines, briefly listed, are as follows:

1. Psychologists are encouraged to recognize that, as cultural beings, they may hold attitudes and beliefs that can detrimentally influence their perceptions of and interactions with individuals who are ethnically and racially different from themselves.
2. Psychologists are encouraged to recognize the importance of multicultural sensitivity and responsiveness, knowledge, and understanding about ethnically and racially different individuals.
3. As educators, psychologists are encouraged to use the constructs of multiculturalism and diversity in psychological education.
4. Culturally sensitive psychological researchers are encouraged to recognize the importance of conducting culture-centered and ethical psychological research among persons from ethnic, linguistic, and racial minority backgrounds.
5. Psychologists strive to apply culturally appropriate skills in clinical and other applied psychological practices.
6. Psychologists are encouraged to use organizational change processes to support culturally informed organizational (policy) development and practices.

Thereafter, these guidelines were applied to a number of areas of psychological practice (e.g., consultation, Arredondo & Reinoso, 2003; see also Pope-Davis, Coleman, Liu, & Toporek, 2003). However, such guidelines originated primarily from the perspective of domestic (in particular, U.S.) concerns with race, ethnicity, and the like and were not created with international issues in mind. Still, many of the guidelines have generic applicability.

Additionally, APA's (2010) *Ethical Principles of Psychologists and Code of Conduct* incorporates multicultural considerations as do those of other professional associations of psychologists (e.g., British Psychological Society, 2009; especially, Canadian Psychological Association, 2000) For example, in the Ethics Code of the APA, part of General Principle D: Justice states, "Psychologists exercise reasonable judgment and take precautions to ensure that their potential biases, the boundaries of their competence and the limitations of their expertise do not lead to or condone unjust practices." Part of General Principle E: Respect for People's Rights and Dignity states,

> Psychologists are aware of and respect cultural, individual and role differences, including those based on age, gender, gender identity, race, ethnicity, culture, national origin, religion, sexual orientation, disability, language and socioeconomic status and consider these factors when working with members of such groups. Psychologists try to eliminate the effect on their work of biases based on those factors, and they do not knowingly participate in or condone activities of others based upon such prejudices.

Additionally, Standard 2, Competence, emphasizes the need to practice only within the boundaries of one's competence. Standard 2.01b states that

> Where scientific or professional knowledge in the discipline of psychology establishes that an understanding of factors associated with age, gender, gender identity, race, ethnicity, culture, national origin, religion, sexual orientation, disability, language or socioeconomic status is essential for effective implementation of their services or research, psychologists have or obtain the training, experience, consultation or supervision necessary to ensure the competence of their services, or they make appropriate referrals, except as provided in Standard 2.02, Providing Services in Emergencies.

Other professional groups have also promulgated relevant guidelines and materials. The Canadian Psychological Association (2000), for example, defines *unjust discrimination* as

> activities that are prejudicial or promote prejudice to persons because of their culture, nationality, ethnicity, colour, race, religion, sex, gender, marital status, sexual orientation, physical or mental abilities, age, socio-economic status, or any other preference or personal characteristic, condition, or status. (p. 6)

Leach and Harbin (1997), however, found that there was only a 21% overlap between the APA Ethics Code standard on nondiscrimination and the psychology ethics codes found in 23 other countries.

It is not only psychologists who have been involved with multicultural guidelines. For example, the American Evaluation Association's *Guiding Principles for Evaluators* (American Evaluation Association, 2009) notes the importance of multicultural competencies, and guidance for teacher education is available (see, e.g., McFadden, Merryfield, & Barron, 1997). Fortier (2010) conducted dissertation research that resulted in recommended internationally relevant multicultural competencies for managers. The *Code of Ethics for Nurses* of the American Nursing Association (which describes itself as being "the profession's nonnegotiable ethical standard"; ANA; 2001a) added a provision to its ethics code in 2001 that states: "The nurse, in all professional relationships, practices with compassion and respect for the inherent dignity, worth and uniqueness of every individual, unrestricted by considerations of social or economic status, personal attributes, or the nature of health problems" (ANA, 2001b). Medical doctors are mandated by the *Code of Medical Ethics* of the American Medical Association (2001; see also Veatch, 1997, 2000) to be "dedicated to providing competent medical care, with compassion and respect for human dignity and rights" and to "support access to medical care for all people." In contrast, the recommended ethics code of the American Bar Association's (2010) *Model Rules of Professional Conduct* makes no reference to multicultural or international issues, only requiring (in Rule 6.1) that an attorney contribute a certain number of hours to pro bono work. In short, many professions in the United States make reference in their ethics codes to multicultural responsibilities (though some do not). Few, however, explicitly deal with international issues.

Most of the published professional guidelines are elaborations of professional expectations of addressing historic issues of discrimination and prejudice. The American versions of such guidelines (e.g., APA, 2003) are generally based on a critique of Western perspectives. For example, the APA (2003) multicultural guidelines state, "Psychology has been traditionally defined by and based upon Western, Eurocentric, and biological perspectives and assumptions" (p. 395). They single out for special consideration race, ethnicity, and the need for psychologists to address multicultural perspectives. Although the guidelines do not say so and although much of what is contained therein could apply to international issues, they are mostly written from the apparent perspective of American diversity issues.

Of course, there have also been some milestones in particular areas in which important books and articles have provided guidance in the international context; some such fields include psychology (e.g., Gerstein, Heppner, Ægisdóttir, Leung, & Norsworthy, 2009; Heppner et al., 2009; Singaravelu

& Pope, 2007), medicine, (e.g., Frenk et al., 2010), nursing, and management. Zakaria (2011) wrote an important book on the expanding role of internationalism in the American context.

My own institution, Alliant International University, has been grappling with the intersection of multicultural and international competencies for some time. As an American-based university with campuses or programs in Latin America and Asia, we have been asking questions about what we should expect our students, faculty, and staff to know in the context of a university with "international" as its middle name. A list of the multicultural–international competencies that we have developed is shown in Exhibit 1.1.

STRUCTURE OF THIS BOOK

This book consists of two major parts. In Part I, each chapter identifies a "traditional" area of multicultural interest and shows how it is enriched by considering the same issues in the context of other countries or immigrants to this country. Here are a few highlights.

Race and Ethnicity

In the United States, *race and ethnicity* generally refer to government-defined groupings (e.g., African American, Asian American, Hispanic). In the international spectrum race and ethnicity may have a number of other categories and meanings, and beliefs equivalent to racism may be found in countries such as those in which most people are of the same skin color but there is prejudice and discrimination among those of different skin color, or those from different tribes. In Chapter 2, Monique Taylor provides a provocative glimpse at concepts of race viewed through African Americans and through Palestinian eyes in the context of the Middle East. She shows the ubiquity of ingroup and outgroup perspectives and of the difficulties of helping those in another country understand how and why race matters. She also shows how her own journey to understanding developed from these experiences.

Gender

Economic and civil rights discrimination against women occur throughout the world. Chapter 3, by Virginia Cawagas, a recognized authority in women's issues, explores the ubiquity of gender discrimination, particularly against women, and notes the various forms it may take in different countries. Her chapter points to major causes of the pervasive discrimination against women, including militarization, but also identifies the differences between

EXHIBIT 1.1
Multicultural and International Competencies, Alliant International University

A. Competencies that apply to faculty, staff, and students
1. A positive, proactive, and nonjudgmental attitude toward diverse cultural and international identities and in their interpersonal and professional interactions
2. A multicultural skill set for understanding oneself and being able to successfully navigate intercultural transactions
3. The ability to engage effectively in difficult dialogues about multicultural and international issues

B. Competencies that apply to faculty and students
1. Ability to transfer and apply insights from one's group, region, or nation-state and culture to another to create knowledge and understanding in areas of professional practice
2. Have general knowledge of various local and international cultures as it relates to one's own field to include cultural differences and similarities, the dimensions of privilege and power, identity, social and political issues, communication, and personal expression
3. Understanding of at least two cultures, preferably covering at least two countries
4. Understanding of problems and issues related to race, gender, social class, and other issues within the two cultures
5. Demonstrate an ability to conceptualize and deliver culturally competent professional services in their respective areas to diverse populations
6. Faculty and students should be able to show respect, affirmation, and adaptability to diverse cultures and nationalities with which they interact
7. Faculty and students should be able to communicate effectively regarding multicultural and international issues

Desired/aspirational: faculty and students should demonstrate skills and abilities in a second language; one of the two languages should be Alliant's language of instruction

C. Competencies applying primarily to faculty
1. Demonstrate familiarity with a different worldview and demonstrate skills, awareness, and knowledge in teaching, international content, and settings
2. Understand and model multiculturalism and respect for international perspectives in their interactions, teaching, professional practice and research

D. Competencies applying primarily to staff
1. Be able to recognize that different cultural styles exist and should be taken into account when working with culturally different student, staff, and faculty populations
2. Be able to demonstrate customer service skills in dealing effectively with multicultural/international communities

Note. Used with permission of Alliant International University.

more developed ("North") and less developed ("South") countries concerning how women are and have been treated.

National Origin

Discrimination on the basis of national origin persists around the world and in many ways is the essence of "internationalism," particularly in the context of immigration of persons from one country to another. Leach, Leong, Inman, and Ciftçi (Chapter 4) demonstrate that *nation* is a relevant level at which to focus in the process of understanding people. They demonstrate how professionals can conceptualize national origin and integrate that learning to better understand and serve the needs of their clients, as well as how national origin can be the basis for inappropriate assumptions and stereotypes.

Sexual Variations

Although there is widespread discrimination and rights violations found throughout the world against those with sexual orientations differing from the norms, countries differ widely in their manifestations of this. In Chapter 5, Sue Kuba explores commonalities and differences among some of the most and least tolerant countries and in so doing notes the near universality of discrimination against sexual minorities around the world. Her chapter helpfully examines three countries in which policies have been fairly supportive of lesbians, gays, bisexuals, and transgendered individuals and three that have been particularly oppressive.

Religion, Nonreligion, and Spirituality

Beth Limberg (Chapter 6) discusses one of the least studied, but highly influential, aspects of multicultural-international issues: religion, nonreligion, and spirituality. She explores how religion can hold different meanings in different cultures and how nonbelievers can experience prejudicial treatment and discrimination in many parts of the world.

Part II of this book considers internationalizing multicultural issues in a variety of applications. These include the following.

Individuals and Groups

Lopez and Ensari (Chapter 7) show how the modern work organization can be a complex combination of international-multicultural issues at both the individual and group level. The modern business context is international, and these authors illustrate the complexities of and opportunities for managing work teams without boundaries. Their case study provides an excellent example of how multiculturalism and internationalism interact at the intersection of the individual and team levels and what can be done to help make international teams function effectively while still recognizing multiculturalism.

Organizations

Kelly and Chung (Chapter 8) extend the Ensari and Lopez chapter to consider how international issues matter at the organizational level. They point to the important role of leaders in creating appropriate climates, and much of what they report is as relevant to nonbusiness organizations. They also provide an illuminating case study.

Mental Health

Hurley and Gerstein (Chapter 9) identify how and why mental health disorders must increasingly be approached as a multicultural and international phenomenon. They note the competencies needed by mental health professionals across a range of settings and applications and extend the thinking on international-multicultural training in mental health professions. Many of their major points may also apply to areas of health care beyond mental health.

Education

How we can best train youth for a multicultural and international world is the focus of the chapter by Matriano and Toh (Chapter 10). They dig deeply into their work on global education and show how a number of important issues are intertwined, including power and control. They demonstrate that international–multicultural issues are the "new normal" for education.

Professional Education Through International Travel and Work

Danny Wedding (Chapter 11) presents a chapter filled with practical guidance on managing the challenges of international travel and development opportunities. This chapter demonstrates that professionals who travel abroad learn much about multiculturalism and internationalism.

In the final chapter of the book, I examine common themes that cut across the various chapters. I make the argument that we no longer have the choice to focus on either multicultural or international issues as independent areas. The new focus for those who care about multiculturalism must also be internationalism. Issues related to "righting wrongs" in the context of a single culture are addressed as well as those that involve extending understanding by considering the ways in which discrimination is found in all cultures.

CONCLUSION

It is difficult to find just the right terms to convey the importance of adding international issues to the repertoire of all professionals. Such a process can lead to intense debates about whether there is really anything novel in integrating international issues into multicultural ones. We believe that international issues are additive to the traditional multicultural ones, that there are general principles that can be extended to these concerns, but also that consideration of international issues will make for better theory and practice in most professional practice disciplines. The ultimate goal is not just to improve academic understanding, it is to change societies everywhere, starting with the professionals, to increase understanding and decrease prejudice and discrimination.

REFERENCES

Allport, G. W. (1954). *The nature of prejudice*. Cambridge, MA: Addison-Wesley.

American Bar Association. (2010). *Model rules of professional conduct: Rule 6.1: Voluntary pro bono public service*. Chicago, IL: Author. Retrieved from http://www.americanbar.org/groups/professional_responsibility/publications/model_rules_of_professional_conduct/rule_6_1_voluntary_pro_bono_publico_service.html

American Evaluation Association. (2009). Guiding principles for evaluators. *American Journal of Evaluation, 29*, 397–398. doi:10.1177/10982140080290040601

American Medical Association. (2001). *Code of medical ethics of the American Medical Association*. Chicago, IL: Author. Retrieved from http://www.ama-assn.org/resources/doc/ethics/ethics-in-hand-physician-version.pdf

American Nursing Association. (2001a). *Code of ethics for nurses*. Silver Spring, MD: Author. Retrieved from http://www.nursingworld.org/MainMenuCategories/EthicsStandards/CodeofEthicsforNurses/Code-of-Ethics.aspx

American Nursing Association. (2001b). *2001 approved provisions*. Silver Spring, MD: Author. Retrieved from http://www.nursingworld.org/MainMenuCategories/EthicsStandards/CodeofEthicsforNurses/2110Provisions.aspx

American Psychological Association. (2003). Guidelines for multicultural education, training, research, practice, and organizational change for psychologists. *American Psychologist, 58*, 377–402. doi:10.1037/0003-066X.58.5.377

American Psychological Association. (2010). *Ethical principles of psychologists and code of conduct (2002, Amended June 1, 2010)*. Retrieved from http://www.apa.org/ethics/code/index.aspx

Amodio, D. M., & Devine, P. G. (2006). Stereotyping and evaluation in implicit race bias: Evidence for independent constructs and unique effects on behavior. *Journal of Personality and Social Psychology, 91,* 652–661. doi:10.1037/0022-3514.91.4.652

Arredondo, P., & Reinoso, J. (2003). Multicultural competencies in consultation. In D. B. Pope-Davis, H. L. K. Coleman, W. M. Liu, & R. L. Toporek (Eds.), *International handbook of multicultural competencies in counseling & psychology* (pp. 330–346). Thousand Oaks, CA: Sage.

Batalova, J., & Terrazas, A. (2010). *U.S. in focus. Frequently requested statistics on immigrants and immigration in the United States.* Washington, DC: Migration Policy Institute. Retrieved from http://www.migrationinformation.org/feature/display.cfm?ID=818

Beiser, M., Feng, H., Hyman, I., & Tousignant, M. (2002). Poverty, family process, and the mental health of immigrant children in Canada. *American Journal of Public Health, 92,* 220–227. doi:10.2105/AJPH.92.2.220

Belkin, G. S., & Fricchione, G. L. (2005). Internationalism and the future of academic psychiatry. *Academic Psychiatry, 29,* 240–243. doi:10.1176/appi.ap.29.3.240

Bernovich, D., II, & Tin, K. M. (2009). IESC Geekcorps: Development for the new millennium. In C. E. Stout (Ed.), *The new humanitarians: Inspiration, innovations, and blueprints for visionaries: Vol. 2. Changing education and relief* (pp. 235–240). Westport, CT: Praeger/Greenwood.

Binder, J., Zagefka, H., Brown, R., Funke, F., Kessler, T., Mummendey, A., . . . & Leyens, J.-P. (2009). Does contact reduce prejudice or does prejudice reduce contact? A longitudinal test of the contact hypothesis among majority and minority groups in three European countries. *Journal of Personality and Social Psychology, 96,* 843–856. doi:10.1037/a0013470

Boisvert, M., Lang, R., Andrianopoulos, M., & Boscardin, M. (2010). Telepractice in the assessment and treatment of individuals with autism spectrum disorders: A systematic review. *Developmental Neurorehabilitation, 13,* 423–432. doi:10.3109/17518423.2010.499889

Bourgeois, J. A. (2011). Academic psychiatry: An international, innovative specialty. *American Psychiatry, 35,* 349–353.

British Psychological Society. (2009). *Code of ethics and conduct. Guidance published by the Ethics Committee of the British Psychological Society.* Leicester, England: Author. Retrieved from http://www.bps.org.uk/sites/default/files/documents/code_of_ethics_and_conduct.pdf

Burke, E. A. (2009). Incorporating internationalism into diversity training. In J. L. Chin (Ed.), *Diversity in mind and in action: Vol. 2. Disparities and competence* (pp. 173–188). Santa Barbara, CA: Praeger/ABC-CLIO.

Callister, L., Beckstrand, R., & Corbett, C. (2011). Postpartum depression and help-seeking behaviors in immigrant Hispanic women. *Journal of Obstetric, Gynecologic, and Neonatal Nursing, 40,* 440–449. doi:10.1111/j.1552-6909.2011.01254.x

Canadian Psychological Association. (2000). *Canadian code of ethics for psychologists* (3rd ed.). Ottawa, Canada: Author. Retrieved from http://www.cpa.ca/cpasite/userfiles/- Documents/Canadian%20Code%20of%20Ethics%20for%20Psycho.pdf

Caplan, S., Paris, M., Whittemore, R., Desai, M., Dixon, J., Alvidrez, J., & Scahill, L. (2011). Correlates of religious, supernatural and psychosocial causal beliefs about depression among Latino immigrants in primary care. *Mental Health, Religion & Culture, 14,* 589–611. doi:10.1080/13674676.2010.497810

Central Intelligence Agency. (2011a). *The world fact book: Country comparison: GDP—per capita income (PPP).* Retrieved from https://www.cia.gov/library/publications/the-world-factbook/rankorder/2004rank.html

Central Intelligence Agency. (2011b). *The world fact book: Country comparison: Net migration rate.* Retrieved from: https://www.cia.gov/library/publications/the-world-factbook/rankorder/2112rank.html

Central Intelligence Agency. (2011c). *The world fact book: Country comparison: Population.* Retrieved from: https://www.cia.gov/library/publications/the-world-factbook/rankorder/2119rank.html

Chaumba, J. (2011). Health status, use of health care resources, and treatment strategies of Ethiopian and Nigerian immigrants in the United States. *Social Work in Health Care, 50,* 466–481. doi:10.1080/00981389.2011.581999

Dealberto, M. J. (2007). Why are immigrants at increased risk for psychosis? Vitamin D insufficiency, epigenetic mechanisms, or both? *Medical Hypotheses, 68,* 259–267. doi:10.1016/j.mehy.2006.07.040

Devine, P. G. (1995). Prejudice and out-group perception. In A. Tesser (Ed.), *Advanced social psychology* (pp. 467–528). Boston, MA: McGraw-Hill.

Eibach, R. P., & Keegan, T. (2006). Free at last? Social dominance, loss aversion, and white and black Americans' differing assessments of racial progress. *Journal of Personality and Social Psychology, 90,* 453–467. doi:10.1037/0022-3514.90.3.453

Etier, B. (2012, February 28). Close-up of an American activist: Oscar Hammerstein II—*Out of My Dreams. Technorati* blog post. Retrieved from http://technorati.com/business/article/close-up-of-an-american-activist

Fortier, D. (2010). Identifying multicultural managerial competencies: Informing the content of a master's program in international management. *Dissertation Abstracts International Section A, 70,* pp. 4353.

Frenk, J., Chen, L., Bhutta, Z. A., Cohen, J., Crisp, N., Evans, T., . . . Zurayk, H. (2010). Health professionals for a new century: Transforming education to strengthen health systems in an interdependent world. *The Lancet, 376,* 1923–1958. doi:10.1016/S0140-6736(10)61854-5

Gaertner, S. L., & Dovidio, J. F. (2005). Understanding and addressing contemporary racism: From aversive racism to the common ingroup identity model. *Journal of Social Issues, 61*, 615–639. doi:10.1111/j.1540-4560.2005.00424.x

Gerstein, L., Heppner, P., Ægisdóttir, S., Leung, S., & Norsworthy, K. (Eds.) (2009). *International handbook of cross-cultural counseling: Cultural assumptions and practices worldwide*. Thousand Oaks, CA: Sage.

Ghods, N. (2010). Distance coaching: The relationship between the coach-client relationship, client satisfaction, and coaching outcomes. *Dissertation Abstracts International Section A, 70*(9A), p. 3532.

Gonsalkorale, K., Sherman, J. W., & Klauer, K. C. (2009). Aging and prejudice: Diminished regulation of automatic race bias among older adults. *Journal of Experimental Social Psychology, 45*, 410–414. doi:10.1016/j.jesp.2008.11.004

Grieco, E. M., Acosta, Y. D., de la Cruz, G. P., Gambino, C., Gryn, T., Larsen, L. J., . . . Walters, N. P. (2012). *The foreign-born population in the United States: 2010. American Community Service Reports*. U.S. Census Bureau. Retrieved from http://www.census.gov/prod/2012pubs/acs-19.pdf

Habermann, M., & Stagge, M. (2010). Nurse migration: A challenge for the profession and health-care systems. *Journal of Public Health, 18*, 43–51. doi:10.1007/s10389-009-0279-0

Held, D., McGrew, A., Goldblatt, D., & Perraton, J. (1999). *Global transformations: Politics, transformations, and culture*. Stanford, CA: Stanford University Press.

Heppner, P. P., Ægisdóttir, S., Leung, S., Duan, C., Helms, J. E., Gerstein, L. H., & Pedersen, P. B. (2009). The intersection of multicultural and cross-national movements in the United States: A complementary role to promote culturally sensitive research, training, and practice. In L. H. Gerstein, P. Heppner, S. Ægisdóttir, S. Leung, K. L. Norsworthy, L. H. Gerstein, . . . K. L. Norsworthy (Eds.), *International handbook of cross-cultural counseling: Cultural assumptions and practices worldwide* (pp. 33–52). Thousand Oaks, CA: Sage.

Jimenez, J. L. (2011, March 8). *U.S. Census: More minorities than Whites in San Diego County*. Retrieved from http://www.kpbs.org/news/2011/mar/08/census-more-minorities-whites-san-diego-county

Johns, M., Cullum, J., Smith, T., & Freng, S. (2008). Internal motivation to respond without prejudice and automatic egalitarian goal activation. *Journal of Experimental Social Psychology, 44*, 1514–1519. doi:10.1016/j.jesp.2008.07.003

Kapiszewski, A. (2006, May). *Arab versus Asian migrant workers in the GCC countries. Migration and development in the Arab region*. Paper presented at the United Nations Expert Group Meeting on International Migration and Development in the Arab Region, Population Division, Department of Economic and Social Affairs, United Nations Secretariat, Beirut, Lebanon. Retrieved from http://www.un.org/esa/population/meetings/EGM_Ittmig_Arab/P02_Kapiszewski.pdf

Kennedy, S., & McDonald, J. (2006). Immigrant mental health and unemployment. *Economic Record, 82*, 445–459. doi:10.11c11/j.1475-4932.2006.00358.x

Lamberg, L. (2008). Children of immigrants may face stresses, challenges that affect mental health. *JAMA, 300,* 780–781. doi:10.1001/jama.300.7.780

Leach, M. M., & Harbin, J. J. (1997). Psychological ethics codes: A comparison of twenty-four countries. *International Journal of Psychology, 32,* 181–192. doi:10.1080/002075997400854

Lee, S. (2011). Racial variations in major depressive disorder onset among immigrant populations in the United States. *Journal of Mental Health, 20,* 260–269. doi:10.3109/09638237.2011.562260

Leong, F. T. L., Pickren, W. E., Leach, M. M., & Marsella, A. J. (Eds.). (2012). *Internationalizing the psychology curriculum in the United States* (pp. 1–9). New York, NY: Springer Science + Business Media.

Malone, M., Baluja, K. F., Costanzo, J. M., & Davis, C. J. (2003). *The foreign-born population: 2000. Census brief.* Washington, DC: Economics and Statistics Administration, U.S. Census Bureau, Department of Commerce. Retrieved from http://www.census.gov/prod/2003pubs/c2kbr-34.pdf

Mattar, S. (2011). Educating and training the next generations of traumatologists: Development of cultural competencies. *Psychological Trauma: Theory, Research, Practice, and Policy, 3,* 258–265. doi:10.1037/a0024477

McFadden, J., Merryfield, M. M., & Barron, K. R. (1997). *Multicultural and global/international education. Guidelines for programs in teacher education.* Washington, DC: American Association for Colleges for Teacher Education.

Merikangas, K. R., Jin, R., He, J.-P., Kessler, R. C., Lee, S., Sampson, N. A., & Zarkov, Z. (2011). Prevalence and correlates of bipolar spectrum disorder in the world mental health survey initiative. *Archives of General Psychiatry, 68,* 241–251. doi:10.1001/archgenpsychiatry.2011.12

Migration Policy Institute Data Hub. (2009). *Ten source countries with the largest populations in the United States as percentages of the total foreign-born population: 2009.* Washington, DC: Migration Policy Institute. Retrieved from http://www.migrationinformation.org/datahub/charts/10.2009.shtml

Military health system pursues telehealth options in mental health care. (2011). *Mental Health Weekly, 21*(18), 1–7.

Most, A. (2000). "You've Got to Be Carefully Taught": The politics of race in Rodgers and Hammerstein's *South Pacific. Theatre Journal, 52,* 307–337.

Murdoch-Eaton, D., Redmond, A., & Bax, N. (2011). Training healthcare professionals for the future: Internationalism and effective inclusion of global health training. *Medical Teacher, 33,* 562–569.

Newheiser, A., & Dovidio, J. F. (2012). Individual differences and intergroup bias: Divergent dynamics associated with prejudice and stereotyping. *Personality and Individual Differences, 53,* 70–74.

Nieves, J. E., Briscoe, G., Edwards, L., & Flores-Carrera, A. (2011). A literature review of videophone use in mental health. *Psychiatric Times, 28*(5), 24–33.

Pettigrew, T. F. (1979). The ultimate attribution error: Extending Allport's cognitive analysis of prejudice. *Personality and Social Psychology Bulletin, 5*, 461–476. doi:10.1177/014616727900500407

Pope-Davis, D. B., Coleman, H. L. K., Liu, W. M., & Toporek R. L. (Eds.). *International handbook of multicultural competencies in counseling & psychology*. Thousand Oaks, CA: Sage.

Rankin, G. (2010, October). So far and yet so near. *Training Journal*, 70–74.

Reynolds, S. J., Leavitt, K., & DeCelles, K. A. (2010). Automatic ethics: The effects of implicit assumptions and contextual cues on moral behavior. *Journal of Applied Psychology, 95*, 752–760. doi:10.1037/a0019411

Scannell-Desch, E., & Doherty, M. (2010). Experiences of U.S. military nurses in the Iraq and Afghanistan wars, 2003–2009. *Journal of Nursing Scholarship, 42*(1), 3–12. doi:10.1111/j.1547-5069.2009.01329.x

Schafer, A., Snider, L., & van Ommeren, M. (2010). Psychological first aid pilot: Haiti emergency response. *Intervention: International Journal of Mental Health, Psychosocial Work & Counselling in Areas of Armed Conflict, 8*, 245–254. doi:10.1097/WTF.0b013e32834134cb

Schininà, G., Aboul Hosn, M., Ataya, A., Dieuveut, K., & Salem, M. (2010). Psychosocial response to the Haiti earthquake: The experiences of International Organization for Migration. *Intervention: International Journal of Mental Health, Psychosocial Work & Counselling in Areas of Armed Conflict, 8*, 158–164. doi:10.1097/WTF.0b013e32833c2f78

Scholte, J. A. (2004). Globalization studies: Past and future: A dialogue of diversity. *Globalizations, 1*, 102–110. doi:10.1080/1474773042000252183

Shome, R. (2012). Mapping the limits of multiculturalism in the context of globalization. *International Journal of Communication, 6*, 144–165.

Singaravelu, H. D., & Pope, M. (Eds.). (2007). *A handbook for counseling international students in the United States*. Alexandria, VA: American Counseling Association.

Subacchi, P. (2008). New power centres and new power brokers: Are they shaping a new economic order? *International Affairs, 84*, 485–498. doi:10.1111/j.1468-2346.2008.00719.x

Takeuchi, D. T., Alegría, M., Jackson, J. S., & Williams, D. R. (2007). Immigration and mental health: Diverse findings in Asian, Black, and Latino populations. *American Journal of Public Health, 97*, 11–12. doi:10.2105/AJPH.2006.103911

Tarver, D. D., & Harden, J. K. (2011). Working with intercultural immigrant families. In A. Zagelbaum, J. Carlson, A. Zagelbaum, & J. Carlson (Eds.), *Working with immigrant families: A practical guide for counselors* (pp. 211–227). New York, NY: Routledge/Taylor & Francis Group.

Turner, L. G. (2011). Quality in health care and globalization of health services: Accreditation and regulatory oversight of medical tourism companies. *International Journal for Quality in Health Care, 23*, 1–7. doi:10.1093/intqhc/mzq078

U.S. Census Bureau. (2010). *Nation's foreign-born population nears 37 million*. Retrieved from http://www.census.gov/newsroom/releases/archives/foreign-born_population/cb10-159.html

U.S. Census Bureau. (2011). *Table 38. Native and foreign-born population by state: 2008. U.S. Census Bureau, statistical abstract of the United States: 2011*. Retrieved from http://www.census.gov/compendia/statab/2011/-tables/11s0019.pdf

U.S. Census Bureau. (2012). *State and county quick facts. San Diego County*. Retrieved from http://quickfacts.census.gov/qfd/states/06/06073.html

van Vugt, M. (2011). The psychology of social conflict and aggression. In J.P. Forgas, A. W. Kruglanski, & K.D. Williams (Eds.), *The Sydney Symposium of Social Psychology* (Vol. 13, pp. 233–248). New York, NY: Psychology Press.

Veatch, R. (1997). *Medical ethics* (2nd ed.). Sudbury, MA: Jones & Bartlett Learning.

Veatch, R. (2000). *Cross cultural perspectives in medical ethics* (2nd ed.). Sudbury, MA: Jones & Bartlett Learning.

Wright, S. C., & Taylor, D. M. (2007). The social psychology of cultural diversity: Social stereotyping, prejudice and discrimination. In M. A. Hogg & J. Cooper (Eds.), *The Sage handbook of social psychology* (concise student ed., pp. 361–387). Thousand Oaks, CA: Sage.

Youngman, S. (2011). The role of the instructional technology coach in improving elementary teachers' perceived ability to meet the national educational technology standards and performance indicators for teachers. *Dissertation Abstracts International Section A, 71*, pp. 3240.

Zakaria, F. (2011). *The post-American world* (2nd ed.). New York, NY: Norton.

I

INTERNATIONALIZING THE TRADITIONAL MULTICULTURAL CATEGORIES

2

INTERNATIONALIZING MULTICULTURAL ISSUES: RACE AND ETHNICITY

MONIQUE M. TAYLOR

فيه الأرياح تخفق لبيتا

منيف قصر من ألي أحب

A tent with the wind coming from all directions is better for me than a great palace. (Arab proverb)

In this chapter, I examine race and ethnicity in the multicultural–international context. I use my international experiences teaching graduate courses in American studies at Al Quds University in Ramallah, Palestine, as a platform for understanding the complexity of race and ethnicity as both a domestic (one's own country) and international issue. My experiences "exporting" U.S. diversity abroad demonstrate how and why adjustments should be made to our approaches and assumptions about race and ethnicity. By comparing the conflicts experienced by the Palestinians in the Israeli context with those of racial minorities in the United States, I consider the conceptualization of race and ethnicity from an international perspective.

DOI: 10.1037/14044-002
Internationalizing Multiculturalism: Expanding Professional Competencies in a Globalized World,
R. L. Lowman (Editor)

THE ROAD TO RAMALLAH

I did not intend to end up in the Middle East, Israel–Palestine, Jerusalem, or the West Bank. My life took this turn when my spouse was offered a foreign correspondent spot based in Jerusalem to cover the Israeli–Palestinian conflict. I had just received tenure and published a book, but I was on maternity leave from my liberal arts teaching position and open to suggestions about how I would fill my time. An international sojourn sounded intriguing, and the timing seemed right. Or so I thought.

My family and I arrived in Jerusalem in fall 2003 when the Second Intifada (Palestinian uprising) was in full swing. The al-Qaeda attacks on the World Trade Center recently had shoved us all into a new world order. The U.S. military invasion of Iraq, launched during the previous spring, had created a dubious moment for Americans on the world stage. Thus, from New York to Jerusalem to Baghdad, an unlikely combination of history and happenstance would structure the narrative of our time in the Middle East.

We made our home in West Jerusalem, and I initially found my way to East Jerusalem to study Arabic at Al-Quds University:

Marhaba . . . Marhabteen

(hello . . . hello to you)

Suu Ismaak . . . Ismi Monique

(What is your name . . . My name is Monique.)

Min ween inti . . . Ana . . . min . . . al welayat al motahida al amrekeya

(Where are you from? . . . I am . . . from . . . the United States of America.)

One evening when class ended, a fellow student introduced me to her father, a dean at one of the Al-Quds campuses. They invited me to their home in East Jerusalem, poured an unending round of cups of tea, and fed me dates, nuts, fruit, and cookies. When my friend's father seemingly had exhausted things to pull from his cupboards, he offered to open a can of tuna. He also offered me a job teaching at the university's American Studies Institute.

And so during the 4 years I lived in Jerusalem with my husband and our toddler, I continued to study Arabic, and I taught graduate courses to master's degree students at Al-Quds University. The first time I went to the Ramallah campus where the program was housed, the director welcomed me warmly and at the same time expressed his amazement that I was not kept away by a fear that keeps many Americans from traveling in the Palestinian West Bank.

Nonetheless, the road to Ramallah was not easy. Initially, but only for a short while, getting to work meant traveling a straight line from Jerusalem to Ramallah and back again. At most, this was a 25- to 30-minute trip each way. From home, I navigated downtown traffic heading east and then north beyond the high-rise side of the West Jerusalem. I drove on through Shoufat, Beit Hanina, Dir Bala, and other Arab neighborhoods still within the boundaries of Jerusalem. The village of Kalandiya, at the farthest edge of Jerusalem, was the meeting point between my life at home and my teaching work in the West Bank.

During my first spring and summer of commuting, Kalandia was the site of a "soft" military checkpoint staffed by soldiers checking identity documents or passports of pedestrian and car traffic. We were guided by concrete cubes painted with English, Hebrew, and Arabic commands: Stop, Checkpoint Ahead, Prepare Your Documents. Coils of barbed wire bounded the space. Ever-present Israeli Defense Forces hovered with their tanks and their guns. Over time, the crossing at Kalandiya changed before my eyes and hardened into something else entirely.

In July 2003, the Israelis began construction of a physical barrier along and within the West Bank. Each day presented evidence of new control: more fences, more barbed wire, patrol roads, meters-high concrete slabs, and observation towers sprouting from the landscape. Soon, crossing would be controlled and channeled by designated lanes, mechanical arms, and turnstiles. When the roads leading to the West Bank competed with the wall, they simply disappeared and my route changed. I could have been zooming along on a drive I made only yesterday, last week, last month and then would come screaming into a concrete barrier or dirt berm that made the road impassable. I was charting a zigzag course to gain entry, all the while watching the side-by-side accumulation of rectangular concrete slabs lowered by cranes taking form as a wall.

As the barrier hardened, passage in and out was routed through a terminal as large and brightly lighted as a toll pass on a U.S. interstate highway. This was the occupation unfolding in real time. Checkpoint Qalandiya took its place in a routine of security found on both sides of the barrier. On the Israeli side, it was a daily occurrence to be asked, "*Eesh neshek? Do you have a weapon?*" Car trunks were inspected to allow entry to supermarket parking lots. Diaper bags, knapsacks, and purses were checked to gain access to banks, shops, and restaurants. At times there were flying checkpoints—strips of spikes set out across the road where soldiers had positioned themselves to profile and stop or wave on travelers. These came and went and could be found anywhere and then not at all. "Why is that man sitting on the road?" my daughter once asked me as we sped by a man who had been stopped at a flying checkpoint. He sat on the curb while his documents were checked, his head and shoulders slumped beneath his red-and-white checked *kaffiya*.

The Palestinians spoke of the concrete colossus as an apartheid wall. In the parlance of the Israeli government, it was a security fence. The British

Broadcasting Corporation (BBC) and others in the media world tried for linguistic neutrality. On its website ("Israel and the Palestinians: Key Terms"), a BBC guide to facts and terminology directed the reader to "see *barrier*" and clicking on the terms *wall* or *fence* brought up the following style guidelines:

> BBC journalists should try to avoid using terminology favored by one side or another in any dispute. The BBC uses the terms "barrier," "separation barrier," or "West Bank barrier" as acceptable generic descriptions to avoid the political connotations of "security fence" (preferred by the Israeli government) or "apartheid wall" (preferred by the Palestinians). The United Nations also uses the term "barrier." Of course, a reporter standing in front of a concrete section of the barrier might choose to say "this wall" or use a more exact description in the light of what he or she is looking at. (BBC, 2010)

This was but one instance of many of the difficulties encountered when trying to speak the "us and them" logic of the Israeli–Palestinian conflict—a task that could make one's tongue go crazy.

Within the first 3 months of our arrival, two suicide bombers attacked busses during the early morning commuting hour (Ellingwood & King, 2004a, 2004b). The explosions were so near to our West Jerusalem apartment that we felt the building shudder and heard a boom so thunderously deep that it settled as a dark crater in the memory. On both occasions, my husband, Ken, ran off, notebook in hand, leaving an unfinished plate of breakfast while I continued to spoon cereal to a hungry toddler. My sense of myself as an outsider, not a part of the conflict, was being shaken.

Passing the checkpoint sat uncomfortably in a corner of my mind. It was difficult to see this as a new variation on a familiar routine: commuting in traffic. Driving to work, I flashed my American passport and I was usually on my way. Occasionally, I had to stop to answer questions: "Where are you going?" "What is the nature of your business?" "Do you know any Palestinians?" Coming home to Jerusalem was an entirely different story: The car was searched. "Open the glove box," they demanded in Hebrew. The flick of a gun indicated the back door: "Open it!" When they pointed to the trunk, that was my cue to pop the release lever, to get out of the driver's seat and stand at the rear of the car, not saying a word, while the trunk was eyeballed, poked through, the spare tire lifted and dropped. I seethed in silent indignation. Always there was the tip of a weapon trained at my feet, a surveillance camera trained on my car, on me.

One day on my commute home, I was caught alongside the crossfire of boys and soldiers. In my youth, I spent this time, twilight, with neighborhood kids playing evening games—king of the hill, kick the can, freeze tag. Here the "play" was *intifada*: a dirt strip the size and length of a football field ran along the edge of the separation barrier. Under the gaze of an observation tower a group of Palestinian boys, *shbaab*, had mounted several concrete cubes and hurled rocks at Israeli soldiers. They wiggled their hips—offering a dance of triumph—taking turns waving an enormous red, black, and green Palestinian flag. The soldiers—seven of them that day—had taken their GI Joe positions behind a white Ford van. From there they took aim. The *shbaab* issued taunting whistles and beckoned with their hands, hooting and tap dancing to the staccato of gunfire . . . *pop-pop-pop*.

I watched this scene unfold through the passenger side window of my car and pondered the insider–outsider distinction that, naively, I thought had kept me at a distance from this situation, these people, this place. I sat in my car, watching with eyes wide open. My heart raced when one of the boys, fleeing a soldier firing rubber bullets, did a dive roll across the hood of my car. But I was just one in a long line of cars that built up and funneled down into the two lanes leading out. Together we waited in traffic that was not moving, stalled by the occupation.

Coming toward me, I saw a mother who had just crossed on foot through the dusty pedestrian lanes at checkpoint Qalandiya with three girls in tow. She led them like baby ducklings—perhaps she was on her way from work and had just collected them from school? Perhaps the same routine I longed to reach on the other side awaited her here on this side: dinner, homework, bedtime stories. One of the girls, the littlest, carried a blond doll dangling from her hand. *Pop-pop-pop*. The girls jumped and clutched at the hem of the mother's *abayah*. Their mother soldiered on, her eyes stone cold, staring straight ahead.

WELCOME, WELCOME: ARRIVING AT AMERICAN STUDIES ABROAD

North of the checkpoint, the road wound past spits of roasting chickens, television repair shops, the Kalandia refugee camp, and an abandoned Israeli Defense Force encampment, the skeletal remains of which bore witness to a recent military incursion and occupation of Ramallah. The El-Bireh suburb was found at the edge of Ramallah. Here, the American studies department shared a four-story stone villa with several of the university's other area studies programs. Our classroom and office space was on the second floor. Like academic hallways anywhere, the bulletin boards held an assortment of announcements: grade notices, class rosters, department memos. The language mix was lots of Arabic and a little English. A sticker proclaiming "RESIST THE WALL TO FALL" caught my eye. (This phrase, found on bumper stickers and graffiti, was akin to the "tear down this wall" mantra once directed against the Berlin Wall.)

The walls leading up the stairway to the second floor were adorned with a time line of framed yellowed *New York Times* front pages. "The Stock Market Crashes." "Kennedy Assassinated!" "Nixon Resigns!" "Neil Armstrong Walks on the Moon." Each line announced the greatest hits pieces of American cultural capital that would land one at the head of a Trivial Pursuit match. Upstairs, the walls of offices and seminar rooms held an assorted collection of American memorabilia. There were framed movie stars: a beaming blonde Olivia Newton John and the young, handsome John Travolta in *Grease*, Ben Affleck in *Pearl Harbor*, and Gary Cooper in *High Noon*. A framed *Saturday Night Fever* album cover and a picture of John Wayne hung close to a Tommy Hilfiger advertisement.

A poster of Martin Luther King Jr. pictured on the mall in Washington, DC, hung on the dining room wall with the "I Have a Dream" speech printed below it. On the same wall, a copy of the U.S. Constitution was hung, printed in Arabic. In the center of the table sat a bag of sugar and a fresh batch of *nana*, mint leaves used to make tea. Down the hall in the library, rows of computer monitors sat atop a conference table, their black screens blank, many still wearing plastic wrapping, slapped with red, white, and blue USAID stickers: from the American People. There was no Internet connection.

The goals of the Al-Quds program were articulated in a vocabulary that would ring familiar to American ears. Students were to be introduced to the values of freedom, democracy, and the free market economy. Their coursework aimed to develop skills of analysis and objectivity, differentiation and comparison, contrast and synthesis. Critical reading and democratic thinking were encouraged. To my approval, there was an explicitly stated place in the curriculum for the respect of tolerance and the reduction of prejudice, racism, and discrimination. Surely this would afford a fine fit for my teaching interests: U.S. multiculturalism brought into the space of an area studies program situated outside of the United States.

A quick glance at its mission statement revealed that the program placed importance on helping to foster better understanding between Palestinians and Americans. Given that the United States is a world power, the program founders argued, too much ignorance remained about U.S. politics, history, and culture. Students were to be encouraged to clarify the distinction between the American people and American foreign policy. "How was this to be possible?" I wondered, my own anger at the U.S. invasion of Iraq still close to the surface.

In the weeks leading up to my first class, disturbing news had come from Abu Ghraib in Iraq. Images of the torture and humiliation of Iraqi prisoners by American soldiers and the desecration and mockery of the Koran made me anxious about the context of my initial meeting with the students. In an essay titled "Education After Abu Ghraib," Henri Giroux (2005) discussed how this episode deepened anti-U.S. anger on the world stage:

Responses from around the world exhibited outrage and disgust over the U.S. actions at Abu Ghraib. The rhetoric of American democracy was denounced all over the globe as hypocritical and utterly propagandistic, especially in light of President George W. Bush's 30 April 2003 remarks claiming that, with the removal of Saddam Hussein, "there are no longer torture chambers or mass graves or rape rooms in Iraq." The protracted release of new sets of pictures of U.S. soldiers grinning as they tortured and sexually humiliated Iraqi prisoners at Abu Ghraib further undermined the moral and political credibility of the United States both in the Arab world and around the globe. (p. 221)

I wondered whether my efforts would be framed by these and other contradictions read between the lines of the Greater Middle East Initiative, launched in 2003, as a part of President Bush's "Forward Strategy of Freedom" (Wittes, 2004). Not only was the distinction between the people and U.S. policy becoming increasingly blurred in the post-9/11 United States, but so, too, for Americans was the gap widening between reality and our ideals. Charged Giroux (2005),

> The media has . . . put into place forms of jingoism, patriotic correctness, narrow-minded chauvinism, and a celebration of militarization that renders dissent as treason, and places the tortures at Abu Ghraib outside of the discourses of ethics, compassion, human rights, and social justice. (p. 221)

I was unsure whether teaching American studies in Palestine could be free from this current disconnect.

From my earliest class sessions, however, my students taught me that the agenda could be broad enough to encompass ideas about the Middle East (Iraq), as sharply defined as opinions about the situation in Palestine (the Gaza Strip and the West Bank), or as narrowly focused as what was going on here and now (Ramallah): "Is it the 'American Dream' to rule the world?" they wondered out loud. "We see the U.S. and America through the eyes of the occupation," they informed me. "What do you think of our situation?" they would ask. Their questions revealed their curiosity and intelligence—and their biases, their ignorance. They had firmly held views, and from the start they put to me questions and points of view that touched on power, politics and place, ideas, ideology, and identities that I was not used to turning around in such a manner. When smiling Malek innocently asked from behind her hijab, "Why do Americans hate us?" her suspicion caught me completely off guard.

Tamara Coffman Wittes (2004), director of the Middle East Democracy and Development Project at the Brookings Institute, pinpointed the basis for this type of mistrust of Americans more precisely than Iraq and Abu Ghraib. Wittes argued that resentment in the Muslim world preceded the war in Iraq and was tied to the decades-long crisis of the unresolved Palestinian–Israeli conflict. In a sense, no matter my intentions, I had stepped into an already unfolding narrative. I took my place among a cast of characters that included good guys and bad guys defined outside of U.S. control.

From Jerusalem to Qalandiya, I traveled in and traveled out. I was an American, a person of color, an academic, using different sets of eyes to observe, reflect, and analyze. From Qalandiya to Ramallah, my students sat alongside me: citizen of a superpower, a minority, an academic expert on race in America, and their eyes were watching me as they observed, reflected, and analyzed. My personal life and my professional work placed me on two sides of the conflict, so I was keenly aware that multiple positions for me and my students existed. These were defined by a variety of narrative constructions and previously developed arguments and assumptions in the contested space(s) between the Middle East and America. The question was (and remains) how to engage these narratives and how to put them in the service of what Giroux (2004) defined as "education after Abu Ghraib" in which "learning is inextricably connected to social change, the obligations of civic justice, and a notion of democracy in which peace, equality, compassion and freedom are not limited to the nation state but extended to the international community" (p. 21).

PLACE, POWER, AND POLITICS: LOCATING POSITIONALITIES AND DEFINING PERSPECTIVE(S)

In the Middle East, any learning I initiated on topics of race, ethnicity, and inequality in America would necessarily sit side by side in a place where the personal collided with the political and the present would engage the past. As Kevin Hovland (1999) noted, "whether in the micro-space of the classroom or in the global realm of international relations," there is an "undeniable centrality of positionality in any global studies conversation" (p. 21). Apart from the geopolitics of the moment, my own positionality, shaped by my social position and subjective experiences, was defined too by life in the U.S. post–civil rights era. My academic approach to teaching and learning about race and ethnicity had been shaped, from the start, within a particular U.S. geographic and historical framework.

Race in Post–Civil Rights America

Born in 1962, I grew up in the vanilla suburbs of Chocolate City (i.e., Washington, DC). A station wagon carried my family across the color line. In suburbia we assumed a middle-class skin, although at home, we always knew we were Black. It seemed annoying when our mother would say no, reinforcing her position with "because you can't do what White kids do" or "because you're not White." Her words would push us smack up against that difference we believed suburban living was peeling away.

I can recall that race followed us each time we moved to a new suburban housing development—places whose pleasantly bucolic names like "Sleepy Hollow" and "River Falls" did not begin to suggest the racism that was attached to the American dream. In one neighborhood, the MacGregors next door built a fence when we moved in, yet they still glared every time we rolled our bikes into the carport, along the edge where the side of our property met theirs.

These early experiences left me with a curiosity about the socio-historical aspects and psychological impact of differences based on race and later guided my career path when I trained as a scholar of race and ethnicity in a sociology program at Harvard University. By the time I held my first tenure-track job, at a college renowned for its early public embrace of multi-culturalism, the culture wars were full blown. Thus, multiculturalism as it was practiced in the classroom carried me so far away from the Black-and-White binary frame of the color line and the melting pot theories about 19th- and early-20th-century White ethnics in America that it seemed as though I had arrived in another country. Old dichotomies simply could not accommodate the broader cast of characters who walked into my Black-and-White universe and made themselves at home.

Moving beyond Black and White, a fundamental piece of my continuing multicultural education came from team teaching with colleagues working on Chicano, Native American, and Asian American issues. Apparently, oppression, inferiority, discrimination, subjugation, second-class citizenship, and injustice knew many colors in the United States. Exploring strategies of resistance, transgression, interrogation, and subversion helped us find commonality in the project of rereading, disrupting, and unsettling constructions of identity in the United States. This was a first moment for me of relocating race in a broader global, albeit domestic, framework.

In March 1991, videotaped images of Los Angeles police officers beating a Black suspect played endlessly on television screens. The Los Angeles Police Department came under scrutiny, and when the police officers involved were acquitted, years of anger about racism and police brutality in minority neighborhoods bubbled over. The 1992 race riots in Los Angeles were sparked by continuing race conflict but cracked open new ethnic fault lines as well as disrupting simple assumptions about the powerful and the powerless.

During the O. J. Simpson trial, my liberal arts community walked on eggshells while the postmodern fluidity of race and class and gender identities had exploded in our faces. At the same time, an angry California electorate introduced ballot initiatives that forced voters to tangle with immigration and affirmative action beyond the "polite" discourse of the classroom. Where these newly racialized and globalized issues spilled beyond the containers of Black and White, race now coexisted in a world full of other "others" in end-of-20th-century America. California and Los Angeles were great places to get down and get dirty in the trenches of the culture wars during the 1990s.

Beyond "Domestic Multiculturalism"

Looking back, I understand the critique from the field of global–international education leveled against that moment of U.S. multiculturalism—that it was becoming "monocultural and self-referential" (Lee, 1995, p. 568), that its most "committed advocates [were] explicit about locating their concerns domestically" (Cornwell & Stoddard, 1999, p. 8), and that there was "a tendency to limit discussion of cultural diversity and multiculturalism to issues affecting populations living within the U.S." (Dominguez & Desmond, 1996, p. 476). However, in this multicultural "retelling the narrative of America" (Cornwell & Stoddard, 1999, p. 17) an immediate struggle brought on by the culture wars was the bare knuckles fight against what Joyce Appleby (1992) noted was an "exceptionalist narrative [used] to foreclose other ways of interpreting the meaning of the U.S." (p. 420). In essence, the domestic focus was pushed in part by a high stakes sense of fighting to attain ideals enshrined in America's very definition of itself.

On the other hand, weren't NAFTA (the North American Free Trade Agreement) with its free-trade-across-borders spirit and the new ethnic diasporas brought on by increased global migration bringing a new zeitgeist and the world to Los Angeles? We needed our students to be equipped (domestically) with perspectives to live and work (domestically) in the new kind of "multiculti" world that late-20th-century cities like Los Angeles were becoming. As performance artist Guillermo Gomez-Pena (1988), linking the logic for U.S. multiculturism to the world, so eloquently noted at the time:

> The demographic facts are staggering: The Middle East and Black Africa are already in Europe, and Latin America's heart now beats in the United States. New York and Paris increasingly resemble Mexico City and Sao Paulo. Cities like Tijuana and Los Angeles, once socio-urban aberrations, are becoming models of a new hybrid culture, full of uncertainty and vitality. And border youth—the fearsome "cholo-punks," children of the chasm that is opening before the "first" and the "third" worlds, become the indisputable heirs to a new mestizaje [the fusion of the Amerindian and the European race]. (Quoted in Simonson & Walker, 1988)

The fact is, however, that leading up to the end of the 20th century, multiculturalism in the United States was rhetorically framed as an adversary to a number of reigning internationalist positions and approaches. Much of this antagonism was created and maintained through institutional planning and prioritization but also reflected cultural and ideological shifts within the American academy. Perhaps it is time to move beyond those moments of conflict over approach(es) because of disciplinary boundaries and funding priorities (Lee, 1995); accusations of an inward orientation of U.S. diversity studies (Dominguez & Desmond, 1996); the lack of mechanisms, spaces, dialogues, and processes (Dominguez & Desmond, 1996); as well as competition for time and space in the school curriculum (Baker, 1999).

Today, arguments abound for building bridges and designing new paradigms to resolve the contradictions between U.S. diversity studies and a move toward international approaches. Dominguez and Desmond (1996) advocated creating "a critical interface" (p. 477) in which we could "see America within a world system" (p. 479) and move away from approaches to internationalism that simply have us "looking outward from the U.S." (p. 487). It is time for "reconciling intersections in the sometimes contentious debates between domestic diversity and globalization," argued Cornwell and Stoddard (1999, p. 10). Yet to resist the temptation of U.S. domestic multiculturalism issues being swept along by today's seductive mantra of "globalization, globalization, globalization," they must be well situated and clearly defined as an essential component of international teaching and learning.

RACE IN RAMALLAH

The domestically defined approach to U.S. multiculturalism and diversity was what I brought to teaching American studies in Ramallah. I felt that studying America through the prism of race and ethnicity would bring an outsider–minority perspective attuned to contradictions that were long inherent in the American rhetoric of freedom, justice, and liberty. Race as it has been lived in the United States had always forced us to adapt caution against treating "Western liberal values as absolute certainties that are readily applicable elsewhere" (Lee, 1995, p. 589). Perhaps, too, I naively assumed that race and ethnicity would serve as protection against peddling a misleading and, in this post 9/11 moment, hard-to-defend exceptionalist narrative (Appleby, 1992) approach to America.

"Why do Americans hate us?" Malek had challenged from the beginning, pushing me to avoid what Dominguez and Desmond (1996) critiqued as a

> tendency to look outward from the United States, seeing similarity to our own situation rather than exploring the possibilities that analyses of the United States generated by quite different contexts might reveal fundamentally different readings of our contemporary cultural formations. (p. 479)

"When we export paradigms," they suggested, "they should be in the service of creating meaningful dialogue" (p. 477). "What do you think of our situation?" Yusef had wanted to know, inviting me into a space of dialogue that is ideally where our U.S. multiculturalism should meet an international perspective.

I must confess, however, that it took a variety of classroom exchanges, which are detailed in the remainder of this chapter, before I fully understood the need to dislocate and displace race and ethnicity from the history and geography of domestic origins. In fact, the opportunity to engage in teaching non-U.S. students challenged much of what I thought I knew as an "expert" on race. Having to design syllabi and choose relevant materials for an audience outside of the United States also allowed me to internationalize my approach as an initial step toward developing a more globally relevant curriculum.

IN THE CLASSROOM: INTEGRATING INTERNATIONAL INSIGHT

"Race, Resistance and Rising Up: Voices From the Harlem Renaissance" was the first class I taught at Al-Quds. The class introduced students to the historical and literary moment known as the Harlem Renaissance. We studied fiction and poetry, philosophical writing, critical and historical analysis, political pamphlets and cartoons, painting, and subway maps. There were not a lot of materials at hand (buying texts in English was prohibitively expensive and thus virtually impossible as an option for the group), so I relied heavily on my personal library and supplemented that with Internet resources. Occasionally, I brought in a boom box, and we listened to cassettes and CDs of Duke Ellington and his contemporaries. In the tradition of American studies, the course placed writers and texts in the context of U.S. and world history. Overall, my goal was that, through an examination of the social and political context of the Harlem Renaissance, students would see the quest for democracy and citizenship in American life viewed from a minority-outsider standpoint.

I began the first day of class with a photo that depicted an organized protest called the Silent March. This event, which marked the founding of the NAACP, was to my mind an elegant and dignified response to the racial violence (lynching) directed against Blacks from the end of the Reconstruction period. I was counting on the image to speak to them, without overwhelming them with text. As a starting point, I was curious to hear what they thought, to know where they were coming from. I gave them some background facts and figures about the epidemic of lynching at the time and then opened the class to discussion. Several hands shot up. (Good. They were engaged.) "But Dr. Monique," a student asked, "why didn't the Black people just kill all the White people?"

The lesson on lynching caused them to want to know why Black Americans did not take revenge for the lynchings. They did not immediately embrace the logic of the NAACP's nonviolent legal approach or its interracial makeup as an organization. Before we took a break, I gave the students printouts of Claude McKay's sonnet, "If We Must Die." We carried our heated discussions out of the classroom and continued them around the kitchen table. Mahmud, a squat, balding, quiet man, the father of 12, and Leila, a young mother of toddler twins who was always full of a maternal bustle, made cups of strong coffee and tea for us while the others sat smoking fetid cigarettes. They got worked up about McKay's suggestion to take up armed struggle and fought among themselves over the censorship and strong reactions the poem had provoked at the time. At one point, Wa'el, one of the darker skinned students, his face pock-marked from acne, removed his cigarette with one hand and with the other thumped his chest near his heart. "We are with you, Dr. Monique," he told me, "We are with the Black people."

I was pleased with this remark, but I noticed throughout the summer that even when I carried them in the class to specific places in New York (uptown and downtown, 125th Street, Central Park, Sugar Hill, the A train), they always ended up back in Palestine, the West Bank, Ramallah. From their own place and perspective, they debated the organizational strengths and weaknesses of the Fatah (the political party founded by Yassar Arafat), for instance, or talked about the generational struggles for power they witnessed today in their own society. These classroom migrations between my world(s) and theirs illustrated the tricky navigation toward creating what scholar Ella Shohat (quoted in Saldivar, 2010) characterized as communities-in-relation: "Our challenge . . . is to produce knowledge within a kind of kaleidoscope framework of communities-in-relation without ever suggesting that their positionings are identical" (p. 823).

One day a few weeks later, the afternoon class session had ended, and we were drinking coffee and eating an ice cream cake and talking more about resistance, the occupation, and the meaning of the *intifada*. I asked the group about the shooting soldiers and the defiant *shbaab* I had seen on my recent commute home. Suleiman, a bespectacled, olive-skinned man with the serious mien of a scholar, told me this about the rock throwers: "It's just what you do," he explained in a flat, matter-of-fact tone. "It's a rite of passage. You have to say to them that 'no, you don't accept their occupation'."

During the semester, the class was introduced to Langston Hughes, W. E. B. Du Bois, and other leading voices of the New Negro movement. We spent a great deal of time talking about identity and the difference between it being imposed from without or constructed from within. "This was why the

New Negro was key to the 20th-century Black experience," I told them. "We were producing our own images, writing poetry, and making art as a civilized people. This display of humanity had to be done. Where Blacks were regarded as inhuman, it was one response to the underlying logic that made lynching possible. Without taking control, our image of ourselves becomes corrupted," I explained while clicking through slides of racist imagery.

"It is like a mental occupation," declared Samia thoughtfully, her dark eyes lighting up.

"Yes," I said, "and one way beyond this mental occupation is for our philosophers and poets and thinkers to articulate us collectively as a race, as a people, to America and to each other." I also introduced them to Du Bois's (1903/1982) essay about double consciousness:

> the Negro is a sort of seventh son, born with a veil, and gifted with second-sight in this American world,—a world which yields him no true self-consciousness, but only lets him see himself through the revelation of the other world. It is a peculiar sensation, this double-consciousness, this sense of always looking at one's self through the eyes of others, of measuring one's soul by the tape of a world that looks on in amused contempt and pity. One ever feels his twoness—an American, a Negro; two souls, two thoughts, two unreconciled strivings; two warring ideals in one dark body, whose dogged strength alone keeps it from being torn asunder. (p. 45)

In response, the students embraced, but adapted, the concept of double-consciousness and made it their own. One student wrote that this idea

> reminded me with [sic] the Palestinian scholar Edward Sa'id, who described this feeling when he was interviewed for a documentary film. Sa'id suffered from being a Palestinian and an American; the two identities he experienced were in conflict. He argued seeing oneself through a distorted unrealistic lens of the others in stereotyped images. These stereotyped images were reflecting inferiority, backwardness, and other passive images about Arabs and Palestinians.

Another student, Yasmeen, heard the same echo from Du Bois to Said (1979); she wrote in a paper that

> I believe that the outstanding Palestinian scholar Edward Sa'id was able to describe such a feeling: "The life of an Arab Palestinian in the West, particularly in America, is disheartening. There exists here an almost unanimous consensus that politically he does not exist, and when it is allowed that he does, it is either as a nuisance or as an Oriental. The web of racism, cultural stereotypes, political imperialism, dehumanizing ideology holding in the Arab or the Muslim is very strong indeed, and it is this web which every Palestinian has come to feel as his uniquely punishing destiny." (p. 27)

In Said (1979), the Palestinians, the Arabs, had the equivalent of an intellectual "midwife," as the Harlem Renaissance's Alain Locke was nick-named, to call forth the existential dilemma of a collective identity. Beyond race, theirs is an identity that is national, ethnic, religious. Like race, this is an imposed construct that does not allow for full humanity.

In response to another exam question about Langston Hughes and W. E. B. Du Bois, a different student recalled a personal experience:

> Right after graduating from university, I was obliged to work in Israel due to lack of job opportunities. . . . I was rejected by the Israelis who were in charge of the West Bank at that time. The first and most difficult shock I received upon starting the work was not, as I expected, the difficulty of the physical work, or the frustration over being educated and have [sic] no job opportunity. All of those hardships I was easily able to overcome because I was a young man who had enough strength and tolerance. The one dif-ficulty I still strive [sic] with is the feeling of inferiority I felt amongst my fellow Palestinians. This almost killed me. . . . I still remember how the workers boasted and narrated to their friends back home about the admi-ration of their superior Israeli bosses of a device [they could operate] or a good job they had done at work. One could easily perceive the acceptance of being inferior to Israelis who were not superior to me at all. What made things even worse [was] the inclination of people to judge their life pat-terns and cultural values according to Israeli standards. To quote Dubois [sic] "measuring one soul by the tape of a world that looked in on amused contempt." Now after reading Langston Hughes and Web Dubois [sic], all of those bad memories jump into my mind to encourage me [to] conclude that whenever and wherever there is oppression, people's reactions have much in common. Let us now leave my own experiences and examine those of Langston Hughes and Web Dubois [sic].

From his own reading of Du Bois on the inferiority and self-loathing that Black Americans experienced because of race, the student translated this com-plex into a split based on Israeli–Palestinian identities. The Occupation, which placed Israelis in control of Palestinians' economic opportunities, left a young university graduate, like his Jim Crow counterparts, with restricted options. His conclusion that our reactions to oppression can be the same "whenever and wherever" wed the universal and particular and took us, through com-parative study, back to underlying sociological and psychological processes of racism, prejudice, and discrimination and their impact on identity.

In my own life and academic work, I have always been sensitive to deconstructing categories and opening them up to a multiplicity of readings. Although I understand the centrality of the Black–White dichotomy as the source of an essentialist–absolute racism needed to enforce slavery, impose Jim Crow, and structure segregation, it also is necessary to use a practice that allows us to turn our analyses of racialization(s) around many axes. When my Harlem research (Taylor, 2003) revealed to me that the Du Boisian expression of a "double consciousness" was expressed by middle-class Blacks' understanding of themselves vis-à-vis White Americans but also about their relationship with working-class and underclass blacks, I wrote of a "double-double consciousness" to which the era of post–civil rights and the declining significance of race had given rise.

One of the students, Omar, borrowed this concept as a way of examining what he named "a Palestinian multi-consciousness." The Palestinian multi-consciousness, wrote Omar,

> is deeply affected by the political and historical developments that Palestine has witnessed. What I mean by multi-consciousness is how the Palestinians perceive themselves from different dimensions. How the Palestinian refugees perceive themselves through the eyes of other Palestinians living in West Bank, and how the West Bankers perceive themselves through the eyes of Palestinians in Gaza Strip, and how the Palestinians in West Bank and Gaza strip perceive themselves through the eyes of the Palestinians holding Israeli IDs and how the Palestinians inside Palestine perceive themselves through the eyes of Palestinians outside Palestine, and how the Palestinian people as a whole perceive itself through the eyes of Israelis and Americans. As a Palestinian, I think that we need a national consciousness to know who we are then to form one identity.

One day in class I was explaining the concept of hypodescent, otherwise known as the "one-drop rule," by which anyone with "one drop" of African American blood was categorized as African American. My intent was to teach the students one version of how race in America has historically been defined. "Why do we need to know this?" Jamal questioned. I presumed that this was his version of my American students' timeworn "will this be on the test?" question, but it forced me to dig deeper. "Why indeed?" I wondered. The point was that race is a sociohistorical construct. We have to understand the role that power and domination play in constructing and defining us. "But why are Americans so obsessed with race?" someone else asked as a follow-up question. "Why do you [Americans] measure race on [your] census?" "Why [sic] the U.S. divide people into groups—isn't it enough just to be American?"

Standing so far from home and centuries removed from this iteration of the construct of race and racism, the one-drop rule sounded illogical, insane, and almost absurd in its retelling. "Well, you all seem obsessed with religion," I remarked. "Are you Muslim, Christian, or Jew?" I countered, repeating to them a question that was often asked of me in the Middle East. "And what about the Israeli and Palestinian labels that are always invoked? These categories—containers, markers, or whatever we choose to call them—hold a social logic that pushes us to explore broader political, economic, and cultural traits of our societies," I explained, remembering beginning lessons imparted to me when I entered Harvard's graduate sociology program decades ago.

"Why is your religion, or national identity, like our race, so fundamental to the conditions you experience here? How?" I demanded of my students; with this question, I recognized the steps I was taking with them that would carry us away from race and ethnicity as the only categories defining shared experiences that we could reach by way of other reference points.

In the next semesters, we moved on to seminars on U.S. history and culture. During the spring term, Rosa Parks died. On a Tuesday, I e-mailed the students obituaries from *The New York Times* and *The Los Angeles Times*. On Wednesday when I arrived for class, long and lanky Hakim, who had a habit of bringing extra reference materials to share, handed me two photos he had downloaded and printed from the Internet: pictures of Rosa Parks being fingerprinted and holding a police number in front of her chest.

I took my place among them at our seminar table and pulled books and papers from my satchel and started toward the chalkboard. But it did not feel right to just start "teaching." Instead, I closed the textbook and asked them to think about history and obituaries and their own lives. Atallah, whose English was not very good, asked, in a mixture of English and Arabic, if we could "do a mourning." With the palms of his hands, he urged the students to their feet. They rose, snapped to attention, and fell silent. Then the room was abuzz with their questions: "Who is she?" "Why do you know her?" Some of the students even took a stab at answers: "Because she is one of the insurgents." "Because she said no." "We know her and respect and admire her," they told me and each other.

Resistance as a concept associated with the narrative of Rosa Parks could get the students engaged, but resistance to what? We took a brief detour from our text. I handed out about 10 detailed pages of Jim Crow laws. They could read, state by state, about different public spaces and facilities and how those laws governed, regulated, and restricted. It was not my intention that they should "bank" the information. I made clear that this was not the type of school material to be associated only with memorization and tests. Rather, I wanted them to grasp an emotion. I wanted them to feel the frustration that this strict regulation of Black bodies in space coexisted with the textbook ideals of American freedom, justice, and liberty that we were studying.

AN INTERNATIONAL MULTICULTURALIST PERSPECTIVE

A few days after our class discussion of Rosa Parks, one of the students, Fatma, sent me an e-mail offering her thoughts: "Rosa walked onto a bus and here we walk into a wall. We need a Rosa Parks to stand up against the wall."

Her words provided a lesson to me on when and how the universal and the particular could connect.

In advocating what he called "critical internationalism," Benjamin Lee (1995) argued against a liberal perspective from which "no essential difference exists between the domestic and the international cases as far as justice as fairness is concerned" (p. 563). An international multiculturalist perspective that fails to take into account this caution of critical internationalism would leave us dependent on universal and transhistorical principles to justify moral values such as justice and freedom. What Lee's critical internationalism offers as an alternative is the opportunity to replace the "universal and cross-contextual view from nowhere" and instead read from "local views from somewhere" that are rooted in specific historical and cultural contexts" (p. 564).

Even as it divided and diminished the world in Palestine, the wall offered a distinct "view from somewhere" as an articulation of oppression. The issue is how lessons learned from a distinct historical experience help us accomplish the shift from one "somewhere" to another "somewhere" successfully. In the case of teaching American studies topics in Palestine, the fluidity of race and ethnicity was revealed by allowing for ways that "our" topic could be processed through "their" narrative(s) of localized experience(s).

In their introduction to "From La Frontera to Gaza," a special issue of *American Quarterly*, Pulido and Lloyd (2010) presented essays from a community forum exploring the connections and differences between the struggles of the Chicana(o) and Palestinian peoples. Their introductory essay, Pulido and Lloyd posed a series of questions highlighting the relevance of finding comparative aspects in social issues.

> Are there lessons from the United Farm Workers boycott that can be applied to the proposed academic boycott of Israeli institutions of higher education? Are there analogies between the wall being constructed on the U.S. border and the separation wall that cuts through the occupied West Bank? (p. 792)

This questioning was driven by what they saw as a need "to undercut or transgress disciplinary boundaries that separate disparate instances of oppression and struggle" (Pulido & Lloyd, 2010, p. 792). At the same time, the questions, left unanswered, invited dialogue prompting me, in a similar vein, to ask: "Is the Montgomery bus boycott (or the sit-ins) a tactic that could be applied in the West Bank?" "Are there analogies between the Jim Crow restrictions and the restrictions imposed by the barrier?" Observations from my students suggest that there are: "Always when I see the wall I think that we are in prison. . . . This is the new racial discrimination," one of my students wrote in a journal entry for class.

From my experiences teaching U.S. racial identity and the history of American race relations in the context of a political occupation, I would argue that to successfully export lessons from U.S. multiculturalism, we need to create theoretical and analytical approaches that bring together (without conflating) experiences of oppression. "Solidarity based on comparative analysis," as Lloyd and Pulido (2010) argued, "is essential to any engagement in global human rights issues" (p. 796). I could teach race abroad, but as a category in this context, race had to be set into constant motion: they are us and I am them, we are here and then we are there, it is then and today is now. My shared reading with Palestinian students of W. E. B. Du Bois and Edward W. Said; Birmingham, Harlem, Ramallah, and Gaza; the Occupation and *Plessy v. Ferguson*; the bus boycotts and *intifada* provided multiple positionalities and perspectives that grounded us with new and necessary "view(s) from somewhere." To disrupt the fixity of race in the service of a global antiracist project would be one approach to wedding U.S multiculturalism and internationalism.

CONCLUSION: THE ROAD FROM HERE

In August 2005, British graffiti artist Banksy traveled to the West Bank, where he created a series of nine controversial but eye-catching murals on stretches of the wall in Bethlehem, Abu Dis, and Ramallah. Several of the images were framed to give the effect of seeing through large cracks in the concrete structure or of taking in a scenic vista through curtained windows. Other image frames, such as the edge of a scrap of paper peeled back and theater curtains being pulled aside, also afforded glimpses of an alternative reality. Painted on the flat, drab, gray concrete blocks, we were exposed to bold color images that suggested something through and beyond this moment in time and space.

The murals, painted as sharp and realistic as photographs, treated the viewer to a tropical beach scene of swaying palm trees blowing over a Windex-blue sea and a white snow-capped mountain towering over the colorful leaves of fall trees. This theme of seeing through and beyond also repeated itself in other Bansky wall images: the black silhouette of a pigtailed girl being carried skyward as she dangled from the end of a bouquet of balloons, a white rope ladder painted to look like a life line thrown from the other side, scissors cutting on a dotted line.

Adopting a perspective that takes us "through and beyond" our own frames of reference can lead the way toward building effective bridges between U.S. and international approaches to diversity. In *Shared Futures*, an American Association of Colleges and Universities report, author Kevin Hovland (2006) argued that the American academy has witnessed such a shift from "master narratives" to "new curricular narratives." These new narratives, which emphasize the convergence between liberal (arts) learning and global learning, suggested a vastly more friendly space that would invite needed productive engagement between U.S. diversity approaches and today's internationalisms: critical internationalism (Lee, 1995), cosmopolitanism (Cheah & Robbins, 1998), postcolonial studies (Cornwell & Stoddard, 1999), global studies, intercultural studies (Bennett & Bennett, 2004; Noronha, 1992), a multicultural globalized curriculum (Baker, 1999), as well as approaches that wed identity and geography through a focus on globalization, diaspora, interculturalism-hybridity, and positionality (Cornwell & Stoddard, 1999).

Whatever our starting point, we would do well to adapt a stance of mixing, melding, and blending that Vanessa Saldivar (2010) termed *mestizaje:*

> [The concept's] utility can be derived from applying characteristics of *mestizaje* to the realm of knowledge production. Crossing boundaries, making connections, and taking elements from different disciplines, different histories, and different communities and bringing them into the same analytical space allows us to better understand questions of power. A *mestizaje* of methods essentially would deviate from disciplinary, geopolitical, and other hegemonic borders and boundaries. By bringing strategies and frameworks from one area or one discipline into another in a hybridity and fusion of knowledge production, we develop ways of combating the erasure and the isolation created by hegemonic discourse. For instance, by making connections between seemingly separate phenomena such as Arab and Latino communities or the U.S.–Mexico border and the apartheid wall in Palestine, we can see more clearly the way similar discourses and the occupation of knowledge are utilized in settler colonial projects. (pp. 827–828)

My own understanding of race and ethnicity was challenged by the experience of participating in the university curricular development of U.S. multiculturalism in the 1990s as well as the chance to teach similar material in an international setting nearly a decade later. The most important lesson I have learned in each of these situations is the need to recognize and embrace the complicated relationship between the universal and the particular when we approach constructs such as race and ethnicity. Between and within groups on the domestic stage and in an international arena there are certainly shared expressions, emotions, and desires (e.g., revenge, rage, solidarity, anxiety, depression, pride) that derive from the similar social positions of outsiders, minorities, and members of underprivileged or oppressed groups. At the same time, it is important to take note of local histories and geographies that provide distinct nuances and subtleties to such identity constructions and the response they give rise to. In the end, perhaps this is something I might never have seen had I not traveled a different road.

REFERENCES

Appleby, J. (1992). Recovering America's historic diversity: Beyond exceptionalism. *The Journal of American History, 79*, 419–431. doi:10.2307/2080033

Baker, F. (1999). Multicultural vs. global education: Why not two sides of the same coin? *Teaching Education, 12*, 97–101.

Bennett, J. M., & Bennett, M. J. (1994). Multiculturalism and international education: Domestic and international differences. In G. Althen (Ed.), *Learning across cultures* (2nd ed., pp. 145–172). Washington, DC: National Association for Foreign Student Affairs.

Bennett, J. M., & Bennett, M. J. (2004). Developing intercultural sensitivity: An integrative approach to global and domestic diversity. In D. Landis, J. M. Bennett, & M. J. Bennett (Eds.), *Handbook of intercultural training* (3rd ed., pp. 147–165). Thousand Oaks, CA: Sage. doi:10.4135/9781452231129.n6

British Broadcasting Corporation. (2010, May 13). *Israel and the Palestinians: Key terms.* Retrieved from http://news.bbc.co.uk/2/hi/in_depth/middle_east/israel_and_the_palestinians/key_documents/6044090.stm

Cheah, P., & Robbins, B. (1998). *Cosmopolitics: Thinking and feeling beyond the nation.* Minneapolis: University of Minnesota Press.

Cornwell, G. H., & Stoddard, E. W. (1999). *Globalizing knowledge: Connecting international and intercultural studies.* Washington, DC: Association of American Colleges and Universities.

Dominguez, V. R., & Desmond, J. C. (1996). Resituating American studies in a critical internationalism. *American Quarterly, 48*, 475–490. doi:10.1353/aq.1996.0031

Du Bois, W. E. B. (1982). *The souls of Black folk.* New York, NY: New American Library.

Ellingwood, K., & King, L. (2004a, January 29). Suicide bomber blows up bus; 8 Palestinians killed in Gaza clash. *The Los Angeles Times.* Retrieved from http://articles.latimes.com/2004/jan/29/world/fg-gaza29

Ellingwood, K., & King, L. (2004b, February 22). Rush hour bus explosion kills 7 in Jerusalem. *The Los Angeles Times.* Retrieved from http://articles.latimes.com/2004/feb/22/world/fg-blast22

Giroux, H. (2004). What might education mean after Abu Ghraib: Revisiting Adorno's politics of education. *Comparative Studies of South Asia, Africa and the Middle East, 24*, 5–27. doi:10.1215/1089201X-24-1-5

Giroux, H. (2005). *Border crossings: Cultural workers and the politics of education* (2nd ed.). New York, NY: Routledge.

Hovland, K. (2006). *Shared futures global learning and liberal education.* Washington, DC: Association of American Colleges and Universities.

Lee, B. (1995). Critical internationalism. *Public Culture, 7*, 559–592. doi:10.1215/08992363-7-3-559

Lloyd, D., & Pulido, L. (2010). In the long shadow of the settler: On Israeli and U.S. colonialisms. *American Quarterly, 62*, 795–809.

Noronha, J. (1992). International and multicultural education: Unrelated adversaries or successful partners. In M. Adams (Ed.), *New directions for teaching and learning* (Vol. 52, pp. 53–59). San Francisco, CA: Jossey-Bass.

Pulido, L., & Lloyd, D. (2010). From La Frontera to Gaza: Chicano–Palestinian connections. *American Quarterly, 62,* 791–794.

Said, E. W. *Orientalism.* New York, NY: Vintage.

Saldivar, V. (2010). From Mexico to Palestine: An occupation of knowledge, a mestizaje of methods. *American Quarterly, 62,* 821–833.

Simonson, R., & Walker, S. (1988). *Multicultural literacy.* Saint Paul, MN: Graywolf Press.

Taylor, M. M. (2003). *Harlem between heaven and hell.* Minneapolis: University of Minnesota Press.

Wittes, T. C. (2004). *The new U.S. proposal for a greater Middle East initiative: An evaluation.* Washington, DC: Saban Center for Middle East Policy at the Brookings Institution. Retrieved from http://www.brookings.edu/research/papers/2004/05/10middleeast-wittes

3

BRINGING GENDER INTO MULTICULTURAL AND INTERNATIONAL COMPETENCIES: STRATEGIES AND CHALLENGES

VIRGINIA FLORESCA CAWAGAS

I received my basic education from the public school system in a small town in the northern island of the Philippines. Although Filipino women were granted the right to vote only in 1937, by the 1950s, boys and girls had equal access to education in most towns, cities, and provinces in the Philippines. Filipino women's professional roles in the formal educational system were widely recognized as more women were appointed school principals, supervisors, and senior administrative officials. In this respect, the Philippine situation was better than other southern countries and regions, where girls and women were marginalized in schooling as well as in higher education opportunities.

In 2010, the Philippines ranked ninth in the World Economic Forum's Global Gender Gap Index, a measure of economic participation and opportunity, educational attainment, political empowerment, and health and survival of women (Hausmann, Tyson, & Zahidi, 2010). The Philippines is the only Asian country included in the top 10 rankings, which are dominated by the

DOI: 10.1037/14044-003
Internationalizing Multiculturalism: Expanding Professional Competencies in a Globalized World,
R. L. Lowman (Editor)

Nordic countries such as Iceland, Finland, Norway, and Sweden. In the same report, the United Kingdom ranked 15th; the United States, 19th; Canada, 20th; and Australia, 23rd. Despite this narrowing of the gender gap in terms of women's economic participation and opportunity, health and survival, and political empowerment, Filipino women continue to face discrimination and all forms of inequalities, whether in their homeland or in their new host countries.

As I joined international educational networks such as the World Council for Curriculum and Instruction and the Peace Education Commission of the International Peace Research Association and shared research work with colleagues, it became more evident that even in highly industrialized societies, gender inequalities persist. Globally, women still face challenges and barriers to full participation in society because of embedded social, cultural, economic, and political structures that continue to marginalize them. Women and girls are more likely to be the poorest and most disadvantaged in many communities worldwide. More often than not, they are excluded from decision making in the economic, social, and political arenas. Few women have independent control of resources, especially in rural communities. Despite this systemic marginalization, they have managed to raise children, put food on the table, and care for the sick.

Through the inspiring advocacy and political struggles of individual women and women's organizations worldwide, progress has slowly been made in overcoming gender-based inequalities and the violations of women's human rights. One key outcome is what is known as *gender mainstreaming* in diverse fields of social, political, economic, and cultural policies, and institutions. In educational systems, for example, gender mainstreaming means the inclusion of policies for equal opportunity for girls and women to access all academic and professional fields, the development of nonsexist curricula, and the use of nonsexist language. This mainstreaming is essential in all fields of educational thought and innovation, including multicultural education and international education. Hence, as this chapter endeavors to show, multicultural and international education needs to integrate concepts and issues of, inter alia, gender inequality and strategies for promoting women's human rights, equitable participation in development, and security from violence of all forms in highly multicultural societies such as the United States, Canada, Australia, and some European countries.

For the purpose of this chapter, the United Nations International Research and Training Institute for the Advancement of Women (INSTRAW; http://www.un-instraw.org) definitions of gender-related terms are used:

- *Sex* refers to the biological characteristics which define humans as female or male. These sets of biological characteristics are not mutually exclusive as there are individuals who possess both, but these characteristics tend to differentiate humans as males and females.

- *Gender* refers to the array of socially constructed roles and relationships, personality traits, attitudes, behaviors, values, relative power and influence that society ascribes to the two sexes on a differential basis. Whereas biological sex is determined by genetic and anatomical characteristics, gender is an acquired identity that is learned, changes over time, and varies widely within and across cultures. Gender is relational and refers not simply to women or men but to the relationship between them.
- *Gender equality* entails the concept that all human beings, both men and women, are free to develop their personal abilities and make choices without the limitations set by stereotypes, rigid gender roles, or prejudices. Gender equality means that the different behaviors, aspirations and needs of women and men are considered, valued and favored equally. It does not mean that women and men have to become the same, but that their rights, responsibilities and opportunities will not depend on whether they are born male or female.
- *Gender equity* means fairness of treatment for women and men, according to their respective needs. This may include equal treatment or treatment that is different but considered equivalent in terms of rights, benefits, obligations and opportunities. In the development context, a gender equity goal often requires built-in measures to compensate for the historical and social disadvantages of women.

The 1995 Beijing Platform of Action produced during the U.N. Fourth World Conference of Women (http://www.un.org/womenwatch/daw/beijing/platform) summarized 12 critical areas of concern that need to be addressed by governments, the international community, and civil society. These concerns can be confronted only by working in partnership with men toward a goal of gender equity around the world. The Platform of Action also recognizes the wide spectrum of women's situations and the varying degrees of barriers to their full empowerment.

Although all these concerns are equally important, because of space limitations, this chapter focuses on three areas within and across societies in which gender interrelates with the daily lives of citizens: militarization and physical violence, culture, and economic and social justice. Through all these dimensions, women's human rights are a pivotal theme. I draw on my personal and social experiences in peace education and peace building in both North (or global North) and South (or global South) contexts to illustrate these interrelationships and offer some gender-sensitive multicultural-international competencies for professionals.

In this chapter, the term *North* is used to describe the wealthy, advanced industrialized nations in Europe and North America as well as the countries of Australia, New Zealand, Japan, Russia, and South Korea; *South* is used to describe the less industrialized and economically poorer countries of the world. However, conceptually, it is also important to recognize that within the South, there are also a minority of rich elites whose income and wealth approximate living standards in the North, and likewise within the North, there is invariably a minority sector of poor citizens who live in Southlike conditions. As explained in the project report of the Jubilee Debt Campaign (A. King, 2010),

> Although it doesn't correspond with exact geography (most obviously Australia is clearly in the "south" of the globe), it is neutral in terms of not assuming poor countries want to develop in the same way as rich countries, and that there are political connections between those countries who have traditionally become wealthy through exploitation, and those that have been exploited. (p. 2)

The other chapters of this book duly acknowledge the multiple layers of discrimination such as ethnicity, sexual orientation, class, religion, age, and disabilities. This chapter focuses on the possibilities of addressing gender issues in the interweaving of multicultural and international competencies for teachers and other professionals in related fields.

GENDER, MILITARIZATION, AND DIRECT VIOLENCE

Humanity today continues to face the serious problem of militarization and the direct violence that accompanies its manifestations from armed conflicts and the cycle of terrorism and counterterrorism to genocidal violence, violent criminal activities, and domestic abuse. Although both sexes are affected, women as a group have been especially victimized (Gnanadason, Kanyuro, & McSpadden, 1996). To understand the role of women in the world today, it is hence crucial that professionals fully understand this intricate web of global and local militarization and the violence and physical abuse that have been inflicted on women in diverse societies. The violence ranges from the use of "comfort women" for the "rest and recreation" (R&R) of military personnel during wartime, to rape as a weapon of war, to trafficking in women and girls for the sex tourism industry, to the violence inflicted in the so-called private sphere in the form of domestic abuse.

It is also important to be aware of the prevalence of symbolic and other institutional manifestations of a culture of war, such as the role of the media in glorifying and promoting a culture of war and violence against women. Consider, for example, the continual presentation of demeaning representations of women as sex objects and "beauty"-obsessed brainless overgrown dolls. Consider, too, the ubiquitous image of the obedient housewife whose whole-day marathon includes cleaning the oven, exterminating the ever-persistent mosquito, spraying the most recent room freshener aroma, and serving meals, while other members of the household rush out to perform the productive roles they play for themselves or the family.

War and Gender Violence

It was 1944. News about the surrender of the Japanese army toward the end of World War II spread quickly in the villages of our province, La Union, in Northern Luzon, Philippines. People silently but tensely awaited the unfolding of each day, praying for the Japanese occupation to end. The rampaging of the retreating Japanese soldiers had created extreme fear among the womenfolk, after hearing horrible stories of how young and old women alike were raped and sexually abused.

My mother was a young married woman with two young children—myself, barely able to walk, and my younger brother, whom she was still nursing. The shock came quite unexpectedly. Two Japanese officials barged into the house and ordered my mother and an aunt, both carrying babies, to go with them to the "cadre" or Japanese camp.

My father, I was told, took me in his arms, and we followed my mother, my aunt, and the two Japanese soldiers. Halfway to the camp in the middle of the rice fields, the soldiers motioned my father to go back. We stopped but followed the group as soon as they started walking away. This was repeated many times, but my father and I would not leave my mother. This angered the soldiers.

Then the soldiers pointed and cocked their rifles at my father. At that moment, my mother with my brother in her arms, my aunt with her baby in her arms, my father, and I myself knelt on the ground, bent our heads, prayed for God's blessings and waited for the burst of firepower. My father used to say it must have been only a few seconds, but it felt like eternity. There was no gunshot.

We heard a loud command: "Go, all of you. Go home!" We looked up and saw the soldiers uncock their guns and walk briskly back to their barracks. The soldiers' decision to let us go was beyond belief, and our family will never know why my mother and aunt were spared.

Although the systematic violation of women during World War II was practiced through the now widely known comfort women phenomenon, in which women in East Asian and Southeast Asian countries occupied by the Japanese military were imprisoned as sex slaves in camps, this news was circulated only in whispers in my province during the war. However, the individual actions of both foot soldiers and their officers were highly dreaded by the womenfolk in every village in the Philippines, especially during the last few months leading up to the expected liberation.

It is difficult to read through pages of personal testimonies of World War II comfort women who have been physically, psychologically, emotionally, socially, and culturally abused and systematically violated (Dolgopol & Pranjape, 1994) as described in the International Court of Justice Report without feeling their anger, pain, humiliation, and frustration. Yet these emotions of empathy can hardly compare with the actual sufferings inflicted on thousands of women by the violence of colonialism and militarism. My reflections on the issue of comfort women concentrate on the underpinning values and motivations for such institutionalized violation of the rights of women and the ensuing complicity of silence (and almost tacit approval) also on a systemic and structural levels.

Although the majority of the comfort women were Korean, there is no shortage of evidence showing that women from China, Indonesia, Taiwan, and the Philippines were also "used" in this role. In these societies, chastity is a virtue every woman is expected to uphold. "In such a society, the rape victim becomes 'soiled goods' bringing shame and dishonor to the family" (Jimenez-David, 1994, p. 1). After the war, the raped women became social outcasts denied the emotional and physical support of families and friends, whereas those who managed to keep secret their conscription to sexual duties had to live with their brutalization in indescribable anguish and loneliness.

Although the violence inflicted on the comfort women took place more than 70 years ago, similar abuses and violence have been and are committed against women in many places of armed conflict and military operations. In 1971, for example, a war broke out in East Pakistan when the people sought their independence from the West. Although the vicious war gave birth to the nation now known as Bangladesh, the toll came in millions dead or made refugees in India, as well as the gruesome rape of the Bengali women. Stories recorded West Pakistan soldiers raping the women in the rebellious territory before the eyes of the horrified menfolk. This systematic and wholesale rape was a deliberate strategy intended to demoralize the Bengali men, to sap them of their will to fight (Brownmiller, 1975). Although an estimated 40,000 women were raped and violated, the strategy did not work. However, after the war, the agony and pain of the raped women did not stop. Although they were "victims," the women were driven out of their homes by their husbands, daughters, and fathers. When the raped women began giving birth to "fairer children with shocks of curly brownish hair," the unmistakable stamp of Pakistani soldiers, the trauma was even more aggravated. The newborn Bangladeshi government had to give "cash incentives" to men who were willing to marry the "marked" women. The women ended up not only as victims of war but also as victims of their own menfolk as well (Jimenez-David, 1994).

Two decades ago, in full view of the whole world, a similar scourge plagued the former Yugoslavia as thousands of Bosnian women and girls were sexually violated, brutalized, and murdered as part of the systematic humiliation and genocide of the Bosnian people. Although there was more international outrage over the mass violation of women in the former Yugoslavia than in previous similar situations, the official sanctions or preventive actions of world governments have not been any more swift and serious than the response to the phenomena of comfort women and the rape of Bengali women. According to Amnesty International (2009), the governments of Bosnia and Herzegovina have failed to provide justice for thousands of women and girls who were raped during the 1992–1995 war.

Systematic mass rape has been frequently used as a weapon of war. During the Armenian genocide, Armenian women and girls were systematically raped and tortured. Indigenous Mayan women and girls were similarly assaulted during the Guatemalan genocide (1981–1983), Tutsi women and girls during the Rwandan genocide (1994), and non-Arab Darfurian women during the counterinsurgency in Darfur (2003–2005).

The evacuation of women and children from war zones to refugee camps has not necessarily ended their exposure to sexual violence. We continually hear about women being raped on their way to and inside refugee camps, the very shelters that have been built supposedly to provide temporary sanctuary for victims of war.

Numerous human rights reports have also amply documented how Thailand and the Philippines were set up as the R&R center for American soldiers during the Vietnam War. In 1967, Thailand and the U.S. military agreed to allow American soldiers stationed in Vietnam to visit Thailand for R&R (Asia Watch and the Women's Rights Project, 1993). In that year alone, the estimated spending of the U.S. military personnel on R&R in Thailand was $5 million, a figure that rose to $20 million by 1970—as much as one fourth of Vietnam's total rice exports for that year (Truong, 1990). In the Philippines, where two of the largest military bases outside the United States were stationed until 1992, the traditional army "camp bordellos" adopted the appearance and organization of a modern industry: R&R for the soldiers. Father Shay Cullen, an Irish priest fighting against trade in women and children, disclosed that during the worst moments of the Vietnam War, thousands of American soldiers came to the Philippines to give vent to their sexual frustrations. During the 1970s and 1980s, Filipinas were imported en masse to Okinawa, the recreation center for Japanese soldiers before it came under American authority, for the pleasure of American military servicemen (De Stoop, 1994).

"Peace" Time and Violence Against Women

As the dehumanization of women in war zones continues, an equally brutalizing trade flourishes "quietly" in all parts of the so-called world at peace. Sex tourism, or the promotion of sex as a purpose of travel in certain Asian and African countries, has long been used by governments (unofficially) and private business (usually with protection from the police and/or military or powerful politicians) as a revenue source (De Stoop, 1994; Enloe, 2000; Jimenez-David, 1994). In many Asian countries, especially Thailand, Taiwan, the Philippines, Indonesia, and South Korea, thousands of foreign male tourists flock in search of the Three S's: sun, sea, and sex. Hundreds of thousands of women have been forced either by socioeconomic circumstances or direct physical threat to work as prostitutes, social escorts, massage parlor girls, sauna bath attendants, dance hostesses, and waitresses in nightclubs and cocktail lounges. The euphemisms for all these trades include "hospitality girls," "artists," "entertainers," "cultural groups," and "ballet groups" (Asia Watch and the Women's Rights Project, 1993; Black, 1994; De Stoop, 1994; Jimenez-David, 1994; O'Kelly & Carney, 1986).

A logical partner of sex tourism is trafficking in women and girls. By the 1970s, the flow of people involved in the sex trade was two-directional: rich men from Japan, Australia, Europe, and the Middle East to Manila and Bangkok, and poor Filipinas to Japan and Europe (Asia Watch and the Women's Rights Project, 1993; De Stoop, 1994). According to Bruckert and Parent (2002),

> the issue of the "trade" or "trafficking" in human beings that started to be raised during the latter part of the 1980s did not really enter into the mainstream until the 1990s. Most of the publications on this subject did not appear until the latter part of that decade. (p. 2)

The small island of Cyprus, with a population of less than a million, is the distribution center for trade in women in the Middle East and transfer station onward to Europe. De Stoop (1994) reported that for many years, the supply of women via Cyprus came from the Philippines and the Dominican Republic, but since the Berlin Wall came down, there has been a massive flow of Romanian, Bulgarian, Hungarian, and Polish women. Regular customers are Cypriot men and soldiers from the United Nations and British bases; during high season, European and Arab male tourists are favored clients. The U.S. Department of State (2011) confirmed that Cyprus is still a destination country for men and women who are trafficked from Russia, Moldova, Ukraine, Hungary, Bulgaria, Romania, Belarus, the Philippines, Morocco, China, Vietnam, Uzbekistan, Greece, the United Kingdom, Colombia, and the Dominican Republic.

Women from Central and Eastern Europe and the former Soviet Union are trafficked through formal and informal channels all over the world (Advocates for Human Rights, n.d.). Up to 18,000 females are working in brothels across Britain after being smuggled into the country. Police revealed that nearly five times more women than previously thought are working under duress in massage parlors and suburban homes (Milmo & Morris, 2008).

Law enforcement and immigration officials reported that entry points for trafficked women into the United States are strategic sites along the U.S.–Canadian border. . . . Military bases were additionally cited as gateways for trafficked women. . . . Upon arrival in the United States, women are housed in various locations, pending movement to other parts of the country. (Raymond & Hughes, 2001, p. 55)

Furthermore, Interpol (2011) reported that

trafficking in women is a criminal phenomenon that violates basic human rights, totally destroying victims lives. Countries are affected in various ways. Some see their young women being lured to leave their home country and ending up in the sex industry abroad. Other countries act mainly as transit countries, while several others receive foreign women who become victims of sexual exploitation.

Millions of women and girls are bought and sold worldwide into marriage, prostitution, or slavery, lured into the hands of traffickers by promises of jobs (United Nations Population Fund, 2000).

The establishment of R&R centers for servicemen and the promotion of sex tourism as well as the local "red districts" are, I argue, all syndromes of structural violence in which women are treated as commodities to be shuffled in the process of trading. Anecdotal evidence of women and girls in the so-called sex industry indicate that a great majority of them have been forced or lured into their "occupation" by powerful economic and social forces operating in the rural and urban poor communities as well as in the international network. Young women and girls living in extreme poverty in rural villages or urban slums in the Philippines, Burma, Thailand, the Dominican Republic, Nigeria, Romania, Bulgaria, Poland, or anywhere else become easy prey when attractive packages of economic improvement and security are flaunted in their or their parents' faces in the process of recruitment. However, if we ask why there is so much poverty in these areas, we need to question the role of governments, private business, and industry in the lopsided "development" of rural and urban communities. Where rural people who have traditionally lived on the land have been dispossessed or relocated because of logging, agribusiness, or hamletting in the case of civil wars, the question of survival drives every member of the family to grab any opportunity for work that can bring immediate relief from the pain of hunger and other forms of deprivation. The paradigm of modernization pushed by governments in the North and South, as well as transnational agencies including international financial institutions, has largely benefitted an elite and middle-class minority, marginalizing urban and rural poor. In "frontier" areas of resource exploitation, women of indigenous peoples displaced by logging, ranching, and mining are pushed into a sex trade to serve the sexual appetites of new or internal colonizers in violent and degrading ways.

Another category of serious violence inflicted on women during "peace" time in the private sphere is legally referred to as *domestic abuse* or *domestic violence*. It is so pervasive that it has been regarded as reaching epidemic proportion (Gracia & Herrero, 2006; W. King, 2006). The National Coalition Against Domestic Violence (NCADV; n.d.) defined domestic violence as the "willful intimidation, physical assault, battery, sexual assault, and/or other abusive behavior perpetrated by an intimate partner against another" (p. 1). The facts provided on their website reveal that an estimated 1.3 million women are victims of physical assault by an intimate partner each year. According to Gracia (2004), this is likely an underestimation because most cases of domestic violence are never reported to the police.

Although advocacy groups like NCADV and the National Organization for Women have worked for decades to stop the epidemic of gender-based violence and sexual assault, there has been no significant reduction in reported cases. This has so alarmed women's advocacy groups that they challenged all government leaders, from the U.S. president down to city councils to make a commitment to end violence inflicted on women and men, girls, and boys through domestic abuse. They further enjoined all those working in offices, schools, churches, the military, courtrooms, law enforcement, entertainment, and the media to be seriously involved in the campaign to reduce, if not eliminate, domestic violence.

Gender-based violence is committed in various communities regardless of the cultural tradition or origin of a group. The violence includes rape, domestic violence, and trafficking in women. Physical abuse is almost always accompanied by psychological abuse (Heise, 1994). Millions of women have suffered from the impact of gender-based violence and yet have little or no recourse to medical attention. Ironically, the women are always under a cloud of fear, thus inhibiting truthful discussion of the issue, a sure condition that the phenomenon will continue. All these exact a heavy toll on the mental and physical health of women that is also now recognized as a public health issue. In all likelihood, many professionals will have contact with the victims of this abuse or mistreatment.

COMPETENCIES FOR CHALLENGING PHYSICAL VIOLENCE AGAINST WOMEN AND FOR ENHANCING GENDER EQUITY

Although the many examples of the impact of militarization, patriarchal cultures, and the neoliberal agenda of globalization on women are life experiences of women miles away from industrialized countries such as the United States and Canada, the continuing oppression and exploitation of women, regardless of location, undermines their dignity and self-confidence and stunts their constructive participation in community life. Hence, multicultural and international competencies for every professional, especially educators, health care providers, social workers, and business executives, need to include sensitivity to problems of physical violence toward women as well as a commitment to help remove or reduce opportunities for continuing abuses.

For example, on the issue of tourism, public education, whether formal or nonformal, should focus on acquiring skills of intercultural understanding and communication to prevent cultural disrespect and conflict, but it is equally important for professionals to be critical of the tourism industry that has included sex tourism so that citizens of the North or West, who may be potential tourists, can be educated and motivated to also help in monitoring cases of trafficking or saving trafficked women. Entrepreneurs and executives in the tourist industry likewise need cultural sensitivity and competency to recognize and reject advertising and promotional strategies that explicitly or implicitly identify women as sexual objects. They should also decline business proposals that facilitate sex tours and advocate for laws against sex trafficking and sexual exploitation.

For professionals providing health care services and social services, another important competency is awareness and critical understanding of the histories and origins of women and their experiences of abuse or oppression so that appropriate interventions can be offered. Survivors of sexual violence are at high risk of experiencing psychological conditions and are at increased risk of revictimization (Olufunmilayo, 2009). As recommended by the American Psychological Association's (APA's; 2007) *Guidelines for Psychological Practice With Girls and Women*, "psychologists are encouraged to recognize and utilize information about oppression, privilege, and identity development as they may affect girls and women" (p. 37). This competence is also essential for other professionals, including those in human resource offices so that they can offer appropriate support and encouragement to members of their organization who come with scars from the past. Given the sensitivity and often the cloud of secrecy accompanying the problem of domestic abuse, it is important for professionals to create an environment of trust that will enhance the promotion of rehabilitation rather than self-righteous judgment. On an individual level, the traditions of patriarchy can legitimize the exploitation and commodification of women as sexual objects by individual men. But when the behavior is promoted by institutions such as the military and government, the rationalization assumes a structural dimension. Hence, it is essential for professionals, as well as advocates, community leaders, and law enforcement officers to have the competencies needed to consider the problems of girls and women in their sociopolitical context, recognizing the role of systems and institutions in sustaining or reinforcing their marginalization and commodification.

GENDER AND CULTURE

Predictably, one of the early images we saw from "liberated" Kabul was a woman "liberated" from the burka. Or was she? Momentarily, possibly to satisfy the whim of a Western news photographer, she lifted the veil. The picture, flashed around the world, reinforced the belief that all that stood between Afghan women and liberation was that piece of cloth (Sharma, 2001, p. 1).

The misguided belief in many parts of the world that a "veiled" woman is not an empowered woman is a typical example of stereotyping Muslim women as embodiments of powerless and submissive beings walking behind men as prescribed in Islamic religious teachings. Following this logic leads to a simplistic conclusion that women in Muslim societies are liberated if they are not obligated to wear a veil or a burka. Thus, the complex issue of women's empowerment is reduced to the symbolic: removal of the veil, access to traditionally male-dominated careers, appointment to top executive positions in business, or holding cabinet positions in government. As Rao (1995) explained,

> Through their clothing and demeanor, women and girls become visible and vulnerable embodiments of cultural symbols and codes. In addition, the primary identification of the woman with the family and home, in the problematic separation of "public" and "private" spheres of existence, contributes to her secondary status in the very realm where her future is debated and even decided: the public. (p. 169)

There is often an unchallenged assumption that economic growth, unprecedented technological advances, modernized means of communication and transportation, and sophisticated political arrangements will be reflected in positive attitudinal and behavior changes in both the public and private spheres. Regrettably, society may have advanced technologically and economically, but the private-sphere issues of identity, traditions, and gender roles in the family have not changed much. The members of many cultures, whether in their original homeland or migrated across the oceans, maintain a traditional patriarchal system in which men are the primary decision makers and women generally acquiesce so as not to incur community disapproval.

Okin (1999) published a provocative essay titled, "Is Multiculturalism Bad for Women?" Her contention came in the midst of national debates in which "critics of multiculturalism commonly argued that it encouraged society to turn a blind eye to abuses of women and children" (Phillips, 2007, p. 73). Despite much criticism from several multiculturalists against Okin's thesis, her claim that minority cultural groups are themselves gendered, with substantial differences of power and advantage between men and women, deserves consideration. Okin argued that the debates on multiculturalism generally lacked a gendered perspective and that multiculturalists like Kymlicka

(1995) had a gender-blind conception of culture, potentially endangering women's and girls' human rights:

> The main reason for the gender blindness of multiculturalists is the failure to see "minority" cultures as internally stratified with uneven power relations between men and women; minority cultural groups are instead conceived of as monolithic, and the differences between them are given more attention than the differences within. (Okin 1999, p. 12)

Sarah Song (2005), in illustrating the conflict that can arise between multiculturalism and gender equality, cited the example of a Supreme Court of New York County decision on the case of *People v. Chen* in 1988. Chen, a New York resident, upon discovering his wife's infidelity, beat and killed her. Chen confessed to killing his wife because she had committed adultery.

> An anthropologist testified that violence against unfaithful spouses was commonplace in Chinese culture. Chen was found guilty of second-degree manslaughter. Relying heavily on cultural evidence, the judge sentenced him to 5 years' probation with no jail time, a much lighter punishment than that usually associated with a second degree manslaughter conviction. (Song, 2005, p. 473)

Several cultural practices carried over to the new countries by immigrants perpetuate the power structure privileging the men and weakening the women. Often these practices are sustained through the multiculturalism policy of respecting and giving space to cultural groups in their exercise of group rights. This becomes problematic as demonstrated in the practice of female circumcision (or female genital mutilation [FGM] as a descriptor formulated by Western societies), "honor" killing, and forced or prearranged marriages.

FGM is the partial or total removal of the female external genitalia of girls generally between 4 to 12 years old, although there are some communities where the procedure is performed much earlier or much later in the girl's life. Advocates of women's rights use the term *female genital mutilation*, but it has been critiqued by women in communities where the practice is prevalent on the basis of being one more imposition of Western feminist cultural imperialism. Hence an alternative term, *female circumcision*, is sometimes used to describe the same process (Center for Reproductive Rights, 2004). The debate about whether FGM is an issue of cultural relativism or of human rights continues. Meanwhile, many human rights organizations agree that the practice is a violation of the rights of girls and children (as it is usually performed on young girls) and therefore should be banned or eradicated. Many non-Western organizations, such as the Egyptian Human Rights Organization, have also joined this movement. The campaign of the latter focuses on educating Egyptians on the harm inflicted to individuals and society and also on clarifying that the practice is not an Islamic tradition.

According to Toubia (1993), FGM is practiced in at least 26 of 43 African and some ethnic groups in Oman, the United Arab Emirates, Yemen, India, Indonesia, and Malaysia. It is important to note that until the 1950s, FGM was performed in England and the United States as a common "treatment" for lesbianism, masturbation, hysteria, epilepsy, and other so-called female deviances (Koso-Thomas, 1987). Although the main reason for the universal objection to FGM is the medical complication, other compelling reasons are more socially, psychologically, and emotionally motivated. Secondary education has been associated with an increase in the disapproval of FGM among communities that practice it. Other reasons include girls' refusal to submit to the procedure, greater access to health education, modernization with its resulting changes in lifestyle, fear of anti-FGM laws, public ridicule, and the realization that FGM has no effect on girls' behavior (Hosken, 1993). Most cultures have officially recognized the practice as a negative tradition or a distortion of religious belief and, above all, dehumanizing to the women who are circumcised.

Despite the banning of the practice in the original countries, FGM has become an important issue in Australia, Canada, England, France, and the United States, where it continues to be practiced by a number of immigrants. Although FGM was prohibited in the United States through the enactment of a federal law in 1996, there may be unintended consequences resulting from such criminalization. As the Ontario Consultants on Religious Tolerance (n.d.) warned,

> It might force the practice deeply underground. Women may not seek medical care later in life because their parents might be [criminally] charged. The operation can be life threatening if performed by untrained individuals; if the operation is botched, the parents may be reluctant to take the child to a hospital out of fear of being criminally charged with child abuse. On the other hand, it does indicate that the government has taken a stand against FGM. This, and potential penalties, may well cause some parents to decide against having their daughter(s) mutilated. (para. 3)

The United Nations Population Fund (UNFPA) estimates that 5,000 women are killed every year in "honor" crimes through various methods such as acid burning, stoning, stabbing, and burying alive (Vlachovd & Biason, 2005). In the United States and Canada, when such crimes occur, the perpetrators provide various reasons including suspected adultery, dressing in American-style clothing, young girls having boyfriends, not honoring prearranged marriage, or the victims seeking a divorce. Such justifications constitute violations of human rights embodied in the Universal Declaration of Human Rights as well as the law of the land. Yet, despite the existence of formal laws, it seems that cultural traditions are given greater value by some cultural groups when it comes to the rights of women.

Narayan (1997), however, cautioned against such cultural framing "when women's issues originating in Third World contexts cross borders, either through migration or media, the use of cultural framing is especially acute" (p. 85). Thus, when dowry murders and honor killings are committed, they are most often identified as culturally driven acts of violence. On the other hand, when, in the West, deaths occur through domestic violence, they are simply referred to as domestic violence, without any cultural ascriptions. As further noted by Volpp (2000), "Culture is invoked in a highly selective way, such that virtually identical misdemeanors by White North Americans and nonwhite immigrants get attributed to culture only when the defendants come from a racialized minority group" (pp. 89–116). Similarly, Razak (2004) argued that

> a contextualized approach to the problem of forced marriages and honour killings has been singularly lacking in law where the idea of culture clash has held sway. In their construction as "honour killings" these murders are not understood as illustrations of a generic violence against women, a violence that majority and minority cultures often fail to condemn. Culture, but minority culture only, assumes a preeminence that is discernible in the efforts made in legal documents and reports to distinguish honour killings from other instances of violence against women. (p. 151)

Although this academic discourse on the appropriate framing of the practice of forced marriages continues, several advocates for women's rights against all forms of violence are actively organizing and mobilizing to provide immediate amelioration as well as long-term solutions. Tahirih Justice Center (2011), an organization protecting immigrant women and girls fleeing violence, has reported a number of cases of forced marriages involving young women from immigrant families now living in the United States. The families in which these forced marriages occur are U.S. citizens, legal permanent residents, refugees, asylum seekers, or have other immigration statuses. In May 2011, Tahirih launched a national survey for service providers, advocates, community leaders, educators, law enforcement officers, and other professionals who may have vital information about cases of forced marriage (either threatened or that have already occurred) in immigrant communities in the United States (http://www.tahirih.org). To preempt any misinterpretations, Tahirih warned that the survey is not intended to stigmatize any community but rather to assist in a better understanding of the nature and scope of forced marriages in immigrant communities in the United States.

COMPETENCIES TO CHALLENGE CULTURE-BASED DISCRIMINATION AND ENHANCE GENDER EQUITY

Given all these challenges to achieving gender equity and equality in both the public and private spheres, professionals can be assisted in the performance of their responsibilities with some guidelines for gender-sensitive and appropriate competencies. One of the competencies recommended by the APA (2007) for psychologists (but it could be equally applicable for most professions) is "to be aware of the effects of socialization, stereotyping, and unique life events in the development of girls and women across diverse cultural groups" (p. 35). For teachers and counselors in schools, it is equally important to be sensitive to possible gender stereotyping and discrimination on the basis of cultural norms and beliefs.

It is also important for all professionals to have an adequate knowledge and understanding of how oppression, racism, discrimination, and stereotyping affect them personally. This allows for self-reflection and interrogation of their own "sexist" or "racist" attitudes and feelings. This understanding is essential for all professionals, but especially for men so that they may be able to better understand how they may have directly or indirectly participated in, or benefited from, individual or institutional sexism. Trainers and teachers should be able to reflect on their own prejudices and how their pedagogies can either oppress or empower their learners (Banks, 2004; Nieto, 2000; Quezada & Romo, 2004). Gender-sensitive competency encourages men to be mindful of how their own belief system and behavior may be governed by stereotypes.

It is also helpful for community leaders, educators, and advocacy groups to have the capacity to raise awareness among elders and other leaders of communities where forced or arranged marriages are practiced and persuade them to give more equity to women to choose their own partners or at least for women in arranged relationships to make the final decision on who is the acceptable spouse.

In dealing with sensitive and complex issues such as culture-driven gender discrimination or violence, all professionals need to have the willingness and skills to engage in respectful conversations. It is inappropriate (and at times irresponsible), for example, to attribute to an entire culture or religion blame for violence. It is also important to open a dialogue, not simply to make pronouncements, about cultural norms that may be presumed as the right to control or punish wives or children. Having the competency to engage in respectful but meaningful dialogue may lead to the illumination or understanding that culture or religion cannot be taken carte blanche as the basis for justifying domestic violence.

Professionals should have the ability to assess and evaluate information to identify gender biases and gaps so that appropriate action and practices may be recommended. It is also helpful for professionals to develop communication and advocacy skills that help them become gender-competent agents of change.

SOCIAL JUSTICE AND GENDER

Another aspect of the discourse in multiculturalism is the depoliticization of multicultural and intercultural education, which has led to what Gorski (2005) described as "conservatized multicultural education." In such a conservative understanding and practice of multiculturalism, the goal of social justice or the elimination of inequalities has been glossed over as teachers and advocates of multiculturalism engage in "cultural plunges" of dress, dance, dialect, and diet.

Underdevelopment, with its symptoms of poverty, hunger, malnutrition, famines, disease, homelessness, unemployment, urban slums, illiteracy, rich–poor inequalities, and growing gaps between developed and developing nations, is no longer a local problem of poor countries but a worldwide phenomenon. Even if women and girls escape the onslaught of direct physical violence, they often become victims of *structural violence,* a term first introduced by Galtung (1969) and now used to describe a form of violence based on the systemic ways in which social, economic, and political structures and institutions may inflict violence on people by preventing them from meeting their basic needs for survival.

Over the decades, most North and South governments have opted for a paradigm of national development premised on modernization or, as it is more commonly described today, globalization. Guided by this paradigm, local, regional, and national economic resources in South countries have been harnessed to fuel rapid growth and a shift from subsistence agriculture to commercialized or cash-crop agribusiness, industrialization, export-oriented manufacturing, free trade zones, urbanization, heavy external borrowings, reliance on foreign aid and transnational corporations, and free-market mechanisms.

In the field of economic development, policymakers, aid agencies, and entrepreneurs likewise have increasingly recognized the need to mainstream gender sensitivity and equality in the private sector. The resultant empowerment of women and girls via their increased participation in the labor force, higher incomes, equal access to resources (e.g., education, training, loans, markets, financial services, business ownership, networks, professional associations) improves the quality of life of the women and girls as well as their society's economic and social development (Danida, 2008).

The integration of many national economies into the globalized economic order has also led to an increasing flow of millions of educated local citizens going abroad as overseas contract workers in Asia, the Middle East, North America, and Europe. This acceleration of global capitalism has also given rise to the gendered labor relations from which the term *feminization of labor* has emerged. This describes the feminization of the workplace characterized by greater employment of women and also of the willingness of men to operate within these more feminized workplaces (Mueller, 2000; Rosales, 1999). Although feminization of labor is a result of expansion of trade, capital flows, and technological advances, it has also led to gender discrimination, violence, sweatshops, and sexual harassment.

In the urban industrialized sectors, the integration of women into the new international division of labor comes in the form of cheap labor in foreign-dominated export processing or free trade zones. Another major international job opportunity for women is the phenomenon of overseas contract or migrant workers, usually as nurses, domestic helpers, or caregivers for families in the rich, industrialized North.

From 1993 to 2003, I taught peace education in the MA and PhD programs in global and international education at the University of Alberta, Canada, where there was a good mix of local and international students. One afternoon my NGO network called for assistance to help Susana, a Filipino live-in caregiver, who was going to be deported the following morning for violating the rules of employment under the live-in caregiver program. After assessing her case and the options available, we mobilized our students and our NGO network, and before midnight Susana was safely sheltered in a sanctuary at the rectory of a Catholic Church near the university. Susana had been a live-in caregiver for 2 years and thus, under the Canadian Caregiver Program, she was entitled to apply for permanent residency; after 3 years or more, she could apply for Canadian citizenship.

This dream and opportunity for Susana suddenly vanished as she remained holed up in a sanctuary for 6 months. During those months, our students, NGOs, churches, media, and a few politicians lobbied the Canadian government to reconsider the deportation order for Susana. Although she was ostensibly being deported for a violation of the live-in caregiver program, ironically, the incident in question was not of her doing but was something done by her Canadian employer. Although we did not succeed in stopping the deportation, we managed to get a commitment from responsible officials of the ministry of immigration to allow Susana to return to Canada and apply for a permanent resident status. It did not take long before Susana returned to Canada under the same live-in caregiver program. Today her family from the Philippines is reunited with her, and they are now living constructive lives in Edmonton, Alberta.

The story of Susana is the tale of millions of migrant workers in the Middle East, Europe, the United States, Hong Kong, and Singapore (International Labor Organization, 2003). Although Susana's case had a happy ending, there is a wealth of evidence showing that many female migrant workers end up being exploited and abused through the confiscation of their passport upon arrival in their country of work, extremely harsh working conditions, curtailment of their basic rights, physical assault, and sexual violence.

The global debt trap has crippled many poor countries that have to pay rich countries for debts from which they did not benefit (Mandel, 2006). As Edwards (2009) also explained, "irresponsible lending has included loans to oppressive regimes; for corrupt, useless or overpriced projects; or on unfair terms, creating huge illegitimate debt burdens that fall on the poorest people" (p. 6). When debt payments drain the poorest countries of resources, the women suffer the most because basic social services are the first to be sacrificed just so indebted countries will not default on their payment. The Jubilee Debt Campaign (http://www.jubileedebtcampaign.org.uk), successor to Jubilee 2000 and Drop the Debt programs, is a U.K. coalition of national organizations, local groups, and individuals that campaigns for the cancellation of unjust debts, borrowed mostly by corrupt leaders or brutal dictators (Edwards, 2009).

> In the year 2000, a petition calling for the cancellation of debts owed by impoverished countries to rich world nations—so-called Third World Debt—was handed to the Secretary-General of the United Nations. It had over 24 million signatures and was entered into the *Guinness Book of Records* twice, as the world's biggest petition and the most international petition, with signatures from more than 166 countries. (A. King, 2010, p. 2)

The campaign has succeeded, although slowly, in obtaining the cancellation of debts of some countries (e.g., Zambia, Uganda, Benin, Bolivia). When countries do get debts cancelled, it can make a big difference for women. For example, "primary school fees abolished in Uganda [resulted] in enrolment doubling and the amount of girls in education increasing to almost equal that of boys" (A. King, 2010, p. 15).

Amid all the challenges, many women have neither internalized their "victimhood" nor remained passive. A number of initiatives by women themselves help them overcome facets of injustice and hence resolve potential root causes that could have led to conflicts or even violence. Many women's advocacy groups have been organized by local NGOs and civil society organizations supported by international solidarity movements to promote fair trade, freedom from debt, human rights of women and children, and the empowering of women to enhance their capacities and contribution to peace building and universal human rights. In the European Union, RESPECT (Rights, Equality, Solidarity, Power, Europe, Co-operation Today), a network of self-organized migrant domestic organizations, support organizations, trade unionists, and academics, campaigns for the rights of migrant women working in private households (Schwenken, 2005, p. 178).

In the 58th Session of the U.N. General Assembly, the summary report on violence against migrant workers recommended that legislative changes should be made by governments "to protect women from all forms of violence, promote women's access to social security services and ensure that women migrant workers do not suffer discrimination in employment-related matters" (United Nations, 2003, p. 18).

Finally, in clarifying the social injustice that women have faced relative to men, it is essential to acknowledge the role of gender inequalities in access to education, as well as the economic compensation for their work. To begin with, in many countries of the South, especially those of Africa and Asia, the schooling of girls continues to lag significantly behind that of boys despite the universal campaign for Education for All (United Nations Educational, Scientific, and Cultural Organization [UNESCO], 2011). The preference of families to allocate scarce resource to sons rather than daughters has accentuated the subordinate position of women as unpaid "workers" in the home (yet they are still often expected or obliged to contribute to the informal economy for survival) and deprived them of opportunities for further schooling and jobs. This inequitable gender distribution of educational resources has also diminished women's access to health and other social dimensions of development.

Hence, in recent decades, many intergovernmental organizations (e.g., UNICEF, UNESCO, the United Nations Fund for Women, United Nations Development Program) and also bilateral agencies (e.g., U.S. Agency for International Development, Canadian International Development Agency, Australian Agency for International Development) have focused on the education of girls and women, including nonformal and adult programs. Such nonsexist education includes not only access issues but also the reorientation of curriculum, pedagogies and institutional culture to help transform the prevailing societal and cultural norms rooted in patriarchy. However, nonsexist education alone will not suffice. There is also the corresponding need for women to be given equal and just compensation for their work.

Although these educational and social justice dimensions of gender inequalities are especially pervasive in Southern countries, it is nonetheless important to acknowledge that women in Northern contexts can and do still face disparities in education and access to jobs as well as income, despite the progress toward gender equality concomitant with modern economic and social development.

COMPETENCIES FOR CHALLENGING STRUCTURAL VIOLENCE AND ENHANCING GENDER EQUITY

What competencies do professionals need for working effectively with women in multicultural and international contexts? A helpful competency for professionals is awareness and understanding of the working conditions of migrant women workers in developed societies. Examples include domestic workers, outwork contractors, seasonal agricultural workers, and other domestic service-related, low-paying jobs. In this regard, professionals can also learn useful lessons and empowerment skills from the dedicated grassroots work of women's NGOs in overcoming gender-based workplace inequalities and human rights violations. A complementary competency is the ability to gain the trust of migrant women workers to enhance their self-confidence and courage to assert their rights. Equally important for professionals, especially those in education, is the skill to conduct empowerment workshops and other educational programs.

Similar to current expectations of leaders and managers in industrialized economies, it is also of utmost importance for international business professionals to gain knowledge, capacities and skills for integrating gender equality and sensitivity in their organizations, programs, and projects. In this regard, appropriate human resource practices play a critical role, including gender awareness in all job specifications; gender competence as a job requirement; nonsexist job titles, specifications, and advertising; gender equitable and nonsexist selection processes; equal remuneration, grading, and promotion; gender-sensitive employee benefits; family-friendly practices (e.g., child-care facilities); nonsexist working environments, cultures, and practices (dress codes, serving tea, meeting places); affirmative action; and clear and effective sexual harassment policies and procedures (Commission on Gender Equality, n.d.).

Educators and other professionals, advocacy groups, and community-based leaders would be more effective if they are able to raise awareness about issues of women in global factories, consumer ethics, fair trade, and workers' rights. The corollary to this competency is the willingness to model the value of gender equity and social justice in teaching, behavior, and relationships. As Gorski (2004) asserted, "I must remain committed to the political, transformative nature of multicultural education and I must *not* turn multicultural education into a relativistic concept that values every perspective" (p. 12).

One of the competencies recommended by the APA (2007) is the ability to foster therapeutic relationships and practices that promote initiative, empowerment, and expanded alternatives and choices for girls and women. *Empowerment* involves both a process of awareness and capacity building toward participation in decision making and the power for transformative action (Karl, 1995). It is a process of challenging existing power relations and being able to participate in the reconstruction of a system that allows for more equitable access to and exercise of power. However, Rowlands (1997) warned that empowerment should not be interpreted narrowly as merely having self-confidence and dignity. Rather, the consequence that flows from having self-confidence and dignity is vital.

When individually empowered individuals use their confidence and dignity to bring about positive changes not only for their personal benefit but also for the larger community, then they are also empowered in a relational and collective way. The Brazilian adult educator Paulo Freire (1990) believed that the poor and dispossessed can initiate social change through collective power.

CONCLUSION

Women have long been subjected to gender-based inequalities reinforced by the dominant development paradigm in conjunction with patriarchal cultural traditions. While being swept up in the "double-day" phenomenon—performing income-generating jobs and also having primary responsibility for domestic work and raising of children—many women additionally are victims of human rights violations through domestic violence. Gender-rooted conflicts therefore also need to be resolved through nonviolent transformation of consciousness of both perpetrators and victims and the empowerment of women to challenge and overcome structures of physical, psychological, and social violence. Moreover, as this chapter has tried to demonstrate, the challenges of recognizing gender-based inequalities and violence of all forms cannot be limited to the province of gender studies or women's studies. Gender is integral to all human and societal relationships and structures and hence also constitutes an essential dimension of the fields of multicultural education and international education.

Throughout the engagement of professionals with their colleagues, students, clients, customers, employees, coworkers, and the wider community, the ideal is not only a matter of competency but, more important, also reflects a personal belief in the inherent dignity and rights of women as one half of humanity. When translated into actions for individual and social transformation, this ideal can lead to a more just, nonviolent, and compassionate world.

REFERENCES

Advocates for Human Rights. (n.d.). *Trafficking in women*. Retrieved from http://stopvaw.org/Trafficking_in_Women.html

American Psychological Association. (2007). *Guidelines for psychological practice with girls and women*. Washington, DC: Author.

Amnesty International. (2009, September 30). *Women raped during Bosnia and Herzegovina conflict still waiting for justice*. Retrieved from http://www.amnesty.org/en/news-and-updates/report/women-raped-during-bosnia-herzegovina-conflict-waiting-justice-20090930

Banks, J. (2004). Multicultural education: Characteristics and goals. In J. Banks & C. Banks (Eds.), *Multicultural education: Issues and perspectives* (pp. 3–30). San Francisco, CA: Jossey-Bass.

Black, M. (1994). Home truths. *New Internationalist, 252.* Retrieved from http://www.newint.org/features/1994/02/05/home

Brownmiller, S. (1975). *Against our will: Men, women and rape.* New York, NY: Fawcett Columbine.

Commission on Gender Equality. (n.d.). *Best practices guidelines for creating a culture of gender equality in the private sector.* Johannesburg, South Africa: Author.

Danida. (2008). *Gender equality in the private sector.* Copenhagen: Ministry of Foreign Affairs of Denmark.

De Stoop, C. (1994). *They are so sweet sir.* Manila, Philippines: Limitless Asia.

Dolgopol, U., & Pranjape, S. (1994). *Comfort women. The unfinished ordeal.* Geneva, Switzerland: International Commission of Jurists.

Edwards, S. (2009). *A new debt crisis.* London, England: Jubilee Debt Campaign.

Enloe, C. (2000). *Maneuvers: The international politics of militarizing women's lives.* Los Angeles: University of California Press.

Freire, P. (1990). *Pedagogy of the oppressed.* New York, NY: Continuum.

Galtung, J. (1969). Violence, peace, and peace research. *Journal of Peace Research, 6,* 167–191. doi:10.1177/002234336900600301

Gnanadason, A., Kanyuro, M., & McSpadden, L. A. (Eds.). (1996). *Violence, women and nonviolent change.* Uppsala, Sweden: World Council of Churches.

Gorski, P. C. (2005). Complicity with conservatism: The de-politicizing of multicultural education and intercultural education. *Intercultural Education, 17,* 163–177. Retrieved from http://www.edchange.org/publications/Complicity_with_Conservatism.pdf

Gracia, E. (2004). Unreported cases of domestic violence against women: Towards an epidemiology of social silence, tolerance, and inhibition. *Journal of Epidemiology and Community Health, 58,* 536–537. doi:10.1136/jech.2003.019604

Gracia, E., & Herrero, J. (2006). Acceptability of domestic violence against women in the European Union: A multilevel analysis. *Journal of Epidemiology and Community Health, 60,* 123–129. doi:10.1136/jech.2005.036533

Hausmann, R., Tyson, L. D., & Zahidi, S. (2010). *The global gender gap report 2010. World Economic Forum.* Retrieved from http://www.weforum.org/issues/global-gender-gap

Heise, L. (1994). *Violence against women: The hidden health burden* (World Bank Discussion Paper). Washington, DC: World Bank.

Hosken, F. (1993). *The Hosken Report: Genital and sexual mutilation of females.* Lexington, MA: Women's International Network.

International Labor Organization. (2003). *Preventing discrimination, exploitation and abuse of women migrant workers. An information guide.* Geneva, Switzerland: Gender Promotion Programme, International Labour Office.

Interpol. (2011, September 13). *Trafficking in women for sexual exploitation*. September 13, 2011.

Jimenez-David, R. (1994). *Woman at large*. Metro, Manila: Anvil.

Karl, M. (1995). *Women and empowerment: Participation and decision-making*. London, England: Zed Books and the United Nations Non-government Liaison Service.

King, A. (2010). *Getting into debt. Dodgy loans, reckless finance and Third World debt*. London, England: Jubilee Debt Campaign.

King, W. (2006, May 16). Studies find epidemic of domestic violence. *The Seattle Times*. Retrieved from http://seattletimes.nwsource.com/html/localnews/2002996949_domesticviolence16m.html

Koso-Thomas, O. (1987). *The circumcision of women: A strategy for eradication*. London, England: Dotesios.

Kymlicka, W. (1995). *Multicultural citizenship: A liberal theory of minority rights*. Oxford, England: Oxford University Press.

Mandel, S. (2006). *Odious lending. Debt relief as if morals mattered*. London, England: New Economics Foundation.

Milmo, C., & Morris, N. (2008, July 3). 18,000 women and children trafficked into UK sex trade. *The Independent*. Retrieved from http://www.independent.co.uk/news/uk/crime/18000-women-and-children-trafficked-into-uksex-trade-859106.html

Mueller, R. D. (2000). *Women and the labour market in changing economies: Demographic issues* (Policy and Research Paper No. 18). Paris, France: International Union for the Scientific Study of Population

Narayan, U. (1997). *Dislocating cultures: Identities, traditions, and Third World feminism*. New York, NY: Routledge.

National Coalition Against Domestic Violence. (n.d.). *Domestic violence facts*. Retrieved from http://www.ncadv.org/files/DomesticViolenceFactSheet%28National%29.pdf

Nieto, S. (2000). *Affirming diversity: The sociopolitical context of multicultural education*. New York, NY: Longman.

O'Kelly, C. G., & Carney, L. S. (1986). *Women and men in society*. Belmont, CA: Wadsworth.

Okin, S. M. (1999). Is multiculturalism bad for women? In J. Cohen, M. Howard, & M. C. Nussbaum (Eds.), *Is multiculturalism bad for women?* Princeton, NJ: Princeton University Press.

Olufunmilayo, F. I. (2009, July). *Sexual violence and primary health workers: Identification of training and collaborative needs*. Paper presented at the Sexual Violence Research Initiative Conference, Johannesburg, South Africa. Retrieved from http://svriforum2009.svri.org/presentations/Fawole.pdf

Ontario Consultants on Religious Tolerance. (n.d.). *Female genital mutilation in North America and Europe*. Retrieved from http://www.religioustolerance.org/fem_cira.htm

Phillips, A. (2007). *Multiculturalism without culture*. Princeton, NJ: Princeton University Press.

Quezada, R., & Romo, J. (2004, Spring). Multiculturalism, peace education, and social justice. *Multicultural Education*, 2–11.

Rao, A. (1995). The politics of gender and culture in international human discourse. In J. Peters and A. Wolper (Eds.), *Women's rights, human rights* (pp. 167–175). New York, NY: Routledge.

Raymond, J. G., & Hughes, D. M. (2001). *Sex trafficking of women in the United States international and domestic trends*. Retrieved from http://www.uri.edu/artsci/wms/hughes/sex_traff_us.pdf

Rosales, L. A. (1999). The feminization of our migrant workers. *KASAMA, 13*(1). Retrieved from http://cpcabrisbane.org/Kasama/1999/V13n1/Kakammpi.htm

Rowlands, J. (1997). *Questioning empowerment: Working with women in Honduras*. Oxford, England: Oxfam.

Sharma, K. (2001, December 19). Opinion: Removing the veil does not empower women. *Women's Enews*. Retrieved from http://womensenews.org/story/commentary/011219/removing-the-veil-does-not-empower-women

Schwenken, H. (2005). The challenges of framing women migrants' rights in the European Union. *Femms, Genre, Migration et Mobilites, 21*, 177–194.

Song, S. (2005). Majority norms, multiculturalism, and gender equality. *The American Political Science Review, 99*, 473–489. doi:10.1017/S0003055405051828

Tahirih Justice Center. (2011). *Forced marriage in immigrant communities in the United States. 2011 national survey results*. Retrieved from http://www.tahirih.org/site/wp-content/uploads/2011/09/REPORT-Tahirih-Survey-on-Forced-Marriage-in-Immigrant-Communities-in-the-United-States-September-20115.pdf

Toubia, N. (1993). *Female genital mutilation: A call for global action*. New York, NY: Women, Ink.

Truong, T. D. (1990). *Sex, money and morality: Prostitution and tourism in Southeast Asia*. London, England: Zed Books.

United Nations Population Fund. (2000). *State of world population 2000*. Retrieved from http://www.unfpa.org/swp/2000/english/ch03.html

United Nations (2003, July 17). *Violence against women migrant workers*. Report of the Secretary-General. United Nations General Assembly Fifty-Eighth Session.

United Nations Educational, Scientific, and Cultural Organization. (2011). *EFA global monitoring report*. Paris, France: Author.

U.S. Department of State. (2011, June 27). *2011 trafficking in persons report—Cyprus*. Retrieved from http://www.unhcr.org/refworld/docid/4e12ee852.html

Vlachovd, M., & Biason, L. (Eds.). (2005). *Women in an insecure world: Violence against women facts, figures and analysis*. Geneva, Switzerland: Geneva Centre for the Democratic Control of Armed Forces.

Volpp, L. (2000). Blaming culture for bad behavior. *Yale Journal of Law and the Humanities, 12*, 89–116.

4

NATIONAL ORIGIN, NATIONAL VALUES, AND CULTURAL CONGRUENCE

MARK M. LEACH, FREDERICK T. L. LEONG, ARPANA INMAN, AND AYŞE CIFTÇI

In keeping with this volume's theme of providing knowledge and information that will be useful for professional practitioners in becoming internationally and multiculturally competent, the purpose of this chapter is to help professionals to better understand the importance of national origin and to move beyond the ethnocentrism commonly encountered in Eurocentric-based approaches to cultural understanding. In this chapter, we also review some of the major models for studying and understanding cultural differences associated with national origin.

National origin has long been a cultural area of study for sociologists, cross-cultural psychologists, political scientists, and many other disciplines. Although progress has been made in integrating multicultural and international issues in professional practice (see Heppner, Leong, & Chiao, 2008), we identify some of the work that remains to be done.

DOI: 10.1037/14044-004
Internationalizing Multiculturalism: Expanding Professional Competencies in a Globalized World,
R. L. Lowman (Editor)

We believe that cultural differences are at the heart of national origin issues, and just as there are many definitions of culture, there are also multitudes of ways to operationalize national origin. Our chosen approach for this chapter comes from cross-cultural psychology, a field in which many studies have used nationality or country of residence or origin as the operationalization of culture. It is true that there are many limitations to this approach (e.g., using broad, stereotypic descriptions to characterize national origin), but the approach is still useful, and a large knowledge base has already been established using it.

CONTEXTUALIZING NATIONAL ORIGIN

The importance of national origin in professional practice can be significant. International businesses that do not accurately assess a country's predominant values may find that mistakes or omissions can be costly. In 2006, for example, Walmart closed all 85 stores in Germany because the American (ethnocentric) business model did not fit with German culture and values. This cost the company approximately $1 billion (http://www.dw-world.de/dw/article/0,,2112746,00.html). Similarly, Starbucks closed a store in China's Forbidden City because it had failed to understand the importance of Chinese cultural expectations and of maintaining a full Chinese presence in this area. (For a more extensive discussion of such problems associated with not understanding national origin issues, see de Mooij, 2010.)

Of course, national origin issues and concerns are not limited to the business world. Given advances in technology, it is easy to consult people from other countries on a variety of, for example, medical and psychological issues. Yet such consultations always need to take national origin into account. For example, a mental health professional may suggest group therapy for a Chinese client as part of a consultation, not realizing that in collectivist cultures it is not common for clients to express themselves in front of strangers, and concerns, if communicated to others at all, are generally kept in the family. Understanding national values helps to reduce cultural mistakes and increases the likelihood of positive outcomes.

Sometimes people characterize others based on stereotypes related to national origin. Readers have likely heard or said something to the effect of, "The Japanese are very business driven," or "Americans are individualistic." At issue, of course, is that these are stereotypes based on dichotomous thinking. There may be many Japanese and Americans who fit these stereotypes, but not all do. Studying individuals to investigate differences on a national level would be very difficult, so cultural variables have been studied to examine the degree to which Japanese and Americans on average differ from people prototypically found in other countries.

Although there may be some underlying truth in broad cultural generalizations (e.g., there is considerable evidence that the United States is one of the most individualistic countries in the world; Triandis, 1989), the use of overgeneralizations can also be problematic. For example, people of Middle Eastern descent are not infrequently pulled from lines for airport screening because they "look Iranian" (or fit a profile that is based, in part, on national origin). Because of our notions about what people in different countries are assumed to be like, we may enter into (or avoid) certain relationships. Likewise, mistaken assumptions may be made that affect professional practice. For example, a physician may attribute the deferential behavior of a Japanese patient to her being Japanese, rather than to the fact that she may simply be introverted or shy. In such cases, it is difficult to differentiate culture from personality, and it becomes even more so when considering someone not from one's own country because we often rely on stereotypes as a basis for rapid characterization of others. Researchers (e.g., Cheung, von de Vijver, Fons, & Leong, 2011; Church, 2010) are only beginning to tease out the differential influences of culture and personality on our perceptions of others. Until more is reliably known, much of how we approach nationalities is accomplished by examining the values associated with each country.

NATIONAL-LEVEL VALUES

National-level values reflect goals and objectives—ideas about what a country characteristically considers good and attractive (Schwartz, 1999; Williams, 1970). They are reflected in shared norms, rituals, and practices that become reinforced in the society (Sagiv & Schwartz, 2007). Because these central trends or tendencies are ingrained into society and become part of the culture, professionals may benefit from knowing them. Additionally, theories developed from studies of national values have been used to predict experiences and behaviors at the individual, group, and organizational levels (see Hofstede, 2001).

How national studies of values are conducted is important to understand in making sense of the results and conclusions of such studies. Typically, large samples of individuals in multiple countries are asked about the values they consider to be important. These values are then categorized into what may, incorrectly, be characterized as being bipolar dimensions. For example, research has suggested that countries can be placed on an *individualism–collectivism* dimension. Such dimensions are based on findings that some countries, such as Australia, have citizens who, on average, have been shown to be more individualistic than those in other countries such as China, which is characterized in such studies as being collectivistic (Hofstede, 1994).

Particularly at the individual or subgroup level, such approaches risk oversimplification because all countries have some individualistic and some collectivistic traits, lying somewhere along the dimension. Examining cultures from a macro, or national, level tends to view a country's citizens from a broader perspective than other cultural approaches. Readers can develop their own approaches to better understanding national cultural values, but in this chapter, we offer some suggestions and practical approaches for understanding the importance of national origin.

CULTURAL VALUES

Many models and approaches have been applied at the national level, but we have chosen to focus this chapter on the importance and roles of cultural values. Therefore, we review the major models of cultural values regarding nations, including the approaches of Florence Kluckhohn and Fred Strodtbeck (1961), Geert Hofstede (1980), Harry Triandis (1996), and Shalom Schwartz (1992, 1997).

We have chosen cultural values as the primary dimension for understanding cultural differences as a function of national origin (alternatively termed *cross-cultural comparison*) for several reasons. First, values, as preferred ways of living in a country, have been a dominant approach for understanding human motivation, judgment, choices, and decision making. It is therefore a common and readily understood variable among psychologists and other social scientists. Second, in the field of cross-cultural psychology (and the approaches of other fields), the values dimension has received a significant amount of empirical research and has been the major framework for comparing human behavior across national cultural groups. Third, many training programs aimed at helping professionals develop international competencies or intercultural communication skills have used cultural values and the associated value conflicts as the major organizing framework.

The Culture Assimilator (also called Intercultural Sensitizer; Leong & Kim, 1991) is an example of one way to discuss intercultural communication. This training tool creates cultural critical incidents with multiple possible outcomes and allows respondents to choose a response and discuss their own and other cultural values based on their responses (see Berry, Poortinga, Breugelmans, Chasiotis, & Sam, 2011). There are a series of training tools in the area of intercultural communication, and the interested reader may want to consult the classic (and frequently revised) text *Intercultural Communication: A Reader* (Samovar & Porter, 2011).

Operationalizing Culture at the Country Level

Space limitations prevent us from providing detailed country-level data. For example, Hofstede's (1980) well-known model and research data are presented in a 474-page volume, *Culture's Consequences: International Work-Related Values*. Here we provide an overview of several programs of research on cultural values followed by case examples. Readers are encouraged to refer to the source materials for each model to locate specific country-level data that may meet their needs for information about a particular target population or for more information about a model.

There are many limitations to the use of country-level or national origin as an operationalization of culture. One is the danger of overgeneralizations and stereotyping based on the country-level data (e.g., the assumption that all Japanese are likely to be introverted). Therefore, an important caveat in using these models is to approach the research findings about national characteristics as a source for hypothesizing about possible group differences that need to be explored and validated in a mindful manner before making inferences or interventions. Leong (2007) provided some guidance in doing this in the context of the cultural accommodation model (CAM) of psychotherapy (which he and his colleagues have also adapted to organizational consulting; see Leong & Huang, 2008).

The complexity of human behavior must also be considered in applying these models. Even though current theories help guide us in understanding human behavior in global settings, culture is a dynamic and complex process that changes over time. It is therefore important to use multiple theories and think in a complex way to reflect the depth of the human behavior. Even though some theories are comprehensive, it may be challenging to apply them to all cross-cultural interactions because no one theory can account for the breadth of culture complexity found in countries.

International Competencies

In a chapter reviewing international developments in counseling psychology, Heppner, Leong, and Gerstein (2008) proposed a model for developing international competencies that were specific to counseling psychology. However, this model also has implications for other areas of psychology as well as for other professions. This model was based on the cross-cultural counseling competencies outlined in the Society of Counseling Psychology's position paper (Sue et al., 1982) and as an extension to the "Resolution on Culture and Gender Awareness in International Psychology" promulgated by the American Psychological Association (2004). The basic purpose of this model was to provide a preliminary conceptual framework for guiding the increasing internationalization of counseling psychology in the United States (although directed at counseling psychology, we believe this recommendation can be applied to work in any profession). Heppner et al. (2008) proposed that the development of international or cross-cultural competencies should begin with a multicultural mind-set (Leong & Hartung, 2000). A multicultural mind-set includes a deep understanding of the contextual basis of human behavior in a cross-cultural and comparative perspective.

The tripartite model of cross-cultural competency includes the following elements: (a) awareness (understanding one's own culture), (b) knowledge (understanding others' culture), and (c) skills (applying the multicultural framework to real-world situations). The model contrasts with the ethnocentric approach (Triandis, 1994) in which people assume that one's own culture's way of thinking, feeling, and behaving is the best and "correct" one, regardless of context. Unfortunately, this approach is still active, although perhaps not intentionally. For example, it can be argued that when therapeutic interventions developed in the United States are transferred to other cultures indirectly via U.S. training programs (e.g., training international students who then return home to practice), the training programs are acting in an ethnocentric manner. Framed this way, ethnocentrism may seem obviously problematic. However, despite multicultural advances, ethnocentrism and monocultural biases reflect common and natural human tendencies and, we argue, require mindful and intentional efforts to overcome (e.g., Berry et al., 2011).

THE CASE OF QUADRI

Here is a brief case example. Quadri (name changed for purposes of confidentiality) moved from Iran to the United States 10 years ago, is married, and has a son. Quadri and his wife's 9-year-old son began to have problems at school. The school's U.S.-trained principal informed Quadri that he and his wife should talk with their son's teacher regarding their son's problematic behavior in class. The teacher explained that their son was being disruptive in class and began discussing with them the use of basic behavioral child-rearing techniques, which they could practice at home. However, Quadri preferred to make an appointment with the family physician, an Arab who was born and raised in the United States. He asked the family physician if there were any pill that would help their son behave better at school. Quadri also informed the physician that he is also requiring his son to attend a religious school. He believed that his son's issues would be resolved once his son practices religion more.

This is an example of professional insensitivity about international–multicultural issues. The teacher did not attempt to understand the parents' culture and worldviews, instead relying on an ethnocentric parenting perspective. One way to avoid the insensitivity would have been for the teacher first to have talked with the parents about their perceptions of their son's behavior. Perhaps through listening and incorporating their worldviews, the teacher might have incorporated a modified approach, such as the family using prayer as a way to introduce more peaceful behaviors in class.

Implications

We propose that an in-depth understanding of our clients', students', coworkers', and supervisees' cultural values is an essential component of any international competency model. It is through awareness and knowledge of our own values and the values of those with whom we interact that we can become more internationally and cross-culturally competent. Furthermore, knowledge of the nexus of cultural values between us and those we serve is a prerequisite for recognizing the potential cultural value conflicts that can serve as barriers to effective research, practice, and training. We now turn to the major models of cultural values that can guide us in becoming culturally and internationally competent professional practitioners.

MODELS OF CULTURAL VALUES

For comparison purposes, the following models are included in Table 4.1.

Kluckhohn and Strodtbeck's Model

Kluckhohn and Strodtbeck (1961) offered one of the first models for the study of cultural (in this context, national) values. Their interdisciplinary approach to the examination of value orientations combined with various methodological approaches such as ethnography and social analyses. In this model, value orientations were characterized by the dimensions that a group considers attractive and that then direct the group's behavior and shape its norms. These dimensions allowed for comparisons within and across groups, so that cultural patterns can be assessed on multiple levels.

Kluckhohn and Strodtbeck (1961) included five universal dimensions that they believed could be observed in every culture. These included assumptions about the following:

1. *Human nature.* What is the basic nature of people? Are people seen as intrinsically good, evil, or a combination?
2. *Person–nature relationships.* What is the relationship of humans and nature? Are humans subordinate to nature, dominant over nature, or living in harmony with nature?

TABLE 4.1
Model Comparisons

Variables	Model			
	Kluckhohn and Strodtbeck	Hofstede	Triandis	Schwartz
Basis	Universality	National cultural differences	Individualism and collectivism	Value orientation differences
Methodology	Ethnography and social analysis	Factor analysis	Construct measurement	Similarity structure analysis
Human nature	Intrinsic human nature	Indulgence vs. restraint	Exchange vs. communal	
Time	Time orientation	Long term vs. short term	Constantly evolving	
Social interaction	Social relations	Individualism–collectivism	Cultural complexity	Embeddedness vs. autonomy
Action	Activity orientation	Masculinity–femininity	Idiocentrism–allocentrism	Mastery vs. harmony
Power and hierarchy	Person–nature relationship	Power distance	Horizontal and vertical	Hierarchy vs. egalitarianism
Flexibility		Uncertainty avoidance	Tight vs. loose cultures	

3. *Time orientation.* How is time considered? Is the importance placed on the past, present, or future?
4. *Activity orientation.* What is the nature of preferred activities? Is the emphasis on doing, becoming, or being?
5. *Social relations.* What is the relationship of humans to each other? Is the relationship collateral, linear, or individualistic?

As an example of applying this model, White, middle-class men from the United States are generally considered to have a dominant (mastery) view of nature, a future time orientation, a doing (achievement) activity orientation, and an individualistic manner of social interaction (see Carter, 1991; House, Hanges, Javidan, Dorfman, & Gupta, 2004). Of course, values are fluid and dynamic, because considering them to be concrete adds to stereotypic thinking.

To the extent that such statements can describe central tendencies that generalize to the national level, these orientations often do not fit well with the assumptions or values of other cultural groups. Using a business example, a marketing friend of the first author who was Turkish once observed that, in her country, many U.S. companies (which, in her view, were composed primarily of White men) have failed in their attempts to conduct business with some companies in Turkey. The Turkish companies chose instead to conduct their business with Middle Eastern and Asian companies. She explained this phenomenon by noting that many U.S. businesspeople tend to fly into Turkey and immediately want to meet and discuss business with their Turkish counterparts. The Turkish executives prefer first to have dinner with the U.S. executives and to engage in a nonbusiness relationship before proceeding to conduct business. Kluckhohn and Strodtbeck's activity orientation ("doing vs. being") and social relations ("individualistic vs. collateral") were clearly at odds, resulting in a failure to develop a business partnership. This is also an example of a misunderstanding between masculine and feminine cultures, a concept we turn to later when discussing the work of Hofstede, Hofstede, and Minkov (2010).

We argue that professional practitioners need to be mindful of how cultural dimensions such as these affect their interactions with people from countries and with cultures different from the professional's own. For example, Budhwar, Woldu, and Ogbonna (2008) found significant value orientation differences in Asian Indians (those living in India), and migrant Indians in the United States, both within and between groups. Yeganeh and Su (2007), in a study of Iranian managers, reported that their managerial culture valued a past orientation, strong hierarchical relationships, collectivism, and an "evil" orientation based on the premise that people cannot be trusted and their behaviors should be controlled as much as reasonably possible.

Obviously, this perspective differs significantly from U.S. business cultures but does have implications for how Americans might best approach Iranians in doing business.

The Kluckhohn and Strodtbeck (1961) model has been criticized as being too static and for not fully addressing the myriad cultural characteristics that make up cultural groups (Carter, 1991). Nevertheless, it still has relevance as a means for professionals to consider their own and their clients' basic cultural values. It has the advantage of being easy to understand. It can also readily be adapted for use in training people in international and cross-cultural perspectives.

Hofstede's Model

There are probably thousands of values on which cultures and societies could be compared (Schwartz, 1997). To reduce those to a manageable number of dimensions to compare them efficiently can be a challenge. When one includes an individual's value dimensions, the issue becomes even more complex. Fortunately, there are models that are useful for dealing with this complexity.

Geert Hofstede (1980, 1991) conducted one of the best known and most widely used internationally relevant cross-cultural studies in which he assessed 116,000 IBM employees from the late 1960s through the early 1970s. This study included 72 countries and three geographic regions and asked about values (Schwartz, 1997). Through factor analysis (a statistical procedure used to reduce a larger number of similar variables into a smaller number), he determined that respondents from the countries represented in his samples differed on four value dimensions. These dimensions are as follows.

1. *Power distance*. This dimension concerns relationships to authority: To what degree is the distribution of power considered legitimate? Some countries, Hofstede noted, have political, business, and educational systems that are more hierarchical than others. Implications of this dimension might include, for example, the case of a meeting in which the input of all group members is needed; if one person defers to another because the latter is of higher social status, it will be difficult to gain the former's candid input.

   Most countries have some degree of power-distance behavior, so readers should consider the degree of distance between the professional and his or her clients. A client may, for example, nod in apparent agreement but privately disagree with the professional, not wishing to embarrass or insult his or her higher social standing, power, and status. However, the client may have no intention of complying with the professional's advice.

2. *Individualism–collectivism.* This dimension addresses the relationship between the individual and the group or society, and the degree to which individuals are primarily expected to care for themselves and their immediate families or are expected to be part of an extended, tightly knit connection of other people. These are not simply opposing dimensions but worldviews in which different issues are considered significant. In collectivistic countries, people are more likely, compared with people in individualistic countries, to become "integrated into strong cohesive in groups, which throughout people's lifetime continue to protect them in exchange for unquestioning loyalty" (Hofstede, 1994, p. 260).

Triandis, Brislin, and Hui (1988) offered explicit suggestions for how those from individualist and collectivist cultures can communicate more effectively with one another. For example, individuals from collectivist cultures should not expect individuals from individualist cultures to readily join workgroups if individual contributions are not recognized. Offering explanations as to the purpose and importance of the group, as well as the collective understanding of the group as the important unit, may help reduce intercultural communication concerns (p. 282).

3. *Masculinity–femininity.* Hofstede himself has acknowledged that in some cultures the terms used for this dimension are viewed as politically incorrect (see Hofstede & Associates, 1998). This dimension concerns the value placed by the culture on assertiveness, achievement, and material success versus interpersonal relationships, caring, and modesty. So-called masculine cultures are associated with excelling and ambition and tend to polarize (e.g., win–lose), whereas cultures labeled feminine are associated with quality of life and relationships. Additionally, feminine cultures tend to have a flexible family structure, have more women working in management positions, are more protective of the environment, and negotiate more than masculine cultures (Hofstede, 2001; Hofstede et al., 2010). The earlier example of the Turkish business associates can also be mentioned here. Inviting new business colleagues for a meal before conducting business is a frequent occurrence in feminine cultures, although it is contrary to expectations found in masculine cultures (Hofstede & Associates, 1998).

4. *Uncertainty avoidance*. This dimension of Hofstede's (1980, 1991, 2001; Hofstede et al., 2010) model concerns the degree to which individuals of a culture feel uncomfortable or comfortable with ambiguity and uncertainty. For example, Germany has been demonstrated to have a fairly high level of uncertainty avoidance (Rauch, Frese, & Sonnentag, 2000) because its culture relies heavily on laws, regulations, and rules as the basis for interacting. In an applied setting, a clinical social worker assigning a homework assignment may consider this dimension of cultural values and be more exacting in his or her presentation of the assignment when working with a recent German immigrant. The United States, particularly in the business domain, is generally considered to have high uncertainty avoidance because Americans tend to avoid long-term planning and rely instead on more controllable, short-range goals. A number of African countries tend to report low uncertainty avoidance (Hofstede et al., 2010).

Extending Hofstede's Model

Hofstede later introduced two additional dimensions to his model that we believe are useful. The first of these added dimensions stemmed from work done by Michael Bond (1988) at the Chinese University of Hong Kong, who had been investigating values among Asian university students using the Rokeach Value Survey (Rokeach, 1973) and found significant overlap with Hofstede's results. Both he and Hofstede were concerned because both methods were developed from a Western perspective, using the Western-developed Rokeach Value Survey. A Chinese Value Survey (Bond, 1988) was then developed and compared with Hofstede's four-dimensional model, independent of the Rokeach Value Survey. There was significant overlap on three of the four Hofstede dimensions, with the uncertainty avoidance dimension showing no equivalency in Bond's work (Bond, 1988; Minkov & Hofstede, 2011). A unique dimension emerged, which Hofstede later incorporated into his model.

5. *Long-term versus short-term orientation*. This added dimension concerned whether people focused primarily on the past, present, or future. Countries such as Japan and Korea have been found to have a long-term orientation (Hofstede, Jonker, & Verwaart, 2008; Lenway & Murtha, 1994), whereas the United Kingdom tends to focus on short-term objectives. In the field of mental health, short-term therapies from psychologists, social workers, psychiatric nurses, and other therapeutic intervention-

ists are not uncommon in short-term orientation cultures, and such approaches tend to be embraced by the third-party payers funding these services.

Still another dimension has been added to the Hofstede model. Inglehart and Baker (2000) found an additional dimension, survival versus self-expression values (Minkov, 2007; Minkov & Hofstede, 2011). After additional examination and analyses, Hofstede et al. (2010) added a sixth dimension to the original Hofstede model.

6. *Indulgence versus restraint*. To what degree are people allowed self-expression, life control, and pursuit of leisure? This dimension concerns how much emphasis countries place on free expression of their people. Countries in which people express greater emotional restraint are more likely to follow rules and less likely to express themselves before strong relationships are formed. On average, many Asian countries tend to show more emotional restraint than Western countries such as the United States and the United Kingdom (Soto, Perez, Kim, Lee, & Minnick, 2011).

Issues With Hofstede's model

There have been some critiques of Hofstede's cultural value dimensions (e.g., Chiang, 2005; Signorini, Wiesemes, & Murphy, 2009). These have included technical measurement issues, questions regarding the samples used for the original research, and conceptual and definitional issues. Still, the individualism–collectivism dimension has been widely used (Shulruf et al., 2011) in practice perhaps because it can be used to explain an assortment of commonly encountered cultural differences (Schwartz, 1997).

Despite the critiques, this work significantly advanced the study of international value dimensions and remains useful when working at the national origin level. It is probably the best known of the cultural values models. Given its prominence in the research literature in psychology, business, economics, and sociology, we elaborate on a major dimension of Hofstede's model, individualism–collectivism, with particular focus on the extensive work by Triandis.

Triandis's Cross-Cultural Model

Given the globalizing trends and the increased interdependence between countries, the *individualism–collectivism cultural syndrome* (Triandis, 1996) provides an important framework to help understand cross-cultural differences and similarities. This dimension has been variously labeled. At the cultural (or country) level, the construct is referred to by Hofstede's term *individualism–collectivism*, whereas at the individual (psychological) level, it is often called *idiocentrism–allocentrism* (Triandis, 1996).

Triandis (1989, 2000) noted that cultural characteristics are dynamic and constantly evolving and influence the way people define themselves privately, publicly, and collectively. Triandis highlighted two broad cultural determinants that help explain the experience of individuals within the individualism–collectivism cultural syndrome: *cultural complexity* and *tight versus loose* cultures.

1. *Cultural complexity.* According to Triandis (1994), in complex societies, "people make large distinctions between objects and events in their environment" (p. 156). The United States is considered a complex society, as evidenced by the number of distinctions made in occupations, for example. According to the *Dictionary of Occupational Titles* (U.S. Department of Labor, 1991), there are more than a quarter million distinct occupations, whereas fewer distinctions are included in less complex societies.

   The complexity of a culture is determined by a number of factors such as population density (relating to the number of possible relationships an individual can have), the number of records kept, fixed residences, individual access to technology, education, and transportation, and a variety of other factors (see Triandis, 1989). Complex cultures and countries tend to be individualistic Triandis (2002) argued, because the greater the number of options, the greater the number of ingroups from which to choose, resulting in lower loyalty toward any one group. These countries also tend to be more affluent, leading to greater financial independence, and therefore greater social and emotional independence (Triandis, 1989). Simple cultures, in contrast, tend to be collectivistic because people from those cultures need to rely on each other for resources and outcomes (Triandis, 1996).

2. *Tight versus loose cultures.* Triandis also suggested that cultures can be characterized as being tight rather than loose, terms that describe the strength of social norms and the degree to which they are sanctioned (Gelfand, Nishii, & Raver, 2006). This dimension can also be conceptualized as homogenous versus heterogeneous cultures. In collectivist cultures, ingroups define values, norms, and identities; there is more inflexibil-

ity (*tightness*) and less tolerance for those who fall outside of the established norms. Such cultures are also generally more homogeneous. Countries such as Pakistan, Japan, and Malaysia fall into this category (Gelfand et al., 2011). Individualist cultures (e.g., the Netherlands, New Zealand, the United States; Gelfand, et al., 2011) tend to have more heterogeneity and are more flexible in tolerating differences from established norms (*loose*). According to Gelfand et al. (2006), families are the first to introduce the type of culture onto children. They teach children in tight societies that one abides by rules, and they are more likely to supervise their children's and grandchildren's behavior. Parents from loose cultures are more likely to allow their children more exploratory flexibility and punish more leniently. Educational institutions act similarly. In tight cultures such as Japan and China, for example, students are expected to obey their teachers, and teachers frequently report on the child's behavior and performance to the parents. These expectations are not as high in loose countries such as the United States.

Overall, on the basis of national tolerance for deviance, individuals would be expected to have different levels of accepted personal expression and varying needs for structure. Professionals, in turn, will need to consider the national origins of their clients and how these factors may apply to working effectively with them. Of course, professionals' own national origins may predispose them to a particular approach, which may require modification and adaption.

As evidenced earlier, the constructs of individualism and collectivism are multidimensional, contextually influenced, and coexist within individuals, communities, and societies (Tamis-LeMonda et al., 2008; Triandis, 1995, 2001). In particular, the literature suggests that there have been great shifts from communal (collectivistic) to exchange (individualistic) relationships across countries and cultures (Adamopoulos & Bontempo, 1986) with increasing affluence (Triandis, McCusker, & Hui, 1990) being a major precursor to this dynamic. This is particularly exemplified in the Asian Indian society (i.e., individuals living in India). Although rising affluence in India has been a result of multiple factors, to illustrate the individualism–collectivism cultural syndrome we focus on one facet of the shift, the current Indian–U.S. subculture related to the information technology (IT) industry.

In recent years there has been increased outsourcing of jobs from countries such as the United States, relying on employees from developing countries where labor costs are considerably cheaper, such as India. According to this chapter's third author, who is from India, the practice of outsourcing is affecting the Indian culture as well as the U.S. culture.

In the process of economic development, India has grown from a less complex culture to a highly complex one, developing greater infrastructure due to its growing IT industry and increased collaborations with the United States in relation to this industry. The large number of call centers outsourced to India, for example, has created an economic boom that has led many people from the rural areas of India to migrate to urban cities, increasing the demands on city life. Traditionally, tightly knit cultures have specific rules, such as expecting deference to authority and great censorship on personal behaviors (e.g., whether to date, who one marries), and therefore we argue that deviance from the norm has typically not been well tolerated in India. Interdependence and group responsibility are characteristic cultural norms, with group goals taking priority over individual ones. Familial or group obligations, familial loyalty, and pressure to maintain harmony at all costs are key attributes valued in this culture. Yet the intermingling of the U.S. culture with the Indian culture has created significant challenges for the Indian family and social structure. The monetary gains from these jobs have also provided greater economic freedom and access to resources and interactions that conflict with Indian cultural expectations and obligations. The expansion of the Indian IT industry through outsourcing has also allowed greater job mobility, which contrasts with the usual practice of job stability. All these aspects have created turmoil within families and in the work environment. Such shifts illustrate how norms, values, and behaviors particular to a geographic region may be influenced by social conditions. In particular, examining the Indian–U.S. IT industry against the backdrop of Triandis's model helps us appreciate how individualism and collectivism intermingle to influence people's experiences and the professional's challenges. The following example is illustrative.

An international student on a U.S. college campus seeks services for depression and anxiety. The counselor might determine that the student wishes to study music, but the client's family wishes her to complete a degree in IT. Although she was raised in a collectivistic country, from an extensive intake interview, it appears that her identity has shifted from a collective, family and community-oriented focus to an individualistic one. She is concerned about how (and whether) to tell her family that she is not interested in studying IT. The therapist concludes that the conflict is causing the client's depression and anxiety. She wishes to maintain her identity and role within her family yet is torn because of her identity shift, a result of increasing resources, social conditions, and individualism. This example reflects a type of conflict seen in many counseling centers across the United States.

Schwartz's National Cultural Values

Another theory of cultural values important in understanding national origin is that of Shalom Schwartz (1992). Schwartz's work has expanded the cross-cultural literature on values significantly. He created two theories of values: (a) one of personal values that describe individuals within cultures and (b) one of cultural value orientations that differentiate among societies (e.g., Bilsky, Janik, & Schwartz, 2011; Knafo, Roccas, & Sagiv, 2011; Schwartz, 1992; Schwartz, Caprara, & Vecchione, 2010). Because of space limitations and the focus of this chapter, we present only his national-level ideas. Interested readers can consult Davidov, Schmidt, and Schwartz (2008); Knafo et al. (2011); Schwartz and Sagiv (1995); and Spini (2003) for more information about Schwartz's individual-level values.

Questions addressed by Schwartz at the national level included the following: What values are embraced at the national level that may differentiate countries? In other words, although both the United States and Canada are North American countries, they may share some values and not others, or perhaps share values but to differing degrees. Schwartz (1997) postulated that these values are not the same as individual level values. National values, he argued, are shared goals and objectives that a society, rather than individuals within it, generally finds desirable. All societies, he argued, rely on values to address issues related to their inevitable need to regulate human behavior,.

In addressing this issue, Schwartz (1997) developed three bipolar cultural value dimensions:

1. *Embeddedness versus autonomy.* This value dimension is similar to the individualism–collectivism value presented by both Hofstede (1994, 2001, 2010) and Triandis (1996), and they are parallel programs of research. "Cultures high on embeddedness regard the family or extended in-group rather than the autonomous individual as the key social unit" (Knafo, Schwartz, & Levine, 2009, p. 875). Autonomous cultures value individuality, personal expression and pleasure, and creativity. For example, countries such as Papua New Guinea and Bangladesh rate much higher on embeddedness scores than do countries such as Canada and New Zealand, which score high on the autonomy value (Allen et al., 2007).

2. *Hierarchy versus egalitarianism.* Hierarchical cultures value assigned roles that help maintain rules and order associated with these roles. These cultures acknowledge and accept the disparate distribution of authority and resources. Cultures that value egalitarianism emphasize equality and social justice. China and

Thailand are considered high in hierarchy, whereas Finland and Spain score high in Egalitarianism.

3. *Mastery versus harmony.* These are cultures that value mastery also value control, success, and self-assertion. Cultures that value harmony attempt to preserve the world and interact with it harmoniously. The United States and Japan tend to hold the mastery value highly, whereas, for example, Latvia and Slovenia value harmony.

TOWARD A MODEL OF CULTURAL CONGRUENCE IN VALUES

An important premise of this chapter is that the multiculturalism movement combined with the efforts to integrate both domestic and international dimensions, will gradually introduce a multicultural mind-set that will replace the Eurocentric, or monocultural, mind-set in the United States. We argue that this shift will not occur rapidly but that it will inevitably take place. In considering how national origin should be understood, we suggest that the major models of cultural values reviewed here will be helpful for analyzing and understanding the psychological similarities and differences among individuals from different countries.

The utility of these models of cultural values lies in their application to the understanding of how values congruence or values conflict can create barriers for effective communication, counseling, or supervision when working with people of different national origins.

In this final section of this chapter, we propose a preliminary model of cultural congruence in values based on Leong's CAM (Leong, 2007; Leong & Lee, 2006). We hope this psychotherapy model will help professionals become more internationally competent. This model is also built upon the work of Sue and Sue (2008), who have argued that cross-cultural competence requires the analysis and understanding of interventions that are culturally appropriate. These authors further divided culturally sensitive and appropriate interventions based on both the process and the outcome. The process includes the mechanisms and the moment-by-moment interactions with the client, whereas the outcomes are the goals of intervention.

Sue and Sue (2008) considered the role of cultural values as a potential barrier to intercultural interactions and have indicated that culture-bound values can operate along various dimensions, consistent with those presented earlier. Therefore, in applying this model of cultural congruence and values, it is important for professionals to be aware of the various models of cultural values and how they may come into play in intercultural interactions. For example, from the Triandis model, if a counselor or manager, to take two examples, is individualistic and supervises or interacts with a client or supervisee who is collectivistic, there are likely to be conflicts along those dimensions if the professional is not aware of the issue of cultural congruence. Using Hofstede's approach, a supervisor who comes from a low power distance culture may expect egalitarian relationships from those who come from a high power distance culture, and such expectations could make the supervisee uncomfortable because of cultural incongruence in their values. Hence, it is incumbent on the internationally competent professional to be aware of where these cultural incongruencies in values, more commonly referred to as cultural conflicts, play out in the interpersonal interactions.

Leong's CAM (Leong, 2007; Leong & Lee, 2006) consists of three phases: (a) identification of cultural gaps in the existing theory that may affect the cultural validity of the theory, (b) selection of culturally relevant constructs and models from the cross-cultural and ethnic and racial minority research to accommodate the existing theory, and (c) examination and analysis of the accommodated theory to assess its incremental validity (Leong, 2007; Leong & Lee, 2006). In reviewing the CAM in relation to Hall, Hong, Zane, and Meyer (2011), Leong and Kalibatseva (2011) proposed that a useful extension of the CAM would be to formulate a new model that is predicated on the concept of cultural congruence. They proposed that effective psychotherapy for Asian Americans or other culturally diverse groups should be conceptualized as an issue of selecting culturally congruent processes and therapeutic goals. Specifically, they proposed that an important element of effective psychotherapy for Asian Americans is understanding the unique cultural values, beliefs, needs, and expectations of Asian American clients in psychotherapy.

Whereas Leong's (2007) CAM delineates the need for therapists to accommodate cultural differences to provide effective psychotherapy for Asian Americans, the cultural congruence model provides a theoretical rationale for making such accommodations. Borrowing from the fields of interactional psychology and person–environment fit models, the cultural congruence approach is predicated on the hypothesis that culturally congruent (vs. incongruent) processes and goals will lead to positive therapeutic outcomes, whether for psychotherapists or international managers. The cultural congruence model argues that professionals engaged in intercultural interactions need select relational processes and outcomes that are congruent with the client's (or subordinate's or supervisor's) cultural values. Conversely, culturally incongruent processes in these relationships will likely lead to negative outcomes for the international professional. Such negative outcomes can range from misunderstandings to interpersonal conflicts and hostilities. Therefore, in the realm of intercultural relations, internationally competent professionals need to analyze the cultural values of their culturally

		PROCESS	
		Culturally congruent	Culturally incongruent
OUTCOMES	Culturally congruent	Congruent process Congruent outcome	Incongruent process Congruent outcome
	Culturally incongruent	Congruent process Incongruent outcome	Incongruent process Incongruent outcome

Figure 4.1. Proposed model of cultural congruence in values.

diverse clients, subordinates, and supervisors to adopt a culturally congruent set of interpersonal behaviors that is consistent with the values of the other. By applying the concept of cultural congruence in values to Sue and Sue's (2008) model, we can derive the model shown in Figure 4.1.

Although this model proposes that culture congruence in values will lead to effective interpersonal communication and interactions between professionals and those they serve, we also need research in support of this model. For this research, we may be able to borrow from the work of John Holland (1997) in his research on the person–environment model of career choice. A key component of Holland's theory has been the hypothesis that congruence with individuals' interest types with those modally found in their work environments will result in person–environment congruence and, therefore, positive outcomes concerning such variables as work satisfaction.

Extending Holland's (1997) person–environment match model, the nature of the "match" between client and professional could be used as the basis for examining desirable results, such as an intervention's outcome, the quality of the professional–client relationship, or the effectiveness in work-team or manager–supervisor relationships. We believe that the match of person and environment in international contexts can, as with Holland's model, also be quantitatively operationalized to measure the degree of compatibility or congruence between a person's environment and personality and the relevant cultural environment in which the professional encounters the client. Thus, an operationalized "cultural congruence index" addressing the match of both client and professional contextual values (e.g., of individualism vs. collectivism) would, we argue, be useful both in research and professional practice. It is a preliminary model, and thus it is left to future research to determine its empirical foundation and value. In the meantime, we offer the proposed model as a key conceptual dimension for developing internationally competent professionals.

REFERENCES

Adampoulos, J., & Bontempo, R. N. (1986). Diachronic universals in interpersonal structures. *Journal of Cross-Cultural Psychology, 17,* 169–189. doi:10.1177/0022002186017002003

Allen, M. W., Ng, S. H., Ideda, K., Jawan, J. A., Sufi, A. H., Wilson, M., & Yang, K. S. (2007). Two decades of change in cultural values and economic development in eight East Asian and Pacific Island nations. *Journal of Cross-Cultural Psychology, 38,* 247–269. doi:10.1177/0022022107300273

American Psychological Association. (2004). *Resolution on culture and gender awareness in international psychology.* Washington, DC: Author.

Berry, J. B., Poortinga, Y. H., Breugelmans, S. M., Chasiotos, A., & Sam, D. L. (2011). *Cross-cultural psychology: Research and applications.* New York, NY: Cambridge University Press.

Bilsky, W., Janik, M., & Schwartz, S. H. (2011). The structural organization of human values—evidence from three rounds of the European Social Survey (ESS). *Journal of Cross-Cultural Psychology, 42,* 759–776. doi:10.1177/0022022110362757

Bond, M. H. (1988). Finding universal dimensions of individual variation in multicultural studies of values: The Rokeach and Chinese value surveys. *Journal of Personality and Social Psychology, 55,* 1009–1015. doi:10.1037/0022-3514.55.6.1009

Budhwar, P. S., Woldu, H., & Ogbonna, E. (2008). A comparative analysis of cultural value orientations of Indians and migrant Indians in the USA. *International Journal of Cross-Cultural Management, 8,* 79–105. doi:10.1177/1470595807088324

Carter, R. T. (1991). Cultural values: A review of empirical research and implications for counseling. *Journal of Counseling and Development, 70,* 164–173.

Cheung, F. M., van de Vijver, F. J. R., & Leong, F. T. L. (2011). Toward a new approach to the study of personality in culture. *American Psychologist, 66,* 593–603.

Chiang, F. (2005). A critical examination of Hofstede's thesis and its application to international reward management. *The International Journal of Human Resource Management, 16,* 1545–1563.

Church, T. (2010). Current perspectives in the study of personality across cultures. *Perspectives on Psychological Science, 5,* 441–449.

Davidov, E., Schmidt, P., & Schwartz, S. H. (2008). Bringing values back in: The adequacy of the European social survey to measure values in 20 countries. *Public Opinion Quarterly, 72,* 420–445. doi:10.1093/poq/nfn035 de Mooij, M. K. (2010). *Consumer behavior and culture: Consequences for global marketing and advertising.* Thousand Oaks, CA: Sage.

Gelfand, M. J., Raver, J. L., & Nishii, L. (2006). On the nature and importance of cultural tightness-looseness. *Journal of Applied Psychology, 91,* 1225–1244.

Gelfand, M. J., Raver, J. L., Nishii, L., Leslie, L. M., Lun, J., Lim, B. C., . . . Yamaguchi, S. (2011, May 27). Differences between tight and loose cultures: A 33-nation study. *Science, 332,* 1100–1104. doi:10.1126/science.1197754

Hall, G. C. N., Hong, J. J., Zane, N. W. S., Meyer, O. L. (2011). Culturally competent treatments for Asian Americans: The relevance of mindfulness and acceptance-based psychotherapies. *Clinical Psychology: Science and Practice, 18,* 215–231. doi:10.1111/j.1468-2850.2011.01253.x

Heppner, P. P., Leong, F. T. L., & Chiao, H. (2008). A growing internationalization of counseling psychology. In S. D. Brown & R. W. Lent (Eds.), *Handbook of counseling psychology* (4th ed.; pp. 68–85). Hoboken, NJ: Wiley.

Heppner, P. P., Leong, F. T. L., & Gerstein, L. H. (2008). Counseling within a changing world: Meeting the psychological needs of societies and the world. In B. W. Walsh (Ed.), *Biennial review of counseling psychology* (pp. 231–258). New York, NY: Routledge.

Hofstede, G. (1980). *Culture's consequences: International differences in work-related values.* Beverly Hills, CA: Sage.

Hofstede, G. (1991). *Cultures and organizations: Software of the mind.* New York, NY: McGraw-Hill.

Hofstede, G. (1994). *Cultures and organizations: Software of the mind.* New York, NY: HarperCollins.

Hofstede, G. (2001). *Culture's consequences: Comparing values, behaviors, institutions and organizations across nations* (2nd ed.). Thousand Oaks, CA: Sage.

Hofstede, G., & Associates. (1998). *Masculinity and femininity: The taboo dimension of national cultures.* Thousand Oaks, CA: Sage.

Hofstede, G., Hofstede, G. J., & Minkov, M. (2010). *Cultures and organizations: Software of the mind* (3rd ed.). New York, NY: McGraw-Hill.

Hofstede, G., Jonker, C. M., & Verwaart, T. (2008). Long-term orientation in trade. In K. Schredelseker & F. Hauser (Eds.), *Complexity and artificial markets: Lecture notes in economics and mathematical systems* (pp. 107–119). Berlin, Germany: Springer-Verlag. http://dx.doi: 10.1007/978-3-540-70556-7_9

Holland, J. L. (1997). *Making vocational choices: A theory of vocational personalities and work environments.* Odessa, FL: Psychological Assessment Resources.

House, R. J., Hanges, P. J., Javidan, M., Dorfman, P. W., & Gupta, V. (2004). *Leadership, culture, and organizations: The GLOBE Study of 62 societies.* Thousand Oaks, CA: Sage.

Inglehart, R. (1997). *Modernization and postmodernization: Cultural, economic, and political change in 43 societies.* Princeton, NJ: Princeton University Press.

Inglehart, R., & Baker, W. E. (2000), Modernization, cultural change, and the persistence of traditional values. *American Sociological Review, 65*, 19–51.

Kluckhohn, F. R., & Strodtbeck, F. L. (1961) *Variations in value orientations.* Oxford, England: Peterson.

Knafo, A., Roccas, S., & Sagiv, L. (2011). The value of values in cross-cultural research: A special issue in honor of Shalom Schwartz. *Journal of Cross-Cultural Psychology, 42*, 178–185. doi:10.1177/0022022110396863

Knafo, A., Schwartz, S. H., & Levine, R. V. (2009). Helping strangers in lower embedded cultures. *Journal of Cross-Cultural Psychology, 40*, 875–879.

Lenway, S., & Murtha, T. P. (1994). The state as strategist in international business research. *Journal of International Business Studies, 25*, 513–535. doi:10.1057/palgrave.jibs.8490210

Leong, F. T. L. (2007). Cultural accommodation as method and metaphor. *American Psychologist, 62*, 916–927. doi:10.1037/0003-066X.62.8.916

Leong, F. T. L., & Hartung, P. J. (2000). Cross-cultural career assessment: Review and prospects for the new millennium. *Journal of Career Assessment, 8*, 391–401. doi:10.1177/106907270000800408

Leong, F. T. L., & Huang, J. L. (2008). Applying the cultural accommodation model to diversity consulting in organizations. *Consulting Psychology Journal: Practice and Research, 60*, 170–185. doi:10.1037/0736-9735.60.2.170

Leong, F. T. L., & Kalibatseva, Z. (2011). Effective psychotherapy for Asian Americans: From cultural accommodation to cultural congruence. *Clinical Psychology: Science and Practice, 18*, 242–245. doi:10.1111/j.1468-2850.2011.01256.x

Leong, F. T. L., & Kim, H. H. (1991). Going beyond cultural sensitivity on the road to multiculturalism: Using the Intercultural Sensitizer as a counselor training tool. *Journal of Counseling and Development, 70*, 112–118.

Leong, F. T. L., & Lee, S. H. (2006). A cultural accommodation model for cross-cultural psychotherapy: Illustrated with the case of Asian Americans. *Psychotherapy: Theory, Research, Practice, Training, 43*, 410–423. doi:10.1037/0033-3204.43.4.410

Minkov, M. (2007). *What makes us different and similar: A new interpretation of the World Values Survey and other cross-cultural data.* Sofia, Bulgaria: Klasika y Stil.

Minkov, M., & Hofstede, G. (2011). The evolution of Hofstede's doctrine. *Cross Cultural Management, 18*, 10–20.

Rauch, A., Frese, M., & Sonnentag, S. (2000). Cultural differences in planning/success relationships: A comparison of small enterprises in Ireland, West Germany, and East Germany. *Journal of Small Business Management, 38*, 28–41.

Rokeach, M. (1973). *The nature of human values.* New York, NY: The Free Press.

Sagiv, L., & Schwartz, S. H. (2007). Cultural values in organizations: Insights for Europe. *European Journal of International Management, 1*, 176–190.

Samovar, L. A., & Porter, R. E. (2011). *Intercultural communication: A reader.* Florence, KY: Wadsworth.

Schwartz, S. H. (1992). Universals in the content and structure of values: Theoretical advances and empirical tests in 20 countries. In M. P. Zanna (Ed.), *Advances in experimental social psychology* (pp. 1–65). San Diego, CA: Academic Press.

Schwartz, S. H. (1997). Values and culture. In D. Munro, J. F. Schumaker, & S. C. Carr (Eds.), *Motivation and culture* (pp. 69–84). New York, NY: Routledge.

Schwartz, S. H. (1999). A theory of cultural values and some implications for work. *Applied Psychology: An International Review, 48,* 23–47. doi:10.1111/j.1464-0597.1999.tb00047.x

Schwartz, S. H., Caprara, G. V., & Vecchione, M. (2010). Basic personal values, core political values, and voting: A longitudinal analysis. *Political Psychology, 31,* 421–452. doi:10.1111/j.1467-9221.2010.00764.x

Schwartz, S. H., & Sagiv, L. (1995). Identifying culture-specifics in the content and structure of values. *Journal of Cross-Cultural Psychology, 26,* 92–116. doi:10.1177/0022022195261007

Shulruf, B., Alesi, M., Ciochina, L., Faria, L., Hattie, J., Hong, F., . . . Watkins, D. (2011). *Social Behavior and Personality, 39,* 173–188. doi:10.2224/sbp.2011.39.2.173

Signorini, P., Wiesemes, R., & Murphy, R. (2009). Developing alternative frameworks for exploring intercultural learning: A critique of Hofstede's cultural difference model. *Teaching in Higher Education, 14,* 253–264. doi:10.1080/13562510902898825

Soto, J. A., Perez, C. R., Kim, Y. H., Lee, E. A., & Minnick, M. R. (2011). Is expressive suppression always associated with poorer psychological functioning? A cross-cultural comparison between European Americans and Hong Kong Chinese, *Emotion, 11,* 1450–1455.

Spini, D. (2003). Measurement equivalence of 10 value types from the Schwartz Value Survey across 21 countries. *Journal of Cross-Cultural Psychology, 34,* 3–23. doi:10.1177/0022022102239152

Sue, D. W., Bernier, J. E., Durran, A., Feinberg, L., Pedersen, P., Smith, E. J., & Vasquez-Nuttal, E. (1982). Position paper: Cross-cultural counseling competencies. *The Counseling Psychologist, 10,* 45–52. doi.org/10.1177/0011000082102008

Sue, D. W., & Sue, D. (2008). *Counseling the culturally diverse: Theory and practice* (3rd ed.). New York, NY: Wiley.

Tamis-LeMonda, C. S., Way, N., Hughes, D., Yoshikawa, H., Kalman, R. K., & Niwa, E. Y. (2008). Parents' goals for children: The dynamic coexistence of individualism and collectivism in cultures and individuals. *Social Development, 17,* 183–209.

Triandis, H. C. (1989). The self and social behavior in differing cultural contexts. *Psychological Review, 96,* 506–520. doi:10.1037/0033-295X.96.3.506

Triandis, H. C. (1994). *Culture and social behavior.* New York, NY: McGraw-Hill.

Triandis, H. C. (1995). *Individualism and collectivism.* Boulder, CO: Westview Press.

Triandis, H. C. (1996). The psychological measurement of cultural syndromes. *American Psychologist, 51,* 407–415.

Triandis, H. C. (2000). Dialectics between cultural and cross-cultural psychology. *Asian Journal of Social Psychology, 3*, 185–195. doi:10.1111/1467-839X.00063

Triandis, H. C. (2001) Individualism–collectivism and personality. *Journal of Personality, 69*, 907–924. doi:10.1111/1467-6494.696169

Triandis, H. C., Brislin, R., & Hui, C. H. (1988). Cross-cultural training across the individualism–collectivism divide. *International Journal of Intercultural Relations, 12*, 269–289. doi:10.1016/0147-1767(88)90019-3

Triandis, H. C., McCusker, C., & Hui, C. H. (1990). Multimethod probes of individualism and collectivism. *Journal of Personality and Social Psychology, 59*, 1006–1020. doi:10.1037/0022-3514.59.5.1006

U.S. Department of Labor. (1991). *Dictionary of occupational titles* (4th ed., rev.). Washington, DC: Author. Retrieved from http://www.oalj.dol.gov/libdot.htm

Williams, R. M., Jr. (1970). *American society* (3rd ed.). New York, NY: Knopf.

Yeganeh, H., & Su, Z. (2007). Comprehending core cultural orientations of Iranian managers. *Cross Cultural Management, 14*, 336–353. doi:10.1108/13527600710830359

5

SEXUALLY AND GENDER-VARIANT INDIVIDUALS: INTERNATIONAL AND MULTICULTURAL PERSPECTIVES

SUE A. KUBA

I remember when I first saw the movie *Bent* (Solinger, Linder, & Mathias, 1997), a powerful film set in Nazi Germany that told the tale of two men living freely as a couple in prewar Europe. It followed them through the devastating consequences of the Nazi extermination and was transcendent in the connections created by gay men under devastation of the Third Reich. Mutually discovered meaning resounded through the film despite the repetitious sadism of the Nazi guards. I wondered why this story of World War II was not told to schoolchildren. I worried that failure to understand how history created such stories could lead us to extermination in another part of the world. In the years since that viewing, I have become familiar with other attempted exterminations and tortures of lesbian, gay, bisexual, and transgender (LGBT) individuals around the world, realizing that such atrocities continue without a specific designated or known name.

At the other extreme, I have marveled at the progress toward LGBT civil rights in undeveloped or religiously constrained portions of the globe. South

DOI: 10.1037/14044-005
Internationalizing Multiculturalism: Expanding Professional Competencies in a Globalized World,
R. L. Lowman (Editor)

Africa, Spain, and Mexico City come to mind. Each has granted full marriage rights to their LGBT citizens when other (presumably more enlightened) countries have not. This struggle continues daily in the United States with advances being so frequent that any specific mention of progress would be hopelessly out of date by the time the book is published.

Such is the struggle and the history of LGBT rights and liberation around the globe. It often makes no sense and engenders fear and anxiety. The factors driving the struggle are not always clear. Yet the ability to work professionally with others in mental health, health, education, business, and law suggests the need for clear knowledge of these factors on the levels of culture, country, historical migrations, and individual efforts. In this chapter, I aim to illuminate some of the international themes emerging from the shadowy world that has been created around the lives of LGBT individuals around the world and to help professionals understand some of the factors that may influence their LGBT clients.

OVERVIEW OF PREJUDICE AND CIVIL RIGHTS ISSUES FOR LGBT INDIVIDUALS

Throughout the world, LGBT individuals face discrimination, hatred, and violence as well as a lack of civil rights. The issues vary significantly in content and process by country and region. The greatest threat occurs to those LGBT individuals who must fear for their lives. Some countries have executed individuals because of the belief or evidence that they were men having sex with men (MSM). Others have forced gender-variant individuals to be stoned or publically humiliated. In some countries, women have been gang raped when they were identified as being lesbian or bisexual. Fear engendered by these experiences frequently leads LGBT individuals to lead lives of silent desperation. Gay men and lesbians may as a consequence marry a heterosexual partner while continuing to have sexual relationships with people of the same sex. These closeted relationships are based on the individual's primary sense of identity, and the other relationship or family is the public face. Depression and suicide can be the outcome. If such individuals' transgressions against the law are discovered, they may, in many countries, be prosecuted for infidelity as well as the charges associated with LGBT acts.

LGBT Identity and Behavior

Identity and behavior are often separated in the understanding of LGBT individuals. Sexual behavior with someone of the same sex is not the same as adopting an identity as gay male or lesbian. Cross-dressing, for example, is not synonymous with a transgendered identity. Having sex with both men and women does not mean one openly declares himself or herself to be bisexual. The failure to identify may represent self-hatred and loathing or merely be self-protective. For example, research in India found that 18% of sexually active males under 19 had experienced sexual contact with another male. Because 50% of the entire sample stated that they were sexually active, this suggests a prevalence rate of 9% for all Indian males under the age of 19. The statistic is related to sexual behavior but not sexual identity. According to the study's authors,

> owing to strict gender identity constructs and associated social taboos and negative consequences of being stigmatized and discriminated, these young men do not openly identify themselves as MSM. (Singh, Mahendra, & Verma, 2008, p. 99)

The lack of identification with the LGBT community is often related to such fear. Yet it seems that public opinion and law change only when such identification becomes widespread; when people know someone who is gender or sexually variant, they change their minds, frequently evolving to a position of support. Enough personal evolution leads to change at the local and national levels.

LGBT Civil Rights

Civil rights consist of a mosaic of specific rights and benefits accorded in one country, state, or province that are denied in others. Subtle forms of prejudice and bias may occur even in supportive countries. These are often related to employment discrimination or the lack of a right to serve in the military or civil service of a country. Employment discrimination may be illegal, but individuals or a panel making the final hiring decision may be unaware of their heteronormative feelings. Individuals experiencing lack of employment based on such discrimination find it difficult to prove legally.

The civil rights tied to the legitimacy of an adult relationship may be more public, but the extent of the legal bias against unrecognized couples is often not well understood. Marriage rights are often center stage in this struggle, but some countries have found unique solutions that respect religious belief and still grant legitimacy to same-sex couples. For example, Great Britain no longer grants any marriage licenses. Marriages are governed only by religious organizations, whereas civil unions are universally tied to legal benefits and are available to any couple regardless of gender or sex. This solution grants all individuals the civil rights usually associated with a marriage. Rights tied to civil recognition of a relationship include the ability to care for a dying partner, provide pension rights, raise children with equal parenting rights, provide untaxed support for a surviving spouse, have equal access to federal benefits and taxes (e.g., Social Security benefits in the United States), and own property with benefit of survivorship. In 1997, the U.S. General Accounting Office identified 1,049 federal laws in which benefits, rights, and privileges were contingent on marital status. These included Social Security benefits, veterans' benefits, employment benefits, and taxation ("A primer on same-sex marriage," 2011). Civil unions or marriages represent the ability for LGBT individuals to function as a family from a financial perspective as well as a social one.

Those who are LGBT in countries with spotty or limited civil rights may migrate within their own country. Young gay or transgendered men often move to urban areas where they may be forced into prostitution to support themselves. Many become vulnerable targets of gay- or trans-related violence. In contrast, the incidence of rural migrant communities of men may have been maintained over time partly to provide a safe environment for MSM. This phenomenon was traced for migrant male communities in the United States by Colin R. Johnson (2008). Such migrant communities continue in the United States and are not being evaluated or considered as part of the LGBT community. Likewise, binational couples face difficulties maintaining a relationship across national lines with differing sensitivity to LGBT issues, even though falling in love does not always respect national boundaries.

Although some countries (e.g., Canada, the Netherlands) welcome and respect LGBT couples as legitimate and provide easy immigration for a partner who is married to a natural citizen, other countries fail to recognize such relationships. These nations may also make it difficult for an individual to immigrate if he or she identifies as LGBT. Couples may be persecuted for attempting to reside in the same nation. However, some nations provide asylum based on sexual orientation when the individual's life might be at risk in his or her home country. Often LGBT individuals do not know the extent of these laws and lack information that might help them live a peaceful and undisturbed life with a partner of their choosing.

PROFESSIONAL PRACTICE WITH LGBT INDIVIDUALS BEGINS WITH KNOWLEDGE AND ATTITUDES

Not infrequently, the ability to work with LGBT individuals, families, and communities is considered in the context of knowledge, attitudes, and skills. It is not sufficient to have factual or contextual knowledge about LGBT issues to work effectively with this population. Confronting personal bias, understanding heterosexual privilege, and having an awareness of heteronormativity[1] throughout the world are also required. Because this information constantly changes, the professional must continually reevaluate his or her skills and be willing to change his or her attitudes.

Because professionals are often armed with mostly incomplete or incorrect information in attempting to understand and work with their LGBT clients, students, and colleagues (Green, Murphy, Blumer, & Palmanteer, 2009; Hernández & Rankin, 2008; Phillips & Fischer, 1998; Pilkington & Cantor, 1996; Semp, 2008), it is important to begin with the known factors that drive individual nations in their attempts to criminalize, marginalize, mainstream, or accept the LGBT individual.

The U.S. psychological and psychiatric communities, including the American Psychological Association (APA) and the American Psychiatric Association (2011), have adopted language supporting gender-variant and sexual minorities (APA, 2000). The APA clearly supports the full integration of human rights for individuals who define themselves as part of the LGBT community (APA, 2011). This perspective is not embraced, however, by many professionals in the United States who may be guided by religious or other beliefs that are frankly discriminatory. Evaluating these disparities internationally adds even more complexity and confusion.

This chapter explores some of the reasons for acceptance or rejection of sexual orientation and related human rights by evaluating factors beyond religious preference. Six specific countries are identified for their unequivocal acceptance (three countries) or unmitigated bias (three countries) toward sexual and gender variations. Common themes from the histories and beliefs of those cultures are evaluated to provide some insight into the evolution of those perspectives. This review helps to identify the wide range of practices associated with LGBT persons in the world. From this understanding, it is possible to begin building international principles for practice with gender- and sexually variant people, couples, families, and communities.

INTERNATIONAL HUMAN RIGHTS FOR LGBT PERSONS

The professional practicing internationally with LGBT clients needs foundational LGBT knowledge about the nations and cultures of those clients. Foundational knowledge includes an understanding of broad historical themes idiosyncratically related to a nation's colonial past, its oppression of others, and its liberation. In other words, in some countries, there has been a tradition of subjecting others to abuse or lowered standing on the basis of

---

[1]Heteronormativity assumes a family construction based on biological and heterosexual parentage inclusive of children. The normality of that construction remains unstated and assumed (Hudak & Giammattei, 2010).

unchosen personal characteristics, and LGBT people may be just one more group in a long tradition of abuse of the less by the more privileged. Certainly there are countries that have accepted the idea that LGBT individuals deserve just and equal treatment. At one end of the spectrum, there are countries that have legalized gay marriage. This represents a liberation for LGBTs. Because it is safe to have an LGBT identity in such countries, the professional can better trust the research on LGBT issues in that country, where citizens may accurately recount their lives and experiences to researchers. However, at the opposite end, there are countries, particularly conservative religious or autocratic ones, where even the presumed expression of gay behavior has led to incarceration, execution, or murder.

When evaluating foundational knowledge, the professional practitioner must always keep the context in mind, even in considering research findings. Some specific examples provide a more personal view of how difficult it is to trust data and research from regions where LGBT people do not have free expression.

Under Egypt's Morality Laws, hundreds were persecuted and tortured. Some have been subject to forced anal examination by medical doctors that included penetration; others have been raped by prisoners—who were encouraged to do so by prison guards. Many have been exposed to torture techniques including burning, electroshock, and hanging in torturous positions (Human Rights Watch, 2004a). In the United States, a gay man named Frederick Mason was detained during a dispute with his landlord in Chicago in 2000. A police officer then raped him using a Billy club while hurling antigay and racist slurs (Amnesty International, 2001).

The pejorative historical references to LGBT individuals are numerous, suggesting the presence of sexual and gender variation throughout history preserved through language. Consider the numerous

> words [that] demonstrate a consciousness (albeit often contemptuous) of a queer stereotype or gay identity. Here are just a few examples: in the Middle East the *xanitha*, who plays the receptive role with older or richer men; in Nicaragua *el cochon*; in Italy the *arruso* and *ricchione*, and *femmenella* ("little female") for the transvestite; *loca* and *maricon* in Latin America; the *teresita* in Argentina; *hicha* and *veado* in Brazil; *masisi* in Haiti; *zamel* in North Africa. . . . Most—but not all—of these labels apply a derogatory stigma to . . . the passive partner in anal intercourse as differentiated from the active partner in that sexual act. (Norton, 1997, p. 39)

Such historical references provide documentation that gender- and sexually variant behavior exists in most regions of the world.

Just as there is differential persecution of gay men on the basis of their role during sex, differential bullying occurs for the woman presumed to take the dominant role in a lesbian relationship. There have also been differences among lesbians, gay men, bisexual persons, and gender-variant individuals, with some receiving greater violence and less legal advocacy on their behalf. Although gay men are often the subjects of torture, criminalization, and execution, lesbians have been targeted for rape or rape in concert[2] to "show them they are women," and this approach is often condoned by family members as a way of correcting them (O'Flaherty & Fisher, 2008). Transgendered youth are most vulnerable to forced heterosexuality due to age and the challenge they pose to binary thinking about gender (O'Flaherty & Fisher, 2008).

Another important set of obstacles is faced by LGBT persons during attempted immigration. These have been documented in the United States but are less well documented in other nations. Because sexual-variant status may be used to document the need for asylum, the imperative to prove one is "gay enough" creates problems for those who have had to hide their sexual status in their country of origin. In addition, they must prove they have suffered discrimination. It is not easy to do this when the punishment in some countries, notably Iran and Saudi Arabia, is execution (Bilefsky, 2011).

International Themes Associated With LGBT Civil Rights

To address the ongoing persecution and criminalization of LGBT individuals in many nations, the nonbinding Yogyakarta Principles (O'Flaherty & Fisher, 2008) were developed by a distinguished group of human rights experts who met in Yogyakarta, Indonesia, to "outline a set of international principles relating to sexual orientation and gender identity. . . . a universal guide to human rights which affirm binding international legal standards with which all States must comply" (The Yogyakarta Principles, n.d.). The principles "offer a way forward by reflecting state obligations under international law to address human rights violations—including violent hate crimes—based on sexual orientation and gender identity" (Human Rights First, 2008a). Likewise, on December 18, 2008, the U.N. General Assembly passed a joint statement on human rights, signed by 66 nations, among them many of the permanent members including Argentina, Brazil, Croatia, France, Gabon, Japan, the Netherlands, and Norway. This statement reaffirmed "the principle of non-discrimination, which requires that human rights apply equally to every human being regardless of sexual orientation or gender identity" (International Lesbian, Gay, Bisexual, Trans and Intersex Association, 2009). These efforts attempted to address a complex history of identification and persecution with bills and policies. Foundational knowledge about these prejudices is important for healing the psychological effects of those who suffer from them.

---

[2]*Rape in concert* is a legal term used to describe rape by multiple attackers during the same time frame.

Many themes related to the historical, cultural, and national factors influencing LGBT civil rights have also been identified. All of these are important factors for the professional practice of psychology, education, and law, among other professions, in the international context. Comprehensive understanding is continually evolving, and these are meant as guidelines for some themes to consider as a professional works at the individual, family, and community levels. Most pragmatic among these themes is the one suggesting definitions of LGBT identity are not universal.

Jeffreys (2007) applied this approach to the expanding definition of prostitution in China. That definition has recently evolved to include same-sex sexual activity, creating a sort of equality that may be misunderstood by Western activists. Chinese prostitution is now punished primarily by targeting the pimp or third parties who benefit from this prostitution. The prostitutes are usually given only a few days in jail. In Nanjing, this new rule of law recently included MSM prostitution, setting a precedent and unveiling a truth about Chinese homosexual activity that was not previously acknowledged.

Jeffreys (2007) suggested that some gay activists wrongly define the ban on MSM prostitution as homophobic, but those accusations would be based on wrongheaded applications of European American values to a different culture. Rather than consider it persecution, the professional needs to understand the complex roles of shame and guilt, as well as the importance of family heirs, in China (Zhou, 2006). Being accused of homosexual activity creates a complex community response to the individual as part of the collective. Negative attitudes are a reaction not only to same-sex experience but to the overall importance of community and culture. Definitions regarding gender- and sexually variant individuals have to become more inclusive of these factors.

Intersecting Identities

Just as people identify with a particular nation, set of cultural values, spirituality, and race, people also have sexual and gender identities. These have a history and can be fluid and multifaceted. These identities can interact and compound or ameliorate bias. For example, historically in South Africa, apartheid-based racial segregation and discrimination caused the same-sex sexual behavior of Black males who were engaged in isolated work (such as in the highly profitable mining industry) to be ignored, whereas homosexual behavior by privileged White males became the focus of discrimination and bias (Lubbe, 2007).

Much binary thinking underlies prejudice against sexually and gender-variant individuals. Marginalization occurs when heterosexual behavior becomes both normalized and privileged and when homosexual behavior becomes marginalized, creating a binary or dichotomous approach to people. This approach ignores multiple, important aspects of individuals' identities. When an individual is sexually or gender variant, this may become the primary focus of the professional, ignoring other identities that may be more significant to the individual or community.

In the United States, some cultural groups require an understanding of the importance of adult family members and the construction of sexuality (Espin, 1984; Greene, 1998; Laird & Green, 1996), yet these complexities are also overlooked. Theoretical perspectives have sometimes proven problematic, especially if rooted in a disease model. For example, Singer (2004) documented that psychodynamic clinical training programs often avoided mention of LGBT issues. Recently, some educational programs have attempted to provide thorough preparation in the delivery of human services to LGBT persons through the offering of certificate programs that take a comprehensive multicultural approach that includes gender, sexual orientation, ethnicity, race, religious preference, age, social class, and language usage (e.g., Kuba, Green, & Giammattei, 2011).

Kaplan (2001) suggested that identification with a particular class makes a person susceptible to different types of discrimination. Gay enclaves exist in many large cities and are often populated by fairly affluent individuals. Same-sex marriage benefits are frequently associated with these privileged enclaves. This may affect the proliferation and acceptance of queer communities in countries with limited access to education, wealth, and privilege of other types (Kaplan, 2001).

Gender identity, like class identity, may serve to maintain a heteronormative atmosphere that blends sexism with heterosexism. Because in many countries the rights of women are limited and sexual privilege is assigned to men, many women must marry men to have access to resources and power. For many lesbians, this means having to choose between being poor or being in a heterosexual marriage. Understanding how gender-based power affects transgendered persons is a significant part of this equation. Those without traditional gender identities are prevented from adequate resources and access to equal opportunities when only heterosexual relationships rooted in male privilege are supported or endorsed.

Thus, miscegenation laws may be used to prohibit same-sex marriage and work "to maintain a caste system based on gender, just as the interdiction of interracial marriage supported white supremacy" (Kaplan, 2001, p. 60). These restrictive laws prevent access to resources that rely on publically recognized intimate connections such as marriage. In cultures with restrictive sex roles, this is even more clearly connected to gender disparity. Two groups that attempt to counter the role of women's equality and therefore reinforce the hegemony of heterosexual (male) privilege are the Taliban in Afghanistan and the Anglican Bishops in South Africa. Both groups also fight the rights of sexually and gender-variant people in those countries.

The damaging effects of class and gender bias are also apparent in limits to medical care required for those desiring to transition using hormones or requiring transsexual surgery. For example, transwomen in Laos often take over-the-counter hormonal supplements without medical supervision and with little knowledge of life-threatening side effects (Winter & Doussantousse, 2009). Similar patterns have been observed in many Southeast Asian countries, especially among those with few resources. Advice about the use of these hormones often comes from friends, with a clear suggestion that "more is better." Irregular use patterns are frequent financial limitations, creating great medical risks. Such self-medication is often tied to lack of money to pay for regular dosages.

Religious Identity

There is great diversity in religious identity among LGBT individuals (Bliss, 2011; Vanderbeck, Andersson, Valentine, Sadgrove, & Ward, 2011; Vidal-Ortiz, 2011). The way those identities are combined with other identifications is complex and difficult to understand. Religious identities vary greatly under the umbrella of fundamentally shared beliefs. LGB couples may marry in the Catholic country of Spain because of an attempt to elevate Catholic marriage over other religious marriages. These non-Catholic civil marriages from another century led to the eventual recognition of gay and lesbian unions as another form of civil marriage, although this was not originally intended. In New Zealand, the difference between Christian denominations is significant; many protestant groups support LGBT civil rights in that country, but nondenominational Christians from unaffiliated churches form the greatest opposition to the same-sex marriage laws (Rishworth, 2007).

Some authors have attempted to understand these variations by articulating four types of factors relevant to religious experience. Whitley (2009) summarized these factors as follows: (a) *intrinsic* factors are related to a personal experience with a deity, (b) *extrinsic* factors provide civic or social motivations for religious beliefs as when one joins a Christian church for the benefit of a social community, (c) *fundamentalist* factors provide affiliation through the belief in one essential truth that is contained in a specific religious tradition, and (d) quest factors relate to an individual's religious beliefs that are divorced from formal religion related to seeking answers to life's most profound questions. The relationships between these factors and prejudice were explored in Whitley's (2009) examination of broad populations in the United States and Canada.

In previous research studies reviewed by Whitley (2009), the quest factor had a negative correlation with prejudice, fundamentalist religions had a positive correlation, intrinsic and extrinsic factors were mixed with more negativity for the intrinsic group and less prejudice for the extrinsic group. Whitley's sophisticated analyses attempted to uncover clearer relationships between these factors of religious experience and the prejudice against LGBT individuals. His approach revealed some important elements of prejudice. Extrinsic factors, such as the need for a social community within the church, did not discriminate between those who were, and those who were not, biased against sexually and gender-variant individuals. Age did matter, with younger persons and college students having less prejudice. Those espousing fundamentalist religious beliefs evidence prejudice regardless of age. The effect size for prejudicial attitudes was larger for Whites when considering their degree of church attendance than it was for African Americans. The frequency of religious attendance increased prejudice more for U.S. citizens than for Canadian citizens. Lesbians received more prejudicial evaluations from those who attended church more often compared with attitudes toward gay men. Men were slightly more prejudicial than women.

Several other issues moderate the religious acceptance of LGBT people. When people believe that sexual orientation is immutable, they are more often accepting. If people perceive LGBT persons as being a threat they are less accepting. Those supporting right wing authoritarian attitudes have also been found to be less accepting. Although religions are often anti-LGBT, not all members of a religious group expressing such official views necessarily are. Thus, in considering support for gender- and sexually variant civil rights, no sweeping generalizations can be made for all Christians, so the Christian LGBT individual may find support for the chosen religious identity or may feel isolated, ostracized, or even removed from the religion by the prejudice of others. For example, persons identifying as LGBT in South Africa report religious discrimination, with 16% reporting religious discrimination and many of those reporting having been forced to leave the church of their choosing due to their sexuality or gender identity (Lubbe, 2007).

Major religions tend to present a unified set of principles and beliefs related to LGBT civil rights and same-sex marriage. Buddhists, for example, are believed to support these rights universally, whereas Muslims are believed to oppose them. Yet there are international exceptions to these broad generalizations. Such biases are just one component of the many difficulties in understanding the progress of civil rights for sexually and gender-variant individuals, couples, and families. When a nation espouses a state religion, the government officials of that country may entrench those religious biases in the national laws. Sometimes those lead to criminalization of LGBT behavior and identity.

Other Experiences of Prejudice

Despite the legalization and decriminalization of LGBT behavior in some countries, evidence of continued discrimination remains. For example, 37% of South Africa's LGBT individuals have reported verbal harassment (Lubbe, 2007). Other authors have described the plight of male sex workers in Kenya relating their persecution to many issues and recommending wide-ranging remedies. As Okal et al. (2009) noted,

> Traditional family values, stereotypes of abnormality, gender norms and cultural and religious influences underlie intense stigma and discrimination. This information is guiding development of peer education programs and sensitization of health providers, addressing unmet HIV prevention needs. Such changes are required throughout Eastern Africa. (p. 811)

Sexual variations and the understanding of them may help to enhance LGBT civil rights or to forestall them. Bisexuality, especially for MSM who are married to women, may be an important theme influencing acceptance or nonacceptance (McLean, 2007). Nondisclosure to female partners by MSM produces negative attitudes. Positive HIV status or having or being at risk of AIDS is another (Holt et al., 1998). Still another factor is the venue for sexual acts. Schrimshaw, Siegel, and Downing (2010) suggested that sexual acts in public locations, such as in bars and parks, negatively affect attitudes toward all sexually variant individuals. Private sexual encounters in homes and hotels are less likely to do so. Continued discrimination and bias against bisexuals may occur in countries in which evaluation of the LGBT culture is negative, whereas in countries with progressive lesbian and gay civil rights, bisexuals may experience greater acceptance (Hatzenbueler, Keyes, & McLaughlin, 2011).

The Role of Family and Children

The importance placed on family relationships by a nation or culture has helped to bolster LGBT families when they are included in the definition or assumptions about what constitutes a family. In some countries, the concern for the welfare of children overrides prejudice about the sexual orientation of parents. South Africa, for example, has a history of highly valued family traditions, and the traditional heterosexual family remains normative (Lubbe, 2007). However, South Africa is highly affected by global culture and deeply concerned about what is in the best interests of the child, so heteronormativity has given way to prioritizing the stability of the family environment over concerns about sexuality. Placement in gay and lesbian homes is now common in South Africa, and child custody laws have changed.

The degree of postmodern thinking and available scholarship may influence definitions of family, creating a noncategorical construct that is fluid and not dependent on marriage. In such cases, the definition of family is revised to include a closely interconnected group of adults and children. This definition also varies depending on urbanization, degree of social discourse, and awareness of LGBT cultural practices (Lubbe, 2007). Often a narrow definition of family can be used to constrict LGBT civil rights and family recognition. Turkey and Poland, for example, have recently attempted to disband or limit free speech of organizations with an LGBT focus based on the heteronormative family and the "lack of morality" expressed in sexually variant behavior (Human Rights First, 2010; O'Flaherty & Fisher, 2008). In the usually LGBT-supportive United Kingdom, a conservative government attempted in the 1980s to redefine families with the intent of excluding LGBT families. In doing so, those in power created Clause 28, which prohibited the discussion of LGBT families in educational settings (Hester, Donovan, & Fahmy, 2010). Such backlashes against sexually and gender-variant civil rights are common and again are rooted in heteronormativity, as is most visible in support for only the heterosexual family.

Family conflict and domestic violence may produce an inadvertent support for LGBT families over time. Access to domestic violence services played a role in beginning acceptance of lesbian women in the United Kingdom and the United States (Hester et al., 2010). Domestic violence was recognized earlier for lesbian women than for gay men, as lesbians began attending domestic violence groups that had been established for heterosexual women. This created a dialogue from which the recognition of domestic violence in the gay male community emerged.

In Spain and many countries influenced by its colonialization (e.g., Mexico), the centrality of family relationships may have helped counter some anti-LGBT religious biases. In Spain, for example, family is defined by its meaning, not by specific persons or by the presence of a heterosexual marriage (Platero, 2007). Thus, the movement toward legitimacy of LGBT couples and families is driven by the valuing of relationship stability, not by a specific set of adults. It may still be driven by specific gendered roles. Mexican American lesbian women living in California often refer to each other as wife, and gay men refer to their husbands. These expressions are differentially emphasized compared with couples from other cultures. Transgender laws have also been loosened in Spain, owing to some of the same factors. One law, the Law of Registration of Rectification of Sex (Platero, 2008), allows a transgendered person to change his or her legal name without completing surgical reassignment. Platero (2008) argued that the failure to integrate other forms of disparity such as class and age in law suggests a perpetuation of discrimination. Thus, a more robust form of legal integration may be required.

National Identity

The presumed right of a country to define the predominant identity of its people is often used as an argument against extending civil rights to sexual- and gender-variant people. In the early 1990s, John Howard ran for prime minister of Australia under a platform that said he would not attempt to create a national Australian identity that excluded diversity. Once elected, Howard reversed his decision and tied the Australian character to "Anglo-Celtic identity, social conservatism, the Christian Right and a neo-liberal 'entrepreneurial culture'" (C. Johnson, 2007, p. 195). In a similar vein, Kollman (2007) suggested that the transnational movements to end LGBT disparity have affected many European nations and much of the world, but Ireland and the United States remain immune. According to Kollman, this may be due to the worldview held by many U.S. and Irish citizens and the resultant belief that national identity should remain free of external influence. Perhaps this informs the attempts to limit same sex-marriage in the United States.

The themes and instances related to gender- and sexually variant individuals' civil rights are numerous. They include the importance of national identity, family definition, family significance, staunchness of gender roles, sense of colonial intrusion, and the relationship between religious dogma and personal religious practice. There are other themes that are significant when polarizing arguments for LGBT discrimination. The next section attempts to address some of these by describing some of the most supportive and some of the most lethal nations in the world in their treatment of LGBT civil rights.

Historical and Psychological Issues for Polarized Nations

Providing comprehensive knowledge of the state of LGBT human rights and supportive networks in all nations would require many volumes. For those practicing in a professional context now, I have chosen to illustrate the issues by selecting several countries from both extremes—countries supportive of LGBT rights and those persecuting LGBT individuals and communities. Depending on specific circumstances, professionals will need to learn more about the international contexts of their clients, but likely there will be some variation of what I present here.

LGBT ISSUES IN THE INTERNATIONAL CONTEXT

In this section, I aim to illustrate the wide diversity of support or nonsupport for LGBT issues internationally and to help professionals understand how clients' behavior may be affected by their experiences, whether in their current countries or those from which they may have migrated.

The Selection of Countries

The criteria I used to select countries with strong LGBT support included the presence of immigration laws that supported LGBT asylum, recognition of LGBT relationship status (domestic partnership, civil unions, or marriage), recognition of the LGBT right to parent through natural childbirth or adoption, and whether LGBT individuals were treated as being part of a protected class. Several organizations' websites provide a compilation of those recognitions. The site create by Human Rights First stated that

> only 12 of the 56 OSCE [Organization for Security and Cooperation in Europe] states have legislation that allows for bias based on sexual orientation to be treated as an aggravating circumstance in the commission of a crime. These are: Andorra, Belgium, Canada, Croatia, Denmark, France, Portugal, Romania, Spain, Sweden, the United Kingdom and the U.S. In the [United States], although federal hate crime legislation does not make violence motivated by sexual orientation a crime, state legislation in 30 states and the District of Columbia provides enhanced penalties for offenses motivated by sexual orientation bias. (Human Rights First, 2008b)

I also examined the presence of specific laws intended to protect against discrimination; to prosecute those who bully, target, or attack others on the basis of LGBT status; and to track hate crimes against LGBT individuals by the state or nation. These criteria led to my selection of three nations representative of those offering the most support for GLBT rights and three most opposed.

Representative LGBT-Supportive Nations

Many nations have provided leadership and strong support for LGBT human rights, and various human rights organizations and the United Nations have recognized this advocacy.

Canada

The evidence for the inclusion of Canada begins with its willingness to sign the U.N. General Assembly joint statement on LGBT rights defining sexual orientation and gender expression as irrefutable parts of an individual's identity that is protected by national law. In Canadian law, sexual orientation is a fundamental part of human identity similar to race or ethnicity, as it relates to refugees and migrants. In an LGBT affirmative statement issued by the Immigration and Refugee Board of Canada, the regulatory agency compared the open expression of LGBT behavior with the open expression of religious beliefs.

> Into the equation must be added the claimant's new found freedom of expression in Canada and his desire to live openly in Sri Lanka as he does

here in Canada. . . . We do not tell claimants that they have a right to practice their religion so long as they hide it. A hidden right is not a right. (Immigration and Refugee Board of Canada, as cited in International Commission of Jurists [ICJ], 2010)

Canada also embraces full marriage rights for couples regardless of sexual minority status and offers that right to nonresidents. Reflecting Canada's support for free expression by LGBT rights groups, the First International Conference on Lesbian, Gay, Bisexual, and Transgender Human Rights was held in Montreal in 2007 (ICJ, 2010).

Three themes related to Canadian history seem especially important in understanding this approach to LGBT individuals. First, Canada was a colony of the United Kingdom, but one that gained its freedom and set its own constitution in the early part of the 20th century. Its power to do so began with legislation in the late 19th century that recognized the important role that Canadians played in the development of material and human resources for World War I (Canadiana, n.d.). Canada gained its independence via a route of recognition rather than war. Another theme that is significant is Canada's general commitment to diversity. For example, the country's commitment to preserving the aboriginal peoples' way of life stands in direct contrast to that of their North American neighbors to the south. This commitment requires an honoring of First Nations' recognition of the "two-spirited" (Taylor et al., 2008), a specific reference to those embodying both masculine and feminine traits. Recent evidence of the Canadian commitment to diversity came in the report they provided related to fair housing, notably that of lesbian women, and the persistent discrimination despite laws to the contrary (ICJ, 2010). Such openness suggests a willingness to evaluate publically acknowledged bias and diversity shortcomings.

Yet even such progressive nations as Canada have experienced a long road to LGBT protection and have not fully arrived at equal rights and protection. A recent national survey of high school students in Canada found that the majority of students (both gay and straight) felt that there is at least one place that is unsafe for LGBT high school students (Taylor et al., 2008). The findings from the same survey suggested that the situation is even worse for transgendered students, 87% of whom identified somewhere—usually a washroom or locker room in their high school—where they felt unsafe. Those surveyed who knew of policies related to LGBT harassment felt safer than those unaware of such policies. The researchers advocated greater awareness and implementation of school policies against antigay bullying.

New Zealand

In a move similar to the one taken by Canada's immigration authority, the New Zealand Refugee Status Appeal Authority created a liberal definition of the term *persecution*, making it clear LGBT individuals should not have to hide their sexual minority status to escape persecution in the countries from which they seek to emigrate. Also like Canada, New Zealand has had a long history of protection of minorities. As early as 1995, for example, New Zealand added sexual orientation to a list of the characteristics protected under asylum laws on the premise that it was a human condition that was "innate or unchangeable" (Amnesty International, 2001, p. 24). New Zealand has also signed the U.N. General Assembly's joint statement on LGBT rights defining sexual orientation and gender expression as being irrefutable parts of an individual's identity that should be protected by national law.

Like all countries, however, this one does not have a perfect record of LGBT human rights. State-supported pensions have been denied to same-sex couples, and a response to queries about this by the ICJ received a negative response. There was no violation of New Zealand law in this action, according to the responders (ICJ, 2010).

South Africa

South Africa holds the distinction of being the first nation in the world to include sexual orientation as a protected class in its constitution. In 1996, the Equity clause of the post-Apartheid Constitution of South Africa included sexual orientation as a protected class, and the prior sodomy laws were simultaneously struck down.

The principle of equality and nondiscrimination embodied in the country's 1996 constitution sees a source of strength in the diversity of a country that has 11 official languages, innumerable religious institutions, and uncounted and often contradictory cultural traditions. The constitution vows in its preamble to "heal the divisions of the past" and to "lay the foundations for a democratic and open society in which government is based on the will of the people and every citizen is equally protected by law." It creates institutions as well as protections toward this goal, striving to accommodate difference while defusing violence (Human Rights Watch, 2003, p. 3)

In May 2000, South Africa was added to a list of countries granting asylum to LGBT refugees. All of these progressive approaches to LGBT rights have taken place in the southern portion of Africa, a continent not known for its tolerance on LGBT issues. It is worthwhile to ask why this has occurred.

To understand the distinction of South Africa, it is necessary to understand the differential effects of British and Dutch colonialism, the reactions of specific nations to that colonialism, and its accompanying rules of law and the specific role of apartheid in South Africa. The existence of sexually and gender-variant behavior, its role before and after colonial reign, and the importance of the AIDS virus in devastating southern Africa are important and controversial components of this history. In some countries (most notably Uganda and Zimbabwe), AIDS has been labeled the "gay plague" and homosexuality "the White man's disease." Same-sex relations are dubbed "unChristian," "unAfrican," "unIslamic" or a "bourgeois decadence" (Amnesty International, 2001, p. 2). Such analyses suggest that homosexuality is identified with the oppressor, and it is a matter of national pride and preservation to oppose these behaviors. They go against nationalism and African identity. Contradictory evidence, however, suggests that sexually and gender-variant behaviors existed before the invasion of the British and the Dutch. It is the law itself that represents the oppressor (Chan-Sam, 1994; Krige, 1974; Potgieter, 1997).

South Africa, as a nation, represented a different view and had other significant influences on its progressive stance. Sodomy, originally used to define any sexually variant behavior other than intercourse with the intention of pregnancy, was eventually narrowed to specify a sexual act between gay men. This differentiation of the sexual act of sodomy, partly influenced by the British rule of law and partly by apartheid, separated this southern African nation from its neighbors. Rather than blame the gender-variant member of a gay coupling, this differentiation found both men culpable when anal intercourse could be proven. This significant shift from criminalization of gendered roles to criminalization of behavior may have led to greater understanding of the relationship between gay men and the emergence of same-sex marriage in this country, while neighboring countries have attempted to revive capital punishment for same-sex conduct (Human Rights Watch, 2003, Appendix). In the meantime, lesbianism has been assumed to be limited and insignificant and has never been regulated in South African law.

South Africa has struggled to define and maintain equity for all of its LGBT citizens. However, Potgieter (1997) documented the differential treatment of Black and White LGBT South Africans as well as the differential treatment of sexually variant women and men. In the early days of the abolition of apartheid, lesbian women experienced triple prejudice from being women, Black, and sexually variant. Such discrimination has persisted in the "new" South Africa, sometimes in horrific form. In 2006, for example, both women of a young lesbian couple were forcibly raped in Cape Town by a group of 20 men and boys. These rapists were assembled by a woman who taunted the young lesbian couple about their sexual orientation. One member of the couple was killed by stabbing and stoning; the other escaped. No public official decried the assault as a hate crime, although several of the perpetrators were arrested (ICJ, 2010). The ICJ inquired about this incident and received no response. According to its report, many members of the new South Africa still believe a lesbian can be converted to a heterosexual through rape.

Representative Nations Opposing or Punishing LGBT Human Rights

Elements considered in selecting the nations opposing or punishing LGBT rights include execution as a punishment for LGBT behavior, imprisonment of LGBT individuals, failure to punish those who inflict bodily harm because of LGBT hate, encouragement for assault on LGBT individuals during confinement, and legislation attempting to disband or limit the free speech of LGBT organizations. According to Flaherty and Fisher (2008), the following nations support the death penalty for gay sexual behavior: Iran, Mauritania, Nigeria (where the death penalty applies in 12 northern provinces), Saudi Arabia, Sudan, United Arab Emirates, Yemen, and Nigeria. Cameroon, Morocco, Uganda, and at least 77 other countries support imprisonment of LGBT individuals. In 2009, Uganda, with the support of some religious organizations in the United States, introduced the Anti-Homosexuality Bill of 2009, which sought to introduce the death penalty for certain same-sex consensual acts and to imprison LGBT-supportive individuals who did not turn in the names of those they knew (Human Rights First, 2010). On the basis of these criteria and such examples, I selected the countries of Egypt, Jamaica, and Zimbabwe.

Egypt

In the past few decades, one of the worst shifts in the recognition of LGBT human rights occurred in Egypt.[3] The ICJ has documented examples, citing incidents related to the arrests of five gay men. These men were allegedly held in inhumane conditions following police arrest for immoral behavior and discovery by the police of their HIV-positive status. Egypt's response to the ICJ inquiry suggested that they had no responsibility for handling these arrests in a discriminatory manner. These five men were charged and imprisoned for 1 year for the crime of homosexuality. Once the men were released, they were forced to undergo police supervision under Egypt's morality laws. These laws gave wide latitude in the interpretation of supervision except to state that it could continue for the length of the original sentence. In this case, the five men were forced to undergo police supervision in jail from 6 p.m. to 6 a.m. every day for another year following release (Human Rights Watch, 2004a).

The crackdown on "immoral" behavior, including any same-sex behavior, had begun 50 years earlier with the end of occupation by the British and

---

[3]In the year since drafting this section, Egypt's journey toward civil rights has taken a dramatic and violent turn. It is unclear whether full rights will be accorded to its LGBT citizens at the end of the revolution, but the potential for change exists.

fear of degradation represented by prostitution, presumed to be a tyranny of the oppressor; Human Rights Watch, 2004a). After the departure of the British from Egypt in 1952 (Treacher, 2007), the "Egyptian Enlightenment" tried to rid Egypt of British moral influences (Human Rights Watch, 2004a, p. 132, footnote 432).

The morality laws targeted sexually variant men differently. Moral laws targeted women specifically for sex work, but men could be arrested for any act of "debauchery." A legal case in 1975 specifically uncoupled the Egyptian term *fujur*, used to describe sex workers, from the act of receiving money and applied the term more specifically to the sexually receptive partner of a male couple having sex in a private residence (Human Rights Watch, 2004a). Since that time, the definition of moral conduct has moved from a focus on sexual role to one of object choice. This has led Egypt to persecute all persons who identified as gender- or sexually variant. The persecution became more universal as the definition expanded. The uncoupling of payment for such services from the sexual act was related to a sexist national belief that no man would consent to penetration voluntarily (only women would).

One of the worst incidents of violence and imprisonment in Egypt occurred in 2001 following a raid on a floating gay nightclub called the Queen Boat. During the raid, many men were injured or tortured, and some were imprisoned. One of the defendants was from a prominent political family in Egypt, and some have suggested that the motive for raiding the club that night was political. Such incidents have occurred historically around the world— one of the first such documented events occurred at the Stonewall bar in New York City nearly 40 years ago. In Egypt, specific events related to postcolonial readjustment, specific police actions, and expansion of persecutory legislation have been a part of a continued oppression of LGBT individuals.

Jamaica

As in many other countries, the fear driven by HIV/AIDS is partly to blame for such violence. "Many Jamaicans believe that HIV/AIDS is a disease of homosexuals and sex workers whose 'moral impurity' makes them vulnerable to it, or that HIV is transmitted by casual contact" (Human Rights Watch, 2004b, p. 1). With this rationale (and others), gay male and transgendered sex is criminally prosecuted in the country. Even those who attempt to intervene on behalf of LGBT persons or persons with HIV/AIDS may be targeted. The Jamaican government did not respond to the U.N. Special Representative requesting investigation of the murder of a man who was a human rights defender working with LGBT and persons with HIV/AIDS in 2005.

Jamaica continues to have sodomy laws prohibiting homosexual contact between adult men. They do not recognize sexual expression between lesbian women, but lesbians' lives may be threatened because of being gender variant. Gay men and lesbians are urged to keep their private lives private in an effort to protect their lives. This constant threat makes organizing difficult and LGBT community culture difficult to access (Glave, 2008; Williams, 2000).

Two incidents illustrate the level of fear and hatred associated with MSM. In one incident, two male friends were seen hugging following a dinner they shared together. Following the dinner, one was assaulted until near death. Neither was gay, but the perception that they might have been was enough to motivate a gang of thugs to protect their national morality. On August 16, 1997, the commissioner of an all-male prison distributed condoms to stop the spread of HIV/AIDS. The contextual homophobia within the prison resulted in the killing of 16 men within 3 days. The targets were those presumed to be homosexual, and the perpetrators were presumed to be proving their manhood (Williams, 2000).

Zimbabwe

Zimbabwe shares many of the postcolonial issues with South Africa but has had little tolerance for LGBT individuals. Lesbians have been specifically targeted in this nation and several surrounding it (Hawthorne, 2006). During the last part of the 20th century, Zimbabwe criminalized LGBT behavior. Differences between these two countries have been tied to the continuation of the rigid Roman Dutch laws. Ironically, those laws are based in Victorian beliefs about sex and morality. The oppressed are defending a historic artifact of the oppressor (Bearak & Cowell, 2010).

In countries such as Zimbabwe, gender- and sexually variant behaviors are described as being "un-African" (Bearak & Cowell, 2010, p.1). However, nonconformity to rigid sexual and gender roles was the product of the Dutch and English colonialism. Native Africa allowed a variety of gender expression, and the variability was often linked to sexual variation. The Dutch and English were much more inhibited in their acceptance of gender nonconformity and homosexual behavior than the Africans who lived there before colonization. Colonial laws reflected European standards prevalent during Victorian England—notoriously repressive and punishing (Human Rights Watch, 2003). Southern African nations retained colonial rule far longer than other parts of Africa, with Zimbabwe gaining free elections only in 1990, the last before South Africa. During liberation, they reified the laws of their oppressors, despite the fact that England and the Netherlands had long since moved away from such laws.

Other potential motives for the criminal penalties associated with sexually variant behavior in Zimbabwe are related to the relentless HIV/AIDs crisis. Despite the overwhelming evidence for predominantly heterosexual transmission of HIV infection in Africa, the LGBT community has continued to be the scapegoat for HIV/AIDS (Human Rights Watch, 2003). This reflects a broader tendency of oppressive governments to spread blame for undesirable events to others, for example, to White landowners and their African employees or to those who oppose the existing government within Zimbabwe. Under such circumstances, the rule of law often lapses, and punishment can be administered by self-appointed vigilantes who are stoked by government hate speech against all of these groups.

Much more rural than its cosmopolitan neighbor South Africa, Zimbabwe retained its White settler class longer. This may have created continued allegiance to the Dutch system and a reticence to identify sodomy specifically and clarify whether lesbianism was part of the law. Independent White rule was maintained in this rural country where the rulers wanted to maintain power and thus may have turned the sodomy laws on their own citizens to keep their morality pure, whereas the morality of the indigenous was seen as not worth being concerned about (Human Rights Watch, 2003; Primorac, 2007).

In Zimbabwe, individuals arrested for the offense of sodomy can be charged with other crimes. These laws are often connected to intimate gay films or periodicals and include statutes against indecent publications and films, media laws requiring the registration of publications and journalists, and laws defining appropriate (gender-specific) clothing. Transgendered persons are targeted under the Zimbabwe's Miscellaneous Offences Act that dates to 1964 (Primorac, 2007). This law punishes "any person who appears in any public place" without "such articles of clothing as decency, custom or circumstances require," a provision that could be and apparently has been interpreted to criminalize gender nonconformity in dress (Human Rights Watch, 2003, Appendix, p. 278). Even private homes in Zimbabwe are considered to be public, effectively prohibiting any "offensive act" that is viewable by the public. Specific broadening of the laws in Zimbabwe related to HIV transmission has resulted in failure to distinguish between HIV-infected consensual sex and HIV-infected nonconsensual sex. Even without evidence, suspected transmission could result in either "offender" receiving a 20-year prison term, thus essentially making it criminal for a male with HIV to have sex with another male (Human Rights Watch, 2003). In Zimbabwe, the underlying element of anti-LGBT laws seems connected to fear, national identity, and sexually transmitted disease.

Similarities in History of Countries Supporting LGBT Human Rights

Comparing human rights for LGBT individuals in Canada, New Zealand, and South Africa suggests some similarity in their histories. Two of these countries obtained independent nation status before the influence of Victorian morality. The lone exception among the countries reviewed was South Africa. Its laws evolved with the changing morality of a people who were free to determine their own fate and who have enjoyed freedom. All of these countries are democracies of long standing. Most do not have a state-endorsed religion. In Europe, the shift to Napoleonic laws seemed to have provided open opportunities for engaging in gender- and sexually variant behavior. Each country differentiated sodomy and defined it as a single type of sexual act as opposed to the more broad definition used to define it as anything not specifically designed to produce a child. Punishing both partners for the act of sodomy may have led to identification with the persecuted, rather than just blaming the receptive individual.

Similarities in History of Countries Punishing or Opposing LGBT Rights

Several themes seem to exist in the histories of those who punish or execute gender- and sexually variant individuals. Many of these countries characterized these activities as divergent from their national identity or morality—a "problem" foisted on indigenous peoples by those who colonized or enslaved them. To some, the HIV/AIDS crisis in their countries bears a striking similarity to the effects of smallpox among indigenous peoples of North America. Countries with a historically high rate of HIV/AIDS (e.g., Jamaica, 1.5%, Uganda, 1.6%) have erroneously tied that disease to MSM, leading to the scapegoating of sexually variant activities in hope of helping their nations survive. These countries are

> burdened by poverty and political uncertainty, and devastated by higher rates of HIV/AIDS . . . infection than any other region in the world. Yet in some countries, politicians, instead of directly addressing those issues, have made calls to persecute and cast out homosexuals. (Human Rights Watch, 2003, p. 1)

Hidden in the background in many of these countries is virulent intolerance for variation in gender expression and sexuality. In Egypt, the White settlers' desire for prostitutes led to a rise in prostitution, which became known as the "oppressor's disease." Differing views of sex roles within LGBT communities further exacerbates this, with prejudice being stronger against the gender-variant individual (e.g., the masculine lesbian, the more feminine gay man). Colonial rule based on Roman law criminalized same-sex acts under vague labels. Rape and prostitution laws remain antiquated in those countries that punish same-sex behavior. Rape is restricted to male-on-female assault and until recently did not include marital rape; prostitution has been viewed as a crime, and prostitutes are not usually able to bring criminal offenses against those who assault or rob them (Human Rights Watch, 2003). These twin dangers of scapegoating and sexism are often accompanied by the presence of overriding religious fervor at the time laws are enacted and the growing political presence of a community of individuals who describe themselves openly as gender- and sexually variant.

Within these themes are the guiding principles that prevent progress toward greater understanding and integration of LGBT individuals into communities. When working in oppressive countries, the professional must create a different map to guide professional practice. Confronting prejudice means understanding the signposts and byways of this map. Its elements include the ability to rigidify behavior based on a sense of superiority that allows one group of individuals to define the appropriate behavior for all others. Often this superiority is based on a moral mandate grounded in religious belief and tradition. The understanding of personal history is limited to elements that continue to support these rigid beliefs. Openness to new ideas and exploration are discouraged, and those supporting change of any kind may be silenced along with the outcasts they attempt to support. To move beyond prejudice and discrimination, dramatic crises or life-altering experiences may be necessary.

ROLES FOR PROFESSIONAL PRACTICE

Professional Practice Advocacy and Needed Research

Professional practice advocacy for changes in LGBT civil rights laws can be achieved through many avenues. Because education and information seem to enhance acceptance of LGBT individuals, couples, and families, one such route to advocacy is the presentation of evidence. The lack of knowledge about factors such as prevalence and the difficulty of understanding the complexity of sexually and gender-variant individuals have resulted in a desire to use methods that vary from standard empirical treatments. Methods for exploring same-sex research differ even among Western nations. For example, the narratives associated with domestic violence need to include understanding of gender and power dynamics (Hester et al., 2010).

Qualitative research strategies are often used to approach topics in which variables are difficult to define or assess adequately. Among these methods are Glaser and Strauss's (1967/2007) approach to grounded theory, which attempts to build theory as it uncovers subjective meaning. Likewise, narrative approaches (Hammack & Cohler, 2009) have explored the narratives of gay and lesbian families as well as the personal construction of gender. Phenomenological approaches (Giorgi, 1985; Moustakas, 1994) have been useful in the careful consideration of a child's view within lesbian families (Kuba, 1981).

Ethnographic studies have evaluated the narratives of those in Asia, including one virtual study in Japan (e.g., Manalansan, 2006; McLelland, 2002).

The practitioner must conduct research that respects cultural differences not only between ethnicities and genders but also between countries and population densities. Thus, a Black gay man living in the rural areas of Zimbabwe will experience a different life course than one living within urban Johannesburg. Understanding how the identity of a gay rural man may be more similar to heterosexual rural men than to gay men living in a city is only one of the many problems requiring creative methodologies for describing the lives of gender- and sexually variant individuals.

Applications to Professional Practice Issues

To provide examples of specific professional practices that are implied by this review, I have chosen to highlight three studies: one related to forensic psychology, one to clinical psychology, and one to educational understanding in different parts of the world.

Many forensic experts are concerned with the perpetuation of domestic violence and its variance within the international context. Walby and Allen (2004) evaluated elements of intersecting identities related to domestic violence and same-sex relationships in the British Crime Survey. They found that lower income levels and lower educational achievement led to greater risk for domestic violence. Age was also significant in that lesbians and gay men having had initial same-sex experiences at a younger age had more often experienced domestic violence later in their lives (Donovan & Hester, 2008). Risks related to income and educational levels were more difficult to explain, but gay men were more likely to have had their spending curtailed as part of a pattern of partner abuse. This survey research evaluates a common forensic problem while attempting to uncover the layers of variables that influence its prevalence in lesbian and in gay male relationships.

One clinical psychology study explored the connections between context and sexual satisfaction in sexually variant relationships. Canadian researchers explored the cultural and relationship factors that led to positive and negative sexual experiences for lesbians and gay men, focusing on the differences between these identities and their sexual expressions. The researchers concluded that sexual experiences need to be contextualized to understand their complexity. In both the lesbian and gay male samples, oppressive cultural factors negatively influenced sexual satisfaction (e.g., lack of community supports, legitimacy, and family disclosure were associated with lower levels of satisfaction). Relationship factors seemed to be positively associated with satisfaction (e.g., connection, intimacy, desirability). More relationship themes were reported by the lesbian women. Community engagement themes suggested that sexual satisfaction may be enhanced for those enjoying the protective effects of identification with the lesbian/gay communities (Cohen, Byers, & Walsh, 2008). The importance of professionals' differentiating among various members of the LGBT community is highlighted in this clinical research.

The educational example of professional practice research comes from an effort to deconstruct the cultural victim narrative often experienced by the youngest members of the LGBT community. Focusing too frequently on the high rates of suicidal ideation of LGBT youth has led to an international culture of the victim. Marshall (2010) suggested that focusing on victimization creates a false narrative for LGBT youth; like other oppressed young people, LGBT youth often develop a strong sense of resilience. The psychological impact of constantly focusing on the need to protect themselves may disable them, and they may fail to recognize their strengths. Marshall called for "after queer educational approaches" (p. 82). Such approaches refer to a distinct and current time period in Western countries, notably the United States and Great Britain. The underlying principle of "after queer" education suggests that queer, meaning unusual or atypical, is no longer "queer" when the media provides many mainstream characterizations of LGBT individuals, and that online access provides gay youth with normalized role models. Instead, he recommended creating multimedia, alternative role models; promoting resilience; and supporting an online youth community that gay youth can create for them. In deconstructing the victim, Marshall provides professionals of all fields with the opportunity to rethink and redefine our approach to working with members of the international LGBT community. These three examples suggest some broader principles for professional practice.

PROFESSIONAL PRACTICE COMPETENCIES WITH THE LGBT POPULATION

How does the competent professional practice in a global community while considering the endless variations of individual difference among the communities, families, and individuals who make up the sexually and gender-variant part of every culture? The preceding material suggests the possible applications and potential stumbling blocks are extensive, yet some guidelines can be offered for the educator, the professional psychologist, the health care professional, the organizational consultant, and the forensic analyst.

Professionals should consider the *history* and *context* of the nation where the client lives (or has lived). Consider, for example, the long-term political movements and how they have supported the development of LGBT acceptance, tolerance, or criminalization. More tolerant, accepting nations such as South Africa and Spain may confound us without this historical perspective because the values of the dominant religions might seem opposed to such acceptance. The Catholic Church played an active role in creating the circumstances for civil marriage in Spain, but this would not be understood without a deep knowledge of history. The way apartheid shaped a unique morality and set of ethics in South Africa paved the way for constitutional support of the sexually variant.

Migration patterns are important for the practicing professional to under. For example, consider the narratives of Nicaraguan women immigrating to the United States through Mexico and that they must make their way past two sets of "coyotes" (men who may victimize them as they provide passage into uncharted new countries). Such experiences create a unique narrative that may alter the gender and sexual expression of lesbian women, resulting in inhibited sexual desire or dependent relationships with subsequent partners. Young rural men migrating to cities may engage in sexually variant behavior or assume gender-variant identities to survive. How do these individuals fit into the gender- and sexually variant community? How do they define themselves in relation to that community and to the rural communities they left? The skilled practitioner seeking to understand the LGBT client's context will need to consider the history of industrialization and its effects on the rural–urban localization of a gay ghetto or a lesbian suburb.

The definition of *national identity* can be an important contextual factor. Here the relationship between religion and state may need to be considered. When a national religious identity is embraced, as it has been by the Taliban in Afghanistan, the criminalization of same-sex sexual behavior may lead to executions accompanied by attempts to escape persecution. Crossing the border to find asylum may pose a life-threatening risk. In Canada, the importance of the separation of church and state paved the way for a distinction between civil and sacred marriages, allowing gays and lesbians to legally wed. Professionals also need to be mindful of nationalized, internalized oppression of people in Zimbabwe, for example, who may have ceased to understand the origin of such bias.

The *importance of family and its definition* has led to the implementation of LGBT civil rights in some jurisdictions and the denigration of them in others. Heteronormative movements (Griffin, 2007; Johnson, 2002; Peterson, 2011) in the United States actively opposing the civil rights of gender- and sexually variant individuals are euphemistically referred to as "family centered." Yet the desire to protect children and families helped create or strengthen same-sex marriage laws in South Africa, Mexico City, and Spain. The meaning of family should ultimately be defined by the family's members, and professionals must respect those definitions. In collectivist cultures such as Laos or China that criminalize or punish LGBT behavior, the role of shame and sadness may be particularly intense.

Professionals should also consider the *multiple and intersecting identities* of the clients they serve. The professional needs to understand the influence on individual identity at the community and personal levels. Professionals' self-awareness is especially important here. When working with an organization to attempt to integrate nonbias policies, trainers have to be willing to challenge others. Finding creative methods for stimulating self-awareness is crucial. People from the LGBT community often do not understand specific ethnic issues that enter into this equation, just as some members of ethnic groups do not fully understand their own heteronormativity (Peterson, 2011). How do professionals help their clients deal with issues of creating a spiritual space for generations of gay men who have been hurt by the Anglican or Catholic churches? Another example comes from the relationship of poor rural young men who move to the cities and support themselves as prostitutes. These "money boys" (Wong et al., 2008) are exploited by various levels of society, but many have accepted the multiplicity of their identities within the urban scene. If these clients identify as gay, mental health professionals might be tempted to see them as victims, when support for their resilience would produce greater strength. In such situations, professionals would do well to consider how the moral stance of a country reflects its potential for insight. Methods for stimulating development toward greater empathy based on understanding of shared hurts might be helpful in replacing attitudes of moral superiority and the need to control others who diverge.

CONCLUSION

This exploration has uncovered some of the themes that provide an international understanding of LGBT politics and law as a background for providing services to gender- and sexually variant clients within families and organizations. In particular, themes related to these legal issues were evaluated in the way that they provide an opportunity for free expression and research accuracy. Problems with lack of definitions, unclear prevalence data, and limited research evidence all flow from the repression that still exists in much of the world. An analysis of six countries provided a deeper understanding of cultural impingement on the rights of LGBT individuals and points the way for advocacy. Examples of research related to specific professional practice in education, psychology, and forensic work were evaluated. The practitioner was encouraged to consider a number of specific issues when working in the professional context. These include the history of a country, national identity, the existence of a state-sponsored religion, the importance of family and its definition, immigration and migration patterns, as well as intersecting identities. This is a demanding task.

In the movie *Bent*, the characters move from being victims to transcendence in simple expressions of self—a self connected to others who have shared the traumatic experience and found meaning in the most difficult of settings. That transcendence can occur because of the understanding that emerges through anger, loss, and denial. Layers of resistance are removed as the watcher finds grace in the lives of intelligent, expressive men who are reduced to moving rocks uselessly from one spot to another and back. This Sisyphean task does not feel unimportant because it is merely the context within which the real revolution occurs. That simplicity lies in contrast to the revolution required to understand and support LGBT individuals, families, and organizations on the international stage. The task confronting the practitioner feels at once hopeless and complex. The meaning between the two men in the film seems far removed from the daily activity of trying to untangle knowledge from history, nations from moral superiority, and identities from each other. Untangling one strand from another to see the entire length of the problem will not bring clarity. Providing a broad overview does not give depth or dimension. Like the heroes in the movie, we may find transcendent understanding by engaging with each other in a repetitive and honest effort to move from one place to another and back again, remaining conscious of ourselves and of others in the process.

REFERENCES

A primer on same-sex marriage, civil unions, domestic partnerships, and defense of marriage acts. (2011). *Infoplease.* http://www.infoplease.com/ipa/A0922609.html

American Psychiatric Association. (2011). *Position statement on homosexuality.* Washington, DC: Author.

American Psychological Association. (2000). *Guidelines for psychotherapy with lesbian, gay, & bisexual clients.* Washington, DC: Author.

American Psychological Association. (2011). *Resolution on marriage equality for same-sex couples.* Washington, DC: Author.

Amnesty International. (2001). *Crimes of hate, conspiracy of silence: Torture and ill-treatment based on sexual identity, AI Index ACT.* London, England: Amnesty International.

Bearak, B., & Cowell, A. (2010, March 27). Zimbabwe shrugs off gay rights. *New York Times*, p. 4.

Bilefsky, D. (2011, January 29). Gays seeking asylum in U.S. encounter a new hurdle. *New York Times*, p. A19.

Bliss, D. L. (2011). Sexual orientation differences in spirituality in a sample of alcoholics anonymous members: Implications for practitioners. *Journal of Gay & Lesbian Social Services, 23*, 335–350. doi:10.1080/10538720.2011.588928

Canadiana. (n.d.). *Canada in the making. Constitutional history. 1867–1931: Becoming a nation*. Retrieved from http://www.canadiana.ca/citm/themes/constitution/constitution13_e.html

Chan-Sam, T. (1994). Black lesbian life on the reef: As told to Tanya Chan-Sam. In M. Gevisser & E. Cameron (Eds.), *Defiant desire* (pp. 186–192). Johannesburg, South Africa: Ravan.

Cohen, J. N., Byers, E., & Walsh, L. P. (2008). Factors influencing the sexual relationships of lesbians and gay men. *International Journal of Sexual Health, 20*, 162–176. doi:10.1080/19317610802240105

Donovan, C., & Hester, M. (2008). "Because she was my first girlfriend, I didn't know any different": Making the case for mainstreaming same-sex sex/relationship education. *Sex Education, 8*, 277–287. doi:10.1080/14681810802218155

Espin, O. (1984). Cultural and historical influences on sexuality in Hispanic/Latina women: Implications for psychotherapy. In C. Vance (Ed.), *Pleasure and danger. Exploring female sexuality* (pp. 149–163). London, England: Routledge & Kegan Paul.

Giorgi, A. (1985). *Phenomenology and psychological research*. Pittsburgh, PA: Duquesne University Press.

Glaser, B. G., & Strauss, A. L. (1967). *The discovery of grounded theory: Strategies for qualitative research*. Chicago, IL: Aldine Transaction.

Glave, T. (2008, June). An open letter to the prime minister of Jamaica. *Callaloo, 31*, 1068–1071.

Green, M. S., Murphy, M. J., Blumer, M., & Palmanteer, D. (2009). Marriage and family therapists' comfort level working with gay and lesbian individuals, couples, and families. *American Journal of Family Therapy, 37*, 159–168. doi:0.1080/01926180701441429

Greene, B. (1998). Family, ethnic identity and sexual orientation: African-American lesbians and gay men. In B. Greene (Ed.), *Lesbian, gay, & bisexual identities in families* (pp. 40–52). New York, NY: Oxford University Press.

Griffin, P. (2007). Sexing the economy in a neo-liberal world order: Neo-liberal discourse and the (re)production of heteronormative heterosexuality. *British Journal of Politics and International Relations, 9*, 220–238. doi:10.1111/j.1467-856X.2007.00280.x

Hammack, P. L., & Cohler, B. J. (2009). *The story of sexual identity: Narrative perspectives on the gay and lesbian life course*. New York, NY: Oxford University Press.

Hawthorne, S. (2006). Lesbians: The invisible torture. *Off Our Backs, 36*(3), 77–78.

Hernández, P., & Rankin, P. (2008). Relational safety and liberating training spaces: An application with a focus on sexual orientation issues. *Journal of Marital and Family Therapy, 34*, 251–264. doi:10.1111/j.1752-0606.2008.00067.x

Hester, M., Donovan, C., & Fahmy, E. (2010). Feminist epistemology and the politics of method: surveying same sex domestic violence. *International Journal of Social Research Methodology: Theory & Practice, 13*, 251–263. doi:10.1080/13645579.2010.482260

Holt, R., Court, P. P., Vedhara, K. K., Nott, K. H., Holmes, J. J., & Snow, M. H. (1998). The role of disclosure in coping with HIV infection. *AIDS Care, 10*(1), 49–60. doi:10.1080/09540129850124578

Hudak, J., & Giammattei, S. V. (2010). *Doing family: Decentering heteronormativity in "marriage" and "family" therapy* (American Family Therapy Monograph Series). Washington, DC: American Family Therapy Academy.

Human Rights First. (2008a). *Violence against LGBT persons. Executive summary*. Retrieved from http://www.humanrightsfirst.org/our-work/fighting-discrimination/2008-hate-crime-survey/violence-against-lgbt-persons

Human Rights First. (2008b). *Violence based upon sexual orientation and gender identity bias: 2008 Hate Crimes Survey*. Retrieved from http://www.humanrightsfirst.org/wp-content/uploads/pdf/fd-080924-lgbt-web2.pdf

Human Rights First. (2010, January 15). *Protect freedom of gay rights in Turkey*. Retrieved from http://www.humanrightsfirst.org/our-work/human-rights-defenders/protect-freedom-of-association-for-gay-rights-activists-in-turkey

Human Rights Watch. (2003, January 1). *More than a name: State-sponsored homophobia and its consequences in South Africa*. Retrieved from http://www.hrw.org/reports/pdfs/g/general/safriglhrc0303.pdf

Human Rights Watch. (2004a, March). *In a time of torture: The assault on justice in Egypt's crackdown on homosexual conduct*. Retrieved from http://hrw.org/reports/2004/egypt0304

Human Rights Watch. (2004b, November). *Hated to death: Homophobia, violence and Jamaica's HIV/AIDS epidemic*. Retrieved from http://hrw.org/reports/2004/jamaica1104/jamaica1104.pdf

International Commission of Jurists. (2010). *Sexual orientation and gender identity in human rights law: References to jurisprudence and doctrine of the United Nations human rights system* (4th updated ed.). Geneva, Switzerland: Author.

International Lesbian, Gay, Bisexual, Trans and Intersex Association. (2008, December 19). *UN Gen. Assembly Statement affirms rights for all*. Retrieved from http://ilga.org/ilga/en/article/1211

Jeffreys, E. (2007). Querying queer theory: Debating male–male prostitution in the Chinese media. *Critical Asian Studies, 39*, 151–175. doi:10.1080/14672710601171772

Johnson, C. (2002). Heteronormative citizenship and the politics of passing. *Sexualities, 5*, 317–336. doi:10.1177/1363460702005003004

Johnson, C. (2007). John Howard's "values" and Australian identity. *Australian Journal of Political Science, 42*, 195–209. doi:10.1080/10361140701319986

Johnson, C. R. (2008). Casual sex. *Interventions: The International Journal of Postcolonial Studies, 10*, 303–320. doi:10.1080/13698010802444728

Kaplan, M. (2001). Constructing queer communities: Marriage, sex, death, and other fantasies. *Constellations: An International Journal of Critical and Democratic Theory, 8*, 857–877.

Kollman, K. (2007). Same-sex unions: The globalization of an idea. *International Studies Quarterly, 51*, 329–357. doi:10.1111/j.1468-2478.2007.00454.x

Krige, E. J. (1974). Women-marriage with special reference to the Lovedu: Its significance for the definition of marriage. *Africa, 44,* 11ff.

Kuba, S. A. (1981). *Being-in-a-lesbian-family: The preadolescent child's experience* (Unpublished doctoral dissertation). California School of Professional Psychology, Fresno, CA.

Kuba, S. A., Green, R.-J., & Giammattei, S. (2011, August). *Initial educational effectiveness for a comprehensive LGBTQ training certificate.* Paper presented the Student Experiences and Expectations of LGBTQ Graduate Training symposium at the Annual Convention of the American Psychological Association, Washington, D.C.

Laird, J., & Green, R.-J. (Eds.). (1996). *Lesbians and gays in couples and families: A handbook for therapists.* San Francisco, CA: Jossey-Bass.

Lubbe, C. (2007). Mothers, fathers, or parents: Same-gendered families in South Africa. *South African Journal of Psychology, 37,* 260–283.

Manalansan, M. F., IV. (2006) *Global divas: Filipino gay men in the diaspora* (Philippine ed.). Quezon City, Philippines: Ateneo de Manila: University Press.

Marshall, D. (2010). Popular culture, the "victim" trope and queer youth analytics. *International Journal of Qualitative Studies in Education, 23,* 65–85. doi:10.1080/09518390903447176

McLean, K. (2007). Hiding in the closet? *Journal of Sociology, 43,* 151–166. doi:10.1177/1440783307076893

McLelland, M. J. (2002). Virtual ethnography: Using the internet to study gay culture in Japan *Sexualities, 5,* 387–406. doi:10.1177/1363460702005004001

Moustakas, C. E. (1994). *Phenomenological research methods.* Thousand Oaks, CA: Sage.

Norton, R. (1997). *The myth of the modern homosexual: Queer history and the search for cultural unity.* London, England: Washington.

O'Flaherty, M., & Fisher, J. (2008). Sexual orientation, gender identity and international human rights law: Contextualising the Yogyakarta principles. *Human Rights Law Review, 8,* 207–248. doi:10.1093/hrlr/ngn009

Okal, J., Luchters, S., Geibel, S., Chersich, M. F., Lango, D., & Temmerman, M. (2009). Social context, sexual risk perceptions and stigma: HIV vulnerability among male sex workers in Mombasa, Kenya. *Culture, Health & Sexuality, 11,* 811–826. doi:10.1080/13691050902906488

Peterson, D. (2011). Neoliberal homophobic discourse: Heteronormative human capital and the exclusion of queer citizens. *Journal of Homosexuality, 58*(6–7), 742–757. doi:10.1080/00918369.2011.581918

Phillips, J., & Fischer, A. (1998). Graduate students? Training experiences with lesbian, gay, and bisexual issues. *The Counseling Psychologist, 26,* 712–734. doi:10.1177/0011000098265002

Pilkington, N., & Cantor, J. (1996). Perceptions of heterosexual bias in professional psychology programs: A survey of graduate students. *Professional Psychology: Research and Practice, 27,* 604–612. doi:10.1037/0735-7028.27.6.604

Platero, R. (2007). Love and the state: Gay marriage in Spain. *Feminist Legal Studies*, *15*, 329–340. doi:10.1007/s10691-007-9064-z

Platero, R. (2008). Outstanding challenges in a post-equality era: The same-sex marriage and gender identity laws in Spain. *International Journal of Iberian Studies*, *21*, 41–49. doi:10.1386/ijis.21.1.41_3

Potgieter, C. (1997). Black South African Lesbians in the nineties. In B. Greene (Ed.), *Ethnic and cultural diversity among lesbians and gay men* (pp. 88–116). Thousand Oaks, CA: Sage.

Primorac, R. (2007). The poetics of state terror in twenty-first century Zimbabwe. *Interventions: The International Journal of Postcolonial Studies*, *9*, 434–450. doi:10.1080/13698010701618687

Rishworth, P. (2007). Changing times, changing minds, changing laws—sexual orientation and New Zealand law, 1960 to 2005. *International Journal of Human Rights*, *11*, 85–107. doi:10.1080/13642980601176282

Schrimshaw, E. W., Siegel, K., & Downing, M. J. (2010). Sexual risk behaviors with female and male partners met in different sexual venues among non-gay-identified, nondisclosing MSMW. *International Journal of Sexual Health*, *22*, 167–179. doi:10.1080/19317611003748821

Semp, D. (2008). A public silence: The discursive construction of heteronormativity in public mental health services and the implications for clients. *Gay & Lesbian Issues and Psychology Review*, *4*, 94–107.

Singer, M. C. (2004). Being gay and mentally ill: The case study of a gay man with schizophrenia treated at a community mental health facility. *Journal of Gay & Lesbian Psychotherapy*, *8*, 115–125. Retrieved from http://EBSCOhost.com

Singh, A. K., Mahendra, V., & Verma, R. (2008). Exploring context and dynamics of homosexual experiences among rural youth in India. *Journal of LGBT Health Research*, *4*, 89–101. doi:10.1080/15574090902913719

Solinger, M. (Producer), Linder, D. (Producer), & Mathias, S. (Director). (1997). *Bent* [Motion picture]. England and Japan: Channel Four Studios.

Taylor, C., Peter, T., Schachter, K., Paquin, S., Beldom, S., Gross, Z., & McMinn, T. L. (2008). *Youth speak up about homophobia and transphobia: The First National Climate Survey on homophobia in Canadian schools. Phase one report.* Toronto, Ontario, Canada: Egale Canada Human Rights Trust.

Treacher, A. (2007). Postcolonial subjectivity: Masculinity, shame, and memory. *Ethnic and Racial Studies*, *30*, 281–299. doi:10.1080/01419870601143950

Vanderbeck, R. M., Andersson, J., Valentine, G., Sadgrove, J., & Ward, K. (2011). Sexuality, activism, and witness in the Anglican Communion: The 2008 Lambeth Conference of Anglican Bishops. *Annals of the Association of American Geographers*, *101*, 670–689. doi:10.1080/00045608.2011.561105

Vidal-Ortiz, S. (2011). "Maricon," "pajaro," and "loca": Cuban and Puerto Rican linguistic practices, and sexual minority participation, in U.S. santeria. *Journal of Homosexuality*, *58*, 901–918. doi:10.1080/00918369.2011.581933

Walby, S., & Allen, J. (2004). Domestic violence, sexual assault and stalking: Findings from the British Crime Survey. *Home Office Research Study 276*. London, England: Home Office.

Whitley, J. E. (2009). Religiosity and attitudes toward lesbians and gay men: A meta-analysis. *International Journal for the Psychology of Religion, 19*, 21–38. doi:10.1080/10508610802471104

Williams, L. (2000). Homophobia and gay rights activism in Jamaica. *Small Axe: A Caribbean Journal of Criticism, 4*, 106–111.

Winter, S., & Doussantousse, S. (2009). Transpeople, hormones, and health risks in Southeast Asia: A Lao study. *International Journal of Sexual Health, 21*, 35–48. doi:10.1080/19317610802554141

Wong, F. Y., Huang, Z. J., He, N. N., Smith, B. D., Ding, Y. Y., Fu, C. C., & Young, D. D. (2008). HIV risks among gay- and non-gay-identified migrant money boys in Shanghai, China. *AIDS Care, 20*, 170–180. doi:10.1080/09540120701534707

Zhou, Y. R. (2006). Homosexuality, seropositivity, and family obligations: Perspectives of HIV-infected men who have sex with men in China. *Culture, Health & Sexuality, 8*, 487–500. doi:10.1080/13691050600847455

The Yogyakarta principles. (n.d.). Retrieved from http://www.yogyakartaprinciples.org

6

RELIGION, SPIRITUALITY, AND SECULARISM IN MULTICULTURAL AND INTERNATIONAL CONTEXTS

BETH LIMBERG

Religion, spirituality, and secularism are often explored as dimensions of multiculturalism—that is, as dimensions of diversity within the borders of a specific country. The intersection of religious, spiritual, and secularist views with politics, law, economics, education, and health care around the world, however, along with increasing globalization and international migration, compels professionals to examine how these views affect their work on an international level as well. Professionals trained in countries that value secularism, countries that seek to clearly define the role and boundaries of religion, may not fully understand the importance of religion to international or immigrant clients from countries where religion touches all aspects of society. Similarly, professionals trained in countries grounded in a particular religious context may not fully recognize the importance of separating religion from their professional ventures with their clients from countries that clearly differentiate religious and secular institutions. This chapter seeks to highlight

DOI: 10.1037/14044-006
Internationalizing Multiculturalism: Expanding Professional Competencies in a Globalized World,
R. L. Lowman (Editor)

some of the ways in which religion, spirituality, and secularism can affect professional endeavors on both the multicultural and the international levels.

RECOGNIZING THE INFLUENCES OF RELIGION

Religion and spirituality are important in many people's lives. In some countries, as many as 99% of people polled answered yes to the question, "Is religion an important part of your daily life?" (respondents surveyed in 114 countries in 2009; Crabtree, 2010). In the United States, which is one of the most religious countries in the industrialized world, 91% of those surveyed reported that they believe in God or a universal spirit (Newport, 2011). Religion and spirituality influence the development of an individual's views of self, other, and the world. These beliefs can interact with other social forces to influence the individual and community values displayed in parenting, work ethic, and engagement in (and role in) the family and activities within the community (e.g., volunteerism, civic engagement; Pelham & Crabtree, 2008; Ruiter & De Graaf, 2006; Smith & Stark, 2009).

Understanding the interactive influence of religion can be complicated, starting with religious affiliation or religious identity. In addition to the spiritual or faith-based identity that comes from the practice of religious or spiritual traditions, cultural aspects of religious identity also exist (Marterella & Brock, 2008). For example, one woman might consider herself Catholic because her family is Catholic and has been Catholic for as long as anyone can remember. Although baptized as an infant and educated throughout her early years in Catholic teaching, she no longer attends church regularly. She may engage in her family's faith traditions to mark major life events (births, weddings, funerals), but the influence of Catholicism is more of a backdrop to her cultural identity than an active force in her spiritual development. On the other hand, another person who considers himself Catholic may be actively involved in his church community, attending daily Mass, serving as a volunteer in his parish, reading scripture, and conscientiously following church teachings. For him, Catholicism actively informs his identity.

Professionals in countries where religion plays only a moderate role in the everyday lives of its citizens may not fully comprehend how religion, culture, and politics are intertwined in other parts of the world, or if they do have this understanding, they may not be aware of how religion and spiritually may affect their clients' experiences and beliefs. For example, a client from Japan may, without thinking, approach her business from a Buddhist perspective, assuming that the international management consultant she has hired would share the assumptions underlying her beliefs because most everyone she knew when she was growing up was Buddhist. A patient from Afghanistan may make assumptions about how his Western doctor will treat him based not only on his perception of how Muslims are treated in the Western world but also on his experience of being recognized as part of the privileged religious majority of his homeland (Sunni) while simultaneously being a part of a marginalized and persecuted religious minority in other parts of the world. For a refugee student from Croatia, her experience of war may include significant religious scarring, intertwining itself in her trauma experience to interfere with her educational pursuits. Finally, a Jewish mental health client may experience subtle or not-so-subtle discrimination in his community, which when coupled with the historical oppression of his ancestors, may exacerbate his experience of depression and anxiety.

Gender roles can also be defined by religious and spiritual belief. Gender expectations provide comfort to some by defining their role in the family and in the community, but these expectations also create disparities that put women at risk for physical and emotional abuse (Aten, Mangis, & Campbell, 2010). In Kuwait, a Muslim state with both conservative and liberal strongholds, Fakhr El-Islam (2008) reported a significant association between mental health symptoms and contraceptive use in women who practiced contraception for economic reasons, despite the prohibition of such by their local Islamic clergy. Meanwhile, in Qatar the removal of some gender disparities represented by advances in the education of women coincided with a dramatic decrease in culture-related somatic symptoms that formerly plagued unmarried and infertile women.

Yet religion is more than an individual matter. Religion is a major political and economic force around the world (Ali, Camp, & Gibbs, 2005; Prothero, 2010; Walsh, 1999). The presence or absence of religion influences the development of cultural and community norms, including the community implementation of education, health care, and community supports. Religion influences organizational structures, management strategies, and professional growth in global business (Ali et al., 2005; Goltz, 2011; Singhal & Chatterjee, 2006). These belief systems influence expectations of conformity within the community and support of community members (e.g., kindness, alms, charity). The influence of religion can even be seen in everyday life such as in the determination of the workweek, weekends (days of rest), and holidays (holy days).

Law and politics are intertwined with religion in many parts of the world, affecting the development of several sociopolitical structures, including the political practices involved in determining who holds power and who is granted "citizenship," how laws are developed, who has access to education, and how geographic boundaries are established and maintained. In some countries (e.g., Malaysia, Kuwait), religious law is the explicit basis of the country's constitution (i.e., the constitutional laws must comply with religious law; Hirschil, 2010). Other countries weave together religious and secular law. In Sri Lanka, for example, individuals are guaranteed freedom of "thought, conscience and religion." Even so, that country's constitution also gives explicit privilege to Buddhism, obligating the state "to protect and foster the Buddha Sasana" (Hirschil, 2010, p. 40). Other countries (e.g., England, the United States) create definitive lines between law and religion, but even in these countries, the influences of religion can be recognized in areas defined as being separate from religion. For example, despite a constitutionally mandated separation of church and state in the United States, religious beliefs are evident in policy debates in education (e.g., teaching of evolution, prayer in school), health care (e.g., stem cell research, abortion, euthanasia) and politics (e.g., gay marriage, inclusion of the word *God* in the pledge of allegiance).

Despite the influence of religious and spiritual beliefs on daily life, professionals may underestimate the importance that religion may play in the lives of their clients. This is especially likely in industrialized countries where religion is reported to be less influential by their citizens. Although professionals tend to value and respect religious diversity, many are not themselves religious. In general, professionals are often less religious than the general population (Pargament & Saunders, 2007; Post & Wade, 2009) and as such may believe that others view religion similarly (Worthington & Aten, 2009). This experience may be reinforced in countries such as the United States where Americans have become less tied to formalized religion over the past 50 years (in the 1950s and 1960s, for example, 2% to 5% of those surveyed did not affiliate with a particular religion, compared with 11% in 2009; Newport, 2010). Nonetheless, poll data suggest that religion and spirituality remain important to more people than not, and with increasing interest that professionals provide culturally competent service, attention needs be paid to the possible religious or spiritual views as one aspect of multiculturalism.

RECOGNIZING THE INFLUENCES OF SECULARISM

Just as religious practice and affiliation can be transmitted from generation to generation, so too can the practice of no religion. For some individuals, secular practice develops in a passive way: Religion has simply never been a part of their lives, or over time, it has become unimportant to their daily living. For others, maintaining secularist views is an active decision, often based in a belief of self-sufficiency, that religion and religious belief are not necessary to one's well-being or the well-being of the community. Secularists may recognize naturalist or rationalist ideologies over the "irrational" ideologies of supreme beings or spirits, or they may aspire to overcome the injustices and inequalities present in most religious institutions. (Consider the aforementioned gender discrepancies or the prejudice demonstrated through the homophobic teachings of many religions.) For these individuals, secularist principles actively inform their worldview.

Worldwide, the number of individuals who identify with a religious or spiritual practice far exceeds the number of individuals who do not. Nonetheless, the influence of secularism is profound, especially in the sociopolitical realm. Many countries maintain the importance of a secular state—a state that takes a neutral stand relative to religion. Often these states support the equality of all citizens, regardless of religion, emphasizing both freedom of religion and freedom from religion. Casanova (2009) asserted that, at a political level, secularism need not involve a theory, either positive or negative, about religion. It may simply describe a

> separation between religious and political authority, either for the sake of the neutrality of the state vis-à-vis each and all religions, or for the sake of protecting the freedom of conscience of each individual, or for the sake of facilitating the equal access of all citizens, religious as well as nonreligious, to democratic participation. (p. 1051)

Political secularism is not an all-or-nothing proposition. Some states support religious pluralism (e.g., the United States); others have a state religion but a secular legislature (e.g., England). Still other states (most notably China and the former Soviet Union) declared religion to be an impediment to a well-run state and devote resources to abolishing religion from within their boundaries (Marsh, 2011). These states accepted atheism as a state philosophy and attempted to force secularism, with only limited success. In India, a debate exists regarding whether Western secularism (state neutrality regarding religion) is in fact superior to a Hindu state. Hinduism, supporters explain, recognizes all religions as "incomplete manifestations of the same truth"; thus, all are equal. Both proponents and opponents of secularism seek a peacefully diverse society, and both support religious pluralism. What differs is the ideological framework surrounding the means to the end (Balagangadhara & De Roover, 2007, p. 68).

Casanova (2009) suggested that secularism moves out of the purely political domain and into the ideological realm when, rather than simply separating political and religious authority, the state attaches value to religion. The range of ideologies can be considered on a continuum of church–state separation, from states that promote religion (e.g., the Vatican) or generously subsidizing religion (e.g., Greece, Norway, Spain) to states in which religions receive no aid or privileges but also no obstruction or interference (e.g., Iceland, Ukraine) to states that impose limitations on religion or severely discriminate against minority religions (e.g., Cyprus) or any religious activity (e.g., the former Soviet Union; Madeley, 2009).

RELIGION, SPIRITUALITY, AND SECULARISM

There is no single, generally accepted definition of religion, spirituality, or secularism, but for the purposes of this chapter, some common characteristics are offered.

Defining Religion

In a general sense, religion is defined by the existence of a particular set of beliefs, practices, and traditions that are commonly held by a community that maintains an expectation that the members will adhere to the commonly held beliefs and practices (Hill et al., 2000). The individual practice of religion may vary. Some individuals may accept all of the commonly held beliefs, and others challenge specific beliefs. Some may participate fully in the prescribed rituals, and others rarely take part in the rites. Some may contribute actively to their religious communities, and others may disengage from the institution. Still, the religion itself is defined by something more than the individual members. Theologian Stephen Prothero identified the common aspects of religion with "4 C's": *creed* (statement of beliefs and values), *cultus* (ritual activities), behavioral *codes* (standards of ethical behavior), and *communities* (institutions). Religion, then, can exist when a community defines its beliefs, practices, and expectations of behavior, and its members act on their agreed-on belief system in a particular way (Prothero, 2010; Walsh, 1999).

Many, but not all, religions are theistic; that is, they share a belief in the existence of a supreme being (e.g., God) or other types of deity or deities. The belief in a soul or souls (i.e., the transcendent part[s] of the self) is also common (Walsh, 1999). Although theist religions have persisted over time and are dominant among diverse cultures, the religions hold vastly divergent views regarding the nature of the divine (Miovic, 2004). As can be expected, religious beliefs and practice, and individual level of adherence, also vary greatly both across and within cultures (Walsh, 1999). Common to most religions, however, are the attention to moral values, standards for living a good life, ultimate concerns regarding life and death and the transcendent, and attention to the sacred, including objects that are set aside for a holy purpose.

Defining Spirituality

Whereas religion relates to specific beliefs and practices, the term *spirituality* is sometimes used to describe a more general feeling of closeness and connectedness to the sacred. What is considered to be "sacred" is defined within a specific social context but may include a perception of a divine being or object or a sense of ultimate reality or truth. This connection to the sacred inspires a sense of intimacy, feelings of awe and wonder, and an experience of "something beyond," perhaps transcendent (Ammerman, 2010; Worthington & Aten, 2009; Worthington, Hook, Davis, & McDaniel, 2011). For many, spirituality is experienced within the context of religion, but not for all.

Worthington and colleagues (Worthington & Aten, 2009; Worthington et al., 2011) described four primary types of spirituality. *Religious spirituality* addresses one's sense of closeness and connection to the sacred as prescribed by a specific religion. Often, religious spirituality supports a sense of closeness to a particular God or Higher Power. *Humanistic spirituality* endorses a sense of closeness and connection to humankind. This may be experienced as a sense of connection to a general group of people and involve feelings of love, altruism, and reflection. Humanistic spirituality finds meaning and fulfillment in relationship. *Nature spirituality* fosters a sense of closeness and connection to the environment or nature. This type of spirituality might be experienced as one watches the waves break on the seashore or stares into the Grand Canyon. Finally, Worthington and colleagues identified *cosmos spirituality*, a sense of closeness or connection with the whole of creation, which may be experienced by meditating on the greatness of creation or reflecting on the vastness of the universe.

On the basis of interviews with people from diverse religious and non-religious communities, Ammerman (2010) developed a framework that can be used to discuss five dimensions of spiritual experience. First, Ammerman recognized *the mysterious*, that which tries to explain the unexplainable. The presence of spirituality in the world is seen as "ordinary events [that] come together in unexpected ways" (p. 158). Spirituality is also recognized in *the majestic*. This seems most closely linked with nature spirituality discussed earlier: the recognition of the natural beauty of the world and the awe experienced through it. *Meaning* is also important to the experience of spirituality, as is *moral compassion* or looking beyond oneself to do what is right. Finally, Ammerman identified in spirituality *connection*, the experience of being a part of something bigger or an awareness that all life is connected (p. 160).

Whereas religion is, by nature, organized or institutionalized, spirituality need not be. It may, in fact, be experienced at a personal, if profound, level. Individuals may be religious and spiritual, religious but not particularly spiritual, spiritual but not religious, or neither religious nor spiritual. Individuals who are not religious or spiritual may describe themselves as secularists, rationalists, materialists, naturalists, atheist, or sometimes agnostic.

Defining Secularism

The term *secular* typically refers to activities or practices that are "not religious." Secularism, however, more precisely refers to a range of consciously held worldviews and ideologies that are often based in a belief of self-sufficiency. These ideologies hold that religion and religious belief are not necessary to one's well-being or the well-being of the community (Casanova, 2009). These views may also include a belief that secularism replaces what is regarded as an irrational dialogue of religion with a more modern, natural ideology. Secularists may identify themselves as atheists and agnostics.

Atheism refers to the belief in the nonexistence of God (or any type of soul or deity). In modern times, this is often expressed as the belief that matter is the only reality (materialism; Miovic, 2004, p. 106), that science and rational thought will ultimately explain all aspects of human existence (rationalism), or as a concern with the natural rather than the supernatural world (naturalism). Like religion, atheism has a long history, dating back to ancient Greece. Atheists tend to focus on logic, reason, science, and life before death, sometimes calling themselves naturalists, secularists, humanists, freethinkers, rationalists, or skeptics (Prothero, 2010). As with any group of people, atheists are not homogeneous. There are those who are vocal advocates of atheism, others who are ultrarational, some who disparage any who would be religious, and many who simply go about their lives quietly, living according to their personal code of belief. Although atheism supports rational discourse and has a tendency to challenge corrupt religious institutions, its adherents account for relatively small numbers across cultures (Miovic, 2004).

Agnosticism is sometimes confused with atheism, but it is correctly defined as the belief that the question of whether God (soul, deity) exists either has not or cannot be answered (Miovic, 2004, p. 106). Agnosticism crosses the divide somewhat, because it can include individuals who are religious or nonreligious. Buddha, for example, historically remained silent on issues of God and soul. As such, Buddhism could be considered an agnostic or nontheistic religion (Miovic, 2004).

PROFESSIONAL SELF-AWARENESS

Understanding a client's religion, spirituality, or secularism as simply one aspect of multicultural competence, many professionals may respond to client beliefs as they would to any other aspect of a client's cultural experience. Even with this acceptance of belief, however, it is important for professionals to examine their own religious, spiritual, or secular experiences and beliefs so that they might bring to their explicit awareness their beliefs, biases, and prejudices about religion, spirituality, and secularism.

Tolerance Versus Acceptance

Professionals are subject to the same implicit and explicit biases about religious difference as anyone else. Professionals who are agnostic or atheist, for example, must be wary of devaluing theist clients with superficial tolerance that merely covers an underlying belief that religion is not necessary or perhaps even harmful. Sensing this bias (or even simply fearing that this bias might exist), the professional's theist clients may restrict their emotional engagement to protect themselves against the negative judgment of a skeptical professional (Aten et al., 2010; Helmeke & Bischof, 2002). Theist professionals must be equally wary of devaluing their atheist or agnostic clients, who may likewise limit their involvement if they fear that their beliefs will be dismissed or challenged. Those with a theist orientation must be especially sensitive to the language they use, so as to avoid defining their clients' problems (implicitly or explicitly) in religious terms. Theist professionals should also remember that their atheist or agnostic clients are, in many countries, members of a minority and often marginalized group. As such, these clients may appear either disengaged or defensive to one who may not be used to defending beliefs.

Professionals are likely to have a zone of tolerance for religious values. They will accept some of their clients' values that differ from their own without hesitation and struggle to understand others as they challenge themselves to appreciate a client's action in light of the client's (rather than their own) value. A counselor may struggle, for example, with how to support a client who laments that her parents expect her to participate in an arranged marriage, but she would rather enter into a "love marriage." The personal and familial consequences of the decision to enter an arranged marriage can be long-lasting and may be difficult to comprehend by a professional whose own religious or secular tradition values individual choice over family obligation. A hotel or restaurant owner may question the advancement of a manager who routinely schedules another employee to cover work on Christmas, a busy day in the industry. The owner may question whether the manager's actions demonstrate a lack of drive or commitment to the business or represent a genuine commitment to one's faith.

In some settings, tolerating different religious or spiritual experiences is most comfortably achieved through avoidance. Passe and Willox (2009), for example, noted that religion is significant to elementary education social studies curriculum (e.g., understanding the Crusades, the formation of India and Pakistan, the significance of John F. Kennedy's faith in his election), and yet many teachers avoid any discussion of religion in their lessons. Passe and Willox suggested that this may occur because teachers are either uneasy or ill equipped to teach the religious content. They cited a political climate in the

United States that discourages the recognition of religion in schools as well as a general lack of knowledge of world religions. They also suggested that unique instructional techniques are needed to teach about world religions in ways that promote tolerance and sensitivity while supporting the acquisition of knowledge about major world religions. Thanissaro (2010) cited similar difficulties in British education, especially in relation to teaching about religious values, despite an increasing demand for the inclusion of "character development" in British schools.

Many professionals in today's world, however, are trained not only to tolerate diversity but also to appreciate and value differing perspectives. When professionals embrace diversity, they may find that they no longer tolerate intolerance well. As such, professionals may struggle to be helpful with clients who hold extreme religious views or who are rigid in their religious beliefs (Worthington & Aten, 2009). This may be especially true when the professional believes that the extreme or rigid views of his client are harmful to the client, to others, or to the business or industry. Professionals who have been trained to work in the "gray" may also struggle with the "black-and-white" thinking of some of their religiously conservative clients (Aten et al., 2010).

Belief or Reality?

Because religion, spirituality, and secularism intersect with other aspects of culture, professionals may find themselves challenged to accept and value beliefs that are outside of their own cultural norms. Those raised in countries where Western belief systems dominate, for example, may struggle to accept beliefs that oppose their own understanding of the world, an understanding that values the tangible and the provable. When faced with a student whose family practices Spiritualism, for example, a Western teacher may struggle to resist her desire to teach that spirits (or ghosts, as she may think of them) are not "real." The family that practices Spiritualism, however, is aware that there exists an invisible world filled with good and evil spirits that influence human behavior. They believe that these spirits can protect or harm people, prevent or cause illness.

This understanding of the supernatural (other than the natural world) is more common than not in the world, and yet many "educated" professionals may be more comfortable with understanding the natural world alone. In Europe and the United States, for example, health professionals have largely accepted a scientific medical model for the diagnosis of physical and mental illness. Professionals evaluate behavior, looking to what they can see or hear or touch as "real" and diagnosable. They allow for cognition to play a role in symptom generation, maintenance, and healing, thus acknowledging some integration of mind and body, but they often continue to focus on the individual organism as central to understanding illness. Western healers tend to place greater confidence in that which can be "proved," believing that they understand depression better, for example, now that they understand which neurotransmitters are out of sync (rather than before when depression was attributed to character or moral weakness or to exposure to an unbearable event; Watters, 2010).

How illness is understood in the United States and Europe, however, is not how illness is understood worldwide. The Yoruba, for example, understand that medical and psychological problems are caused by disconnection, and as such, they seek to remedy the problems through reunion. Traditional diviner-doctors, known as *babalawo* ("father of secrets") or *iyalawo* ("mother of secrets"), serve as mediators between the *orishas* (divine spirits) and their clients; they are able to utilize *Ifa* (divination) to summon certain invisible agents who know about the sickness of misfortune and to question them about how to resolve the difficulties (Prince, 2004; Prothero, 2010). Ultra-orthodox Jews recognize that illness is rooted in the divine and not the organic. Mental illness, in particular, may be viewed as being a punishment for past sins, or God may have given the individual special challenges for reasons as yet unknown. Given this, a change in the individual's relationship with God is necessary for healing (Popovsky, 2010). Fundamentalist Christians are likely to consider mental illness in the same way. Muslims are aware that emotional problems stem from weakness of personality or faith, from neglect of religious values or from deviation from *fitrah* (state of inherent goodness; Fakhr El-Islam, 2008; Haque, 2010). Unprovoked aggression may be caused by the supernatural influence of demons and calls for traditional healers (Fakhr El-Islam, 2008).

Hindus may turn to the *vedic* sacred texts for an understanding of illness. They will read that mental health depends on *karma* (action), *vayu* (air), and *swabhav* (personal nature). Mental illness can result from disrespect toward the creator, religious scholars, or teachers. Spirit possession can result from neglect of one's duties to God, cruelty, lust, or extortion. Those who do good deeds and maintain their social obligations are not likely to be possessed by spirits (Haque, 2010, p. 128). Buddhists recognize that good health results from following the spiritual teachings of Buddha, which leads to enlightened self-awareness. Meditation and yoga are helpful in maintaining a tranquil state of mind. Many Chinese (who identify with a mixture of Tao and Buddhist philosophies and ancestor worship) realize that good health is attributed to their state of emotions. They accept that excessive, unbalanced or undisciplined emotions are the primary reason for illness (Haque, 2010). Although highly religious clients may define their concerns as being spiritual in nature, clients who take a scientific approach to atheism or agnosticism may take an equally naturalistic approach to illness.

Western professionals need be cautious not to judge faith traditions that value spirits (or any other experiences that do not conform to Western belief systems) as inferior or primitive (Walsh, 1999). Worthington and Aten (2009), for example, found that therapists are more likely to make errors when they work with clients from religions with which they are not familiar, including pathologizing what would be considered normative experiences within the client's own religious context. Other studies demonstrate that the further the religious beliefs are from mainstream religious belief (e.g., Christianity in the United States), the higher the clinical rating of pathology, regardless of whether the symptom was explained as a part of the religion (Post & Wade, 2009).

Miovic (2004) recommended that professionals investigate these types of judgments at a fundamental level. He asked professionals to consider whether they view their clients' reports of religious and spiritual experiences as *beliefs* (without relationship to facts of existence) or as *perceptions* (actual spiritual realities; p. 105). As Miovic pointed out, people value differently those things that they evaluate to be "actual experiences" than those things they assess to be the product of a belief system. He asked healers, for example, whether they value as equally real the experience of a client who reports intimate partner violence and the experience of a client who reports that her deceased husband is communicating with her in her dreams. The professional's answer to this question may play out in subtly distancing statements such as "It sounds important to you, tell me about your beliefs" as opposed to more empathic statements such as "Yes, I can see how your (deceased) husband continues to look out for you." With the first statement, the healer responds with respectful interest in another's belief, but with the second, the healer responds with empathy to another's experience. As professionals examine their own beliefs, they must examine if they can genuinely hold open the possibility that the client's differing worldview "may reflect correct perceptions about the actual nature of reality" (p. 106).

Along a similar vein, Cohen (2003) cautioned that professionals' beliefs may pull them in another direction, that of seeing spirituality as transcendent and science (naturalism) as mundane. She called to mind the lack of attention to existential concerns amid the practicality of science and questioned whether some professionals placed less value on naturalism because of the absence of a "higher purpose." She also cautioned against the polarizing ideology that would place spirituality at odds with "organized religion," an ideology that derisively describes religious institutions as bogged down in the "rote repetition of empty rituals and beliefs" (p. 271). Cohen warned that these polarizing ideologies interfere with the ability to assess clients' religious, spiritual, or secularist lives accurately.

To explore personal beliefs and biases, professionals are encouraged to use their own supervision or consultation to become aware of and develop responses to their beliefs and biases as they interfere with their work (Marterella & Brock, 2008; Post & Wade, 2009; Worthington & Aten, 2009). As professionals know themselves better, they will be in a better position to understand the beliefs of their clients.

Organizational Beliefs

Like individuals, organizations also are embedded in culture and therefore subject to implicit and explicit biases about religion, spirituality, and secularism. Gozdz (2000) reminded us that the fundamental assumptions that drive society also guide organizations within that society. He suggests that many businesses today, for example, are embedded in "Western orthodox science," a worldview that favors, among other things, empiricism, rationalism, objectivity, and the quantification of reality (p. 1267). Without awareness, organizations that function under these assumptions may overlook spirituality as a source of power within the dynamics of an organization (Goltz, 2011). Vasconcelos (2010), however, noted that organizations increasingly are considering the implications of spirituality in the workplace, especially how nurturing such can be beneficial to the organization. He suggested that because spirituality and religion are "closely intertwined on human beings' journey on this planet," understanding these topics in an organizational setting makes sense; organizations, after all, exist entirely with the human experience (p. 607).

Organizations that seek to integrate spirituality into their management structures may do so through a specific religious model (e.g., a Baptist university or an Islamic halal market) or more broadly by emphasizing and rewarding spiritual values such as respect, balance, and integrity. Singhal and Chatterjee (2006), for example, suggested that highlighting meaning and purpose within the organizational culture strengthens employee commitment to that organization. The actions of the organizational leaders can also demonstrate the values of the organization (whether religious, spiritual, or secular). Business practice is rife with ethical decisions and moral ambiguities: individual versus community well-being, service versus wealth, integrity-at-each-step versus ends-justifies-the-means mind-set. Without exploration, organizational leaders may find themselves torn between competing values and expectations. Gozdz (2000) cautioned that the assumptions of the Western science orthodox are limited and may not be sufficient to guide and regulate business institutions in ethical action. A more holistic "transpersonal" approach, he argued, can transform business by integrating spirituality and psychology with (the currently favored) science in understanding the human experience. The process of becoming aware of one's assumptions and biases, then, becomes important at an organizational level, just as it is at the individual level.

DEVELOPING PROFESSIONAL RELATIONSHIPS

Religious, spiritual, and secular beliefs can provide meaning to life events and ways to integrate experiences into a coherent whole. They can contribute to people's beliefs about themselves, others, and the world and motivate people to act in certain ways. Communities with shared beliefs can provide social support and personal comfort to their members. Religious belief and practice has been associated with psychological well-being, sense of purpose, and health and with psychological distress, intolerance, and prejudice (Marterella & Brock, 2008; Pargament & Saunders, 2007; Post & Wade, 2009; Walsh, 1999). To understand the impact of religion, spirituality, or secularism on the lives of their clients, professionals need a consistent way of assessing the influence.

Gathering Information

Often there is opportunity early in the professional relationship to gather information about the client as rapport is developed. If intake paperwork is a part of this process, a question regarding the client's religious, spiritual, or other beliefs can be added with a follow-up question regarding the importance of those beliefs. Among other things, as relevant, professionals can assess their client's commitment to spiritual or religious practices, which can indicate the extent to which the client will view the world through a religious lens. Religious or spiritual affiliation, for example, can be based in tradition or demographics ("My family is Irish Catholic") or can be the driving force behind core values, life goals, and everyday behavior. Josephson and Peteet (2007) suggested using the FICA model to assess level of religious or spiritual commitment: importance of *faith* or beliefs in daily life, degree to which faith has *influenced* one's life, involvement in a *community* related to one's faith, and *addressing* how the client would like to integrate faith into the professional endeavors. (See Josephson & Peteet, 2007, for additional tools for interviewing techniques and strategies.)

When relevant, the professional may wish to take a more extensive belief history, the focus and extent of which will depend to some degree on the type of professional relationship. For example, medical professionals may be particularly interested in the family and community supports available to their clients. Understanding the role of religious, spiritual, or secular communities in the client's life may assist in identifying key supports (transportation, in-home caregivers) following an upcoming surgery. Mental health professionals may be interested in how changes in religious beliefs or practices have strengthened or strained family (especially intergenerational) relationships. Lawyers may be interested in how religion, spirituality, or secularism informs a client's worldview, recognizing that their client may be more willing to accept a particular legal strategy if the strategy is framed within the client's religious, spiritual, or secular values.

Taking a thorough belief history requires a knowledge of what questions to ask and what the answers mean (Cohen, 2003), so professionals will benefit from a working knowledge of religious, spiritual, and secular beliefs and practices and resources to research specific beliefs and practices as the need arises. This knowledge would include an understanding of the significance of specific actions within the client's religious or nonreligious affiliation (e.g., divorce; regular church, synagogue, or temple attendance; tithing or alms-giving practices; importance of prayer), as well as an appreciation for how the systems of belief and practice intersect with other important client factors, including gender, age, ethnicity, socioeconomic status education, sexual orientation, immigration or refugee experience, and country of origin. Colbert, Jefferson, Gallo, and Davis (2009), for example, identified the prominence of religious expression within the African American community and highlighted the interaction of this with age: the older the African American adult becomes, the more he or she depends on his or her religion to deal with difficult life events. Advertisers may be especially interested in how religious or spiritual beliefs intersect with other demographic factors as they assess consumption of particular products or brands within specific communities (Lindridge, 2010). Similarly, businesses that use lifestyle advertising may be interested in how cultural and religious value systems influence the success of various marketing strategies (Javaid, Khan, & Baig, 2010).

Professionals also benefit from understanding how religious, spiritual, and secular beliefs influence the ways people cope with adversity, how they experience pain and suffering, what is labeled as a problem, and the meaning of symptoms, especially as these beliefs shape the way people communicate their distress and their beliefs about its causes and future course (Walsh, 1999, p. 3). For example, in different parts of the world, emotional distress may be expressed through somatic concerns (headaches, stomachaches, concerns about specific organs), low energy, or conduct problems. In Armenia, where children are recognized as having the ability to see souls and dead people, pseudohallucinations are not uncommon. Sometimes, the absence of an expected response has religious significance. For example, hopelessness is not likely to be reported as a symptom of distress in Muslim clients because, according to Islamic belief, one should never give up hope for relief of suffering because endurance is rewarded in the afterlife. If we observe their experience through the lens of Western psychology, we may see hopelessness, but the individual does not report it that way because he or she does not experience it that way (Fakhr El-Islam, 2008).

Religious and spiritual experiences can also affect how individuals respond in organizational settings. Ali et al. (2005) examined the concept of "free agency" in light of religious teachings about free will in Christianity, Judaism, and Islam and identify possible differences in response to organizational structure (hierarchical vs. flat or matrix organizations), authority (can it be questioned), change (approached with caution or anticipation), and professional growth (self- or other-directed). For example, because both Christianity and Judaism emphasize the role of authority figures within the religious context, adherents may be more responsive to authority and organizational hierarchies. In contrast, Islam places more emphasis on group alliance and personal relationships. As such, flatter organizational structures, such as partnerships, may be preferred (pp. 108–109). Osisioma (2009) similarly hypothesized that religious adherence may affect a manager's choice of conflict management strategies, especially related to authoritarian versus accommodating or compromising dispositions.

Part of the belief history may include a discussion of the client's religious, spiritual, or secularist development. The client's developmental path may be relatively smooth (a client finds peace in the spiritual practices of her family, practiced for generations) or comparatively complicated (e.g., the decision to marry outside of the family's religion leads to the client's ostracism). Decisions about participation or nonparticipation in the family religious, spiritual, or secularist practice may be supported by significant others or may strain principal relationships. Cohen (2003) suggested listening carefully to see whether a shift in belief or practice reflects other difficulties in family structure. Professionals may also assess whether the client's decision to change belief or practice is accompanied by grief and mourning or by confidence in a newfound understanding of the world.

Finally, professionals should assess what their clients expect from their services, paying particular attention to expectations related to religious, spiritual, or secular needs and expectations. Many clients see education or health care as secular ventures and as such may not bring up religious or spiritual matters when entering into these settings. In mental health settings, in fact, clients may intentionally avoid introducing religion, for fear that they will be pathologized for their beliefs, that the therapist will blame religion for causing their mental illness, or that the therapist will try to undermine their religious beliefs (Popovsky, 2010). A simple statement of acceptance in these situations can be quite powerful and open to therapy (and education and health care) the fullness of the client's life. Similarly, asking questions about religious, spiritual, or secular beliefs at the beginning of the professional relationship (on intake forms or through a religious history) lets the client know that religious and spiritual issues are acceptable areas of exploration.

Assessing Supports and Hindrances

As the relationship develops, the professional will start to assess the client's strengths and weaknesses, including what supports and hinders client goals. Opening the door to religious and spiritual issues can become especially important when the issues at hand are intertwined with religious and spiritual beliefs. For example, religious, spiritual, and secularist traditions prescribe certain responses to difficult experiences including loss, trauma, death of a loved one, and serious illness of self or a loved one. To address these issues well, professionals have to work with the whole individual, in the context of the family and community, rather than focusing solely on the difficult experiences of the individual. Accurately assessing for supports and hindrances, however, is not always easy. Clients may choose to hold private certain information that they consider irrelevant or that might bring shame to their family. For example, religious directives to "honor thy parents" or to refrain from gossip may prevent a client from speaking negatively about others, even when the information is true (Fakhr El-Islam, 2008; Popovsky, 2010). A business client may be silent about the poor business practices of her partner, for example, if she believes that her statements could be construed as gossip. She may be confused or even offended by her consultant's questions, especially if she has a different understanding of the cause of her problems. The client's response, based in her religious or spiritual beliefs can be misinterpreted as resistance, evasiveness, or even denial of reality (Popovsky, 2010). Following clients' lead and using their language encourage exploration while being sensitive to clients' desires (Helmeke & Bischof, 2002).

Evaluating the client's manner of relating to his or her religion is one way to understand what supports (or hindrances) are available (Aten & Worthington, 2009). Many people turn to religion to inform their moral and spiritual values, basing life decisions in this more so than counseling, parent education, or community laws or policies (Walsh, 1999). People especially turn to religion and spirituality for guidance, strength, and healing during stressful times (Marterella & Brock, 2008; Miovic, 2004; Pargament & Saunders, 2007). Religious and spiritual communities can provide stability, resources for the physical needs of their members, social activities, family and marriage enrichment, child care, support groups, and celebrations and rituals for life events (Marterella & Brock, 2008). Lindridge (2010), for example, noted that several Sikh interviewees reported weekly attendance at the *gurdwara* (a Sikh temple) but explained that their participation reflected an active desire to be connected with their Sikh community rather evidence of particular religious adherence. These communities can also provide structure that enhances a spiritual life, access to sacred texts and teachings, and rituals and rites that signify spiritual transformation. This connection to community can enrich one's spiritual life beyond what can be achieved alone (Cohen, 2003). In a recent U.S.-based Gallup poll, Americans of all faith traditions who identified themselves as "very religious," even those who do not claim affiliations with a specific religion, reported higher overall wellbeing than those who are moderately religious or nonreligious (controlling for age, income, education, gender, race/ethnicity, marital status, and religion; Newport, Agrawal, & Witters, 2010).

Not all religious or spiritual beliefs are healthy, however, and some can be quite harmful. Religious beliefs may lead a patient to refuse medication or a guardian to refuse lifesaving medical intervention for a loved one because such treatments demonstrate a lack of faith in God's ability to heal (Aten et al., 2010; Vess, Arndt, Cox, Routledge, & Goldenberg, 2009). A patient may also refuse medication on days of religious observance that require fasting over several days (e.g., Yom Kippur, Ramadan; Popovsky, 2010). Homophobia and homonegativity, present in most world religions, have led to prejudice, ostracism, injury, and death. Interfaith marriage, infertility, or conflict with religious leaders or member of one's congregation may be cause for distress because of religious or spiritual standards for behavior (Helmeke & Bischof, 2002). Divorce and remarriage can lead to family schisms and removal of support at times when support is most needed. Separation from the family's faith traditions can create significant conflict, especially when the next generation of children (grandchildren) enter the picture (Walsh, 1999) or when a family business is ready to be passed down. In making a decision that is contrary to the family's religious beliefs, an individual may be exposed to a harsh or rejecting response from the family (and community).

Some issues may be related directly to conflict with one's religious, spiritual, or secularist beliefs or communities, or the beliefs themselves can be a source of frustration, as clients search for answers or meaning or challenge their existing belief system (Marterella & Brock, 2008). Pargament and Saunders (2007) noted, for example, that some spiritual experiences create risk for poorer health and well-being, including feelings of anger toward God, conflicts with congregation and clergy, and spiritual doubts and confusion. In a 2003 survey of college counseling centers, for example, 20% of student clients reported clinical levels of distress related to religious or spiritual problems, including confusion about values and beliefs and thoughts of being punished for one's sins (Post & Wade, 2009).

Professionals may take a pragmatic approach to assessing their clients' relationship to their religion: It is healthy if it provides an adaptive source of support or growth-promoting meaning; it is unhealthy if it does not. Even this reflects the professional's values and bias, however, so caution is warranted (Miovic, 2004).

Working With Highly Religious Clients

Highly religious clients may choose to work with professionals who have similar beliefs to their own, perhaps believing that they will be better understood and therefore better served. If beliefs or values differ too much (as defined by the client), the professional relationship may stall or fail. In mental health settings, for example, highly religious clients may be especially sensitive to their therapist's religious beliefs or practices, possibly asking directly about the therapist's religion. If the client perceives that the therapist is similar enough, the relationship proceeds. If the client perceives that the therapist is too different, the client may resist treatment, make poor progress, or terminate early, usually without confrontation (Worthington & Aten, 2009). Professionals who have been taught to keep their private lives separate from their professional persona may be surprised when a client asks directly about the professional's own religion, and the professional may be tempted to respond with a neutral attempt to assess the motivation behind the question "Why is this important to you?" However, this type of response may be interpreted as evasive or as undervaluing the client's religious beliefs. The client may assume that beliefs are not shared and disengage from the relationship (Aten et al., 2010; Worthington & Aten, 2009). Aten et al. (2010) recommended answering these questions directly and honestly to avoid miscommunication. The initial discussion may be awkward, but it allows for discussion later, should the client suspect that value differences are interfering with the goals of the project.

Some highly religious clients are fundamentalist. *Fundamentalism*, found in all major world religions and denominations, refers to the strict and rigid adherence to an undisputable interpretation of truth, as revealed in scripture, prophecy, or sacred text. Fundamentalism typically demands the rejection of beliefs, practices, opinions, facts, positions, or persons that are inconsistent with the accepted "truth." Adherence to the doctrine is expected in every aspect of life (Aten et al., 2010; Walsh, 1999). Fundamentalist groups tend to create closed systems, restricting contact with the "outside world" to avoid the threats posed by those who do not adhere to their beliefs or standards of conduct (Aten et al., 2010; Popovsky, 2010). For some highly religious clients, a professional's acceptance of religious pluralism can itself be suspect because it confirms that the professional is an "outsider." Being aware of these potential conflicts and responding sensitively can help the professional and client move forward together. Popovsky (2010) highlighted the need to consider each client individually. Fundamentalists do not represent a homogenous group, and making assumptions about one client's needs or religious adherence based on a previous experience with others in the client's religious or spiritual group can create unnecessary obstacles.

Although professionals may struggle with the absolute nature of fundamentalism, its structure and absolute certainties can provide a sense of inner peace, wholeness, coherence, and meaningful connection with others (Walsh, 1999). Heilman and Witztum (1997) reminded professionals that religious and spiritual beliefs can be profoundly felt. They encouraged professionals (especially professionals of the healing arts) to be sensitive and creative in developing strategies that support the client's values, even when those values appear at odds with common practice. In this way, the client may be served without also being "converted" to a set of values that may conflict with deeply held beliefs.

ATTAINING CLIENT GOALS

Some clients may make explicit the ways in which they expect their religious, spiritual, or secularist beliefs to be incorporated into the achievement of their goals. They may state their desire to have their business practices align closely with the teachings of Buddha or their Christian values, for example. Religious and spiritual interventions have been successfully integrated into education, nursing, and medical and mental health practice for years. In countries in which the constitution is based in sacred texts, religion is incorporated into law. In business, religious, spiritual, and secularist themes may be incorporated in a practical way into a growth plan or in an aspirational way into a mission statement, and marketing might use religious imagery or religious language to reflect client values.

Religious, spiritual, and secularist concepts may be introduced in consultation as additional coping resources or problem-solving strategies. Existing strategies (those that do not require a change in religious, spiritual, or secularist belief) may be used, or the professional may introduce transformative coping strategies. Transformative coping strategies challenge clients to modify their religious schema to deal with their problems or to attain their goals (e.g., modifying the belief that one is punished by God to a belief that one is protected by God; Worthington & Aten, 2009). Karakas (2011) outlined a management strategy to assist with this type of transformation at an organizational level. His model encourages consultants and change agents to consider six dimensions of transformation: complexity, community, creativity, spirituality, flexibility, and positivity. Professionals who can assist in transforming coping strategies and organizational structures (in a way that honors rather than disregards or diminishes religious, spiritual, or secularist beliefs, even those that may be blocking growth) can have great impact on long-term functioning of the client, who can maintain the adaptive, resource-filled aspects of their religion while reexamining potentially maladaptive aspects.

Few professionals would intentionally interfere with a client's religious observance, but this may occur without an understanding of the intricacies of these observances. Issues of gender-match between professional and client, for example, may be significant to some highly religious clients. Ultra-orthodox Jews may demonstrate anxiety when working with a professional of the opposite sex (Popovsky, 2010). Similarly, Muslim women may be resistant to working with a male professional who is not Muslim (Haque, 2010). Fundamentalist Christian clients may be sensitive to perceived attempts to change even a single religious belief. Because fundamentalist Christians do not believe that Christian doctrine was created by humans, they do not believe that they can "pick and choose" which beliefs to uphold. Their beliefs are not isolated but part of a larger, interwoven belief system. Trying to change one belief may lead client to feel like his or her entire religious belief system is being challenged (Aten et al., 2010). Plante (2007) recommended as a guide for religiously sensitive professionals, one that he has labeled RRICC: *respect* (different beliefs, traditions, and practices), *responsibility* (to serve clients well, to seek appropriate consultation and referrals to religious and spiritual professionals), *integrity* (honesty and openness about skills and limitations), *competence* (appropriately trained and supervised), and *concern* (report and prevent harm).

Understanding the key tenets of major religious and nonreligious belief systems can help professionals recognize when the discussion of religious, spiritual, or secularist interventions may be appropriate. Hinduism, for example, values the enlightened self and attention to the phenomenology of consciousness. Mindfulness techniques (i.e., contemplative practices that assist in centering or grounding the individual in the "here and now") may be useful, then, whether in a medical, educational, or management setting. Use of the Koran and Hadith with observant Muslim clients may assist in the exploration of negative thoughts and beliefs that interfere with the achievement of client goals (e.g., Allah is always in control, the client can trust Allah to be with him or her and to comfort him or her; Worthington et al., 2011). Fakhr El-Islam (2008) added that with Muslim clients, using metaphor may allow for greater exploration of beliefs without direct challenge to religious concepts. The recent popularity of mindfulness and relaxation extends from Buddhist tradition and practice, in which mind–body medicine, relaxation, and "mindfulness" meditation (nonjudgmental awareness of the present moment) have been practiced for centuries. Buddhism offers a highly developed method of self-investigation that may be compatible with the goals of some clients. Others may find the Buddhist ethical principles of nonviolence and nonharming and compassionate action, livelihood, and speech in line with their beliefs (Rubin, 2004). When these constructs are integrated into Western therapies associated with illness and pain management, evidence demonstrates a reduction in anxiety symptoms, chronic pain, fibromyalgia symptoms, cancer treatments, and addiction recovery (Worthington et al., 2011). In keeping with Buddhist expectation that basic happiness comes from harmonious interpersonal relationships, Naikan therapy (practiced in Japan) assists those who wish to improve their interpersonal relationships with others and to control those of their own actions that interfere with their ability to be in harmony with others (Tanaka-Matsumi, 2004). The focus of self-reflection, then, is on the effect of self on other so that positive relationships can be developed and maintained by mutually fulfilling obligations within the hierarchical and collectivistic structure of Japanese culture (Tanaka-Matsumi, 2004).

COLLABORATION

Many human endeavors are value based (Greenberg, Kalian & Witztum, 2010; Miovic, 2004; Popovsky, 2010). Professional goals of self-agency, self-fulfillment, and self-reflection support Western cultural goals of individualism, achievement, and self-sufficiency. This contrasts directly with cultures that value collectivism and obligation to the community, precedence of group interests over individual interests, harmonious relationships in the family, respect for elders, control of undesirable emotions, and avoidance of open expression and conflict (Fakhr El-Islam, 2008; Haque, 2010; Popovsky, 2010). Promoting self-actualization may be at odds with collectivistic cultures and associated religions in which a focus on family may be more in line with these religious and cultural worldviews (Fakhr El-Islam, 2008; Haque, 2010; Worthington & Aten, 2009). Involving family and community members becomes essential when working with religious, spiritual, or secularist clients whose belief systems support and honor the collective.

This goes beyond politely engaging with family members who unexpectedly join the client in a meeting to fully accepting the members as valuable members of the team. In medical settings, for example, Muslim family members may expect to make treatment decisions for their ill family member, just as they would make decisions for their healthy members. If not thoughtful about this experience, medical professionals may incorrectly interpret the family presence as interference, enmeshment, or intrusiveness (Fakhr El-Islam, 2008). Engaging religious and spiritual leaders can also strengthen the professional's work with clients, especially with those who value religious or spiritual guidance. Ultra-orthodox Jews, for example, often consult their rabbis about major life decisions, including marriage, work, and health care, and the rabbi's advice will almost always override that of others, including physicians (Popovsky, 2010). Consultants will be more effective, then, if they are willing to include significant members of the community (as determined by the client) in planning and decision-making processes. Issues related to confidentiality and patient self-determination must be considered, of course (Aten et al., 2010; Fakhr El-Islam, 2008; Popovsky, 2010), but when included, religious and spiritual leaders can serve as cultural liaisons between professionals and clients.

SUMMARY AND CONCLUSION

Religion, spirituality, and secularism have far-reaching influence. Professionals are encouraged to look anew at the world, recognizing in a potentially new way the influences of religion, spirituality, and secularism in day-to-day living and in their own professional practice. The practice of exploring personal and professional beliefs and assumptions strengthens professional practice. This exploration is more than just opening oneself to new understandings, although this is a likely result; it also requires a sincere evaluation of the new experiences. When the old assumptions are put aside ("bracketed," as phenomenologists would say), does the new understanding better account for success? Can former practices be enhanced by approaching the problem from a different perspective? Does a different approach allow for a better professional relationship with the client? Do new ideologies create problems of their own? Along with the evaluation of the new perspective, ideology, theory, or strategy, professionals must also evaluate their own willingness to change their practice. Understanding does not (and should not) automatically lead to acceptance; professionals must assess for themselves what they can and cannot tolerate. Professionals are encouraged to be creative and at times uncomfortable as they explore new areas or evaluate the effectiveness of new techniques. This dedication to self-exploration and sincere evaluation of new perspectives is essential now more than ever. Professionals who can expand their multicultural competence to include a truly global perspective will be ready for the fast-approaching transcultural future of international partnerships in business, education, medicine, and law.

A CLOSING NOTE

In this chapter, I have identified the need for professionals to understand their own context, that which defines the lens through which they see the world. It seems fair, then, that I should identify my own context, at least in part, for the reader. I have spent most of my career working with children and their families, and my interest in multiculturalism and internationalism develops out of this work. Over time, I have come to recognize that the visions parents have for their children (and, accordingly, the decisions that they make about parenting) are often grounded in their values, both explicit and implicit. Parents who value independence provide opportunities for their children to practice self-reliance. Parents who value interdependence reinforce actions that demonstrate sensitivity to another's needs. Parents who value respect for elders expect their children to use respectful language when talking to adults. Parents who value innovation may place less emphasis on respectful language and stress instead the clear articulation of new ideas.

These values stem from ethnic tradition, national heritage, socioeconomic status (or caste), religious, spiritual or secularist belief, and myriad other social influences. Parents do not need to be able to articulate these values for them to affect their parenting. In fact, family conflict often arises when unarticulated values are in conflict. Consider, for example, a Japanese mother married to a European American father, living together with their newborn daughter in the United States. In Japan, this mother would expect her infant to sleep with her for several years, fostering the collectivist values that are dominant in Japan. In the United States, the father would expect his infant to sleep in a crib, often in a separate room, supporting the individualistic values of the dominant European culture in the United States. The conflict can be heightened by the families of this mother and father, who "know" that their way is the best way, based on years of experience. In my role of clinical psychologist, I find that I am best able to assist families when I can join them in understanding how all of these values interact to create the parents' vision for the future of their family.

My attraction to religion, spirituality, and secularism is a part of this interest in understanding how families determine their values, but my interest in religious differences began long before my career as a psychologist. I grew up around families with different faith traditions, sometimes from different parts of the world. Just as I was raised in the religion of my parents (who were raised in the religion of their parents), the other kids on the block were raised in the religion of their parents. This was my first experience of religion—that religion was inherited, just like eye color. The religious pluralism on my block did not appear to bother any of the adults, so it never bothered me. In fact, it gave me an opportunity early on to appreciate the similarities and differences between beliefs. My reasons for accepting religious pluralism have matured since childhood, as has my development in my own faith. However, with this development has also come a continued fascination with (and respect for) the diversity of personal and group belief and values and practices. This fascination (and all of its accompanying biases) is likely evident throughout this chapter.

REFERENCES

Ali, A. J., Camp, R. C., & Gibbs, M. (2005). The concept of "free-agency" in monotheistic religions: Implications for global business. *Journal of Business Ethics, 60*, 103–112. doi:10.1007/s10551-005-5749-x

Ammerman, N. T. (2010). The challenges of pluralism: Locating religion in a world of diversity. *Social Compass, 57*, 154–167. doi:10.1177/0037768610362406

Aten, J. D., Mangis, M. W., & Campbell, C. (2010). Psychotherapy with rural fundamentalist clients. *Journal of Clinical Psychology, 66*, 513–523. doi:10.1002/jclp.20677

Aten, J. D., & Worthington, E. L. (2009). Next steps for clinicians in religious and spiritual therapy: An endpiece. *Journal of Clinical Psychology: In Session, 65*, 224–229. doi:10.1002/jclp.20562

Balagangadhara, S. N., & De Roover, J. (2007). The secular state and religious conflict: Liberal neutrality and the Indian case of pluralism. *Journal of Political Philosophy, 15*, 67–92. doi:10.1111/j.1467-9760.2007.00268.x

Casanova, J. (2009). The secular and secularisms. *Social Research, 76*, 1049–1066.

Cohen, M. (2003). Frontline: The affirmation of a religious (not merely spiritual!) orientation in clinical treatment. *The Journal of the American Academy of Psychoanalysis and Dynamic Psychiatry, 31*, 269–273. doi:10.1521/jaap.31.2.269.22111

Colbert, L. K., Jefferson, J. L., Gallo, R., & Davis, R. (2009). A study of religiosity and psychological well-being among African Americans: Implications for counseling and psychotherapeutic processes. *Journal of Religion and Health, 48*, 278–289. doi:10.1007/s10943-008-9195-9

Crabtree, S. (2010). *Gallup Global Reports: Religiosity highest in world's poorest nations.* Retrieved from http://www.gallup.com/poll/142727/Religiosity-Highest-World-Poorest-Nations.aspx#2

Fakhr El-Islam, M. F. (2008). Arab culture and mental health care. *Transcultural Psychiatry, 45*, 671–682. doi:10.1177/1363461508100788

Greenberg, D., Kalian, M., & Witztum, E. (2010). Value-sensitive psychiatric rehabilitation. *Transcultural Psychiatry, 47*, 629–646. doi:10.1177/1363461510383745

Goltz, S. M. (2011). Spiritual power: The internal, renewable social power source. *Journal of Management, Spirituality & Religion, 8*, 341–363. doi:10.1080/14766086.2011.630171

Gozdz, K. (2000). Toward transpersonal learning communities in business. *American Behavioral Scientist, 43*, 1262–1285. doi:10.1177/00027640021955856

Haque, A. (2010). Mental health concepts in Southeast Asia: Diagnostic considerations and treatment implications. *Psychology, Health & Medicine, 15*, 127–134. doi:10.1080/13548501003615266

Heilman, S. C., & Witztum, E. (1997). Value-sensitive therapy: Learning from ultra-orthodox patients. *American Journal of Psychotherapy, 51*, 522–541.

Helmeke, K. B., & Bischof, G. H. (2002). Recognizing and raising spiritual and religious issues in psychotherapy: Guidelines for the timid. *Journal of Family Psychotherapy, 13*, 195–214. doi:10.1300/J085v13n01_10

Hill, P. C., Pargament, K. I., Hood, R. W., McCullough, M. E., Swyers, J. P., Larson, D. B., & Zinnbauer, B. J. (2000). Conceptualizing religion and spirituality: Points of commonality, points of departure. *Journal for the Theory of Social Behaviour, 30*, 51–77.

Hirschil, R. (2010, Summer). Holy glocalization: Constitution and sacred texts in the "non-secular" world. *Harvard International Review, 32*, 38–42.

Javaid, H., Khan, S., & Baig, E. (2010). Lifestyle advertising—Emerging perspective in advertising. *European Journal of Economics, Finance and Administrative Sciences, 20*, 115–118.

Josephson, A. M., & Peteet, J. R. (2007). Talking with patients about spirituality and worldview: Practical interviewing techniques and strategies. *Psychiatric Clinics of North America, 30*, 181–197. doi:10.1016/j.psc.2007.01.005

Karakas, F. (2011). Positive management education: Creating creative minds, passionate hearts, and kindred spirits. *Journal of Management Education, 35*, 198–226. doi:10.1177/1052562910372806

Lindridge, A. (2010). Are we fooling ourselves when we talk about ethnic homogeneity? The case of religion and ethnic subdivisions amongst Indians living in Britain. *Journal of Marketing Management, 26*, 441–472. doi:10.1080/02672571003633644

Madeley, J. T. S. (2009). Unequally yoked: The antinomies of church–state separation in Europe and the USA. *European Political Science, 8*, 273–288. doi:10.1057/eps.2009.16

Marsh, C. (2011). Religion after atheism. *Society, 48*, 247–250. doi:10.1007/s12115-011-9425-8

Marterella, M. K., & Brock, L. J. (2008). Religion and spirituality as a resource in marital and family therapy. *Journal of Family Psychotherapy, 19*, 330–344. doi:10.1080/08975350802475072

Miovic, M. (2004). An introduction to spiritual psychology: Overview of the literature, East and West. *Harvard Review of Psychiatry, 12*, 105–115. doi:10.1080/10673220490447209

Newport, F. (2010). *Gallup: In U.S., increasing number have no religious identity.* Retrieved from http://www.gallup.com/poll/128276/Increasing-Number-No-Religious-Identity.aspx

Newport, F. (2011). *Gallup: More than 9 in 10 Americans continue to believe in God.* Retrieved from http://www.gallup.com/poll/147887/Americans-Continue-Believe-God.aspx

Newport, F., Agrawal, S., & Witters, D. (2010). *Gallup: Religious Americans enjoy higher wellbeing.* Retrieved from http://www.gallup.com/poll/144080/Religious-Americans-Enjoy-Higher-Wellbeing.aspx

Osisioma, H. E. (2009). Effect of gender, age, and religion on choice of conflict management style in Nigerian organizations. *African Journal of Business and Economic Research, 4*, 90–105.

Pargament, K. I., & Saunders, S. M. (2007). Introduction to the special issue on spirituality and psychotherapy. *Journal of Clinical Psychology, 63*, 903–907. doi:10.1002/jclp.20405

Passe, J., & Willox, L. (2009). Teaching religion in America's schools: A necessary disruption. *Social Studies, 100*, 102–106. doi:10.3200/TSSS.100.3.102-106

Pelham, B., & Crabtree, S. (2008). *Gallup: Worldwide, highly religious more likely to help others.* Retrieved from http://www.gallup.com/poll/111013/Worldwide-Highly-Religious-More-Likely-Help-Others.aspx

Plante, T. G. (2007). Integrating spirituality and psychotherapy: Ethical issues and principles to consider. *Journal of Clinical Psychology, 63*, 891–902. doi:10.1002/jclp.20383

Popovsky, M. A. (2010). Special issues in the care of ultra-orthodox Jewish psychiatric in-patients. *Transcultural Psychiatry, 47*, 647–672. doi:10.1177/1363461510383747

Post, B. C., & Wade, N. G. (2009). Religion and spirituality in psychotherapy: A practice-friendly review of research. *Journal of Clinical Psychology, 65*, 131–146. doi:10.1002/jclp.20563

Prince, R. (2004). Western psychotherapy and the Yoruba: Problems of insight and nondirective techniques. In U. P. Gielen, J. M. Fish, & J. G. Draguns (Eds.), *Handbook of culture, therapy, and healing* (pp. 311–319). Mahwah, NJ: Erlbaum.

Prothero, S. (2010). *God is not one: The eight rival religions that run the world—and why their differences matter.* New York, NY: Harper One.

Rubin, J. B. (2004). Psychoanalysis and Buddhism. In U. P. Gielen, J. M. Fish, & J. G. Draguns (Eds.), *Handbook of culture, therapy, and healing* (pp. 253–276). Mahwah, NJ: Erlbaum.

Ruiter, S., & De Graaf, N. D. (2006). National context, religiosity, and volunteering: Results from 53 countries. *American Sociological Review, 71*, 191–210. doi: 10.1177/000312240607100202

Singhal, M., & Chatterjee, L. (2006). A person-organization fit-based approach for spirituality at work: Development of a conceptual framework. *Journal of Human Values, 12*, 161–178. doi:10.1177/097168580601200205

Smith, B. G., & Stark, R. (2009). *Gallup: Religious attendance relates to generosity worldwide.* Retrieved from http://www.gallup.com/poll/122807/Religious-Attendance-Relates-Generosity-Worldwide.aspx

Tanaka-Matsumi, J. (2004). Japanese forms of psychotherapy: Naikan therapy and Morita therapy. In U. P. Gielen, J. M. Fish, & J. G. Draguns (Eds.), *Handbook of culture, therapy, and healing* (pp. 277–291). Mahwah, NJ: Erlbaum.

Thanissaro, P. N. (2010). Finding a moral homeground: Appropriately critical religious education and transmission of spiritual values. *International Journal of Children's Spirituality, 15*, 175–187. doi:10.1080/1364436X.2010.502223

Vasconcelos, A. F. (2010). Spiritual development in organizations: A religious-based approach. *Journal of Business Ethics, 93,* 607–622. doi:10.1007/s10551-009-0243-5

Vess, M., Arndt, J., Cox, C. R., Routledge, C., & Goldenberg, J. L. (2009). Exploring the existential function of religion: The effects of religious fundamentalism and mortality salience on faith-based medical refusals. *Journal of Personality and Social Psychology, 97,* 334–350. doi:10.1037/a0015545

Walsh, F. (1999). Religion and spirituality: Wellsprings for healing and resilience. In F. Walsh (Ed.), *Spiritual resources in family therapy* (pp. 3–27). New York, NY: Guilford Press.

Watters, E. (2010). *Crazy like us: The globalization of the American psyche.* New York, NY: Free Press.

Worthington, E. L., & Aten, J. D. (2009). Psychotherapy with religious and spiritual clients: An introduction. *Journal of Clinical Psychology: In Session, 65,* 123–130. doi:10.1002/jclp.20561

Worthington, E. L., Hook, J. N., Davis, D. E., & McDaniel, M. A. (2011). Religion and spirituality. *Journal of Clinical Psychology: In Session, 67,* 204–214. doi:10.1002/jclp.20760

II

APPLICATIONS

7

FOSTERING MULTICULTURALLY AND INTERNATIONALLY COMPETENT INDIVIDUALS AND TEAMS

PATRICIA DENISE LOPEZ AND NURCAN ENSARI

National or cultural boundaries are blurred when considering a Korean female CEO of an African production company based in California or a Turkish marketing manager of an internationally known Japanese electronics company based in Germany, Brazil, Japan, and the United States. The complexities and challenges of multicultural and international issues have occupied academicians and businesses for many decades. Now, however, society is faced with massive dynamic, global, and overarching challenges that force us to break the borders of specific countries. Within organizations, the focus is shifting from diversity-related programs and legal requirements such as affirmative action, sexual harassment, and adverse impact to more global issues such as immigration, acculturation, global talent management, outsourcing, and networked organizations (Bartlett, Ghoshal, & Birkinshaw, 2004).

DOI: 10.1037/14044-007
Internationalizing Multiculturalism: Expanding Professional Competencies in a Globalized World,
R. L. Lowman (Editor)

The starting point of this chapter was our own experiences in struggling to construct and reflect our subjectivities and identities and in facing the challenges of living and working in culturally diverse and international settings. Both authors moved to the United States several years ago from their native countries of the Philippines and Turkey (Lopez and Ensari, respectively), to pursue their doctoral studies and eventually to live and work in California. Denise, the first author, went back to the Philippines for a few years to teach at the Asian Institute of Management (AIM) and to do management training and consulting for Asian companies. While teaching at AIM, she was asked to use the case-method teaching style, a highly participatory and inductive teaching technique made popular by the Harvard Business School. This pedagogy, which is contrary to the Asian traditions of respect and acceptance of authority, challenged Denise and her Asian students and colleagues to expand and modify their thinking processes and interactions. A common personal and professional dilemma Denise and other Asian professionals have faced is how to integrate Western theories and concepts while trying to preserve one's values, expanding one's interpersonal and management repertoire, and ultimately defining a personal style that works in increasingly diverse international organizations. Denise later moved back to the United States and, before joining Alliant International University, worked at a global survey consulting firm, where she managed large-scale research projects, frequently working virtually with internal staff members, clients, and service providers around the world. The various challenges of working with diverse and international colleagues and virtual teams, such as differing languages, local norms and policies, mind-sets, and work styles, demonstrated to her how task demands and social interactions become more complex as the context becomes broader and more global. These experiences contributed to the core message of this chapter—namely, that the kinds of competencies one needs to be effective interpersonally and within teams in today's multicultural and international environment need to expand to meet these more complex challenges.

Nurcan moved to the United States from Turkey about 15 years ago for her doctoral studies but continued to live two separate lives in two culturally distinct countries as she tried to integrate into a culture in which her Turkish identity was perceived by most as unfamiliar, even strange. She continues to experience role conflict and incongruence between her role as a Muslim, a mother of two, and a daughter of highly traditional and collectivistic parents and her role as a professor in a highly diverse American university, a scientist, a liberal, and a modern Turkish woman. Her life is constantly influenced by the intersection and interaction of these multiple identities, experiences, and background. Often, she experiences identity interference as a result of holding multiple identities. For example, the pressures of being a Muslim woman in the United States interfere with the image of a modern liberal woman, or her role as a female professor often leads her to minimize her identity as a mother and a wife to fit in with her male peers. She shares these challenges and struggles with many individuals and team members as they consider their intersectional and interactive identities and roles within and outside the work environment.

The stories of both authors represent just two examples of the complexities of living and working in a multicultural and international context. In this chapter, we discuss these complexities in more detail and present ideas for fostering effective multicultural and international individuals and teams. We begin first by defining multiculturalism and internationalism. We then present a case that illustrates multicultural and international challenges among individuals and teams. Next, we analyze the case using various social psychological and management theories and offer recommendations for managers and business consultants. Finally, we present a framework of multicultural and international competencies for individuals and teams.

DEFINING MULTICULTURALISM AND INTERNATIONALISM

Agreeing on common definitions of *multiculturalism* and *internationalism* has been challenging for academicians. Some scholars (Cokley, Dreher, & Stockdale, 2004) have viewed multiculturalism as it relates to local, domestic issues (e.g., racism in United States, class differences in Mexico) and consider internationalism to be related to international relations outside of the United States (e.g., an American expatriate in Vietnam, a Japanese employee in New York). Others (Baker, 1983; Berry, Poortinga, Segall, & Dasen, 2002) have broadly defined multiculturalism as inclusive of all cultures with respect to age, sex, race, place of residence, nationality, religion, and other characteristics and have used the concepts of multiculturalism and internationalism interchangeably. Finally, although the term *multiculturalism* is defined as sensitivity to and awareness of other cultures, *internationalism*, and increasingly, the term *globalization*, seem to be associated more with a political and business agenda to gain competitive advantage in the marketplace (Gooderham & Nordhaug, 2003). Thus, in today's global organizations, multicultural and international issues can arise simultaneously or independently.

In this chapter, we conceptualize multiculturalism as a set of values and goals focusing on issues and interactions primarily to those "within country" (e.g., based on gender or ethnicity), and internationalism as a set of values and goals related to issues and interactions "across nations or countries." Although multicultural and international issues may come up independently in some situations, they may converge or interact in others depending on an individual's cultural and national identity, his or her work role, and the organization's characteristics. In today's global environment, it is rare for individuals, teams, and organizations to interact with others in a purely domestic, or purely international, context. Rather, people need to be prepared to interact with colleagues, customers, and other partners who are diverse not only in terms of traditionally defined multicultural dimensions such as gender and race–ethnicity but also in terms of, for example, nationality, sociopolitical and cultural background, geographic location, and language.

BEYOND A SINGLE SET OF COMPETENCIES

We believe that determining a single set of multicultural and international competencies expected of all leaders and managers in all situations is no longer viable. This principle also applies to teams that work virtually, with members of different cultures and from various countries collaborating. At the individual level, the role of a multiculturally or internationally competent leader may require a different set of skills for a Korean female CEO of an African company than for a Turkish manager of an international Japanese company. Leaders with multicultural awareness and knowledge may not have global skills (Connerley & Pedersen, 2005) or vice versa. At the same time, there are basic individual-level competencies that leaders need to develop in order to respond appropriately to multicultural and international problems. These competencies should be developed in light of the reality of multiple identities. Similarly, at the team level, competencies that allow for successful collaboration and productive outcomes differ for heterogeneous teams that work within a country versus those that interact globally (across nations). These competencies, along with advanced communication technologies, will allow dispersed teams to work globally and virtually with relative ease while maintaining and enhancing common collective identities.

The objective of this chapter is to review and analyze these individual, interpersonal, and team-level competencies divided into three categories: fundamental, multicultural, and international–global. Our starting point is a case of a global team and a manager who are working on a demanding project with high client expectations and short time frames. On the basis of the experiences of various managers we have interviewed in the high-tech and business process outsourcing industries, this fictional case illustrates various personal, interpersonal, and team challenges, some of which stem from work roles and task and organizational demands, and some of which stem from multicultural and international issues, such as multiple social identities, work roles, ethnocentrism, sexism, and prejudice. Through this case, we aim not only to draw attention to the reality of complex lives of today's employees and teams but also to make suggestions on how to foster and develop key competencies and offer potential solutions to some challenges.

A Client Emergency: The Argos Customer Relationship Management Global Team

Tanisha is a global project manager for Phoenix Systems, a global information systems provider.[1] Phoenix Systems designs and implements customer relationship management (CRM) software that allows client organizations to track, organize, and synchronize interactions with their sales prospects and customers. Tanisha is 29 years old, African American, and a software engineer who has risen through company ranks to become one of its few minority global managers. She reports to Jim, vice president (VP) of global service operations. Jim is in his early 50s, a Caucasian American with an old-school attitude focused primarily on the bottom line.

In this fast-paced industry, Phoenix's strategy is to leverage its innovative technology and global talent. At Phoenix, projects are staffed by highly skilled employees regardless of where they are located. These global cross-functional team structures allow employees to be close to their customers and to be available to them 24/7. The company has adopted a results-oriented work environment that allows employees to set up flexible work schedules and work virtually using various technologies. Typically employees communicate through e-mail and web chat; occasionally senior managers visit various work sites. Projects have internal websites where team members can post, view, and exchange information.

Tanisha is based in California and manages a team of 20 people (known as the Argos CRM global team). The team is in charge of developing, implementing, and maintaining a customized CRM system for their client organization, Argos, a major player in the European travel and hospitality industry. Team members are located in the United States, Spain, India, Israel, and the Philippines. U.S. and Spanish team members handle North American and European sales and client relations. Those in India and Israel do software programming and system maintenance, and employees in the Philippines provide customer service and tech support.

After 8 months, the Argos CRM team has completed the CRM design and is in its first phase of implementation. Despite a few snags in software development and testing, the system was implemented on schedule. Argos CRM's 3-year contract includes regular testing, upgrading, and 24/7 customer support. Tanisha's team of 20 meets regularly by teleconference once a week for 2 hours. The weekly global call occurs at 8 a.m. Pacific time, 5 p.m. Madrid time, 6 p.m. Tel Aviv time, 8:30 p.m. Chennai time, and 11 p.m. Manila time. The language used is English, which all team members speak at varying fluency levels and with various accents.

---

[1]This composite case represents an integration of a number of specific situations. All names and case details are assumed.

While Tanisha was trekking in Kilimanjaro on a much-needed 1-week vacation, the CRM system broke down, and the problem remained unresolved for 18 hours. The situation had been escalated to Tanisha's boss, Jim, by the senior VP at Argos, who complained that the breakdown had resulted in lost sales and poor servicing of their major clients. Apparently, before this, the people at Argos had not been overly impressed by the quality of customer service received; this breakdown was a major disaster for them, and they were threatening to take their business elsewhere. Jim sent Tanisha an urgent voicemail to fix the system ASAP. He ended his voicemail with a scathing comment undermining her competence and reliability and questioning her fitness as a leader for this highly visible global assignment.

Internally, as soon as the European-based Argos client group detected this breakdown, the group leader immediately contacted the customer tech support hotline, which was based in Manila, in the Philippines. Unfortunately, this incident happened on Good Friday, and most of the senior managers in Manila, including Evelyn (head of Philippines support), were on vacation. When the Argos call came in, the Filipino customer support team was on skeleton crew, staffed by newbies who did not know the intricacies of the Argos system. Furthermore, these support agents had been trained to assist on typical system issues; more difficult problems were to be passed to the software engineers in Chennai, India. However, in an attempt to prevent bad news from escalating, the Filipino agents spent several hours trying to resolve the issue; they also left an e-mail message for the software team in Chennai requesting assistance but did not hear from them for 4 hours. The agents finally called Evelyn, who then had to page Manish, the lead systems engineer, to emphasize the situation's urgency.

The Argos client group also left a voicemail for Jose, the Madrid-based client relations manager for the project. Unfortunately, Jose was attending a family affair and did not have his mobile phone on for the entire day. Upon accessing his voicemail, Jose instantly started sending voicemails and e-mails to Evelyn and Manish emphasizing the gravity of the situation.

With Manish personally involved, the Indian engineers sprang into action. They were able to identify most of the issues and apply the necessary fixes. However, despite rebooting, the Argos system still did not work quite right. After 4 hours of frustrating investigation, they located the Israeli programmer, David (based in Tel Aviv), who had collaborated with the Indian team on major portions of the system. Manish, David, and the Indian programmers eventually realized there was a system error that needed to be reprogrammed, but because of the shortened windows for internal testing plus constant pressure from the U.S.- and Spain-based client relations staff to deliver the system, this mistake had not been discovered before implementation.

By this point, the Argos system had been down for 14 hours, and the clients were livid. Jose in Madrid was upset because he had taken the brunt of the client's anger and was trying to coordinate all "those unreliable support teams." After 4 more hours, the issue was resolved, but by then, Argos had expressed their dissatisfaction with the system's quality, the customer support, and the travel and hospitality revenues lost to its competition.

Upon returning from Africa late Easter Sunday night, Tanisha immediately concentrated her efforts to pacify Argos. Despite Jim's skepticism, she even went out of her way to help the Argos sales team by making joint Argos/ Phoenix presentations to key customers about the quality of Argos's CRM systems. This gesture was viewed positively and actually helped Argos retain many of its clients and even attract new business.

Tanisha realized there were underlying issues in the way her global team worked that needed to be resolved. During and after the recent crisis with Argos, her subteams seemed more focused on defending their actions and blaming others. Tanisha had a feeling these issues had to do with more than just task and relational problems. She wondered whether multicultural and international factors also played a role in the dynamics of her global team.

Case Analysis: Underlying Interpersonal, Multicultural, and International Issues

Some relevant details and interpersonal–cultural nuances require elaboration in this case. For one thing, although Tanisha was an ambitious and exceptionally talented engineer, she was conscious of her minority status. Even as a global project manager, she did not feel included by her peers and by upper management. Her relationship with Jim was stilted; she did not perceive him to be a supportive boss in terms of providing her with the requisite feedback and mentoring for this, her first global assignment. She felt he paid more attention to other project managers. Tanisha was also concerned about Jim's voicemail, which only confirmed her perception that he did not really expect her to succeed in this job. According to the self-fulfilling prophecy phenomenon (Wilkins, 1976), personal expectations about future events may lead individuals to behave in particular ways that, on occasion, can cause the expected event to occur. Furthermore, others' expectations may also, unwittingly, shape future outcomes (Wilkins, 1976). This has important implications for leader–follower relationships, particularly in a diverse organizational setting where a leader's expectations about a minority employee such as Tanisha may be based on stereotypes; these in turn may have a negative impact on the employee's motivation and performance (Kierein & Gold, 2000; Rosenthal & Rubin, 1978).

Tanisha had a relatively good relationship with Jose (a Spaniard in his mid-30s), although things had not started off well. Tanisha preferred a casual, democratic leadership style, and she perceived Jose to be arrogant and auto-cratic in his dealings with others. There were a few instances when she directly contacted Jose's subordinates while he was away, resulting in some tensions with Jose, who did not like to be bypassed. Jose's team seemed to work at a more relaxed pace than the Americans. It was not a secret that there were differences in compensation among the Phoenix employees around the world, with the Americans receiving the highest salaries and the European employees having much more vacation time. American members sometimes felt they had to carry more of the workload while their Spanish colleagues were on vacation.

Tanisha assumed she would have an easier relationship with Manish and David since all three were engineers. However, throughout the project, Manish and David (both male, mid-30s) frequently interrupted her (and others) and sometimes seemed to take over the meetings. Tanisha could always tell when Manish and David were agitated because their accents would be more pronounced and harder to understand. She was irritated that they did not keep her posted on the nitty-gritty details of tech development. Moreover, she and Jose became frustrated when software completion dead-lines were not met and had to be pushed back. It was as if, for Manish and David, deadlines were "soft" and could always be negotiated.

Manish and the Indian software team had issues with the weekly global call. Aside from the fact that the meeting occurred in the evening, after they had already worked an excessively long day, they felt their concerns were not given enough time. Also, now that the software design was complete and they were doing systems maintenance, the work was less exciting for them. Evelyn, who was in charge of customer tech support, often felt that Filipinos were treated as third-class citizens on the team. Not only was the meeting time always set to almost midnight their time, their issues came last on the agenda. They felt the least valued even though they did a lot of grunt work answering client calls. Evelyn and her team members rarely said anything during meetings unless they were formally prompted. Tanisha knew they were uncomfortable on these calls, especially when it came to participating in open discussion and debate.

Integration of Psychological and Management Concepts and Theories

Team Issues

In analyzing the case, we first pay attention to basic task, structure, and functioning issues that would generally apply to all teams regardless of composition or context. The team's task is difficult and complex (high tech), with several subgroups that are sequentially interdependent (Stewart & Barrick, 2000; Thompson, 1967). The Argos CRM team has the challenge of performing tasks that occur in a sequential or predetermined order, that is, selling and client relations, to software design and testing, to systems implementation, and then customer service and technical support. The potential for operational problems is higher in sequentially interdependent work than it is in pooled work in which members or subgroups simply combine their efforts in no particular order (e.g., making as many sales calls as possible). This is because sequential interdependence requires greater communication and coordination between subgroups (George & Jones, 2005). The vulnerability to such operational problems is magnified by the team's operation in a global and virtual environment. Moreover, members and subgroups may affect product and service quality or delivery if some or all individuals or subunits have skill deficiencies or if there is low motivation to perform or collaborate. These process issues were clearly seen in the Argos CRM case.

The lack of communication and coordination among these subgroups also suggests that the different units within the Argos CRM team were not fully aligned toward a common identity and purpose. The Argos CRM members seemed to be more concerned about meeting their personal and subgroup goals and defending their own scope of responsibilities than being jointly accountable for the entire systems design and delivery process for their client. The group as a whole did not have clear norms or procedures for working together, especially for responding to major problems necessitating concerted action from multiple units. There did not appear to be a history of or process for identifying who to contact, who would lead if the project manager was not available, how to back each other up, or how to make difficult decisions, for example. Relationships among the subgroups were weak, and there was a lack of trust among the members. Trust issues are common among groups for which the majority of interactions are virtual with little of the face-to-face contact that is so crucial for facilitating positive impression management, understanding, and relationship building (Gibson & Cohen, 2003).

The common ingroup identity model (Gaertner, Dovidio, Anastasio, Bachman, & Rust, 1993) offers ways in which previously segregated work groups can be successfully merged into a superordinate unit. This model argues that when a new team is formed, a new social identity for team members is always created. Previous memberships are replaced by new superordinate social identities; loyalties to previous teams are transferred to the new common category for collective welfare. Alternatively, the superordinate group identity can be created by making salient an existing inclusive categorization (e.g., the organization as a whole; Gaertner et al., 1993). In the case of Argos, a common ingroup identity can be created by (a) reminding subgroups that their common interest is the success of the organization as a whole,

(b) forming heterogeneous work teams consisting of members from different work units with accountability to the larger organization, and (c) enhancing subgroup members' awareness of their interdependence within a superordinate organization (Brewer & Schneider, 1990). Related to this, experts on team performance have also stressed the importance of creating a common mission and vision and clarifying team goals, norms, and procedures around information exchange, communication, and coordination (Beatty & Barker Scott, 2004; Marquardt & Horvath, 2001).

Although the case indicates that there was a global weekly call, having all 20 team members at the same meeting (especially without visual interaction) was too cumbersome. It is likely that the agenda was frequently large, with several portions being irrelevant to most attendees. Our interviews with global managers suggest that large (especially virtual) meetings tended to involve more "reporting out" than "decision making," which become disengaging to participants. It may be better to reorganize the global call to involve fewer key participants at the highest levels of the team or organization and at the same time create structures such as cross-functional task forces to encourage more frequent interactions among members across different functions and levels (Brett, Behfar, & Kern, 2006).

Team experts (e.g., Gassmann, 2001; Gibson, 2011) also emphasize that the organization as a whole as well as senior leaders must provide sufficient support to ensure maximum functioning of their global teams. In this case, although there were flexible work policies and technologies in place, the employees appeared to need more team development, technical and cultural training programs, senior management support and coaching, and incentives and support systems to build relationships outside their immediate units.

Cultural Issues at Individual, Interpersonal, and Multicultural–International Levels

The members of the Argos CRM team came from diverse backgrounds that influenced their worldviews, cultural identities, attitudes, perceptions, behaviors, and interactions with others. The case illustrates some of the challenges brought about by multicultural and international team compositions, such as subtle but important differences in power and status (e.g., U.S.- and Euro-centered project leadership vis-à-vis outsourcing of support roles to India and Philippines, U.S.-centric schedule of global calls, male–female work interactions). According to social identity theory (Tajfel & Turner, 1986), the mere act of individuals categorizing themselves as "us versus them" leads those individuals to display ingroup favoritism. The positive differentiation of the ingroup from a comparison outgroup on some valued dimension helps ingroup members achieve positive self-esteem (Brewer, 1991). The motivation to enhance self-image can lead to stronger intergroup differentiation and prejudice (Tajfel & Turner, 1986). These intergroup processes can be seen within the Argos CRM team in that differentiation among the employees led to social categorizations ("we" vs. "them," or "my team" vs. "others"), which contributed to intergroup conflict and prejudice. Intergroup tensions detracted from the members' ability to create a common team identity and foster collaboration (e.g., Jose's comment about unreliable Indian and Filipino support groups, the Filipinos' perception of being third-class citizens).

Stereotyping and prejudice are manifested in different ways in the case of Argos. For instance, Tanisha's boss, Jim, as well as a number of international male managers who come from highly masculine, hierarchical cultures (Indian) and highly competitive cultures (Israeli), appeared to have unfavorable attitudes toward her as a younger minority female. Stereotypes of women as more communal (selfless and concerned with others) and less agentic (self-assertive and motivated to master) than men (Eagly & Steffen, 1984) can damage perceptions of women as successful leaders. In their role congruity theory of prejudice, Eagly and Karau (2002) argued that perceived incongruity between the female gender role and leadership roles leads to prejudice toward female leaders. As a result, competent and qualified female leaders, such as Tanisha, face unfavorable gender stereotypes and have to work harder to overcome prejudicial attitudes and achieve success in leadership roles in their organizations.

Culture clashes frequently occur as a result of different worldviews or cultural assumptions. Several frameworks are available for professionals to map out important cultural dimensions that may affect interactions with individuals and teams across cultures. Among the most notable are Hofstede (2001; see chapter 4) and his dimensions of individualism–collectivism, power distance, uncertainty avoidance, masculinity–femininity, and Confucian dynamism or long-term orientation; Hall and Hall (1995) with their dimensions of time, space, and high–low context; and Kluckhohn and Strodtbeck (1961) with their cultural orientation framework differentiating people's assumptions about basic human nature, relationships among people, relation to nature, human activity, and orientation to time and space.

Although it is beyond the scope of this chapter to describe these cultural frameworks in detail, some of these dimensions are useful in the case. For example, Tanisha and Jose have different management preferences that may stem from individual and cultural preferences related to power distance and hierarchical–democratic values. The Filipino team members' reluctance to voice objections in front of senior people and their response of trying to solve the breakdown problem before bringing it up directly to authority figures reflect high collectivism, high power distance, and the importance of preserving "face." This contrasts with American and Israeli preferences for frank, open, challenging discussions and debates. In this case, some team members come from high-context cultures characterized by less direct and more formal communication styles in which meanings are conveyed not simply by oral or written words but also by nonverbal and behavioral cues (Hall & Hall, 1995). These differing perspectives could present a problem, especially in a global and virtual team environment in which the modes of communication are not as rich as face to face, thus providing much less access to contextual cues. Perspectives about time differ across cultures and could also create conflict when managing projects, as was illustrated in this case. For some cultures (e.g., the United States), time is finite, deadlines are treated literally, and there is a strong short-term focus. For other cultures (e.g., many Asian, Latino, and Middle Eastern cultures), time is fluid, deadlines are viewed as adjustable, and orientations tend to be longer term (Hall & Hall, 1995; Zweifel, 2003).

The case also illustrates the additional challenges faced by this global team in working across differing time zones, geographies, and linguistic differences. Although English was the common language and technologies were in place to facilitate non-face-to-face communication, these factors were not sufficient to ensure the high levels of trust, cohesion, knowledge transfer, and coordination required for optimal response to the emergency. Although some authors (e.g., Jarvenpaa & Leidner, 1999) have argued that trust can be built swiftly among virtual teams, many experts have underscored the importance of face-to-face interactions interspersed with virtual communication, intensive technology training, and the establishment of team identity and team norms (Gibson & Cohen, 2003; Marquardt & Horvath, 2001; Zweifel, 2003). The case also illustrates the perception of certain non-U.S. team members related to their lower levels of English fluency, accents, and reserved communication styles. Experts (Lev-Ari & Keysar, 2010; Ruscher, 2001) have noted that these factors not only can lead to misunderstandings but also may fuel negative perceptions of individuals' knowledge, skill, and credibility, thus limiting their potential contributions and feelings of inclusion.

Finally, the case highlights the importance of understanding how key elements of national cultures such as religion, history, politics, and economic factors may impact team performance (Marquardt & Horvath, 2001). This information facilitates understanding of international team members and is critical for planning and decision making. For example, had the Argos CRM team leaders appreciated the importance of Easter holidays in the Filipino Catholic culture, they might have coordinated work schedules and tasks globally so that overall service levels would not be vulnerable. The case also illustrates perceived equity issues stemming from international human resources (HR) differences (e.g., compensation mismatches, differences in vacation days) between the United States and other countries. Among multinational organizations, it is typical for salaries and benefits to be anchored in the markets where the employees are located, and these markets differ in terms of cost of living expenses, cultural and legally mandated practices, and other factors. Nevertheless, such differences can create misperceptions about the fairness or unfairness of compensation packages. Team leaders who are aware of such differences can mitigate potential issues by communicating openly, distributing workloads fairly, and involving members in identifying various modes of rewards and recognition.

Cases like that of Tanisha and her team are becoming more and more common in today's global environment. Our analysis suggests several steps that managers can take to prevent or address the various issues described in the case. We also outline various ways in which business consultants can help diverse and global employees and teams work more effectively together (see Table 7.1).

MULTICULTURAL AND INTERNATIONAL COMPETENCIES FOR INDIVIDUALS AND TEAMS

Individuals who wish to be effective in working with others and within teams in multicultural and international contexts need to possess important knowledge, skills, and attitudes (KSATs). Since the late 1990s, there has been increased interest in identifying competencies for diverse leadership and the management of multicultural and global teams (e.g., Connaughton & Shuffler, 2007; Connerley & Pedersen, 2005; Gibson, 2011). We have integrated these competencies into a two-dimensional framework that organizes the KSATs by (a) level (individual, interpersonal, and team) and (b) context (fundamental, multicultural, and international-global; see Table 7.2). Concerning organizational levels, we consider certain KSATs to be basic competencies for individuals; additional KSATs, identified from top to bottom of the table, become important for working with other individuals or with teams. With regard to context, we consider some individual, interpersonal, and team KSATs to be foundational. Moving from left to right in Table 7.2, additional KSATs become critical when working in a multicultural (domestic) context, and even more so when the work entails individuals or teams from another country (international) or from multiple countries (global). Our notion of competencies is cumulative; as people interact with others at various levels and social contexts, they need to expand their KSATs.

At the individual level, the importance of self-awareness, self-management, and openness to experience cannot be overemphasized. There is strong agreement among psychologists, managers, and other experts of human behavior (e.g., Fouad & Arredondo, 2007; Sue, 2001; Whetten & Cameron, 2007) that knowing one's values, goals, personal strengths, and weaknesses is the

TABLE 7.1
Recommendations for Managers and Business Consultants

Level	Managers	Business consultants
Individual/self	Reflect on your own values and biases, work and role schemas, stereotypes, and preferred ways of working. Be aware of how these may color your perceptions and behaviors.	Enhance managers' self-knowledge and self-awareness through self- and peer assessments.
Interpersonal	Communicate clearly, honestly, and with respect. Actively look for opportunities to get to know your colleagues deeply. Develop open and trusting relationships. Acknowledge personal, cultural, and power differences. Discuss underlying assumptions and ways to overcome interpersonal conflicts. Learn and practice diverse ways of communicating. Use richer modes of communication (e.g., face-to-face, videoconferences). Practice perspective taking. Be sensitive to nonverbal behaviors and contextual cues.	Provide coaching and training on interpersonal and intercultural relations, especially communication, negotiation, and conflict resolution. Promote mentoring and other career development activities, especially for women and minorities. Provide support for mentors and mentees. Encourage formal and informal organizational activities that allow increased contact between members of diverse groups. Get the organization to promote and value multiple ways of communicating and relating while maintaining high performance standards.
Team	Align members and subgroups on a common identity and goal. Encourage members to "think globally." Clarify team norms and procedures around information exchange, communication, and coordination. Examine work structure and flow. Redesign or build in mechanisms that allow for greater flexibility. Understand how individuals and subgroups from different cultures work. Emphasize respect and inclusion. Provide incentives (e.g., recognition) for collaborating and achieving overall goals. Rotate meeting times and agenda so different members or subgroups are heard first. Explore and maximize use of synchronous and asynchronous communication technology.	Design and implement cross-cultural and international management development programs. Encourage selection and development of diverse team leaders (including those outside host country). Provide coaching. Help managers design more effective meetings especially among diverse and geographically dispersed teams. Consult on meeting design and use of technology. Facilitate teambuilding, problem solving, knowledge exchange, and other collaborative activities (both in-person and virtual). Make relevant information about specific cultures and countries (e.g., religion, history, politics) easily accessible to employees. Provide expertise about new structures and processes to enhance team effectiveness. Consult with the organization about designing appropriate and equitable reward programs for diverse international employees.

TABLE 7.2

Basic, Multicultural, and International–Global Competencies for Individuals and Teams

Level	Fundamental	Multicultural	International-global
Individual			
Knowledge	Self-awareness	Cultural self-awareness	Global self-awareness
Skills	Self-management	Cultural self-management	Continuous global learning
Attitudes	Openness to experience	Tolerance of ambiguity	International and global mind-set
Interpersonal			
Knowledge	Interpersonal intelligence	Cultural intelligence (metacognitive and cognitive CQ)	International and global intelligence
Skills	Perspective taking Communication, negotiation, and conflict resolution	Cultural intelligence (behavioral CQ) Cross-cultural communication, negotiation, and conflict resolution	Diverse communication skills International and global adaptability Creating innovation
Attitudes	Respect, trust	Cultural intelligence (motivational CQ); Cultural empathy	Courage
Team			
Knowledge	Group dynamics Team leadership	Multicultural and diverse teams	Global and virtual teams
Skills	Managing intra- and interteam processes Building team relationships	Bridging and integrating cultural differences Equitable participation and information exchange	Shared understanding Global integration and knowledge transfer Trust and supportive climate
Attitudes	Motivation to collaborate	Inclusiveness	Passion for excellence and social transformation

foundation for personal control and self-management, which, in turn, serves as a building block for understanding, empathizing, and working productively with others (Whetten & Cameron, 2007). The concept of emotional intelligence (EI), generally defined as the ability to manage oneself and one's relationship with others (Goleman, 1995; Mayer, Salovey, & Caruso, 2004), has resonated strongly among managers, even though its theoretical clarity and empirical measurement are still debated among researchers (e.g., Conte, 2005). There is an increasing body of research demonstrating the links between EI and performance outcomes (Amabile & Kramer, 2007; Lopes, Grewal, Kadis, Gall, & Salovey, 2006). Being open to experience is a foundational attitude because it facilitates individual motivation for growth and development. Although openness to experience has often been presented as one of the Big Five personality traits, we conceive of it here as a personal belief or mind-set that can and should be encouraged and developed, consistent with Dweck's (1999, 2008) research on malleable or incremental self-attributes.

At the interpersonal level, people need interpersonal intelligence to be effective in their relationships with others. By *interpersonal intelligence*, we mean not only being aware of others' perspectives and emotions (the second half of EI) but also having knowledge about effective communication, power and influence, conflict resolution, and motivation. Interpersonal intelligence provides people with a platform for understanding, but for this intelligence to be effective, it needs to be translated into behavior in skill areas including perspective taking, oral and written communication skills, and influence tactics; application of strategies for reaching agreement and resolving conflicts constructively; and diagnosing interpersonal and motivational problems and providing feedback. Developing interpersonal intelligence and skills can be accomplished through various means, such as reading, formal instruction, case analysis, structured skill practice and application, and feedback and coaching (Whetten & Cameron, 2007). Having a respectful attitude and a willingness to trust others supports interpersonal intelligence and allows skills to flourish.

At the team level, the individual and interpersonal competencies discussed here must be supplemented by knowledge specific to group dynamics and leadership. To work effectively in a team requires a basic understanding of the stages of group development, task and social processes, communication, cooperation, competition, group motivation, and cohesion (Levi, 2010). It also requires knowledge about leadership (e.g., formal and informal bases of power, leadership theories and styles) as well as best practices for setting up teams for success through various task, social, and commitment-building strategies (Beatty & Barker Scott, 2004; Hackman, 2003; Wagerman, Fisher, & Hackman, 2009). Team leaders can develop skills to manage intrateam processes such as selecting team members; clarifying team vision and mission; setting goals; clarifying roles; identifying norms and protocols for communication, problem solving, decision making, and conflict resolution; and fostering member relationships. At the same time, team leaders can develop skills to manage processes and relationships with other teams inside and outside their organizations because the team typically exists and contributes as part of a larger entity. Appropriately, the motivation to collaborate with others, stemming from an appreciation of the potential power of the team, is the requisite attitude for working effectively within teams. Team skills can be developed through formal and informal instruction; within organizations, they can also be developed through team development interventions.

The KSATs we have discussed provide a basic foundation for working effectively with others. However, as people interact in increasingly multicultural contexts, either within the United States or within other countries or regions, additional KSATs become vital. Several multicultural competency models emphasize cultural self-awareness as the foundation for multicultural competence (Fouad & Arredondo, 2007; Hansen, Pepitone, Arreola, Rockwell, & Greene, 2000; Sue, 2001). This means knowing oneself culturally, in terms of one's heritage, personal identity, values, and assumptions. At the skills level, the person is able to acknowledge how such cultural characteristics influence personal goals, attitudes, and behavior toward others. This includes the ability to acknowledge that one's beliefs represent just one of many ways of looking at the world. A culturally aware individual recognizes the dangers of personal biases and assumptions and consciously seeks opportunities to expand one's learning and cultural repertoire. Tolerance for ambiguity is an important attitude for the multiculturally competent individual, given the need to deal with cultural uncertainty and balance multiple worldviews (Matveev & Nelson, 2004).

In the multicultural context, we argue that interpersonal-level cultural self-awareness needs to be coupled with cultural intelligence (CQ). Earley and Ang (2003) described CQ in terms of the individual's mental (metacognitive and cognitive), behavioral, and motivational capabilities to function effectively in a culturally diverse settings. These factors correspond neatly with the requisite knowledge, skills, and attitudes for working interpersonally and multiculturally in Table 7.2. *Cognitive* CQ refers to having knowledge and knowledge structures regarding different cultures, such as knowledge of cultural norms and conventions. *Metacognitive* CQ refers to personal consciousness and awareness able to be used during intercultural interactions. Having cultural knowledge allows the individual to anticipate and diagnose cultural difficulties that may emerge and identify suitable responses (Offermann & Phan, 2002). At the skill level, *behavioral* CQ refers to the person's capacity to enact "situationally appropriate behavior from a broad repertoire of verbal and nonverbal behaviors" (Ng, Van Dyne, & Ang, 2009, p. 515). Having high behavioral CQ means being able to identify and adapt various strategies to communicate, negotiate, and resolve conflicts with an individual from a different culture. In terms of attitude, the motivational CQ component highlights the importance of being confident and intrinsically motivated to interact with others in a multicultural setting (Earley & Ang, 2003). Additionally, *cultural empathy* (the capacity to understand and appreciate the world from the cultural lens of others) is critical in multicultural interactions (Matveev & Nelson, 2004).

CQ and empathy can be developed through experiential learning methods (Ng et al., 2009). Experiential learning takes place (Kolb, 1984) through a deliberate cyclical process of experiencing, reflecting, conceptualizing, and experimenting on new behaviors (Kolb, 1984). This process can be applied in, for example, classrooms, leadership programs, and domestic and international assignments. At the multicultural team level, knowledge about how diversity affects team functioning is essential (Connaughton & Shuffler, 2007; Levi, 2010; Mannix & Neale, 2005). Although diversity within teams is typically expected to enhance creativity and innovation, actual research evidence has shown that this potential is often not reached because of social categorization of team members into ingroups and outgroups that may foster stereotyping, create intergroup conflict, slant participation in favor of majority members, reduce team cohesion, and interfere with overall team functioning (Mannix & Neale, 2005). Diverse team members often have differing cultural assumptions about what it means to be part of a team and thus operate from different behavioral norms (Gibson & Zellmer-Bruhn, 2001). Team leaders need the skills to identify, bridge, and integrate differences among the team members to enhance information exchange (Lane, DiStefano, & Maznevski, 2000). This process can be accomplished through mechanisms we described earlier, such as creating a common identity, setting superordinate goals, and encouraging equitable participation (Van der Vegt & Bunderson, 2005). Team leaders must also be comfortable using strategies to bring diverse opinions to the surface, especially from minority group members. These multicultural team knowledge and skills can be developed through reading, classroom training, team process observation and facilitation, and coaching. The requisite attitude should be inclusiveness, a "pluralistic value frame" that values and strives to accommodate multiple cultural perspectives (Mor Barak, 2005, p. 8).

Finally, when working in an international and global context, individuals need to add more components to their set of competencies. Unfortunately, current research on diversity management still tends to be U.S.-centric and does not fully address issues related to the cultural contextualization of diversity, language, and social class diversity (Jonsen, Maznevski, & Schneider, 2011). These three areas, with the addition of time, geographic dispersion, increased technological usage, and virtuality, are most pertinent to international and global contexts.

At the individual international–global level, we encourage individuals to cultivate a stronger global self-awareness (Buchan et al., 2011). That is, in addition to personal and cultural identities, national identity influences the way we interpret and respond to others from other countries. Even those who have completed diversity training (Rynes & Rosen, 1995) recognize that the cultural differences and models they have been exposed to in the United States do not necessarily apply to the same extent or in the same way in other countries and regions. As such, they would do well to hone skills related to continuous global learning, continuously acquiring new knowledge about international and global matters and continually testing and evaluating personal or national assumptions vis-à-vis other worldviews. From an attitudinal perspective, to be effective in the contemporary world of work, individuals can begin to adopt an international and global mind-set, in which they consider themselves as being "citizens of the world" (Bartlett, Ghoshal, & Birkinshaw, 2004; Cummings & Worley, 2009). In this manner, they will develop interest in global issues and believe they have personal or professional roles and responsibilities within the worldwide arena instead of just their local or domestic spheres.

As people work with others in the international–global context, they enhance their international–global intelligence by understanding the key drivers of the business and how it is conducted in various countries and cultures where the organization maintains partners, employees, customers, suppliers, and other stakeholders (Dalton & Ernst, 2004). They can build on their knowledge of the histories, laws, and customs of these countries so that they can leverage organizational and employee capabilities to meet organizational goals within these international contexts. Working with other people internationally requires diverse communication skills. Ideally, individuals would possess foreign language skills or, at the very least, knowledge of key words and phrases to demonstrate respect for other cultures. They are adept at using various communication media—in-person, e-mail, phone, and web-conferencing, for example. They become internationally and globally adaptable, that is, able to take their behavioral CQ to the next level by demonstrating culturally appropriate words, tones, gestures, and other responses when interacting with others from various countries. Furthermore, truly international leaders are able to create innovation by leveraging the positive aspects of different countries and cultures and creating synergistic results in the form of new ideas, policies, practices, products or services (Dalton & Ernst, 2004). Working internationally takes courage, strength of mind, and will was well as willingness to take risks by trying new ways of thinking and behaving.

Finally, working with teams at the international–global level requires knowledge of the unique issues and challenges faced by global and virtual teams. Marquardt and Horvath (2001) outlined five challenges facing global teams: (a) managing cultural diversity, differences, and conflicts; (b) dealing with geographic distances, dispersion, and despair; (c) solving coordination and control issues; (d) maintaining communication richness over distances; and (e) developing and maintaining teamness. In particular, virtual teams have to deal with technological challenges, which are complicated not only by technological sophistication and reliability but also by the differing levels of access, resources, technological support, and norms around the use of technology (Cramton & Orvis, 2003).

With these considerations in mind, team leaders must have the skills to create three conditions that enable global, virtual team success (Gibson, 2011; Hinds & Mortensen, 2005): (a) shared understanding and identity, (b) integration, and (c) a trusting and supportive communication climate. To facilitate shared understanding and identity, leaders can engage the team in a discussion of their shared vision and goals; to reach agreements about tasks, norms, and work processes; and to foster appreciation for what individual team members and subgroups bring to the table. Integration in this model refers to the global coordination of work across individuals, subgroups, geographic distances, and time zones. Recent studies have highlighted the ability to facilitate knowledge management and transfer within and across geographically dispersed business units as critical to performance and innovation (Hajro & Pudelko, 2010; Zakaria, Amelinckx, & Wilemon, 2004). Team leaders must be particularly competent with various information-sharing and communication modalities in virtual environments (Grosse, 2002).

Global integration can also be enhanced through structural partnerships between team members in similar roles across work sites; social mechanisms such as virtual and face-to-face orientations and informal gatherings, role clarification, and the deliberate facilitation of information exchange during meetings (Gibson, 2011). Team leaders can build a supportive and trusting communication climate through active listening, framing and follow-up, encouraging the exchange of social information, acknowledging "risky" disclosures and celebrating supportive responses, and paying regular attention to levels of openness, trust, and psychological safety within their teams (Gibson & Cohen, 2003).

Concerning attitude, international and global leaders seek to motivate and inspire others (Hajro & Pudelko, 2010) and are passionate about excellence and social transformation. These attitudes are particularly crucial in a complex, uncertain, global environment. In the words of an American HR director working with an international team to craft a global HR strategy and system, "Beyond learning and working through our differences, it is as if we are all driven to create a new and better world for ourselves and our employees through the work we are doing" (Lopez & Ensari, 2011).

CONCLUSION AND FUTURE DIRECTIONS

There is a growing and urgent need to acknowledge and understand the complexities of working with diverse and global teams consisting of members from different regions and countries who have multiple cultural identities. In this chapter, some of these complexities were depicted in the case of Tanisha and the Argos CRM team, followed by potential solutions to these challenges and the presentation of key competencies for individuals as well as teams in a multicultural and international setting. Despite the threats of group separatism, assimilation, and ethnic hierarchies (Frederickson, 1999), organizations, in general, seek to acquire a diverse workforce in an attempt to maximize human capital, creativity, collaboration, and competitive advantage in the global market. We believe that understanding these competencies and creating an organizational culture and structure that supports individual and team development are the key components of truly multicultural organizations.

Projecting into the future, there are emerging concepts, such as post-multiculturalism transnationalism, and super-diversity (Vertovec, 2010), that organizational psychologists are starting to address. For instance, is multiculturalism truly desired universally? How do various individuals, teams, or organizations perceive diversity? For example, researchers have found that multiculturalism tends to appeal more to U.S. minority group members such as African Americans than to majority group members such as White Americans (Lambert & Taylor, 1988). Simple categorization along a single dimension does not necessarily capture the dynamics of today's complex relationships (Ensari & Miller, 2001); thus, a postmodernist approach offers a new perspective that recognizes the coexistence of multiple realities and perspectives and emphasizes multiple, local truths rather than a singular, universal truth (D'Andrea, 2000; White & Epston, 1990). We suggest that today's organizations become more familiar with the postmodernist approach and understand its consequences. One consequence of multiple categorization is that identification with more than one salient social group changes well-established fundamental psychological processes such as perception, personality, cognition, attributions, social interaction, and identity formation (Benet-Martínez, Leu, Lee, & Morris, 2002; Vera & Quintana, 2004). Another implication of this perspective is that social identities can have an interactive effect such that, for instance, gender, race, and sexual preference aspects of identity may combine in complex ways (Bowleg, 2008). This interactive effect is called *intersectionality* and refers to the manner in which multiple aspects of identity may combine in different ways to construct social reality (Cole, 2009; Shields, 2008).

We recommend that future research empirically examine the complexities associated with the intersection of the multiple identities to enhance ecological validity. Moreover, organizations seeking to make strides in multiculturalism and internationalism would do well to acknowledge that employees come with multiple identities that may interact and affect individual, interpersonal, or organizational outcomes. The use of these modern and postmodernist perspectives will likely have a positive impact on various strategic initiatives, including the training and development of multicultural and international competencies.

REFERENCES

Amabile, T. M., & Kramer, S. J. (2007). Inner work life: Understanding the subtext of business performance. *Harvard Business Review, 85,* 72–83.

Baker, G. C. (1983). *Planning and organizing for multicultural instruction.* Reading, MA: Addison-Wesley.

Bartlett, C., Ghoshal, S., & Birkinshaw, J. (2004). *Transnational management* (4th ed.). New York, NY: McGraw-Hill.

Beatty, C. A., & Barker Scott, B. A. (2004). *Building smart teams. A roadmap to high performance.* Thousand Oaks, CA: Sage.

Benet-Martínez, V., Leu, J., Lee, F., & Morris, M. (2002). Negotiating biculturalism: Cultural frame-switching in biculturals with "oppositional" vs. "compatible" cultural identities. *Journal of Cross-Cultural Psychology, 33,* 492–516. doi:10.1177/0022022102033005005

Berry, J. W., Poortinga, Y. H., Segall, M. H., & Dasen, P. R. (2002). *Cross-cultural psychology: Research and applications* (2nd ed.). Cambridge, England: Cambridge University Press.

Bowleg, L. (2008). When Black + lesbian + woman ≠ Black lesbian woman: The methodological challenges of qualitative and quantitative intersectionality research. *Sex Roles, 59,* 312–325. doi:10.1007/s11199-008-9400-z

Brett, J., Behfar, K., & Kern, M. C. (2006). Managing multicultural teams. *Harvard Business Review, 84*(11), 84–91.

Brewer, M. B. (1991). The social self: On being the same and different at the same time. *Personality and Social Psychology Bulletin, 17,* 475–482. doi:10.1177/0146167291175001

Brewer, M. B., & Schneider, S. (1990). Social identity and social dilemmas: A double-edged sword. In D. Abrams & M. A. Hogg (Eds.), *Social identity theory: Constructive and critical advances* (pp. 169–184). London, England: Harvester-Wheatsheaf.

Buchan, N. R., Brewer, M. B., Grimalda, G., Wilson, R. K., Fatas, E., & Foddy, M. (2011). Global social identity and global cooperation. *Psychological Science, 22,* 821–828. doi:10.1177/0956797611409590

Cokley, K., Dreher, G., & Stockdale, M. S. (2004). Toward inclusiveness and career success of African Americans in the workplace. In M. S. Stockdale & F. J. Crosby (Eds.), *The psychology and management of workplace diversity* (pp. 168–190). Malden, MA: Blackwell.

Cole, E. R. (2009). Intersectionality and research in psychology. *American Psychologist, 64,* 170–180. doi:10.1037/a0014564

Connaughton, S. L., & Shuffler, M. (2007). Multinational and multicultural distributed teams: A review and future agenda. *Small Group Research, 38*, 387–412. doi:10.1177/1046496407301970

Connerley, M. L., & Pedersen, P. B. (2005). *Leadership in a diverse and multicultural environment: Developing awareness, knowledge and skills.* Thousand Oaks, CA: Sage.

Conte, J. M. (2005). A review and critique of emotional intelligence measures. *Journal of Organizational Behavior, 26*, 433–440. doi:10.1002/job.319

Cummings, T. G., & Worley, C. G. (2009). *Organization development and change* (9th ed.). Cincinnati, OH: South-Western College Publishing.

Cramton, D. C., & Orvis, K. L. (2003). Overcoming barriers to information sharing in virtual teams. In C. Gibson & S. G. Cohen (Eds.), *Virtual teams that work: Creating conditions for virtual team effectiveness* (pp. 214–230). San Francisco, CA: Jossey-Bass.

Dalton, M., & Ernst, C. T. (2004). Developing leaders for global roles. In C. McCauley & E. V. Elsor (Eds.), *The Center for Creative Leadership handbook for leadership development* (pp. 361–382). San Francisco, CA: Jossey-Bass.

D'Andrea, M. (2000). Postmodernism, constructivism, and multiculturalism: Three forces reshaping and expanding our thoughts about counseling. *Journal of Mental Health Counseling, 22*(1), 1–16.

Dweck, C. S. (1999). *Self-theories: Their role in motivation, personality and development.* Philadelphia, PA: Taylor & Francis/Psychology Press.

Dweck, C. S. (2008). Can personality be changed? The role of beliefs in personality and change. *Current Directions in Psychological Science, 17*, 391–394. doi:10.1111/j.1467-8721.2008.00612.x

Eagly, A. H., & Karau, S. J. (2002). Role congruity theory of prejudice toward female leaders. *Psychological Review, 109*, 573–598. doi:10.1037/0033-295X.109.3.573

Eagly, A. H., & Steffen, V. J. (1984). Gender stereotypes stem from the distribution of women and men into social roles. *Journal of Personality and Social Psychology, 46*, 735–754. doi:10.1037/0022-3514.46.4.735

Earley, P. C., & Ang, S. (2003). *Cultural intelligence: Individual interactions across cultures.* Palo Alto, CA: Stanford University Press.

Ensari, N., & Miller, N. (2001). Decategorization and the reduction of bias in the crossed categorization paradigm. *European Journal of Social Psychology, 31*, 193–216. doi:10.1002/ejsp.42

Fouad, N., & Arredondo, P. (2007). *Becoming culturally oriented: Practical advice for psychologists and educators.* Washington, DC: American Psychological Association.

Frederickson, G. M. (1999). Models of American interethnic relations: A historical perspective. In D. Prentice & D. Miller (Eds.), *Cultural divides: Understanding and overcoming group conflict* (pp. 23–34). New York, NY: Russell Sage Foundation.

Gaertner, S. L., Dovidio, J. F., Anastasio, P. A., Bachman, B. A., & Rust, M. C. (1993). The common ingroup identity model: Recategorization and the reduction of intergroup bias. *European Review of Social Psychology, 4*, 1–26.

Gassmann, O. (2001). Multicultural teams: Increasing creativity and innovation by diversity. *Creativity and Innovation Management, 10,* 88–95. doi:10.1111/1467-8691.00206

George, J. M., & Jones, G. R. (2005). *Understanding and managing organizational behavior* (4th ed.). Upper Saddle River, NJ: Prentice Hall.

Gibson, C. B. (2011). Collaborating with virtuality: Leveraging enabling conditions to improve team effectiveness. In J. S. Osland & M. E. Turner (Eds.), *The organizational behavior reader* (9th ed., pp. 298–309). Upper Saddle River, NJ: Prentice Hall.

Gibson, C. B., & Cohen, S. G. (Eds.). (2003) *Virtual teams that work: Creating conditions for virtual team effectiveness.* San Francisco, CA: Jossey-Bass.

Gibson, C. B., & Zellmer-Bruhn, M. E. (2001). Metaphors and meaning: An intercultural analysis of the concept of teamwork. *Administrative Science Quarterly, 46,* 274–303. doi:10.2307/2667088

Goleman, D. (1995). *Emotional intelligence.* New York, NY: Bantam.

Gooderham, P. N., & Nordhaug, O. (2003). *International management: Cross-boundary challenges.* Malden, MA: Blackwell.

Grosse, C. U. (2002). Managing communication within virtual intercultural teams. *Business Communication Quarterly, 65*(4), 22–38. doi:10.1177/108056990206500404

Hackman, J. R. (2003). *Leading teams.* Cambridge, MA: Harvard Business School Press.

Hajro, A., & Pudelko, M. (2010). An analysis of core-competences of successful multinational team leaders. *International Journal of Cross Cultural Management, 10,* 175–194. doi:10.1177/1470595810370910

Hall, E. T., & Hall, M. R. (1995). *Understanding cultural differences.* Yarmouth, ME: Intercultural Press.

Hansen, N. D., Pepitone-Arreola-Rockwell, F., & Greene, A. F. (2000). Multicultural competence: Criteria and case examples. *Professional Psychology: Research and Practice, 31,* 652–660. doi:10.1037/0735-7028.31.6.652

Hinds, P. J., & Mortensen, M. (2005). Understanding conflict in geographically distributed teams: The moderating effects of shared identity, shared context, and spontaneous communication. *Organization Science, 14,* 615–632. doi:10.1287/orsc.14.6.615.24872

Hofstede, G. (2001). *Culture's consequences: Comparing values, behaviors, institutions, and organizations across nations* (2nd ed.). Thousand Oaks, CA: Sage.

Jarvenpaa, S. L., & Leidner, D. E. (1999). Communication and trust in global virtual teams. *Organization Science, 10,* 791–815. doi:10.1287/orsc.10.6.791

Jonsen, K., Maznevski, M., & Schneider, S. (2011). Special review article: Diversity and its not so diverse literature: An international perspective. *International Journal of Cross Cultural Management, 11*(1), 35–62. doi:10.1177/1470595811398798

Kierein, N. M., & Gold, M. A. (2000). Pygmalion in work organizations: A meta-analysis. *Journal of Organizational Behavior, 21,* 913–928. doi:10.1002/1099-1379(200012)21:8<913::AID-JOB62>3.0.CO;2-#

Kluckhohn, F. R., & Strodtbeck, F. L. (1961). *Variations in value orientations*. Evanston, IL: Row, Peterson.

Kolb, D. A. (1984). *Experiential learning: Experience as the source of learning and development*. Englewood Cliffs, NJ: Prentice Hall.

Lambert, W. E., & Taylor, D. M. (1988). Assimilation versus multiculturalism: The views of urban Americans. *Sociological Forum, 3*, 72–88. doi:10.1007/BF01115124

Lane, H. W., DiStefano, J. J., & Maznevski, M. L. (2000). *International management behavior. Text, readings and cases* (4th ed.). Malden, MA: Blackwell.

Lev-Ari, S., & Keysar, B. (2010). Why don't we believe non-native speakers? The influence of accent on credibility. *Journal of Experimental Social Psychology, 46*, 1093–1096. doi:10.1016/j.jesp.2010.05.025

Levi, D. J. (2010). *Group dynamics for teams* (3rd ed.). Thousand Oaks, CA: Sage.

Lopes, P. N., Grewal, D., Kadis, J., Gall, M., & Salovey, P. (2006). Evidence that emotional intelligence is related to job performance and affect and attitudes at work. *Psicothema, 18*, 132–138.

Lopez, P. D., & Ensari, N. (2011). *An interview study on managers' and diversity experts' perceptions of multiculturalism and internationalism in organizations*. Unpublished manuscript, California School of Professional Psychology, Alliant International University/Los Angeles, Alhambra, CA.

Mannix, E., & Neale, M. A. (2005). What differences make a difference? The promise and reality of diverse teams in organizations. *Psychological Science in the Public Interest, 6*(2), 31–55. doi:10.1111/j.1529-1006.2005.00022.x

Marquardt, M. J., & Horvath, L. (2001). *Global teams: How top multinationals span boundaries and cultures with high-speed teamwork*. Palo Alto, CA: Davies-Black.

Matveev, A. V., & Nelson, P. E. (2004). Cross cultural communication competence and multicultural team performance: Perceptions of American and Russian managers. *International Journal of Cross Cultural Management, 4*, 253–270. doi:10.1177/1470595804044752

Mayer, J. D., Salovey, P., & Caruso, D. R. (2004). Emotional intelligence: Theory, findings, and implications. *Psychological Inquiry, 15*, 197–215. doi:10.1207/s15327965pli1503_02

Mor Barak, M. E. (2005). *Managing diversity: Toward a globally inclusive workplace*. Thousand Oaks, CA: Sage.

Ng, K., Van Dyne, L., & Ang, S. (2009). From experience to experiential learning: Cultural intelligence as a learning capability for global leader development. *Academy of Management Learning & Education, 8*, 511–526. doi:10.5465/AMLE.2009.47785470

Offermann, L. R., & Phan, L. U. (2002). Culturally intelligent leadership for a diverse world. In R. E. Riggio, S. E. Murphy, & F. J. Pirozzolo (Eds.), *Multiple intelligences and leadership* (pp. 187–214). Mahwah, NJ: Erlbaum.

Rosenthal, R., & Rubin, D. (1978). Interpersonal expectancy effects: The first 345 studies. *Behavioral and Brain Sciences, 1*, 377–415. doi:10.1017/S0140525X00075506

Ruscher, J. B. (2001). *Prejudiced communication: A social psychological perspective*. New York, NY: Guilford Press.

Rynes, S., & Rosen, B. (1995). A field survey of factors affecting the adoption and perceived success of diversity training. *Personnel Psychology, 48*, 247–270. doi:10.1111/j.1744-6570.1995.tb01756.x

Shields, S. A. (2008). Gender: An intersectionality perspective. *Sex Roles, 59*, 301–311. doi:10.1007/s11199-008-9501-8

Sue, D. W. (2001). Multidimensional facets of cultural competence. *The Counseling Psychologist, 29*, 790–821. doi:10.1177/0011000001296002

Stewart, G., & Barrick, M. R. (2000). Team structure and performance: Assessing the mediating role of intrateam process and the moderating role of task type. *Academy of Management Journal, 43*, 135–148. doi:10.2307/1556372

Tajfel, H., & Turner, J. C. (1986). The social identity theory of inter-group behavior. In S. Worchel & L. W. Austin (Eds.), *Psychology of intergroup relations* (pp. 7–24). Chicago, IL: Nelson-Hall.

Thompson, J. D. (1967). *Organizations in action*. New York, NY: McGraw-Hill.

Van der Vegt, G. S., & Bunderson, J. S. (2005). Learning and performance in multidisciplinary teams: The importance of collective team identification. *Academy of Management Journal, 48*, 532–547.

Vera, E. M., & Quintana, S. M. (2004). Ethnic identity development of Chicana/o children. In R. J. Velasquez, B. M. McNeill, & L. Arellano (Eds.), *Handbook of Chicana and Chicano psychology* (pp. 43–59). Mahwah, NJ: Erlbaum.

Vertovec, S. (2010). Towards post-multiculturalism? Changing communities, conditions and contexts of diversity. *International Social Science Journal, 61*, 83–95. doi:10.1111/j.1468-2451.2010.01749.x

Wagerman, R., Fisher, C. M., & Hackman, J. R. (2009). Leading teams when the time is right: Finding the best moments to act. *Organizational Dynamics, 38*, 192–203.

Whetten, D. A., & Cameron, K. S. (2007). *Developing management skills*. Upper Saddle River, NJ: Prentice Hall.

White, M., & Epston, D. (1990). *Narrative means to therapeutic ends*. New York, NY: Norton.

Wilkins, W. E. (1976). The concept of a self-fulfilling prophecy. *Sociology of Education, 49*, 175–183.

Zakaria, N., Amelinckx, A., & Wilemon, D. (2004). Working together apart? Building a knowledge-sharing culture for global virtual teams. *Creativity and Innovation Management, 13*, 15–29. doi:10.1111/j.1467-8691.2004.00290.x

Zweifel, T. D. (2003). *Culture clash: Managing the global high-performance team*. New York, NY: Selectbooks.

8

ORGANIZATIONS IN MULTICULTURAL AND INTERNATIONAL CONTEXTS: INSIGHTS FOR THE GLOBAL LEADER

LOUISE KELLY AND WENDY CHUNG

Globalization, which refers to the increasing integration of the world's economic system through the reduction of barriers to international trade (Croucher, 2004, p. 10), has collapsed the barriers of time and space internationally. The concept of globalization is certainly not relegated to economic integration. As De Mooij (2011) suggested, it could be applied to a series of developments related to the creation and reproduction of the social systems of the world as a whole. These include the rise of capitalism, Western imperialism, and the development of the global media system, all made manifest in a mind-set that facilitates cultural, educational, technological, and service-orientated integration. It has created interdependence among businesses and countries that encompasses many diverse cultures (Ergeneli, Gohar, & Temibekova, 2007). Along with organizational diversity comes the resulting interconnectedness of peoples around the world, which has created networks of multiculturally diverse organizational members from across international

DOI: 10.1037/14044-008
Internationalizing Multiculturalism: Expanding Professional Competencies in a Globalized World,
R. L. Lowman (Editor)

borders. These changes, growing more rapid and expansive with each passing year, have also produced many new problems and challenges.

Globalism has created a demand for organizational leaders who are sophisticated in international management and leadership strategies. The goal of this chapter, therefore, is to explore global leadership in contemporary organizational contexts. The focus is particularly on the overlap of internationalism with, and its divergences from, multicultural (diversity) concepts in organizations. We argue that for the global organization to succeed, its leadership must invest significantly in embedding a global mind-set into the organization's culture. The role of leaders in creating an organizational culture that advances and supports globalism is elaborated. Alternative approaches to examining the globalization process and the diversity phenomenon within organizations are explored, along with issues in the integration of these approaches. Strategies and considerations are identified for leaders as they create the *third culture*—a negotiated organizational culture—in which globalism can thrive. Finally, issues and needs in globalizing leaders and organizations are discussed and approaches identified that are currently being used in leadership research across nations, governments, and industries.

We do not come to this topic randomly. The first author (Kelly) has lived on two continents, been an immigrant twice, and dealt with minority status in two of three countries where she has lived. The second author (Chung) has triple minority status through emigration, ethnicity, and gender. As a result of the intersection of their international and multicultural identities, both authors have taken leadership positions in their institutions around international and multicultural issues.

GLOBALIZATION IN BUSINESS

Although we use the terms *international* and *multicultural* in this chapter, the more widely used terms in business are *globalization* and *diversity*. As a general term, *globalization* has to do specifically with markets and market-driven decisions that arise from the greater integration across markets and the resultant increased flows of foreign direct investment (Ghemawat, 2011). We argue that many businesses—with varying degrees of success and innovation—are in fact working to embrace both of these perspectives (here termed *global diversity* and *global leadership*).

The concept of global leadership emerged in part from the needs of corporations since the 1990s to adopt global strategies, to expand internationally, and to compete in the global marketplace (Reade, Todd, Osland, & Osland, 2008). Corporate leaders have become more concerned with these issues as they have realized that their employees were often not prepared for the challenges of operating in a global business environment. In addition, it was clear that managers with global capabilities were increasingly needed to develop and implement new international strategic initiatives and to create the third culture—an organizational culture that is a strategic blend of diverse organizational members (Rhinesmith, 1993).

Not surprisingly, the globalization of business entities has been driven largely by the profit motive, which is the essence of free-market capitalism. Economic gains from globalization have been possible because of the reality of competitive (and comparative) advantage, primarily deriving from differing labor rates around the globe. These drivers are changing, however, and cultural and leadership factors are taking on increasing importance (Byrne & Bradley, 2007). We suggest in this chapter that improvement in the organizational culture and climate (enhancement of the level of commitment of workers, as well as of their growth and development) and improvement of the organization's chances of global success by any measure will come with careful nurturing of a diverse workforce and respect for cultural differences internationally. In this chapter, we acknowledge the convergence and divergence approaches to examining the globalization process and the global diversity phenomenon in organizations. The *convergence* approach considers the need for organizations to adapt to the global marketplace, whereas the *divergence* approach focuses more on how organizational norms and functions affect the ways in which meaning is constructed in various cultural environments (Stohl, 2001). There is an obvious tension between these two approaches, so we consider first their integration at both the organizational and individual levels. We also discuss ways to leverage this integration when creating an organizational culture in which global diversity can thrive. Finally, we discuss implications of our major points for leadership in organizations.

THE GLOBAL DIVERSITY PHENOMENON: AN INTEGRATED CONCEPT

There has been a great deal of interest in and debate about the cultural effects of globalization (Eisenberg, Goodall, & Trethwey, 2010; House, Hanges, Javidan, Dorfman, & Gupta, 2004; Miller, 2003; Stage, 1999; Zahra, 1999). The discussion has included whether globalization changes are utopian or dystopian (Miller, 2003). The *utopian* perspective views globalization as a catalyst for escalating the transfer of technologies, for bringing cultures and societies together, and for creating a community of peace-loving, intelligent citizens (Samovar & Porter, 1991). In this view, continued globalization will help facilitate cooperation and goodwill among nations. It has the potential to become an instrument for world peace as well as for progress and prosperity across nations. In stark contrast is the *dystopian* argument that globalization will undermine the integrity of a country's political and social institutions and therefore weaken its cultural makeup. Some are also concerned about the possibility of less developed economies becoming more technologically, politically, and economically dependent on developed-nation economies (Zahra, 1999).

As organizations globalize, changes often become evident. One of the most salient of these, according to Monge (1998), is that global consciousness and self-reflexivity become manifest within the organization. *Global consciousness* refers to the sense that there is a collective consciousness in which all individuals participate (Barnes, 1994; Robertson, 2003; Surowiecki, 2004). *Self-reflexivity*, in this discussion of intercultural communication, means to analyze one's own behavior consistently to understand how culture influences one's actions (Nagata, 2004). With these two changes, awareness of one's own culture and the culture of others is heightened.

We believe that all employees, but especially the leaders, of global organizations, must be conscious of the impact of multiculturalism and internationalism (global diversity) on organizational processes. Equally important, they must be cognizant of the inevitable tensions between *cultural convergence*—the need for contemporary organizations to conform, on the one hand—and *cultural divergence*, the pull of cultural identification and of maintaining traditional values and conventional practices—on the other hand (Stohl, 2001).

Global organizational leaders, we argue, must be able to deal effectively with these tensions, beginning with the recognition of the multicultural and international dynamics in a globally diverse organizational context. One way of dealing effectively with these tensions is the recognition and integration of the so-called third culture, which refers to a phenomenon that emerges when two cultures are negotiated and transformed into one common, "third" culture through a strategic blending of beliefs, values, and ways of conducting business (W. V. Schmidt, Conaway, Easton, & Wardrope, 2007). When approached from this perspective, global diversity efforts shift from a focus on either the convergent or divergent approach to one that creates a third, negotiated culture in which, for example, the multinational organization and host country can successfully coexist (W. V. Schmidt et al., 2007). As an integrated concept, global diversity's key goal is to use the third culture to create synergy between culturally diverse organizational members. The objective, as P. L. Schmidt (2007) suggested, is to increase effectiveness by sharing perceptions, insights, and knowledge. Such an integrated approach of using cross-cultural knowledge may require some of or all of the five conditions for learning suggested by Peterson (2007): insight, motivating, capabilities, real-world practice, and accountability. The coaching system that Peterson outlined shifts individuals from their usual thinking, behaviors, and performance patterns to expanded thinking and enhanced performance, toward a more integrated sense of self with a view to sustainable development, and ultimately to greater success.

In the first stage of this process, the manager or leader gains new insights from interviews and surveys within the organization. Then, through appreciative inquiry, information is gathered on abilities, goals, and values as self-identified. These self-identified abilities, goals, and values are then synthesized with the views of others in the organization, with the goal of defining a common view of success factors in the organization.

As organizations strive toward authentic global diversity, not only do they combine their workforces to produce goods and services, they also invest significant efforts in negotiating and converging worldviews, values, and ways of doing business. This creates the third culture in which critical business decisions are made and complex international business problems can be successfully solved. Extensive research (Marquardt & Horvath, 2001; McLeod & Lobel, 1992; Watson, Kuman, & Michaelson, 1993) has suggested that the culturally diverse workforce, whether domestic or international, outperforms homogenous groups when identifying and solving problems. As an example, culturally diverse groups produce a significantly higher number of realistic and useable ideas and solutions than do homogeneous groups (Daily, Whatley, Ash, & Steiner, 1996).

Global diversity strategies, then, must address the management of multiculturalism but within an international context. Because multicultural and unique individuals make up the fabric of any organization in search of a global stance, they must be identified and managed. Global diversity management, anchored in a convergent approach, was defined by Karabacakoglu and Ozbilgin (2010) as being "a set of activities and strategies that seek to leverage the individual distinctions of organizational members in internal and external markets—and among consumers and community groups—in an effort to enhance the global strength of the organization" (p. 79).

A study of Brazilian managers by Canen and Canen (2008) illustrated the costs of not having multicultural leadership. Their research, based on a combination of firsthand information and reconstruction of facts, demonstrated that in an organization in which there has been a tradition of constructing "otherness" and isolating the "others," the likelihood of the bullying of the outgroups (those who have been treated as "others") increases. The authors viewed this approach as a direct organizational consequence of having had extremely monocultural leaders. We suggest that more multiculturally competent leaders would have been able to provide tools and avenues for organizational conflict resolution that would minimize culturally motivated bullying of the type reported in this research.

INTRAORGANIZATIONAL DIVERSITY

There is a likely relationship between multiculturalism and internationalism. Organizational diversity suggests a network of members who are diverse in age, gender, ethnicity, religion, educational level, social class, for example. Organizations that embrace multiculturalism, according to P. Johnson (2007), will also seek to establish diversity as a competitive advantage in their quest for globalism. Such organizations value and respect all diversity and seek to create an organizational culture in which diversity is embraced as the key ingredient in generating a third culture—termed a negotiated culture—and inevitably adds to the ability of the entity to thrive.

An example of such a global organization is the company Ericsson, one of Sweden's largest telecommunication and data communication organizations. Ericsson operates in 175 countries and has had great success in focusing on, and leveraging, individual differences. This company attributes its success to the value it places on the distinctiveness of the organizational members, as a necessary first step, because it has allowed them to feel welcome to contribute their unique perspectives to enhance organizational effectiveness and improve the bottom line (Karabacakoglu & Ozbilgin, 2010). In this company, diversity of membership has been treated as an organizational asset. Holmberg and Åkerblom (2008) came to similar conclusions about the positive impact of diversity in organizations in their study of the interaction of Swedish culture and leadership styles.

Many studies of international and multicultural issues (e.g., Holmberg & Åkerblom, 2008) have used the Global Leadership and Organizational Behavior Effectiveness (GLOBE) dimensions, such as humane orientation, gender egalitarianism, and performance orientation, derived from an important study by House et al. (2004). House et al. investigated culture and leadership in organizations in 62 societies, including 17,000 middle managers. The empirical findings of the GLOBE study reinforced the idea that leadership is culturally contingent and that sensitivity to cultural differences among leaders is of increasing importance.

Although the GLOBE study (House et al., 2004) did not focus on within-country diversity, we argue that there are important links and interdependencies between the global and multicultural diversity dimension (Verbos, Gerard, Forshey, Harding, & Miller, 2007). We argue that it is multicultural identity that determines the socialization and enculturation experiences likely to be experienced within national cultures.

One trend among global organizations interested in enhancing both diversity and internationalism is the increasing prevalence of alliances between nongovernmental organizations (NGOs) and corporations (Linton, 2005). An understanding of the globalized world and the shifting political economic landscape, we believe, needs to include the study of the role of NGOs. Such organizations often provide a voice for emerging social trends and movements (e.g., sustainability). NGOs often rely on "bottom of the pyramid" (BoP) business strategies such as social entrepreneurship (Teegen & Doh, 2004). BoP strategies include selling existing goods to and sourcing familiar products from the world's four billion poorest people (Simanis, 2009). In addition, there are also specific BoP innovations, techniques, and business models that allow one to build successful business ventures, create sustainable business ecosystems, and design new technologies with the BoP in mind. Such BoP strategies can even transform entire sectors through collaborative entrepreneurship. NGOs in developing countries using BoP strategies can act as complements to both the private and government sectors and have begun to pursue alliances or to be pursued as alliance partners with multinational enterprises (MNEs) that are seeking to gain legitimacy in the areas of some of the social movements mentioned earlier.

Alliances between for-profit corporations and NGOs can allow both types of organizations to pursue commitments such as the eradication of social oppression in all forms within societies, thus helping to ensure greater participation of members of diverse social and cultural groups in the economic system. Such alliances can be mutually beneficial, increasing the corporation's engagement with broader external social responsibilities, including environmental concerns.

We see examples of such alliances in the case of fair trade coffee certification and Starbucks (Taylor, 2005). Starbucks, the international coffee purveyor, has taken seriously measures such as reforestation efforts and has helped bridge economic and social needs by paying the highest price for its coffee, even above the market price. Such practices can not only fortify goodwill but also change the concept of sustainable supply. Truly sustainable practices involve helping producers to help themselves by focusing on environmental renewal.

Another example of a successful NGO corporation alliance with a sustainable business model is that of the Rain Forest Alliance (RFA). This NGO encourages family planning and fosters organic farming, but it also tolerates the use of some chemicals that may be less than 100% organic when the suppliers can demonstrate that such practices are necessary for local economic advantage (Fridell, 2009). Sara Lee, Nestle, Smuckers, and Kraft are some of the major food producers that have entered into alliances with the RFA to pursue a sustainable business strategy. Kraft, for example, offers a product with a Rain Forest brand that will have the same price as its well-known brand, but some of the proceeds go to RFA. This is an example of how global strategies can be pursued with a global consciousness and multicultural awareness through engagement with broader external social issues like environmental concerns. Farmers in this example are a particular subset within the larger culture, and the corporate alliance with RFA allows the corporation to address the unique needs of this farming subculture in a sensitive way that does not impose the standards of the corporation's own country of origin.

As MNEs and small- to medium-sized enterprises (SMEs) seek alliances with NGOs in developing countries, they may experience conflicts in styles of communication and leadership, cooperation, and collaboration across differing cultures. One way of framing this type of conflict is to use the model of Hendry, Pettigrew, and Sparrow (1988) in which they describe the so-called best-fit practices—that is, practices that are appropriate to the culture from which they emerge.

In Hendry et al.'s (1988) model, organizations inevitably develop unique business models that best fit into the cultures in which they thrive. There is evidence (e.g., House et al., 2004) that societal factors can and do influence the characteristics of organizations within the society. With an emphasis on human resource management practices, the Hendry model stresses that best-fit practices should take precedence over attempts to create a universal set of prescriptions that apply in all organizational contexts. Similarly, by finding organizational leadership and management methods that fit the cultural context, multicultural and international organizations can develop practices that serve to enhance organizational success.

Globalization is not only a process of organizations becoming more internationally interdependent but also a revised perspective from which to view the world, influencing values and behaviors. Eisenberg et al. (2010) asserted that the culture of an organization induces its members to think, act, and behave in particular ways, and it reinforces these. It is for this reason that the organization's culture also holds the power to inculcate the global perspective or worldview throughout the organization. By holding corporate leaders accountable, the likelihood is increased that a global perspective will be diffused and sustained.

CULTURAL CHALLENGES IN GLOBAL ORGANIZATIONS

The changes associated with globalization often create stresses of one kind or another. Richmond, McCroskey, and McCroskey (2005) observed that when large and diverse cultural subgroups come together in an organization, there is an increase in clashes (confrontations and conflict) in which one group may be perceived as winning and others as losing. House et al. (2004) also predicted that with continued cultural convergence and dismantling of economic boundaries an amplification of cultural conflict commonly occurs. This can be costly in a variety of ways for any organization. Richmond et al. (2005) also noted that when organizations branch into new cultures, despite the inevitable diversification that follows, they try to maintain their organizations' own cultural features. This, too, can be counterproductive and must be proactively addressed if conflict is to be minimized.

Organizations have responded in a variety of ways to the challenges of diversification. Conrad and Poole (2005) suggested that such responses vary widely and can include *denial* (that diversification is occurring) and the tendency to minimize the impact of diversity by *homogenizing* the differences or *marginalizing* others by accepting the diverse groups only superficially while falsely claiming otherwise. We suggest that the key to dealing with globalization in organizations is to fully embrace the consequent diversity as an organizational strength by acknowledging and celebrating it and by promoting cultural diversity as an inherent competitive advantage (Conrad & Poole, 2005), dealing directly with the inevitable conflict that might occur.

House et al. (2004) suggested that to convert the cultural hurdles and latent cultural conflicts into globalization opportunities, successful global leaders need to be open to a diversity of others' ideas and opinions. More specifically, these researchers identified the need for flexibility in responding positively and effectively to the beliefs, values, and business practices that may be drastically different from their own. In this manner, an organizational culture can be created that encourages participants to embrace the unexpected when conducting business in different countries or with different subcultures within a given culture.

Relevant expertise may also be needed. To understand multicultural and international differences and the potential difficulties and conflicts that might arise, it may be desirable to seek insight from experts with relevant knowledge and experience. This may include knowledge of demographics, geography, and history. Cummings (2004) elaborated on how making use of such knowledge is most valuable when groups are structurally diverse with members from different affiliations, roles, or positions.

The contemporary global organization, we argue, requires special leadership skills to facilitate the organic transformation to a negotiated third culture. In this way, cultural polarities that can spawn organizational conflicts may evolve into organizational subsystems that generate new meaning and understanding. The resulting organizational culture will facilitate successful globalization, allowing businesses to optimize the management of their diverse organizational components and, as W. V. Schmidt et al. (2007) noted, they will "create a stronger, more flexible, and adaptive organization ready to compete in the world market" (p. 49).

FACILITATING A GLOBAL ORGANIZATIONAL CULTURE THROUGH LEADERSHIP

International organizations seek globally oriented leaders—those who are skilled, knowledgeable, and globally aware. Such leaders also need to be competent in managing and leading internationally diverse employees. With the rapid expansion of globalism, it has become increasingly important to know how to train such managers.

Because global leadership is a relatively young field of study, there is no widely accepted agreement in the research literature on the required competencies (Oddou, Osland, & Blakeney, 2009). For now, there are calls for subjective input in the study of globalization to capture the insights of expert, or successful, global leaders and to integrate what is learned into prescriptive models (Burke & Cooper, 2006). Additionally, there is a growing awareness of the link between corporate social responsibility and global leadership, and some have labeled this *responsible global leadership* (Pruzan & Miller, 2005). We suggest, based on our own consulting and teaching experience, an approach to global leadership competencies that emphasizes developing cognitive flexibility that would allow the leader and employees to move (cognitively) from separate "contested territories" to shared "negotiated spaces" where meaningful encounters and purposeful deliberation between cultures can take place. This negotiated space is similar to the notion of the third culture discussed in this chapter.

A new conceptualization of excellence in global leadership is emerging that is predicated on demonstrating leadership by acting as responsible stewards of human and natural resources while promoting economic, social, biological, and ecological development (Petrick, Scherer, Brodzinski, Quinn, & Ainina, 1999). Further theoretical, conceptual, and empirical investigations of the process of developing global leadership expertise are needed, and a good starting point would be an analysis of best practices among successful global leaders (McFarland, Senen, & Childress, 1993; McGregor, 1960).

The challenges faced by any manager or leader entering the global scene are considerable. Without adequate training, the pitfalls can be unseen or unexpected, and the errors costly, as can be seen in many of the studies of expat managers (Carraher, Sullivan, & Crocitto, 2008; Harzing, 2002).

The research on outcomes and diversity in top management teams is mixed (Barsade, Ward, Turner, & Sonnenfeld, 2000), but it tends to show a curvilinear relationship between diversity and performance of top management teams such that very low or very high levels of diversity negatively affect overall performance (Simons, Pelled, & Smith, 1999).

Not everyone views global leadership positively. Some (e.g., Ayres, 2004) see it as simply the export of Western ideas, products, and managers to foreign markets with the goal of transforming other cultures to fit with (at least for business purposes) those of the West. This is certainly what has been done in the past, but it is not what we mean by global leadership.

As they enter leadership positions in global organizations, many managers may find that they have cultural blind spots or may be somewhat culturally myopic. Such leaders bring with them the values and worldviews dominant in their own cultures. They may be adept at articulating preferences for diversity in the way things are done in the organization but nonetheless challenged to actually apply this mind-set in their leadership roles and practices. On the other hand, finding the quintessential global manager who understands, respects, values, and accepts all "other" cultural beliefs, values, and behaviors may be a utopian goal.

Authentic Leadership

We believe that global organizations benefit from striving toward the development of authentic leadership in their efforts to facilitate the creation of a third organizational culture. Cohen (2011) suggested that the authentic leader is relatively devoid of personal ego and is instead concerned with so-called higher purposes and principles and goals that transcend personal ones. Although this may sound utopian, it is clear that global leadership requires awareness of the fact that organizational success is fueled not only by individual efforts but the widespread synergies from teamwork and integration. Leaders need to know how the social and political issues of various international venues in which business is being done interact with the human conditions both within the cultures of those countries and within the organization. The global leadership mandate, we argue, is to build interdependencies between, on the one hand, the cultural distinctiveness of organizational employees, individually and as a whole, and the external interfaces.

To operate successfully in the global marketplace, we believe that leaders must be holistic and systemic thinkers who embrace their roles as the organization's key cultural monitors but who are also willing to share these responsibilities. As Schein (2010) aptly argued, neither culture nor leadership can be understood independently. This means that leadership and culture are conceptually intertwined, and the leader as the monitor of the global organizational culture must be mindful that the leader's actions become a basis for assessing and appropriately changing the embedding culture.

In this approach, leadership actions must reinforce the espoused assumptions about globalism. This suggests the need for leaders to be aware of what they stress as being important in the organization, what they measure and control, how they react to critical incidents and organizational crises, how they allocate resources, their role-modeling behavior, and how they allocate rewards (Bass & Riggio, 2005; Yukl, 2010).

Although these leadership responsibilities are not different in kind from those of leaders in any setting, the existence of human diversity and organizational subcultures in the global setting makes for a challenging matrix of variables that must be managed. Global leadership, we suggest, is mostly concerned with creating a third and negotiated organizational culture. It therefore will need to be centered on coordinating, aligning, and integrating employee diversity and the organizational subcultures by applying an integrated international–multicultural mind-set. This is best accomplished if there is a conceptual understanding of the three levels on which organizational culture exists and an intuitive understanding of the role communication plays in negotiating the links between the levels.

Leading Through the Three Levels of Organizational Culture

Authentic global leaders are mindful of the paradox generated by the need to nourish diversity in ways of doing things within their organizations versus the need to create a single, well-integrated organizational culture with which everyone in the organization can identify (Casimir & Waldman, 2007). More important, the global leader, in the quest to globalize the organization, must be sensitive to his or her basic assumptions about how the global organization must operate as it survives and adapts to the external environment and how those assumptions will be manifested in the values and practices within the organization.

A global organizational culture can be created and managed at the three levels at which it manifests itself (Schein, 2010). At the deepest and least visible level are the basic assumptions on which the organization operates. These reflect organizational members' beliefs about the appropriate actions for human beings to take with regard to their environment, the relational orientations among employees, the organization's relationship with its environment, the organization's time orientation, homogeneity versus diversity, and information and training (Kluckhohn & Strodtbeck, 1961). Global organizations generally are anchored on the worldview or basic assumption that globalization is inevitable and that most—if not all—human activity happening around the world is interconnected and interdependent (Friedman, 2005). This basic assumption is then reflected in the organization's valuation and overt manifestations of globalism and diversity.

Organizational values—the second level of organizational culture—that nourish globalism are usually congruent with the basic assumption that is manifested in the organization's support for cultural diversity. It is, however, at the artifactual or surface level—the third level—that organizational globalism is evident. It is at this level that organizational features, behaviors, climate, and processes that reflect a global culture are visible and can be experienced. It is at the surface level of the organization's culture that the authentic leader manifests skills in facilitating the creation of a global organizational culture. Leadership strategies at this level reinforce the importance placed on cultural distinctiveness within the organization and address the paradox of using this distinctiveness to create a truly global organization. This challenge is compounded when there are several national, multicultural, and occupational macrocultures involved, as is the case in most global organizations.

Manifesting the Authentic Global Culture

Anchored on basic assumptions and values that endorse cultural diversity and the drive to generate overt reflections of an authentically global organization, the global leader who values decisions made from culturally diverse teams strives to create synergy by seeking the broadest input, combining the best in the available cultures and building on the very differences among employees to achieve mutual growth and accomplishment through cooperation (Cumming & Schmidt, 2010). In addition, in culturally sensitive global organizations, there will be a level of autonomy among the employees rather than top-down management (Gilbert & Ivancevich, 2000). In this way, culturally diverse employees will feel validated and be motivated to contribute their unique perspectives to the decision-making process.

Such an approach was evident in Stage's 1999 study of Thai managers in subsidiaries of U.S. corporations. The managers were happy with some aspects of American management. For example, respondents reported that one distinction of American companies that they perceived as positive was that they did not engage in micromanagement, as did Thai leadership, giving them adequate latitude to implement their personal management skills.

The global leader can strategically use the surface culture to create a safe and nondefensive communication climate in which culturally diverse employees can uncover and share their own cultural assumptions and worldviews that have an impact on the way they perceive organizational life. Leaders can then create what Schein (2010) called "cultural islands"—symbolic places within the organization in which culturally diverse organizational members achieve cultural insights and mutual understandings. If this space becomes an entrenched surface-level feature of the organizational culture, we argue, it is likely to facilitate the creation of the third culture, which spawns a learning organizational climate in which diversity is discussed, negotiated, and leveraged as an organizational asset.

Other surface-level organizational cultural strategies allow for the creation of physical spaces that reflect the cultural diversity of the organization's employees, which helps to establish a sense of mutual respect among and value for organizational subcultures. Leaders can also choose names for buildings and organizational artifacts that reflect the unique culture of employees. Religious and spiritual practices can also be honored and observed. Although such measures may seem trivial and even condescending to some, the people so honored will appreciate the gestures, and their levels of commitment will be raised (Bove, Pervan, Beatty, & Shiud, 2009). All surface elements of culture can be treated in a way that facilitates the reinforcement and/or acceptance of the organizational assumptions and values and can, with time and consistent reinforcement, lead to a deeper penetration to the more intractable levels of the organizations culture and establish that the globalization efforts have taken root.

Other useful leadership approaches may be relevant to global organizations. For example, Hale and Fields (2007) compared Ghanaian and U.S. leaders' effectiveness, particularly with respect to the concept of servant leadership. Although there were differences found between the North American and African leaders on their views of servant leadership (with Ghanaians reporting much less experience with this approach), there was significant congruence among the North Americans and Africans on their view of the effect of service and humility on leader effectiveness (Hale & Fields, 2007). Other studies also support the idea that national culture has an influence on leadership styles. For example, the paternalistic leadership style is widely embraced in the Chinese culture (Hao & Lirong, 2007) but is not as well regarded in other cultures.

THE CASE OF MYTEK: GLOBAL LEADERSHIP AND INNOVATION CHALLENGES

We are including here a case that illustrates the leadership dilemmas that monocultural companies may face as they encounter the need to globalize and the emerging challenges they encounter because of tensions between intergenerational leadership mind-sets.[1] This is particularly true of global family businesses that at some point have to negotiate the transition from family management to a more professional orientation. The matrix of global culture, business culture, and family culture adds to the complexity of the leadership challenges.

Mytek is a leader in the production of household appliances in Mexico and South America. Two Taiwanese brothers founded the company 25 years

---

[1]This case study is based on a real-life example. It is used with permission of the company.

ago and continue to be the key strategic decision makers. Now they have a second-generation Taiwanese American senior executive in charge of business development, Dr. Ping Wang, the son of one of the founders, and a Mexican American manager runs the day-to-day operations of the company in Mexico. These four constitute the company's top management.

This company is currently facing this mixture of global and intergenerational family leadership challenges. Mytek, which has manufacturing operations in Tijuana, Mexico, and headquarters in San Diego, California, has been leveraging its manufacturing and supply chain strengths to enter new product markets. The company was forced to change the low-margin commodity strategy it had used successfully for the past 20 years because of the increasing threat from competition from China in producing commodity-like products. As a result of aggressive global competition, Mytek's senior management began to conduct strategic analysis and leadership development. The company's leadership needed to find a way to drive both financial and environmental sustainability by identifying new profitable businesses while also having to create a company with an appropriate degree of readiness for globalization. They have experienced significant growth in sales and have achieved a substantial market share in various home appliance segments in Mexico and have established operations in several countries.

After 25 years, Mytek continues to be a family-owned enterprise that has managed to maintain its original organizational culture rooted in Taiwanese business practices. Mytek today is in the midst of a transition from a first- to a second-generation family business. As the company advances through its generational transition, the overall family culture seems to remain strong and is perhaps creating some resistance to the development of a third culture in which organizational subcultures negotiate a collective meaning and mind-set. The language used in meetings in a multilingual, transnational company has an impact on the success of its global strategy. At Mytek, management meetings are conducted in Mandarin, Taiwanese, Spanish, and English at various times. However, strategic issues are more likely to be discussed in Taiwanese. This prevents the Mexican manager, who is not fluent in Taiwanese, from participating. The use of Taiwanese here could also impede the full integration of future hires of American or Mexican MBAs into the strategy process. And it could limit employees' professional development and keep the company as an exclusively Taiwanese family culture.

So far there has been minimal focus on creating that global company culture that integrates the worldviews and values of the cultures represented. The attention paid to consciously globalizing the organization's culture has perhaps been insufficient, and the company's focus on the profit motive may have limited its attention to this dynamic.

Dr. Wang: The Challenges of a Contemporary Global Leader

Dr. Ping Wang, the son of one of the founding brothers who started the North American operation and who has graduate degrees in electrical engineering and interdisciplinary sciences from the University of California at San Diego and Stanford University, respectively thinks that Mytek has reached "a fork in the road" (P. Wang, personal interview, April 12, 2012). Dr. Wang is poised to be promoted to president of Mytek in the next couple of years and thus take over the strategic decision making for the company. He assumes this position with a global mind-set and a strategic plan that involves taking the company "beyond a family-owned company to one that is more corporate like," one that not only increases its portfolio of products and continues diversifying but also has the ability to scale national and cultural boundaries. However, his quest for cultural globalization is in sharp contrast to the operational approach that this company, led by his Taiwanese father and uncle, has taken. He encounters a divergent mind-set that does not place the same emphasis as he does on the cultural diversification approach to organizational globalization or on taking risks and pursuing innovation.

To fully understand the divergent mind-sets, it is necessary to understand the evident generational and cultural divide between Dr. Wang and his father and uncle who founded the company in Taiwan 25 years ago. Despite this generational divide, the Taiwanese family business culture mandates that company leadership should stay in the family and consequently should be taken over by the subsequent generation—in this case the son, Dr. Wang. Even though his father founded the North American operation and speaks multiple languages, a homogeneous Taiwanese organizational culture prevails with regard to strategic decision making. It is a reflection of the Taiwanese culture of its founders, who continue to occupy the leadership roles in the organization.

The cultural divide between the first and second generation is largely derived from the contrasting life and industry experience of the first- and second-generation leaders. Dr. Wang's background is one of a young Western entrepreneur, scientist, and engineer who learned how to do business in Silicon Valley, who focuses on bridging and finding synergies between disparate realms of technical and business disciplines as well as between cultures. His mind-set is an outgrowth of his own hybrid Taiwanese American culture. He considers himself steeped in Eastern worldviews but acculturated to Western worldviews through his experiences growing up and being educated in the United States and working in high-tech American companies in Silicon Valley. The distinctions in the microcultural experiences of these two generations of leaders results in a parallel distinction in their leadership mind-sets in which Dr. Wang is willing to generate a compromised, negotiated organizational culture that conflicts with the current strong family culture leadership.

Dr. Wang is cognizant of the challenges he will face if he were to address globalization from within Mytek. Taiwan is an entrepreneurial culture that is ruled by midsized family-based businesses. As within any organization, there will be inevitable resistance to any perceived attempts to challenge embedded cultural norms. This is compounded by the reality of an inherent generational hierarchy in the Taiwanese culture in which age and experience are valued in business decisions. Because of his youth, hybrid culture, and comparatively minimal business experience, Dr. Wang's strategic plans, unless similar to the traditional Taiwanese way of doing business, will not be seriously considered.

Hybridization and the Third Culture

The tension created by the evident need to globalize Mytek's organization's culture and the realities of the continued resistance to it has spawned a nontraditional third-culture company that Dr. Wang, calls "a company within a company." VEA Technologies, founded by Dr. Wang, is a consumer electronics company focused on next-generation, innovative products—more specifically, display technology. He is a also the founder of the Ansir Innovation Center technology accelerator and incubator in San Diego, which is a think tank that connects with the entrepreneurial community in San Diego. He seeks to establish an organizational culture that nurtures and facilitates the growth of innovative ideas across microcultures and especially professional subcultures such as manufacturing, branding, and marketing, among others.

Dr. Wang has manifested in these companies the characteristics of the third, negotiated culture. His participatory leadership style focuses on building consensus and collective thinking. This style is particularly well suited for a think tank or a high-tech company such as VEA. It should be noted that the only reason Mytek is involved in these two new ventures is because the second generation, Dr. Wang, was exposed to these types of business ventures in his time in the Silicon Valley. In contrast, his father has only experience in commodity-type manufacturing that is prevalent in the industrial base in Taiwan. Dr. Wang's mission, as he states, is to establish a team with an open mind and ability to scale national and cultural boundaries, organically and multiculturally.

VEA Technologies is a core part of Mytek, because it is funded by Mytek. It has a signature third culture that emerged as a product of tensions created by the distinctions in leadership styles across the generations and the need to create an authentically globalized organization. The current challenge is to determine how operations can be integrated to avoid the further calcification of and distinctions between the Mytek and VEA cultures. This integration must occur in a way that maintains and endorses the authenticity of VEA Technologies and supports a negotiated third culture. In essence, it is the organizational culture that supports and facilitates the growth of a global organizational culture. Today, Mytek is poised to meet these challenges with a focus on the strategic development of the organization's global leadership.

Dr. Wang understands that he needs to navigate the middle road between the extremes of Taiwanese commodity manufacturing culture, with its strong respect for family and hierarchy, and the more freewheeling, innovation-based Silicon Valley culture. He sees this as a delightful challenge rather than a perplexing contradiction. He knows that the way forward will require a delicate balancing of these two equally strong cultural traditions, both of which inspire him. Because he actually embodies the mixture of the two cultures and has practiced self-reflexivity, he believes he is the authentic global leader who is able to successfully create a negotiated space or third culture that respects all traditions.

TWO CONSIDERATIONS FOR GLOBALIZING

Two additional elements to consider when approaching globalization from a cultural perspective are the stage of development of the organization and the widespread integration of a globalization culture throughout the organization.

The Developmental Stages of the Organization

A newly formed or developing organization has no (or few) traditions or existing patterns that are entrenched, and this lack allows it to adapt to and take advantage of opportunities in the external environment with relative ease. Furthermore, a new organization usually does not have well-entrenched internal understandings of how to integrate internal processes to combat entropy. In some ways, then, these deficiencies are beneficial because the leaders in such a setting typically have more latitude to vary and change, or even to experiment (Hackman & Johnson 2004). Unlike well-entrenched cultures of every kind and size, newly formed organizations are blessed with the opportunity to form all cultural standards from scratch and to reinforce them. As they progress, they can make diversity-orientation a basic and vital part of their emerging culture.

Continued growth of an organization through midlife, however, often leads to the parallel emergence of subcultures formed around similar experiences, skill sets, functions, challenges, rank, and status. Although such subcultures are inevitable in the global organization, the leader's responsibility is not to suppress but to manage the inevitable conflicts in such a way that the overall milieu is not impaired.

As an organization advances through its developmental stages, the overall culture becomes more entrenched and, with time, more difficult to change. Similar processes occur in most organic processes or systems. Inevitably, there is cultural calcification. As new members enter the organization, their prior experiences have some influence on the ways in which the organization functions, but in large and complex entities, such influence is slight. In smaller concerns, a single new person can have more of an impact. Leaders must understand the dynamics of these variables and deal with them effectively and openly.

The global leader must therefore understand the challenges of embedding and maintaining a global culture within organizations at varying stages of development. Certainly, new organizations or ones in the early stages of development present an opportunity to implement globalizing strategies with minimal hindrance. The challenge increases, however, as organizations evolve through midlife into maturity. In their attempts to create organizational cultures that promote globalism, leaders may encounter homogeneous organizational cultures. At this stage of organizational development, there is an increase in the likelihood of conflict among the multiple organizational subcultures that emerge, especially around occupational communities (Gladwell, 2008).

Integration of International and Multicultural Perspectives

Effective global organizational leaders need to ensure the salience of an integrated international and multicultural perspective throughout the organization. We contend that to truly understand the dynamics that occur within the global organization, it is necessary to understand the interplay between the multicultural and international identities of organizational members. This will facilitate the creation of a culture that provides system-wide reinforcement of behaviors that enhance globalization (Eilers & Camacho, 2007).

We argue that leaders who integrate international and multicultural perspectives will at the very least increase the likelihood for harmonious internal relations and also better interface with those outside the organization. To the degree that such harmony enhances attitudes and acceptance, it may also increase productivity and other measures of success.

Schein (2010) noted that with growing technological complexity and globalization come a parallel emphasis on multicultural groups, called *collaborations*, composed of members from different macrocultures and occupational subcultures. We contend that when societal conflicts between social identity groups spill over into organizations, the global leader with the integrated international–multicultural perspective can better face the challenges of attempting to bridge differences and to manage the inevitable cultural conflicts to accomplish work. Global leaders who understand their subordinates from an integrated multicultural and international mind-set will, we believe, understand and appreciate the multicultural distinctions and consequent behaviors of employees within the same national culture. The leader who, for example, understands the complex differences between the 50-year-old, middle-income, professional Caribbean female employee and the 30-year-old, middle-income, professional Caribbean male employee has a better chance of leading effectively. In this example, each culturally induced identity is inextricably tied to the practices of the individuals. Although the two employees might share a similar work ethic, their individual behaviors could differ because they do not share similar age and gender expectations. Male and female Caribbeans (such as the second author of this chapter) are socialized differently. Males in such cultures are expected to be more assertive than their female counterparts. Age could also be a defining feature of their workplace behavior. Sociopolitical and socioeconomic realities may also significantly influence enculturation across generations and have a consequent impact on behaviors attitudes and expectations of the leader (McCray, Wright, & Beachum, 2007).

Kawahara (2007) demonstrated this nuanced view in her qualitative study of Asian American leadership in which she found gender and culture and their complex interaction had a significant impact on leader effectiveness. Leadership styles and practices do indeed vary internationally (across national boundaries) but are also influenced by multicultural diversity within national cultures (Walumbwa, Lawler, & Avolio, 2007). A study based on the GLOBE data, for example, concluded not only that Mexican managerial regional differences were too significant to make a general conclusion about Mexican culture but also that the strong influence of U.S. management practices muddled any consistencies that could be drawn about the "Mexican manager." However, they were still able to show that leaders' effectiveness does, to some extent, depend on their alignment with their country's culturally endorsed implicit leadership theory (Howell et al., 2007; L. Johnson, Møller, Jacobson, & Wong, 2008).

Clearly, professionals must consider an array of cultural variables and their impact on leadership styles and practices (Euwema, Wendt, & van

Emmerik, 2007) in understanding a global organization. Cultural and local sensitivity must always be considered. One example of how leadership dimensions vary across cultures and subcultures is found in research on conflict resolution styles that vary along individualistic versus collectivist cultural dimensions. A study conducted in Hong Kong and Sydney (Wan, 2007) demonstrated that respondents from these two cities were significantly different in their preferred conflict resolution styles.

Global leadership styles that recognize microcultural variances in the global workforce allow leaders to understand their own culturally influenced styles and are more likely to value each employee as an individual with cultural distinctions (Liu, 2010). This gives them a heightened sense of how to address these distinctions when creating and managing the organizational culture to facilitate diversity and maximize outcomes on every dimension (Magnuson, 2007).

Learning From Global Leadership Examples

In addition to the need for more and better research on global leadership, there is also a need for careful analysis of the approaches already being used in the practice of global leadership across nations, governments, and industries. Inductive methodologies that are aimed at surfacing global leadership successes and failures can be of immense value, but only if such experiences are properly analyzed and documented and then built into prescriptive formulae.

One program of interest that exemplifies this approach is the INSEAD Global Leadership Program (IGLC), which was launched in 2003. This program aims to identify best managerial practices on a global scale and to find ways to develop leaders more effectively. Manfred Kets De Vries, one of the principal researchers in this endeavor, has described the mission of this program as being to help leaders create results-driven, sustainable organizations by creating reflective leaders, high-performance teams, and good places to work. The idea is that you can have the best technology and the greatest economies of scale and other positive attributes, but if you do not have the people equation right, you will not go very far. As is noted in the IGLC's newsletter: "We try to help create companies where people are result oriented, entrepreneurial team players and responsible corporate citizens" (INSEAD Alumni Association, 2006).

IGLC's vision of "responsible corporate citizens" includes an understanding of the nuances of cultural diversity within a particular national culture. Usable findings from this program are long overdue, however, and so there remains a continuing and largely unfulfilled need for further empirical validation of these assertions.

SUMMARY

Global leadership can be a key to international success for many organizations, but the skills and approaches needed do not develop in managers automatically. Leaders of global organizations are held accountable for authentic globalization, but for that objective to succeed, the goal and responsibility must be shared at all levels. Strategic decisions in global organizations with multicultural awareness are undertaken in such a way as to create an atmosphere of inclusion and empowerment, and this can be challenging, especially if not handled appropriately, carefully, and with clear goals and desired outcomes that are fully understood by employees at every level. Approaching the challenge from an organizational culture perspective, with a sincere appreciation for human diversity and a deep understanding of cultural identity as a function of the integration of one's international and multicultural experiences, allows the leader to embrace the unique diversity of employees at every level. It also facilitates the enlistment of their help in building a foundation from which to globalize.

As leaders embed and manage global organizational cultures, they must consider critical organizational factors, including the organization's stage of development (early development, maturity, or decline) and the various levels of the existing and evolving culture. Global leaders must especially be prepared to encounter significant challenges as organizations evolve through midlife, when there is a proliferation of subcultures centered on functions and occupations, location, product and technology, divisions and hierarchy, among other factors. This, in addition to the diversity among employees, creates demands on the leader's ability to create a global organizational culture by leveraging the distinctive features inherent in the diversity among employees. Additionally, surface (and seemingly trivial) cultural flexibility is helpful to build confidence in the globalization process that ultimately will penetrate to deeper levels and become the dominant or embedded culture.

As daunting as it may seem, globalizing an organization's culture can be facilitated if authentic and well-prepared global leaders pay attention to the nature of variety among human beings and develop the skills needed to manage the organizational culture effectively. Such leadership calls for actions and behaviors that are consistent and sincere and requires that they continuously demonstrate a strong commitment in the quest to globalization.

REFERENCES

Ayres, J. A. (2004). Framing collective action against neoliberalism: The case of the "anti-globalization" movement. *Journal of World-Systems Research, 10,* 11–22.

Barnes, A. K. (1994). *Management maturity: Prerequisite to total quality*. Lanham, MD: University Press of America/Rowman, Littlefield.

Barsade, S. G., Ward, A. J., Turner, J. D. F., & Sonnenfeld, J. A. (2000). To your heart's content: A model of affective diversity in top management teams. *Administrative Science Quarterly, 45*, 802–836. doi:10.2307/2667020

Bass, B. M., & Riggio, R. E. (2005). *Transformational leadership*. Mahwah, NJ: Erlbaum.

Bove, L. L., Pervan, S. J., Beatty, S. E. & Shiud, E. (2009). Service worker role in encouraging customer organizational citizenship behaviors. *Journal of Business Research, 62*, 698–705.

Byrne, G. J., & Bradley, F. (2007). Culture's influence on leadership efficiency: How personal and national cultures affect leadership style. *Journal of Business Research, 60*, 168–175. doi:10.1016/j.jbusres.2006.10.015

Burke, R. J., & Cooper, C. L. (2006). *Inspiring leaders*. New York, NY: Routledge.

Canen, A. G., & Canen, A. (2008). Multicultural leadership: The costs of its absence in organizational conflict management. *International Journal of Conflict Management, 19*, 4–19. doi:10.1108/10444060810849155

Carraher, S. M., Sullivan, S. E., & Crocitto, M. M. (2008). Mentoring across global boundaries: An empirical examination of home- and host-country mentors on expatriate career outcomes. *Journal of International Business Studies, 38*, 1310–1326.

Casimir, G., & Waldman, D. A. (2007). A cross cultural comparison of the importance of leadership traits for effective low-level and high-level leaders: Australia and China. *International Journal of Cross Cultural Management, 7*, 47–60. doi:10.1177/1470595807075171

Cohen, A. (2011). *What is authentic leadership?* Retrieved from http://www.andrewcohen.org/andrew/authentic-leadership.asp

Conrad, C., & Poole, M. S. (2005). *Strategic organizational communication in a global economy* (6th ed.). Victoria, Australia: Thomson/Wadsworth.

Croucher, S. L. (2004). *Globalization and belonging: The politics of identity in a changing world*. Lanham, MD: Rowman & Littlefield.

Cumming, D., & Schmidt, D. (2010). Legality and venture capital governance around the world. *Journal of Business Venturing, 25*, 54–72.

Cummings, J. N. (2004). Work groups, structural diversity and knowledge sharing in a global organization. *Management Science, 50*, 352–364. doi:10.1287/mnsc.1030.0134

Daily, B., Whatley, A., Ash, S. R., & Steiner, R. L. (1996). The effects of a group decision support system on culturally diverse and culturally homogeneous group decision making. *Information & Management, 30*, 281–289. doi:10.1016/S0378-7206(96)01062-2

De Mooij, M. (2011). *Consumer behavior and culture: Consequences for global marketing and advertising*. Thousand Oaks, CA: Sage.

Eilers, A. M., & Camacho, A. (2007). School culture change in the making: leadership factors that matter. *Urban Education, 42,* 616–637. doi:10.1177/0042085907304906

Eisenberg, E., Goodall, H., Jr., & Trethwey, A. (2010). *Organizational communication: Balancing creativity and constraint.* Boston, MA: Bedford/St. Martin's.

Ergeneli, A., Gohar, R., & Temirbekova, Z. (2007). Transformational leadership: Its relationship to culture value dimensions. *International Journal of Intercultural Relations, 31,* 703–724. doi:10.1016/j.ijintrel.2007.07.003

Euwema, M. C., Wendt, H., & van Emmerik, H. (2007). Leadership styles and group organizational citizenship behavior across cultures. *Journal of Organizational Behavior, 28,* 1035–1057. doi:10.1002/job.496

Fridell, G. (2009). The co-operative and the corporation: Competing visions of the future of fair trade. *Journal of Business Ethics, 86,* 81–95. doi:10.1007/s10551-008-9759-3

Friedman, T. (2005). *The world is flat: A brief history of the 21st century.* New York, NY: Farrar, Straus & Giroux.

Ghemawat, P. (2011). *World 3.0: Global prosperity and how to achieve it.* Cambridge, MA: Harvard Business School Press.

Gilbert, J. A., & Ivancevich, J. M. (2000). Valuing diversity: A tale of two organizations. *The Academy of Management Executive, 14,* 93–105. doi:10.5465/AME.2000.2909842

Gladwell, M. (2008). *Flirting with disaster.* New York, NY: Union Square.

Hackman, M. Z., & Johnson, C. E. (2004). *Leadership: A communication perspective.* Long Grove, IL: Waveland Press.

Hale, J. R., & Fields, D. L. (2007). Exploring servant leadership across cultures: A study of followers in Ghana and the USA. *Leadership, 3,* 397–417. doi:10.1177/1742715007082964

Harzing, A. (2002). Are our referencing errors undermining our scholarship and credibility? The case of expatriate failure rates. *Journal of Organizational Behavior, 23,* 127–148. doi:10.1002/job.125

Hao, Z., & Lirong, L. (2007). Relationship between paternalistic leadership and organizational justice. *Acta Psychologica Sinica, 39,* 909–917.

Hendry, C., Pettigrew, A. M., & Sparrow, P. R. (1988). Changing patterns of human resource management. *Personnel Management, 20,* 37–47.

Holmberg, I., & Åkerblom, S. (2008). "Primus inter pares": Leadership and culture in Sweden. In J. S. Chhokar, F. C. Brodbeck, R. J. & House, J. S. (Eds.), *Culture and leadership across the world: The GLOBE book of in-depth studies of 25 societies* (pp. 33–74). Mahwah, NJ: Erlbaum.

House, R., Hanges, P., Javidan, M., Dorfman, P., & Gupta, V. (2004). *Culture, leadership and organizations: The globe study of sixty-two societies.* Thousand Oaks, CA: Sage.

Howell, J.P., DelaCerda, J., Martínez, S.M., Prieto, L., Bautista, J., Ortiz, J., & Méndez, M.J. (2007). Leadership and culture in Mexico. *Journal of World Business, 42*, 449–462. doi:10.1016/j.jwb.2007.06.006

INSEAD Alumni Association. (2006, April). Professor Manfred Kets De Vries [Interview]. *INSEAD Alumni Newsletter.* Retrieved from http://www.insead.edu/alumni/newsletter/April2006/Manfredinterview.htm

Johnson, L., Møller, J., Jacobson, S.L., & Wong, K. (2008). Cross-national comparisons in the International Successful School Principalship Project: The USA, Norway and China. *Scandinavian Journal of Educational Research, 52*, 407–422. doi:10.1080/00313830802184582

Johnson, P. (2007). *Astute competition: The economics of strategic diversity.* Oxford, England: Elsevier.

Karabacakoglu, F., & Ozbilgin, M. (2010). Global diversity management at Ericsson: The business case. In L. Costang (Ed.), *Cases in strategic management* (pp. 79–91). London, England: McGraw-Hill.

Kawahara, D.M. (2007). Making a difference: Asian American women leaders. *Women & Therapy, 30*, 17–33. doi:10.1300/J015v30n03_03

Kluckhohn, F.R., & Strodtbeck, F.L. (1961). *Variations in value orientation.* New York, NY: Row, Peterson.

Linton, A. (2005). Partnering for sustainability: Business–NGO alliances in the coffee industry. *Development in Practice, 15*, 15–21.

Liu, L. (2010). *Conversations on leadership: Wisdom from global management gurus.* New York, NY: Wiley.

Magnuson, E. (2007). Creating culture in the mythopoetic men's movement: An ethnographic study of micro-level leadership and socialization. *The Journal of Men's Studies, 15*, 31–56. doi:10.3149/jms.1501.31

Marquardt, M.J., & Horvath, L. (2001). *Global teams: How top multinationals span boundaries and cultures with high-speed teamwork.* Palo Alto, CA: Davies-Black.

McCray, C.R., Wright, J.V., & Beachum, F.D. (2007). Beyond *Brown:* Examining the perplexing plight of African American principals. *Journal of Instructional Psychology, 34*, 247–255.

McFarland, L.J., Senen, S., & Childress, J.R. (1993). *Twenty-first century leadership.* New York, NY: Leadership Press.

McGregor, D. (1960). *The human side of enterprise.* New York, NY: McGraw-Hill.

McLeod, P.L., & Lobel, S.A. (1992). The effects of ethnic diversity on idea generation in small groups. In J.L. Wall & L.R. Jauch (Eds.), *Academy of Management Best Paper Proceedings* (pp. 227–231). Columbia, SC: Academy of Management.

Miller, K. (2003). *Organizational communication: Approaches and processes* (3rd ed.). Victoria, Australia: Thomson/Wadsworth.

Monge, P.R. (1998). Communication structures and processes in globalization. *The Journal of Communication, 48*, 142–153.

Nagata, A. (2004). Promoting self-reflexivity in intercultural education. *Journal of Intercultural Communications, 8,* 139–167.

Oddou, G., Osland J. S. & Blakeney, R. N. (2009). Repatriating knowledge: Variables influencing the "transfer" process. *Journal of International Business Studies, 40,* 181–199. doi:10.1057/palgrave.jibs.8400402

Peterson, D. B. (2007). Executive coaching in a cross-cultural context. *Consulting Psychology Journal: Practice and Research, 59,* 261–271. doi:10.1037/1065-9293.59.4.261

Petrick, J., Scherer, R., Brodzinski, J., Quinn, J. F., & Ainina, M. F. (1999). Global leadership skills and reputational capital: Intangible resources for sustainable competitive advantage. *The Academy of Management Executive, 13,* 58–69. doi:10.5465/AME.1999.1567322

Pruzan, P., & Miller, W. C. (2005). *Spirituality as the basis of responsible leaders and responsible companies.* London, England: Routledge.

Reade, C., Todd, A. M., Osland, A., & Osland, J. (2008). Poverty and the multiple stakeholder challenge for global leaders. *Journal of Management Education, 32,* 820–840. doi:10.1177/1052562908317445

Rhinesmith, S. (1993). *A manager's guide to globalization: Six keys to success in a changing world.* Alexandria, VA: Irwin.

Richmond, V. P., McCroskey, J. C., & McCroskey, L. L. (2005). *Organizational communication for survival: Making work, work.* Boston, MA: Allyn & Bacon.

Robertson, R. T. (2003). *The three waves of globalization: A history of a developing global consciousness.* London, England: Zed Books.

Samovar, L. A., & Porter, R. E. (1991). *Communicating between cultures.* Belmont, CA: Jossey-Bass.

Schein, E. (2010). *Organizational culture and leadership* (4th ed.). Belmont, CA: Jossey-Bass

Schmidt, P. L. (2007). *In search of intercultural understand: A practical guidebook for living.* Vienna, Austria: Meridian World Press.

Schmidt, W. V., Conaway, R. N., Easton, S. S., & Wardrope, W. J. (2007). *Communicating globally: Intercultural communication and international business.* Thousand Oaks, CA: Sage.

Simanis, E. (2009, October 26). At the base of the pyramid. *Wall Street Journal,* pp. R7.

Simons, T., & Pelled, L. H., & Smith, K. A. (1999). Making use of difference, diversity, debate and decision comprehensiveness in top management teams. *Academy of Management Journal, 42,* 662–673. doi:10.2307/256987

Stage, C. W. (1999). Negotiating organizational communication cultures in American subsidiaries doing business in Thailand. *Management Communication Quarterly, 13,* 245–280. doi:10.1177/0893318999132003

Stohl, C. (2001). Globalizing organizational communication. In F. M. Jablin & L. L. Putman (Eds.), *New handbook of organizational communication: Advances in theory, research, and methods* (pp. 323–375). Thousand Oaks, CA: Sage.

Surowiecki, J. (2004, July 4). The wisdom of the crowd. *Orlando Sentinel*, pp. G1, G4.

Taylor, P. (2005). In the market but not of it: Fair trade coffee and Forest Steward-ship Council certification as market-based social change. *World Development, 33*, 129–147. doi:10.1016/j.worlddev.2004.07.007

Teegen, H., & Doh, J. P. (2004). The importance of nongovernmental organizations (NGOs) in global governance and value creation. *Journal of International Business Studies, 35*, 463–483. doi:10.1057/palgrave.jibs.8400112

Verbos, A., Gerard, J. A., Forshey, P. R., Harding, C. S., & Miller, J. S. (2007). The positive ethical organization: Enacting a living code of ethics and ethical organizational identity. *Journal of Business Ethics, 76*, 17–33. doi:10.1007/s10551-006-9275-2

Walumbwa, F. O., Lawler, J. J., & Avolio, B. J. (2007). Leadership, individual differences, and work-related attitudes: A cross-culture investigation. *Applied Psychology: An International Review, 56*, 212–230. doi:10.1111/j.1464-0597.2006.00241.x

Wan, H. (2007). Conflict management behaviors of welfare practitioners in individualist and collectivist culture. *Administration in Social Work, 31*, 49–65. doi:10.1300/J147v31n01_04

Watson, W. E., Kuman, K., & Michaelson, L. K. (1993). Cultural diversity impact on interaction process and performance: Comparing homogeneous and diverse task groups. *Academy of Management Journal, 36*, 590–602. doi:10.2307/256593

Yukl, G. (2010). *Leadership in organizations* (7th ed.). Upper Saddle River, NJ: Prentice Hall.

Zahra, S. A. (1999). The changing rules of global competitiveness in the 21st century. *Academy of Management Executive, 13*, 6–42.

9

THE MULTICULTURALLY AND INTERNATIONALLY COMPETENT MENTAL HEALTH PROFESSIONAL

ERICA J. HURLEY AND LAWRENCE H. GERSTEIN

The composition of the United States has undergone dramatic shifts in recent years. Now, with approximately 38.5 million foreign-born residents (12.5% of the U.S. population; U.S. Census Bureau, 2010), an estimated 10.8 million undocumented immigrants (U.S. Department of Homeland Security, 2011), and an unprecedented number of U.S.-based mental health organizations providing assistance internationally, U.S. mental health professionals have opportunities to work with foreign-born persons more than ever. Although U.S. mental health professionals have been trained to acknowledge diversity as an integral part of providing services, additional competencies are needed as the "diversity within diversity" (Healy, 2004, p. 307) of the population grows. This increased international diversity within the United States (paralleled by similar phenomena in many other countries) requires that mental health professionals provide adequate services while navigating complex issues such as differences in language, dissimilarities in cultural

DOI: 10.1037/14044-009
Internationalizing Multiculturalism: Expanding Professional Competencies in a Globalized World,
R. L. Lowman (Editor)

values, and cultural variations in the ways in which mental health problems are manifested. International competencies are therefore needed not only for those U.S. mental health professionals who provide services abroad but are essential for all.

In this chapter, we address the need for an emphasis on international competencies for mental health professionals working with international clients even if they plan to work only within the boundaries of their countries. We begin by reviewing the multicultural counseling movement (MCM) and past attempts to address the needs of the culturally diverse. Next, we highlight the salient themes from this movement that are also relevant to the international movement. We then review various conceptions of international competencies that have been put forth for mental health professionals, we describe current efforts aimed at promoting these competencies, and we address the implications for mental health professionals. Finally, we explore some challenges associated with international competencies and present future directions for promoting such competencies among mental health professionals.

THE MULTICULTURAL COUNSELING MOVEMENT

A discussion of international competencies would not be complete without first providing an overview of the MCM and mental health professionals' past efforts to address the needs of the culturally diverse. Such a review is helpful because the international movement has paralleled the MCM in many respects. In this section, we describe the historical context in which the MCM has occurred, its necessity for mental health professionals, obstacles to this movement, and the progress that has occurred over the past 50 years. Although we focus on this movement in the context of the United States, a similar discussion could be presented of such movements in other countries, particularly those in Europe and more recently in Asia.

In the United States, the MCM among mental health professionals coincided with the civil rights movement in the 1950s and 1960s. As civil rights legislation was passed (e.g., the Civil Rights Act of 1964 outlawing segregation), mental health professionals took an increasingly strong stance in acknowledging the role of culture in addressing mental health needs (Arredondo & Perez, 2003). Rather than accepting that the Eurocentric values of male Caucasians could be universally applied, proponents of the MCM argued that an understanding and appreciation of the role of culture was integral to enriching mental health practice, research, training, and theory.

Indeed, at this time, it became increasingly apparent that U.S. racial minorities (e.g., African American, Hispanic, Asian) were not benefitting from mental health services to the extent that Caucasians were. S. Sue and colleagues (S. Sue & McKinney, 1975; S. Sue, McKinney, Allen, & Hall, 1974) reported that approximately 50% of African American, Asian, Hispanic, and Native American clients did not return to counseling after their first session compared with 30% of Caucasian clients, even when controlling for gender, age, income, marital status, education, and type of service received. D. W. Sue and Sue (1977) cited counselors' inattention to language variables, class-bound values, and cultural values as primary reasons for the underutilization of mental health services among minority persons. Differences between service providers and clients were largely ignored, and thus, although mental health services were becoming increasingly available in communities at this time (President's Commission on Mental Health, 1978), many racial minorities did not use them.

This inattention to cultural variables contributed to more problems than the underutilization of services. Caplan and Nelson (1973) analyzed the literature on African Americans found in the *Psychological Abstracts* over a 6-month period. They found that 82% of the articles attributed African Americans' problems to personal shortcomings as opposed to societal problems. Such findings underscored the ways in which mental health professionals were perhaps unintentionally further stigmatizing racial minorities within the United States. By the late 1970s, other publications, such as *Psychological Testing of American Minorities: Issues and Consequences* (Samuda, 1975) and *Even the Rat Was White: A Historical View of Psychology* (Guthrie, 1976), similarly criticized psychologists' efforts to work with racially diverse populations because of the ethnocentrism within their approaches. Such evidence highlighted the potential for harm when working with racially diverse clients.

The MCM gained momentum as proponents presented critiques of Eurocentric mental health practices. Not all mental health professionals, however, were supportive of this movement. The movement was met with a certain degree of resistance as some mental health professionals argued that (a) current mental health practices were already relevant to the culturally different and (b) cultural issues were irrelevant to mainstream mental health issues because minority populations constituted only a small segment of the population (Clark, 1990). Although the MCM originated with the civil rights movement, decades passed before many mental health professional organizations formally adopted policies related to issues of diversity.

Even though it has been a slow journey, the MCM in the United States has made significant strides in advancing multicultural research, theory, training, and practice since its inception (Leung, 2003). Mental health organizations such as the American Counseling Association (2005), the National Organization of Human Service Professionals (2000), the American Psychological Association (APA; 2003), and the National Association of Social

Workers (2001), to name a few, have all officially endorsed multicultural-ism as a central ethical issue. Moreover, mental health accreditation bodies such as the Council for Accreditation of Counseling and Related Educational Programs (2009), APA (2009b), and the Council on Social Work Education (2008; CSWE) now require that multicultural content be infused throughout the training curriculum for mental health professionals. Although mental health professionals still have a long way to go before eliminating all men-tal health disparities in the United States (U.S. Department of Health and Human Services, 2001), most would contend that much progress has been made since the MCM began.

This brief review of the MCM underscores the fact that mental health practices have not remained constant over time but have evolved to meet the demands of a diverse society. Not only were mental health services under-used by racial minorities, research has suggested that some mental health professionals contributed to harming such populations with their inattention to cultural contexts. Clearly, mental health professionals needed to change their practices. As stated earlier, advances in the MCM took time, and fur-ther progress is needed. Yet the world in which we live is not static, and it appears that further initiatives are urgently needed. Many of these initiatives, we argue, will be enacted through the international movement.

THE INTERNATIONAL MOVEMENT

The importance of identifying international competencies for U.S. mental health professionals is apparent when comparisons between the inter-national and multicultural movements are drawn. Such comparisons not only provide a foundation for understanding the evolution of the international movement, they also offer insight into the development of additional com-petencies that may be needed and bases for future directions.

Even though the international efforts of U.S. mental health profession-als have been somewhat inconsistent over time, such efforts have intensi-fied in recent years because of the advances of globalization. Because the world in which we live is now characterized by economic, social, and cultural interconnectedness (Heppner, 2006), an international focus for U.S. mental health professionals is no longer optional but essential. Nonetheless, in the same way that such professionals were underprepared to work with racially diverse clients in the United States 50 years ago, evidence suggests that U.S. mental health professionals are underprepared to work with international populations today (Wessells, 2008; Whitley, Kirmayer, & Groleau, 2006).

Earlier we noted that although U.S. racial minorities had opportunities to make use of mental health services, they frequently opted not to because the services lacked cultural relevance. Now a similar trend appears to be occurring with international persons. Although there are more opportunities for U.S. mental health workers to work with international persons, research suggests that the latter are less likely to seek mental health services than are persons born in the United States (U.S. Department of Health and Human Services, 2001).

The United States attracts more international students than any other country in the world. Currently more than 690,000 international students are studying in U.S. colleges and universities (Institute for International Education, 2011). However, they rarely seek counseling services, even though they may experience a variety of stressors, including language barriers, difficulty in adjusting to the U.S. educational system, cultural differences, and homesickness (Olivas & Li, 2002). In a study examining utilization rates at a university counseling center, Nilsson, Berkel, Flores, and Lucas (2004) found that only 2% of international students sought counseling, and approximately one third of those dropped out after the initial intake. Although international students represented 8% of the student body, they represented only 2.6% of clients seen during that year. These rates were considerably lower than, for example, those of U.S. racial minorities, including African Americans, who comprised 13% of the student body and 15% of the counseling center clientele; Asian Americans, who comprised 12% of the student body and 13% of clientele; and Hispanic persons, who comprised 4% of the student body and 5% of the clientele. The overall base rate of the U.S. student body using counseling services, however, was not reported in this study.

A similar trend may exist in community mental health care settings. Vega, Kolody, Aguilar-Gaxiola, and Catalano (1999) found that for Mexicans and Mexican Americans living in Fresno County, California, 12% of those born in the United States with diagnosable mental health disorders sought out mental health specialists, compared with only 5% of those born in Mexico. Similarly, a nationwide study with more than 2,000 Asian Americans and Asian immigrants found that Asian Americans (6%) were more likely to seek mental health services than were Asian immigrants (2%; Abe-Kim et al., 2007).

Many possible reasons exist as to why international persons in the United States may not seek mental health services. The negative stigma of mental illness has been frequently linked with a lack of help seeking among international populations (Dadfar & Friedlander, 1982; Heggins & Jackson, 2003; Ibrahim & Ingram, 2007). Nonetheless, other barriers may be present, and qualitative studies have provided alternative explanations. Ang and Liamputtong (2008) found that lack of confidence in speaking English, preference for personal social support networks, and lack of knowledge about university counseling services were the primary reasons that international students in Australia did not seek services. Whitley, Kirmayer, and Groleau (2006) conducted in-depth interviews with 15 West Indian immigrants living in Canada to understand their reluctance to use mental health services from primary health care providers. They found that a perceived overwillingness of doctors to rely on pharmaceutical medications as interventions, dismissive attitudes, and lack of time from physicians in previous encounters, as well as a belief in the curative powers of nonmedical interventions, all contributed to their reluctance. Thus, although mental health professionals may have relatively little control over factors such as stigma, they can adapt their practices in other ways to provide more internationally appropriate services.

In the same way that advocates of the multicultural movement challenged U.S. professionals to explore reasons as to why mental health services were not being used by U.S. racial minorities, we extend the same challenge to mental health professionals regarding their practices for working with international clientele. Given the extremely low rates of mental health service utilization by international persons in the United States, one must question whether mental health services as they are currently implemented are perceived as appropriate sources of assistance. Thus, increased efforts are needed to internationalize mental health services in the United States.

As noted, opportunities for harm emerge when mental health professionals practice beyond the scope of their competencies and/or when competencies for working with a particular population have not been identified. Up to this point, we have focused exclusively on working with international populations in the United States, but it is also important to mention the impact of U.S. mental health professionals providing services abroad. Globalization has resulted in more opportunities to provide psychosocial assistance internationally. These opportunities include participation in global initiatives that address barriers that prevent access to mental health services through international agencies such as the World Health Organization, as well as participation in nongovernmental organizations (NGOs) that provide psychosocial assistance in emergency settings, including regions of the world affected by natural disasters and war.

Wessells (2008) described some of the unintended consequences of mental health workers providing international assistance. He explained that international psychosocial assistance in emergency settings has become increasingly professionalized but that there are few empirically supported interventions for international emergency settings, and mental health workers therefore often rely on "preconceptions, personal preferences, and ideologies rather than [on] applied science that takes into account the unique historical, political, cultural, and social realities of the affected people and their situation" (p. 7). Wessells described one such example from Kosovo. Mental health professionals attempted to conduct experiential trauma work with Kosovar Albanians in response to an onslaught by the Serbian people. The processing of the painful experiences, however, led to increased hostility among the Kosovar Albanians, some of whom in turn left the trauma group to attack the Serbian people. In this situation, mental health professionals' attempts to help the Kosovar Albanians resulted in fueled hostilities. This example shows a failure to comply with Principle A (Beneficence and Non-maleficence) of APA's (2010) *Ethical Principles of Psychologists and Code of Conduct*, which states that psychologists "take care to do no harm."

The Kosovo incident is a particularly disturbing example of the potential to do harm, but more indirect opportunities for harm exist as well. Wessells (2008) also described the unintended consequences that occurred after the 2004 tsunami in Southeast Asia, which was said to be followed by the "Golden Tsunami." During the latter, NGOs (including those with a mental health focus) flooded the region, intent on helping, but they actually contributed to the already chaotic environment because of their lack of coordination, competition for providing services, and imposition of outsider approaches. Again, mental health professionals were underprepared to work effectively in an international setting.

However, some U.S. mental health organizations take great care to ensure that services are offered in a culturally appropriate way. For example, the National Board of Certified Counselors International (NBCC-I) Mental Health Facilitator Program (MHF) focuses on improving access to community-based mental health care at an international level but only at the request of local mental health experts (NBCC-I, 2011). MHF international workers collaborate with communities in various countries to identify people who are already involved in counseling-related services (i.e., teachers, nurses, clergy) rather than developing a new mental health profession. After identifying these people, the MHF workers train them to develop mental health facilitation skills. Community members, therefore, retain their professional identities and roles but add mental health facilitation skills to their practice. In addition, MHF programs are evaluated and modified as needed to fit cultural norms. Thus, although the potential for harm may exist when providing mental health services internationally, there is also the potential for good when services are provided in culturally appropriate ways.

The examples described here are not intended to insinuate that mental health professionals from outside the country generally provide inadequate service in international settings; rather, the examples are intended to highlight the need for mental health professionals to develop international competencies given the serious potential for harm. The cases suggest that there currently may be extreme variations in mental health professionals' international competencies even for professionals practicing abroad. Thus, a greater emphasis on international competencies is needed.

We have highlighted examples of the way in which U.S. mental health professionals might contribute to harm at an international level, but it is also important to consider how similar problems can occur within a professional's own country. It might be argued that mental health professionals, as with, for example, the racial issues in the 1960s in the United States, may need to further strengthen their multicultural competencies to mitigate the challenges of working with international clients. Using this logic, if U.S. mental health professionals were to become more multiculturally competent, then they would be better prepared to work with international populations. Yet there is evidence to suggest that multicultural competencies may not translate readily to work with international populations or in international settings.

Leung and Chen (2009) contended that although U.S. multicultural counseling theories acknowledge cultural variables more than do other theories, their applicability in an international context within the United States is limited. These limitations exist because U.S. multiculturalism is embedded in "the ideals, principles, and philosophical beliefs that are the core foundation of the U.S. political and social structure" (p. 947). These "ideals, principles, and beliefs" include culturally nuanced definitions of social justice, cultural democracy, and equity that were born out of the civil rights movement.

Graham (1999) stated a similar concern about the values of social work being applied in international contexts. He argued that the core principles of social work that guide intervention methods, such as social justice, equal interventions, and self-determination, were hard to operationalize in diverse contexts because the social work knowledge base was still dominated by a Eurocentric worldview. Thus, professional dialogues about ethics may inadvertently result in "culture wars" (Holtzhausen, 2011) in which U.S. values take precedent over other values.

Some scholars have provided examples of such cultural conflicts. For instance, Leung and Chen (2009) explained that in traditional Chinese societies, social relationships were hierarchical rather than lateral, individual rights were granted rather than assumed, and the value of social responsibility was viewed as ranking above that of individual freedom. Therefore, those who apply social justice principles related to multicultural diversity developed in the United States could provoke suspicion and resistance among Chinese clients and might even risk sanctioning or prosecution if the behaviors were considered to be a challenge to the current Chinese political system. Likewise, Cobbah (1987) contended that the problem of the oppression of women in Africa would not be answered by focusing on individual freedom but rather through values of communalism, including hierarchy, respect, restraint, responsibility, reciprocity, and commonality. These explanations suggest that multicultural values may not be synonymous with international values. Given the two examples just mentioned and many others that could be highlighted in different countries, it is critical that mental health professionals carefully balance their responsibility to adhere to their profession's code of ethics while respecting and obeying their culture's values, norms, and laws. Obviously, in instances in which individual and societal freedoms are highly restricted, it becomes more challenging, dangerous, and even criminal to openly and aggressively confront oppression and human rights violations. In such cases, mental health professionals must carefully navigate how they address these issues and strive to create small changes in their profession's code of ethics or culture that can eventually result in improved and more ethical services.

As mental health professionals have more opportunities to work with immigrants in their countries and with international persons who may identify with different value systems than those that are predominant in their own country, such issues are expected to become increasingly common. Even within the United States, some have questioned whether ethical principles developed in the United States should be universally applied and whether the core values of mental health professions are universally relevant (Healy, 2007; Knapp & VandeCreek, 2007).

Consider the following examples:

- Parents from Laos refuse medication to treat their daughter's epilepsy because in Hmong culture epileptic attacks are perceived as opportunities to communicate with the spiritual realm (Fadiman, 1997).
- A Mexican family is upset because the 17-year-old daughter recently attended a service at an evangelical Protestant church, dated a non-Hispanic student, and wants to attend a college that is far away from home (Knapp & VandeCreek, 2007).
- The parents in an East Asian family use physical punishment of their children to ensure obedience and conformity to their standards, including a high level of respect for elders (Healy, 2007).
- Parents from a Middle Eastern culture insist that their two daughters in elementary school act with such modesty that they do not speak in front of the class or express any desire to excel in any subject (Knapp & VandeCreek, 2007).

Bearing in mind these examples, how should internationally competent mental health professionals provide services to ensure that they are respecting cultural differences? What follows are some suggestions for how such professionals can function effectively and, at the same time, use culturally appropriate and respectful strategies.

The multicultural competencies that were originally developed in the United States to address racial (and other forms of) diversity may not be sufficient to encompass the increasing within-country international diversity, and as such, they also may not fully respect cultural differences in attitudes, behaviors, and cognitions. Although multicultural competencies may indeed highlight the role of culture, the values of multiculturalism are still embedded in U.S. nationalist ideals. In an increasingly international society, it is expected that mental health professionals will be working with clients whose values are not based on U.S. ideals. Thus, it is essential that U.S. mental health professionals develop the competencies to navigate these differences appropriately.

A final similarity between the international and multicultural movements should be mentioned. Although there has been an expressed need for international competencies among U.S. mental health professionals, progress toward formally incorporating an international focus into training has been slow. The mental health professions in the United States have responded to the need for international competencies at different rates.

Calls for U.S. mental health professions to internationalize have grown exponentially within the past decade (Douce, 2004; Gerstein, Heppner, Ægisdóttir, Leung, & Norsworthy, 2009; Heppner et al., 2008), and a number of mental health professional organizations have become more involved in internationally focused initiatives. For example, the APA now invites psychologists to collaborate with the United Nations to address a variety of global issues including gender equality and human rights (APA, 2009a). Moreover, the APA passed a "Resolution on Culture and Gender Awareness in International Psychology" in 2004 to offer guidance in the internationalization process (Norsworthy, Heppner, Ægisdóttir, Gerstein, & Pedersen, 2009). Nonetheless, the APA Commission on Accreditation has not yet specifically addressed the need for international competencies in psychology training programs.

The field of social work, in contrast, has made considerably more progress regarding its international focus. In 2000, the International Federation of Social Workers (IFSW) and the International Association of Schools of Social Work (IASSW) collaborated to adopt an international definition of social work (Sewpaul & Jones, 2004). Furthermore, the CSWE requires that baccalaureate and master's level social work programs include an international learning component to prepare social workers to recognize the global context of social work practice. Although it has been observed that there is considerable variation in the extent to which such training is provided (Lyons, 2006), this evidence does suggest that the social work profession is striving to promote international competencies among trainees.

It is encouraging that many U.S. mental health professions have acknowledged the significance of an international focus. However, we argue that it is as equally important that mental health training programs incorporate international competencies into their curricula. Without such training, the positive impact that mental health professionals will have when working with international populations will likely be limited. We note that in a parallel situation, decades passed before multicultural counseling competencies were added to the training of mental health professionals. International competencies, we argue, should not suffer a similar fate.

In summary, the international movement among U.S. mental health professionals has paralleled the progression of the multicultural counseling movement. Both movements evolved as it became apparent that additional competencies were needed to meet the needs of increasingly diverse societies. Although mental health professionals enhanced their abilities to meet the needs of culturally diverse clients by developing multicultural competencies, research has suggested that these professionals may not be appropriately addressing the needs of the international population. Therefore, U.S. mental health professionals must acquire additional competencies to function effectively and appropriately in an internationally diverse society.

INTERNATIONAL COMPETENCY MODELS

Here we review two models that have been proposed for enhancing mental health professionals' international competencies: Heppner, Leong, and Gerstein's (2008) cross-cultural competencies model and Ægisdóttir and Gerstein's (2010) international counseling competencies model. Although these models were originally developed for counselors and counseling psychologists, we contend that they are also relevant to other mental health professionals. In this section, we also highlight a new integrative paradigm of international counseling competencies.

Heppner et al. (2008) identified a set of characteristics that were said to describe the internationally competent counselor. They stated that such professionals should (a) use an ecological model (Bronfenbrenner, 1977, 1979) to understand the cultural contexts of their clients' microsystems, mesosystems, exosystems, macrosystems, and chronosystems and recognize this knowledge as culture specific; (b) understand how these systems affect ethnic minorities in their home country; (c) acquire knowledge about these systems in other parts of the world; (d) apply such knowledge when engaged in international activities; and (e) use their knowledge and skills to accommodate cross-cultural differences that would otherwise hinder their ability to work effectively. Specifically, Heppner et al. (2008) argued that these competencies were relevant for both those who planned to engage in international activities and individuals working with international persons in the context of their own countries.

Heppner et al.'s (2008) model embodies several strengths. First, the ecological perspective of Bronfenbrenner's (1977, 1979) model is intended to ensure that mental health professionals do not narrowly focus on the intrapsychic processes of individuals but also examine how the various systems in which a person resides (e.g., families, local communities, nations) may influence thoughts, feelings, beliefs, and behavior. For mental health professionals working domestically with international persons, it is critical to recognize the role of the larger sociocultural systems (macrosystems) and the history of systems (chronosystem) in providing culturally appropriate services, given that such systems may look very different in various parts of the world. Another strength of Heppner et al.'s (2008) model is its focus on cultural specificity. Rather than assuming that knowledge and skills are universal, internationally competent mental health professionals view knowledge and skills as a truth within a particular culture. Such an approach is essential to ensure that such professionals do not assume that U.S. theories and practices are universal truths, perpetuating a U.S.-centric bias that has existed for many years (Gergen, Gulerce, Lock, & Misra, 1996; Gerstein, Heppner, Ægisdóttir, Leung, & Norsworthy, 2009).

Limitations of Heppner et al.'s (2008) model also should be mentioned. While the model takes into account the interactions between the various systems in which a person lives (e.g., family, community, nation), it places less emphasis on the interactions occurring between the mental health professional and the client. Relatively little attention is given in this model to explaining how mental health professionals' values and assumptions influence their work, which increases the potential for unintentionally providing ethnocentric services. In a similar way, questions arise as to how to understand and negotiate cross-cultural differences in behavior, attitudes, and values given that Heppner et al. (2008) asserted that internationally competent mental health professionals regard knowledge as culture specific. More information is needed to determine whether an internationally competent mental health professional embraces a purely cultural-relativist stance within this model.

Ægisdóttir and Gerstein (2010) provided another model of international competencies for counselors and counseling psychologists. They adapted the widely used awareness, knowledge, and skills model of enhancing multicultural counseling competencies (Arredondo et al., 1996; D. W. Sue, Arredondo, & McDavis, 1992) to reflect international counseling competencies. Their model is composed of four dimensions—motivation, awareness, knowledge, and skills (MAKS)—related to offering international services in diverse settings. Specifically, Ægisdóttir and Gerstein suggested that counselors should (a) be *motivated* to seek out opportunities to develop cross-cultural competencies; (b) be *aware* that microsystems and macrosystems may vary significantly by culture and country; (c) be *knowledgeable* about their own cultural heritage and customs, other cultural groups, and international topics; and (d) increase their cross-cultural competency *skills*. They further contended that the development of these cross-cultural competencies would assist counseling professionals in successfully addressing international issues.

Ægisdóttir and Gerstein's (2010) model also possesses a number of strengths. One strength is that it focuses on dimensions of both the client and the mental health professional. That is, it not only highlights the importance of gathering information about the client but also stresses the necessity of mental health professionals reflecting on their own awareness and cultural knowledge. Given that such professionals' actions are inevitably influenced by their values, this type of awareness is essential to address biases that might influence how services are provided. Another strength is that the model underscores the affective component of working in international settings and with international populations. That is, it stresses the importance of motivating mental health professionals to be engaged in this type of work. Indeed, given the complexities of providing services in an international context that were mentioned earlier, motivation appears essential to the process of mental health professionals seeking knowledge, engaging in self-reflection about their own biases and assumptions, and developing new skills.

This model also has limitations. Although its proponents noted four domains integral to international competencies, the components of the model were not linked with any psychological or learning theories. Thus, it is unclear how competencies in any one of the four domains apply to other domains and whether there is an inherent order in which mental health professionals should attend to these various domains. Another limitation is that the model is somewhat ambiguous in describing the degree and type of motivation, knowledge, awareness, and skills that are necessary for mental health professionals to be internationally competent. Further discussion is required, therefore, to establish what differentiates minimal and more advanced international competencies for mental health professionals.

Each of these models is useful for conceptualizing the competencies needed for international work, but each lacks specificity, clearly testable hypotheses, and a strong philosophical foundation. More information about each model is also needed regarding how to train professionals systematically in these international competencies and how to integrate them into curricula. We believe that systematic learning is essential, given that many scholars have suggested that the acquisition of competencies is a developmental process (Ægisdóttir & Gerstein, 2010; Marsella & Pedersen, 2004).

TOWARD A NEW, INTEGRATED MODEL

In this section, we introduce our dynamic-systemic-process (DSP) model of international competencies, which was developed to address the limitations of other models. The DSP is based on previous models of international competencies for counselors (e.g., Ægisdóttir & Gerstein, 2010; Heppner et al., 2008), as well as dynamic systems theory (Thelen & Smith, 1994) and expectancy theory (Vroom, 1964). It is guided by the assumption that psychologists' development of international competencies is continuous, recursive, constantly evolving, cumulative, and dynamic and that this developmental process is in a reciprocal relationship with the environment (Gerstein, Hurley, & Hutchison, 2012).

Gerstein et al. (2012) defined *international competencies* as the possession of the motivation, awareness, knowledge, and skills required to provide culturally appropriate services to individuals whose primary country of identification differs from that of the service provider. This definition parallels that of Ægisdóttir and Gerstein (2010). The current definition and model differ from their work, however, in that the DSP model incorporates other variables thought to be related to the development of international competencies. It is also informed by an extensive literature review of the research on international effectiveness. More specifically, the DSP model integrates both the stable and dynamic characteristics of persons (person variables, person process variables), as well as the stable and dynamic characteristics of the environment (environmental variables, environmental process variables).

According to the DSP model, the development of international competencies is influenced in part by *person variables*, which are the relatively stable characteristics of a person that contribute to his or her effectiveness when working with international clientele (Gerstein et al., 2012). Specifically, research suggests that an individual's personality (Mol, Born, Willemsen, &Van Der Molen, 2005; Shaffer, Harrison, Gregersen, Black, & Ferzandi, 2006) and previous international experiences (Bhaskar-Shrinivas, Harrison, Shaffer, & Luk, 2005; Hechanova, Beehr, & Christiansen, 2003) are two variables that may influence his or her effectiveness in an international context. *Person process variables*, which are the dynamic characteristics of a person that interact with the environmental context, also must be understood in relation to the development of international competencies. Person process variables identified in the literature on international effectiveness include emotion recognition (Taylor, 1994), motivation to learn (Ægisdóttir & Gerstein, 2010; Black & Mendenhall, 1990; Johnson, Lenartowicz, & Apud, 2006; Noe, 1986), cultural adaptability (Hammer, Gudykunst, & Wiseman, 1978), cultural intelligence (Johnson et al., 2006), coping skills (Feldman & Thomas, 1991, 1992, 1993), cognitive complexity and flexibility (Detweiler, 1975, 1978), cognitive closure (Kashima & Loh, 2006), ethnorelativism (Wiseman, Hammer, & Nishida, 1989), and interpersonal skills (Abbe, Gulick, & Herman, 2007; Kealey, 1989). All of these variables are incorporated into the DSP model.

In addition, in the DSP model, it is assumed that the development of international competencies is also shaped by environmental variables and environmental process variables (Gerstein et al., 2012). *Environmental variables* are the stable aspects of the host culture and organization. In the literature on international effectiveness and for the DSP model, these variables include cultural distance (Hechanova et al., 2003) and characteristics of the job and organization (Bhaskar-Shrinivas et al., 2005). In contrast, *environmental process variables*, or the dynamic environmental influences affecting the development of international competencies, include the delivery, timing, and rigor of international training (Black, Mendenhall, & Ouddou, 1991; Littrell, Salas, Hess, Paley, & Riedel, 2006; Mendenhall & Oddou, 1986). These variables are incorporated into the DSP model as well.

In summary, the DSP model of international competencies is guided by the belief that the development of international competencies is a process that must be understood within context. Although this model is admittedly more complex than the two previous models of intentional competencies that have been described, it is believed that it more closely reflects the reality of international work. Moreover, it offers a possible road map for implementing training programs to better prepare mental health professionals for international work. It is hoped that this model can provide a framework for investigating how international competencies may develop over time.

Clearly, there is a great deal of complexity involved in defining international competencies. Each of the models reviewed embodies a number of strengths, including their emphasis on mental health professionals' awareness of the greater historical, political, and societal forces that influence the way in which services should be provided and the development of skills in light of this awareness. Although there are limitations linked with these models, they provide a general overview of what it may mean to be an internationally competent mental health professional.

INTERNATIONAL COMPETENCY TRAINING

We next discuss some ways in which such competencies are developed. More specifically, we highlight various recommendations that have been offered for promoting international competencies and review the research regarding how training programs prepare students to acquire these skills.

Many recommendations have been made about ways to increase the international competencies of mental health professionals (e.g., Ægisdóttir & Gerstein, 2010; Gerstein & Ægisdóttir, 2007; Heppner, 2006; Leong & Ponterotto, 2003; Marsella & Pedersen, 2004). Marsella and Pedersen (2004), for example, described 50 ways to internationalize psychology, including actions to be taken by professional psychology associations and actions to be implemented by academic departments. These actions include increasing awareness of the social, political, historical, and cultural determinants of all the psychologies, as well as encouraging academic minor concentrations that focus on global problems. Leong and Ponterotto (2003) recommended having training programs support travel to international conferences, integrating international publications into the curriculum, and encouraging internships at internationally focused sites. Similarly, Ægisdóttir and Gerstein (2010), relying on the MAKS model, provided suggestions for ways that training programs could enhance international competencies.

Although such recommendations are helpful, training programs must also consider the extent to which they plan to offer students training in international competencies. The CSWE identified three approaches for helping programs identify the level of curricular intensity for international training: selective, concentrated, and integrated (Estes, 2009). The *selective* approach is aimed at helping students gain a fuller understanding of international dimensions of domestic social work problems. Limited coursework and field practice in cross-cultural settings are offered within this approach. The *concentrated* approach, in contrast, is geared toward promoting international social work as a discrete field of professional practice. Students may focus on international dimensions of poverty, racism, and sexism. Finally, for the *integrated* approach, highly specialized programs exist to prepare students for leadership roles in national and international social work practice. Applying the CSWE model more broadly, mental health training programs could be more intentional and systematic when offering international training opportunities if they first embrace one of the three approaches to incorporating international content just mentioned.

Given the numerous recommendations in the literature about how to provide international training opportunities, it is important to determine whether U.S. mental health training programs are indeed using them. Research regarding the presence of international training opportunities in such programs, however, is limited. Moreover, although international immersion programs have frequently been described as a way to enhance students' international competencies (Greatrex-White, 2007; Lindsey, 2005; Wang & Heppner, 2009), there has been considerably less attention given to other types of international training opportunities.

International immersion programs have been offered in many mental health training programs, including nursing (Greatrex-White, 2007; Tabi & Mukherjee, 2003; Zorn, 1996), social work (Boyle, Nackerud, & Kilpatrick, 1999; Krajewski-Jaime, Brown, Ziefert, & Kaufman, 1996; Lindsey, 2005), school counseling (Alexander, Kruczek, & Ponterotto, 2005), and counseling psychology (Friedlander, Carranza, & Guzman, 2002; Wang & Heppner, 2009). The reported benefits of these immersion experiences include the development of an international perspective (Zorn, 1996) and new ways of expressing empathy, as well as culture-specific practices learned from host countries (Ruddock & Turner, 2007) and increased awareness and knowledge of the host culture (Boyle et al., 1999). Such results are not surprising when one considers that counselors most frequently describe field experiences as being highly influential in their professional development (Furr & Carroll, 2003).

Although the research suggests that immersion programs do provide trainees the opportunity to develop international competencies, training programs should be cautious about relying solely on immersion programs to provide international training opportunities. Logistical and financial barriers often limit the number of students who can participate (Gerstein & Ægisdóttir, 2007), and those who do commit the time and resources to an international experience may already have an interest in working internationally. That is, although international immersion programs might be more geared for those who work internationally, other avenues for internationally focused training must be included for those professionals who may not have the time or resources to travel internationally.

Turner-Essel and Waehler (2009) examined the ways in which U.S. counseling psychology training programs provide students with international training opportunities using Leong and Ponterotto's (2003) eight recommendations for internationalizing programs. More than half of the responding training directors indicated that their respective programs incorporated international issues by focusing on multiculturalism (70.2%), promoting travel to international conferences (71.1%), incorporating works by non-Americans in the curriculum (59.5%), and considering international experience as somewhat or extremely important in the admissions process (89.2%). Less than half of the respondents indicated that international learning was incorporated through training experiences with an international focus (45.5%), inviting international guests (41.6%), offering international exchanges (4.4%), and requiring foreign language competency (0%). A follow-up study conducted by Hurley, Gerstein, and Ægisdóttir (2012) 3 years later yielded similar results. No statistically significant changes occurred regarding the presence of international opportunities with the exception that international issues were increasingly being incorporated into multicultural training content in 2010 (92.3%) compared with 2007 (70.2%).

Hurley et al. (2012) also examined differences in training directors' and doctoral students' perceptions of international training opportunities. They found that directors perceived international training opportunities integrated into programs to a greater extent compared to what their students reported. In addition, directors were significantly more knowledgeable in the areas of international research and curriculum initiatives compared with their students. Nonetheless, on average, both directors and doctoral students reported that international training opportunities were available only "to a small extent" or "to some extent." These results suggest that there is considerable room for improvement in the implementation of international training opportunities.

Systematic research regarding the availability of international training opportunities in other types of U.S. mental health training programs is limited. For example, the U.S. social work profession has stated that international content must be integrated into the curriculum, but we found no studies that examined how this content had been integrated other than through immersion experiences. Thus, although international content is required as part of the accreditation process for baccalaureate and master's level social work programs, it is unclear how programs are meeting these requirements. This lack of research parallels Lyons's (2006) observations that there may be considerable variation in the extent to which international content is included in training.

In summary, although many recommendations have been offered for enhancing international competencies, little information is available about the extent to which mental health training programs are structuring their programs to teach these competencies. Obviously, some delay is inevitable between the time recommendations are made and the reality of their implementation. Nonetheless, now is the time for mental health training programs in the United States to conduct more research in this area. Such research is essential to ensure that programs are, indeed, training mental health professionals to possess these international competencies.

Implications for Mental Health Professionals

Although systematic change is necessary in training programs, mental health professionals also can strive to enhance their services at the individual and organizational level. Nonetheless, navigating the practical implications of globalization may seem like a formidable process for such professionals. Indeed, there are challenges linked with each specific field of mental health (e.g., psychology, social work, psychiatry) when providing national or international services. Although it is impossible to capture sufficiently the breadth and depth of all of the practical implications of globalization, we highlight a few broad implications that are likely to be generalizable across various mental health disciplines.

As globalization continues to result in major demographic shifts within countries, mental health professionals will need to become more reflective about how well their services address the needs of international persons. It may be useful to ask oneself the following questions:

- To what extent does your organization currently provide services to international persons in the community?
- How do the rates of international clients using your services compare with the number of international persons in the community?
- If differences exist, what are some possible reasons?
- How does your organization accommodate language barriers or other differences that may interfere with the provision of services?
- What have been the experiences of the international clientele who have used your services?

The growing internationalization of the mental health professions will also require that mental health professionals familiarize themselves with ecological approaches to the provision of services, such as that proposed by Bronfenbrenner (1977, 1979) and adapted to an international context by Heppner et al. (2008). As Heppner et al. (2008) discussed, and as discussed earlier in this chapter, mental health professionals will need to actively seek out information about the various systems in which a client resides (e.g., family, local community, national community) to determine how they may need to accommodate for cultural differences that could interfere with their ability to work effectively. Because cultural and international differences between the client and mental health professional will add complexity in how services are provided, relying on a systems approach can offer a useful heuristic tool to navigate the process.

In a similar way, mental health professionals will have more opportunities to work with clients who may be dramatically different in terms of family values, conceptualizations of mental illnesses, and attitudes toward medication. In light of such differences, we expect that mental health professionals will need to become increasingly familiar with ethical decision-making models that address the role of culture in the provision of services. The decision-making model outlined by Knapp and VandeCreek (2007) serves as one such example. In their model, conflict is analyzed from the perspective of *soft universalism*, which assumes that all cultures share basic values, although these values may be expressed differently across cultures. As mental health professionals continue to work with increasingly internationally diverse clients, we expect that a reliance on such models will take on greater relevance and importance for mental health professionals.

Globalization will inevitably continue to influence the way in which mental health services are delivered in both expected and unexpected ways. Therefore, continuing to acquire knowledge and skills over time when working with international clients may be the most integral competency for mental health professionals to possess. Although a foundation in international competencies is necessary, we anticipate that an unending and dynamic openness to learning from those elsewhere around the world will be most beneficial in addressing the changes brought forth by globalization.

CHALLENGES AND FUTURE DIRECTIONS

Enhancing international competencies among mental health professionals is not without its challenges. In this section, we further explore a few challenges that were previously outlined in this chapter and suggest future directions for overcoming them. Specifically, we discuss the complications that arise from the tensions between the international and multicultural counseling movements, problems with conceptualizing international competencies, and issues regarding training persons to possess such competencies.

Heppner et al. (2009) described several areas of contention between the multicultural and international movements, including the lack of integration of multicultural counseling into the cross-cultural counseling movement, the misapplication of U.S. psychology methodologies to nondominant cultural groups, and the implications of limited resources. Because the concept of multiculturalism has not been clearly defined within the international movement, some scholars have expressed concern that mental health professionals might inadvertently impose the values of dominant cultures onto others in an international context. In addition, multicultural (Quintana, Troyano, & Taylor, 2001) and international (Ægisdóttir, Gerstein, Leung, Kwan, & Lonner, 2009) scholars have warned that, for example, U.S. methodologies could be used to impose U.S. perspectives. For instance, because linguistic equivalence of measures has been associated with cultural equivalence, some mental health professionals who conduct international research might wrongly assume that attention to statistics is equivalent to attention to cultural variables. Finally, professionals within the two movements have had to compete for limited financial resources, as well as for attention within the discipline. For example, some fear that working abroad with people in Mexico would be highly regarded, whereas working with Mexican Americans would be shunned (Gerstein, Heppner, Stockton, Leong, & Ægisdóttir, 2009). Heppner and colleagues therefore encouraged mental health professionals to explore how the two movements might complement one another in the areas of research, training, and practice.

Another challenge for the international movement is the lack of research on the dimensions and specifics of international competencies. In particular, although models such as Heppner et al.'s (2008) cross-cultural competency model, Ægisdóttir and Gerstein's (2010) international competencies model, and Gerstein et al.'s (2012) DSP model of international competencies have been proposed, no research has been conducted to ascertain whether competencies proposed in these models are beneficial to working with international clients. Clearly, more research needs to be conducted not only to measure the international competencies of trainees and professionals but also to link these competencies with actual client outcomes. Research is needed as well on whether there is a universal set of international competencies or whether both universal and unique competencies are needed by U.S. mental health professionals and other professionals living abroad. Additionally, researchers should compare the effectiveness (i.e., trainee outcomes) of various curricula designed to teach different international competencies.

A final challenge is the lack of information about the training process. Although we offered recommendations for promoting international competencies, there is currently a lack of research on what types of training experiences and classes are, indeed, effective in shaping international competencies. Just as it is important to link specific competencies with client outcomes, it is critical to determine whether specific training practices lead to culturally appropriate international competencies.

None of the challenges just highlighted are insurmountable. Rather, they can serve as a reminder that the international movement must remain accountable to its mission. It is hoped that this chapter will stimulate additional dialogue and solutions about how the objectives detailed herein can be best achieved. It is the responsibility of the community of mental health professionals to make certain that we are properly equipped to function in this ever changing, rapidly shrinking, and increasingly interdependent global society.

REFERENCES

Abbe, A., Gulick, L. M. V., & Herman, J. L. (2007). *Cross-cultural competence in army leaders: A conceptual and empirical foundation* (SR 2008-01). Arlington, VA: U.S. Army Research Institute for the Behavioral and Social Sciences.

Abe-Kim, J., Takeuchi, D. T., Hong, S., Zane, N., Sue, S., Spencer, M., . . . Alegría, M. (2007). Use of mental health-related services among immigrant and U.S.-born Asian Americans: Results from the National Latino and Asian American Study. *American Journal of Public Health, 97,* 91–98. doi:10.2105/AJPH.2006.098541

Ægisdóttir, S., & Gerstein, L. H. (2010). International counseling competencies: A new frontier in multicultural training. In J. G. Ponterotto, J. M. Casas, L. A. Suzuki, & C. M. Alexander (Eds.), *Handbook of multicultural counseling* (3rd ed., pp. 175–188). Thousand Oaks, CA: Sage.

Ægisdóttir, S., Gerstein, L. H., Leung, S.-M. A., Kwan, K. L. K., & Lonner, W. J. (2009). Theoretical and methodological issues when studying culture. In L. H. Gerstein, P. P. Heppner, S. Ægisdóttir, S.-M. A. Leung, & K. L. Norsworthy (Eds.), *International handbook of cross-cultural counseling: Cultural assumptions and practices worldwide* (pp. 89–109). Thousand Oaks, CA: Sage.

Alexander, C. M., Kruczek, T., & Ponterotto, J. G. (2005). Building multicultural competencies in school counselor trainees: An international immersion experience. *Counselor Education and Supervision, 44,* 255–266. doi:10.1002/j.1556-6978.2005.tb01754.x

American Counseling Association. (2005). *Code of ethics and standards of practice.* Alexandria, VA: Author.

American Psychological Association. (2003). Guidelines on multicultural education, training, research, practice, and organizational change for psychologists. *American Psychologist, 58,* 377–402. doi:10.1037/0003-066X.58.5.377

American Psychological Association. (2009a). *APA at the United Nations.* Retrieved from http://www.apa.org/international/un

American Psychological Association. (2009b). *Guidelines and principles for accreditation of programs in professional psychology.* Washington, DC: Author.

American Psychological Association. (2010). *Ethical principles of psychologists and code of conduct (2002, Amended June 1, 2010).* Retrieved from http://www.apa.org/ethics/code/index.aspx

Ang, P. L. D., & Liamputtong, P. (2008). "Out of the circle": International students and the use of university counseling services. *Australian Journal of Adult Learning, 48,* 109–130.

Arredondo, P., & Perez, P. (2003). Expanding multicultural competence through social justice leadership. *The Counseling Psychologist, 31,* 282–289. doi:10.1177/0011000003031003003

Arredondo, P., Toporek, R., Brown, S. P., Jones, J., Locke, D. C., Sanchez, J., & Stadler, H. (1996). Operationalization of the multicultural counseling competencies. *Journal of Multicultural Counseling and Development, 24,* 42–78. doi:10.1002/j.2161-1912.1996.tb00288.x

Bhaskar-Shrinivas, P., Harrison, D. A., Shaffer, M. A., & Luk, D. M. (2005). Input-based and time-based models of international adjustment: Meta-analytic evidence and theoretical extensions. *The Academy of Management Journal, 48,* 257–281. doi:10.5465/AMJ.2005.16928400

Black, J. S., & Mendenhall, M. (1990). Cross-cultural training effectiveness: A review and a theoretical framework for future research. *Academy of Management Review, 15,* 113–136.

Black, J. S., Mendenhall, M., & Oddou, G. (1991). Toward a comprehensive model of international adjustment: An integration of multiple theoretical perspectives. *Academy of Management Review, 16,* 291–317.

Boyle, D. P., Nackerud, L., & Kilpatrick, A. (1999). The road less traveled: Cross-cultural, international experiential learning. *International Social Work, 42,* 201–214. doi:10.1177/002087289904200208

Bronfenbrenner, U. (1977). Toward an experimental ecology of human development. *American Psychologist, 32,* 513–531. doi:10.1037/0003-066X.32.7.513

Bronfenbrenner, U. (1979). *The ecology of human development: Experiments by nature and design.* Cambridge, MA: Harvard University Press.

Caplan, N., & Nelson, S. D. (1973). On being useful: The nature and consequences of psychological research on social problems. *American Psychologist, 28,* 199–211. doi:10.1037/h0034433

Clark, R. (1990). Minority influence: The role of argument refutation of the majority position and social support for the minority position. *European Journal of Social Psychology, 20,* 489–497.

Cobbah, J. A. M. (1987). African values and the human rights debate: An African perspective. *Human Rights Quarterly, 9,* 309–331. doi:10.2307/761878

Council for Accreditation of Counseling and Related Educational Programs. (2009). *2009 standards.* Alexandria, VA: Author.

Council on Social Work Education. (2008). *2008 educational policy and accreditation standards.* Alexandria, VA: Author.

Dadfar, S., & Friedlander, M. L. (1982). Differential attitudes of international students toward seeking professional psychological help. *Journal of Counseling Psychology, 29,* 335–338. doi:10.1037/0022-0167.29.3.335

Detweiler, R. A. (1975). On inferring the intentions of a person from another culture. *Journal of Personality, 43,* 591–611. doi:10.1111/j.1467-6494.1975.tb00724.x

Detweiler, R. A. (1978). Culture, category width, and attributions: A model-building approach to the reasons for cultural effects. *Journal of Cross-Cultural Psychology, 9,* 259–284. doi:10.1177/002202217893001

Douce, L. A. (2004). Society of Counseling Psychology Division 17 of APA Presidential Address: Globalization of counseling psychology. *The Counseling Psychologist, 32,* 142–152. doi:10.1177/0011000003260009

Estes, R. J. (2009). *United States–based conceptualization of international social work education.* Retrieved from http://www.cswe.org/File.aspx?id=31429.

Fadiman, A. (1997). *The spirit catches you and you fall down: A Hmong child, her American doctors, and the collision of two cultures.* New York, NY: Farrar, Straus & Giroux.

Feldman, D. C., & Thomas, D. C. (1991). From Desert Shield to Desert Storm: Life as an expatriate during the Persian Gulf War. *Organizational Dynamics, 20,* 37–46. doi:10.1016/0090-2616(91)90070-P

Feldman, D. C., & Thomas, D. C. (1992). Career management issues facing expatriates. *Journal of International Business Studies, 23,* 271–293. doi:10.1057/palgrave.jibs.8490268

Feldman, D. C., & Thomas, D. C. (1993). Expatriation, repatriation, and domestic geographical relocation: An empirical investigation of adjustment to new job assignments. *Journal of International Business Studies, 24,* 507–529. doi:10.1057/palgrave.jibs.8490243

Friedlander, M. L., Carranza, V. E., & Guzman, M. (2002). International exchanges in family therapy: Training, research, and practice in Spain and the U.S. *The Counseling Psychologist, 30,* 314–329. doi:10.1177/0011000002302009

Furr, S. R., & Carroll, J. J. (2003). Critical incidents in student counselor development. *Journal of Counseling & Development, 81,* 483–489. doi:10.1002/j.1556-6678.2003.tb00275.x

Gergen, K. J., Gulerce, A., Lock, A., & Misra, G. (1996). Psychological science in cultural context. *American Psychologist, 51,* 496–503.

Gerstein, L. H., & Ægisdóttir, S. (2007). Training international social change agents: Transcending a U.S. counseling paradigm. *Counselor Education and Supervision, 47,* 123–139. doi:10.1002/j.1556-6978.2007.tb00043.x

Gerstein, L. H., Heppner, P. P., Ægisdóttir, S., Leung, S.-M. A., & Norsworthy, K. L. (2009). Cross-cultural counseling: History, challenges, and rationale. In L. H. Gerstein, P. P. Heppner, S. Ægisdóttir, S.-M. A. Leung, & K. L. Norsworthy (Eds.), *International handbook of cross-cultural counseling: Cultural assumptions and practices worldwide* (pp. 3–32). Thousand Oaks, CA: Sage.

Gerstein, L. H., Heppner, P. P., Stockton, R., Leong, F. L., & Ægisdóttir, S. (2009). The counseling profession in- and outside the United States. In L. H. Gerstein, P. P. Heppner, S. Ægisdóttir, S.-M. A. Leung, & K. L. Norsworthy (Eds.), *International handbook of cross-cultural counseling: Cultural assumptions and practices worldwide* (pp. 53–67). Thousand Oaks, CA: Sage.

Gerstein, L. H., Hurley, E., & Hutchison, A. (2012). *The dynamic-systemic-process model of international competencies for applied psychologists.* Manuscript in preparation.

Graham, M. J. (1999). The African-centered worldview: Toward a paradigm for social work. *Journal of Black Studies, 30,* 103–122. doi:10.1177/002193479903000106

Greatrex-White, S. (2007). A way of seeing study abroad: Narratives from nurse education. *Learning in Health and Social Care, 6,* 134–144. doi:10.1111/j.1473-6861.2007.00157.x

Guthrie, R. (1976). *Even the rat was white: A historical view of psychology.* Boston, MA: Allyn & Bacon.

Hammer, M. R., Gudykunst, W. B., & Wiseman, R. L. (1978). Dimensions of intercultural effectiveness: An exploratory study. *International Journal of Intercultural Relations, 2,* 382–393. doi:10.1016/0147-1767(78)90036-6

Healy, L. M. (2004). International dimensions of multicultural social work. In L. Gutierrez, M. Zuniga, & D. Lum (Eds.), *Education for multicultural social work practice: Implications for economic and social justice* (pp. 307–318). Alexandria, VA: Council on Social Work Education.

Healy, L. M. (2007). Universalism and cultural relativism in social work ethics. *International Social Work, 50*, 11–26. doi:10.1177/0020872807071479

Hechanova, R., Beehr, T. A., & Christiansen, N. D. (2003). Antecedents and consequences of employees' adjustment to overseas assignment: A meta-analytic review. *Applied Psychology: An International Review, 52*, 213–236. doi:10.1111/1464-0597.00132

Heggins, W. J., & Jackson, J. F. L. (2003). Understanding the collegiate experience for Asian international students at a Midwestern research university. *College Student Journal, 37*, 379–391.

Heppner, P. P. (2006). The benefits and challenges of becoming cross-culturally competent psychologists: Presidential address. *The Counseling Psychologist, 34*, 147–172. doi:10.1177/0011000005282832

Heppner, P. P., Ægisdóttir, S., Leung, S.-M. A., Duan, C., Helms, J. E., Gerstein, L. H., & Pedersen, P. B. (2009). The intersection of multicultural and cross-national movements in the United States: A complementary role to promote culturally sensitive research, training, and practice. In L. H. Gerstein, P. P. Heppner, S. Ægisdóttir, S.-M. A. Leung, & K. L. Norsworthy (Eds.), *International handbook of cross-cultural counseling: Cultural assumptions and practices worldwide* (pp. 33–52). Thousand Oaks, CA: Sage.

Heppner, P. P., Leong, F. T. L., & Gerstein, L. H. (2008). Counseling within a changing world: Meeting the psychological needs of societies and the world. In W. B. Walsh (Ed.), *Biennial review of counseling psychology*. New York, NY: Taylor & Francis.

Holtzhausen, L. (2011). When values collide: Finding common ground for social work education in the United Arab Emirates. *International Social Work, 54*, 191–208. doi:10.1177/0020872810372364

Hurley, E. J., Gerstein, L. H., & Ægisdóttir, S. (2012). Examining internationalization in U.S. counseling psychology training programs. *The Counseling Psychologist*. Advance online publication. doi:10.1177/0011000012436432

Ibrahim, F. A., & Ingram, M. A. (2007). Counseling South Asian international students. In H. Singaravelu & M. Pope (Eds.), *A handbook for counseling international students in the United States* (pp. 195–209). Alexandria, VA: American Counseling Association.

Institute for International Education. (2011). *Open doors 2010: International students in the U.S.* Retrieved from http://www.iie.org/Research-and-Publications/Open-Doors/Data

Johnson, J. P., Lenartowicz, T., & Apud, S. (2006). Cross-cultural competence in international business: Toward a definition and a model. *Journal of International Business Studies, 37*, 525–543. doi:10.1057/palgrave.jibs.8400205

Kashima, E. S., & Loh, E. (2006). International students' acculturation: Effects of international, conational, and local ties and need for closure. *International Journal of Intercultural Relations, 30*, 471–485. doi:10.1016/j.ijintrel.2005.12.003

Kealey, D. J. (1989). A study of cross-cultural effectiveness: Theoretical issues, practical applications. *International Journal of Intercultural Relations*, *13*, 387–428. doi:10.1016/0147-1767(89)90019-9

Knapp, S., & VandeCreek, L. (2007). When values of different cultures conflict: Ethical decision making in a multicultural context. *Professional Psychology: Research and Practice*, *38*, 660–666. doi:10.1037/0735-7028.38.6.660

Krajewski-Jaime, E. R., Brown, K. S., Ziefert, M., & Kaufman, E. (1996). Utilizing international clinical practice to build inter-cultural sensitivity in social work students. *Journal of Multicultural Social Work*, *4*(2), 15–29. doi:10.1300/J285v04n02_02

Leong, F. T. L., & Ponterotto, J. G. (2003). A proposal for internationalizing counseling psychology in the United States: Rationale, recommendations, and challenges. *The Counseling Psychologist*, *31*, 381–395. doi:10.1177/0011000003031004001

Leung, S. A. (2003). A journey worth traveling: Globalization of counseling psychology. *The Counseling Psychologist*, *31*, 412–419. doi:10.1177/0011000003031004004

Leung, S. A., & Chen, P.-W. (2009). Developing counseling psychology in Chinese communities in Asia: Indigenous, multicultural, and cross-cultural considerations. *The Counseling Psychologist*, *37*, 944–966. doi:10.1177/0011000009339973

Lindsey, E. W. (2005). Study abroad and values development in social work students. *Journal of Social Work Education*, *41*, 229–249. doi:10.5175/JSWE.2005.200303110

Littrell, L. N., Salas, E., Hess, K. P., Paley, N., & Riedel, S. (2006). Expatriate preparation: A critical analysis of 25 years of cross-cultural training research. *Human Resource Development Review*, *5*, 355–388. doi:10.1177/1534484306290106

Lyons, K. (2006). Globalization and social work: International and local implications. *British Journal of Social Work*, *36*, 365–380. doi:10.1093/bjsw/bcl007

Marsella, A. J., & Pedersen, P. B. (2004). Internationalizing the counseling psychology curriculum: Toward new values, competencies, and directions. *Counselling Psychology Quarterly*, *17*, 413–423. doi:10.1080/09515070412331331246

Mendenhall, M., & Oddou, G. R. (1986). Acculturation profiles of expatriate managers: Implications for cross-cultural training programs. *Columbia Journal of World Business*, *21*, 73–79.

Mol, S. T., Born, M. P., Willemsen, M. E., & Van Der Molen, H. T. (2005). Predicting expatriate job performance for selection purposes: A quantitative review. *Journal of Cross-Cultural Psychology*, *36*, 590–620. doi:10.1177/0022022105278544

National Association of Social Workers. (2001). *Standards for cultural competence in social work practice*. Washington, DC: Author.

National Board of Certified Counselors International. (2011). Mental health facilitator. Retrieved from http://www.nbccinternational.org/mhf

National Organization of Human Service Professionals. (2000). Ethical standards of human service professionals. *Human Service Education*, *20*, 61–68.

Nilsson, J. E., Berkel, L. A., Flores, L. Y., & Lucas, M. S. (2004). Utilization rate and presenting concerns of international students at a university counseling center:

Implications for outreach programming. *Journal of College Student Psychotherapy*, *19*, 49–59. doi:10.1300/J035v19n02_05

Noe, R. A. (1986). Trainee's attributes and attitudes: Neglected influences on training effectiveness. *The Academy of Management Review*, *11*, 736–749.

Norsworthy, K. L., Heppner, P. P., Ægisdóttir, S., Gerstein, L. H., & Pedersen, P. B. (2009). Exportation of U.S.-based models of counseling and counseling psychology: A critical perspective. In L. H. Gerstein, P. P. Heppner, S. Ægisdóttir, S.-M. A. Leung, & K. L. Norsworthy (Eds.), *International handbook of cross-cultural counseling: Cultural assumptions and practices worldwide* (pp. 3–32). Thousand Oaks, CA: Sage.

Olivas, M., & Li, C. (2006). Understanding stressors for international students in higher education: What college counselors and personnel need to know. *Journal of Instructional Psychology*, *33*, 217–222.

President's Commission on Mental Health. (1978). *Report to the president*. Washington, DC: U.S. Government Printing Office.

Quintana, S. M., Troyano, N., & Taylor, G. (2001). Cultural validity and inherent challenges in quantitative methods for multicultural research. In J. G. Ponterotto, J. M. Casas, L. A. Suzuki, & C. M. Alexander (Eds.), *Handbook of multicultural counseling and psychology* (pp. 604–630). Thousand Oaks, CA: Sage.

Ruddock, H. C., & Turner, D. S. (2007). Developing cultural sensitivity: Nursing students' experiences of a study abroad programme. *Journal of Advanced Nursing*, *59*, 361–369. doi:10.1111/j.1365-2648.2007.04312.x

Samuda, R. (1975). *Psychological testing of American minorities: Issues and consequences*. New York, NY: Doubleday.

Sewpaul, V., & Jones, D. (2004). Global standards for social work education and training. *Social Work Education*, *23*, 493–513. doi:10.1080/0261547042000252244

Shaffer, M. A., Harrison, D. A., Gregersen, H., Black, J. S., & Ferzandi, L. A. (2006). You can take it with you: Individual differences and expatriate effectiveness. *Journal of Applied Psychology*, *91*, 109–125. doi:10.1037/0021-9010.91.1.109

Sue, D. W., Arredondo, R., & McDavis, R. J. (1992). Multicultural counseling competencies and standards: A call to the profession. *Journal of Counseling & Development*, *70*, 477–486. doi:10.1002/j.1556-6676.1992.tb01642.x

Sue, D. W., & Sue, D. (1977). Barriers to effective cross-cultural counseling. *Journal of Counseling Psychology*, *24*, 420–429. doi:10.1037/0022-0167.24.5.420

Sue, S., & McKinney, H. (1975). Asian Americans in the community mental health care system. *American Journal of Orthopsychiatry*, *45*, 111–118. doi:10.1111/j.1939-0025.1975.tb01172.x

Sue, S., McKinney, H., Allen, D., & Hall, J. (1974). Delivery of community mental health services to Black and White clients. *Journal of Consulting and Clinical Psychology*, *42*, 794–801. doi:10.1037/h0037579

Tabi, M. M., & Mukherjee, S. (2003). Nursing in a global community: A study abroad program. *Journal of Transcultural Nursing*, *14*, 134–138. doi:10.1177/1043659602250637

Taylor, E. W. (1994). Intercultural competency: A transformative learning process. *Adult Education Quarterly, 44*, 154–174. doi:10.1177/074171369404400303

Thelen, E., & Smith, L. B. (1994). *A dynamic systems approach to the development of perception and action.* Cambridge: MIT Press.

Turner-Essel, L., & Waehler, C. (2009). Integrating internationalization in counseling psychology training programs. *The Counseling Psychologist, 37*, 877–901. doi:10.1177/0011000009336149

U.S. Census Bureau. (2010). *Place of birth of the foreign-born population: 2009.* Retrieved from http://www.census.gov/population/foreign

U.S. Department of Health and Human Services. (2001). *Mental health: Culture, race, and ethnicity—A supplement to "Mental Health: A Report of the Surgeon General."* Rockville, MD: U.S. Department of Health and Human Services, Substance Abuse and Mental Health Services Administration, Center for Mental Health Services.

U.S. Department of Homeland Security. (2011). *Immigrant population residing in the United States: January 2010.* Washington, DC: U.S. Department of Homeland Security, Office of Immigration Statistics, Policy Directorate.

Vega, W. A., Kolody, B., Aguilar-Gaxiola, S., & Catalano, R. (1999). Gaps in service utilization by Mexican Americans with mental health problems. *The American Journal of Psychiatry, 156*, 928–934.

Vroom, V. H. (1964). *Work and motivation.* New York, NY: McGraw-Hill.

Wang, L., & Heppner, P. P. (2009). Cross-cultural collaboration: Developing cross-cultural competencies and yuan-fen. In L. H. Gerstein, P. P. Heppner, S. Ægisdóttir, S.-M. A. Leung, & K. L. Norsworthy (Eds.), *International handbook of cross-cultural counseling: Cultural assumptions and practices worldwide* (pp. 141–154). Thousand Oaks, CA: Sage.

Wessells, M. G. (2008). Do no harm: Challenges in organizing psychosocial support to displaced people in emergency settings. *Refuge: Canada's Periodical on Refugees, 25*, 6–14.

Whitley, R., Kirmayer, L. J., & Groleau, D. (2006). Understanding immigrants' reluctance to use mental health services: A qualitative study from Montreal. *Canadian Journal of Psychiatry, 51*, 205–209.

Wiseman, R. L., Hammer, M. R., & Nishida, H. (1989). Predictors of intercultural communication competence. *International Journal of Intercultural Relations, 13*, 349–370. doi:10.1016/0147-1767(89)90017-5

Zorn, C. R. (1996). The long-term impact on nursing students of participating in international education. *Journal of Professional Nursing, 12*, 106–110. doi:10.1016/S8755-7223(96)80056-1

10

MULTICULTURAL EDUCATION, GLOBAL EDUCATION: SYNERGIES FOR A PEACEFUL WORLD

ESTELA MATRIANO AND TOH SWEE-HIN (S. H. TOH)

This chapter focuses on two recognized innovative and transformative education movements: multicultural education and global education. These two movements seek to help build societies and a world order capable of meeting the needs, protecting the rights, and ensuring the ecological security of all humanity. Acknowledging that multicultural education has contributed valuable ideas and practices in responding to the growth of cultural diversity in many countries, the case is made for linking the work of educators and other professionals in promoting multiculturalism with the vision, goals, and strategies of global education. Drawing on a growing body of conceptual and theoretical analysis, professional and community practice and research, as well as personal experiences, we demonstrate why the integration of multicultural and international perspectives is important in education. We aim to provide relevant and helpful guidance for education professionals to become global educators, optimizing their contributions to these specific fields of

DOI: 10.1037/14044-010
Internationalizing Multiculturalism: Expanding Professional Competencies in a Globalized World,
R. L. Lowman (Editor)

transformative education and in the process become aware of synergies that can mutually strengthen the capacities of multicultural education and global education and help to build a more peaceful world for all humanity.

OUR ROADS TO GLOBAL EDUCATION

Over a number of decades, the paths of the two authors of this chapter have often crossed, especially within the international professional educator organization called the World Council for Curriculum and Instruction (WCCI). In the conferences, workshops, and research activities of WCCI, we discovered that we shared many common values, principles, ideas, and strategies in educational fields underpinned by the vision of building a more peaceful world. Of these, two are especially meaningful—namely, multicultural education and global education—given our parallel journeys from Asian birthplaces (the Philippines [Matriano] and Malaysia [Toh]) to becoming migrants in global North or advanced industrialized societies, the United States in Estela Matriano's case and Australia and Canada in Toh Swee-Hin's case.

As newcomers to "Western" societies that had already become multicultural due to migrations from many regions, each of us could not escape the dynamics and complexities of living and working in social and professional contexts in which issues of cultural "identities" were daily realities. Moreover, as we developed our intellectual and social interest in the field known as multiculturalism and multicultural education, we were increasingly challenged by those realities to make distinctions between alternative paradigms of theory and practice. Some of the questions we struggled to address included the following: What does it mean to be a "multicultural" society, institution, or community? What role does or can education play in promoting multiculturalism? And, especially, what are the responsibilities of professionals in all sectors in providing education in support of a multicultural society?

Before we arrived in our new countries (the United States and Australia), our conceptions and worldviews of the goals and purposes of multiculturalism and multicultural education had already been influenced by our experiences of growing up in Asia. Hence, multiculturalism for each of us could not be grounded only in the domestic context of our new place of permanent residence and eventual citizenship. Rather, "global" was already present within what multiculturalism meant to us, both in terms of our identities and envisioning scholarly, professional, and social commitments. For example, an early influence of the global aspects of our lives occurred during World War II, when our respective homelands, the Philippines and Malaya (now Malaysia), were occupied by the Japanese military forces. We share our respective experiences in this and other sections of this chapter, along with our reflections on our experiences and how they influenced our models of education.

Estela Matriano (EM):   It was 4 long and difficult years of living in the war-torn country that the Philippines then was. Every day was filled with fear, running away from the Japanese military and seeking shelter from bombings and all kinds of atrocities. Life then was so uncertain, and basic needs were not easily available. Toward the end of the war, in 1944, the Japanese soldiers reacted to their impending defeat with anger and brutality, exacting revenge on notably innocent civilians. Sadly, one day in the orchard in our village home, my mother became an easy target and was killed by a Japanese soldier, leaving me and my sister orphans. This most painful experience, in addition to the many tragic incidents others in my country had also suffered, led me, as a young 14-year-old girl, to vow that I would never condone war. Instead, I vowed to work in every way I could to promote peace at all levels of life, a pledge I have kept to this day. In this regard, my later decision to settle in the United States was a form of self-imposed exile because my commitment to build peace, which includes upholding democracy and human rights, led me into visible opposition to the Marcos era of political repression in the Philippines, which increasingly put my life under threat.

Toh Swee-Hin (TSH):   Although I was born after World War II had ended, I learned as a child that my father had joined with other leaders of his home village to try to protect a British soldier seeking refuge from the Japanese military. However, their effort was discovered, and in retribution, a number of village leaders, including one of my granduncles, were executed. My father survived 3 years in a war prison, a time during which my mother endured considerable hardships raising my baby sister while also helping to look after my uncles and others in the extended family. Even without directly experiencing war and all its suffering and inhumanity, I learned from my parents' stories that war and violence need to be abolished for the well-being of all peoples, even the soldiers.

Although we both shared the pains of those tragic personal memories, we were also moved that each of us raised the theme of forgiveness and reconciliation.

> EM: Years later, a new Japanese student moved into the graduate residential house where I lived. The landlady was surprised and asked me, "How can you wake up every morning and see a Japanese roommate with you when your mother was killed by Japanese?" I responded by noting that the Japanese student was not responsible for the soldier's action and that forgiveness, not revenge, and was a virtue to be followed. It was valuable that my own mother had always encouraged me in my upbringing. The Japanese student and I soon became very good friends.

> TSH: In my case, I remembered that not once did my father ever voice hatred or a desire for revenge toward his former captors, and many years later, upon his retirement, he happily included Japan on his holiday tour of East Asia. Forgiveness, as my later involvement in peace and global education affirmed, is, we both argue, an essential value for building a peaceful world. In addition, our felt experiences of pain ought not to lead to stereotypes of the "enemy," as we learned when Japanese people already settled in the United States and Canada were being unjustly displaced and detained in internment camps during World War II.

Although they carry sad reminders that the violence of wars or armed conflicts affects not only those who are direct victims but also their loved ones and relations, our personal stories are also a hopeful sign that destructive and negative responses such as hatred are not inevitable. We revisit this theme through the lens of 9/11, an event that has not only reverberated in recent U.S. history but has also had an impact on other societies and that has continued to generate reactions of bitterness and vengefulness. In short, we argue that a multicultural society is formed not only by historical and contemporary circumstances found within the boundaries of a society but is also profoundly shaped by external international and global forces and events.

As this chapter aims to clarify, multicultural education also needs to link integrally with educational work and initiatives that merge the "global" with the "local" through what we call *global education*. Drawing on a growing body of conceptual and theoretical analysis, professional or community practice and research, as well as our personal, work, and social experiences, we articulate our preferred perspectives and practices in both multicultural education and global education.

FROM LIBERAL TO CRITICAL MULTICULTURALISM AND MULTICULTURAL EDUCATION

The emergence and growth of policies promoting multiculturalism and multicultural education in Western countries has been shaped by varying historical, political, and social forces. Yet all of these policies share an underpinning concern with the need for peoples of different cultures in a culturally diverse society to better understand and respect each other and in turn live together in harmony. In Canada, Australia, and the United Kingdom, from the 1970s on, the changing demographic profile due to immigrants arriving from non-European regions prompted explicit or de facto national multiculturalism policies (Kivisto, 2002). Educational institutions were called on to integrate awareness of this growing cultural diversity in their curricula, in contrast to the earlier predominant emphasis on the Anglo-Saxon and the broader Western European heritage, and to promote attitudes of intercultural sensitivity. In the United States, however, as Grant (2006) sketched, the process was more gradual, beginning from the 1930s with the intercultural education and intergroup movements that acknowledged the cultural contributions of new settlers as they became new "Americans" as well as with programs to reduce prejudices. Then, from the 1950s, a key impetus to U.S. multicultural education was provided by the civil rights movement in its struggle for justice and equality for African Americans. This in turn led to the ethnic studies movement, which argued for a curriculum that included the histories and cultures of minority groups (Banks, 2008; Grant & Sleeter, 1989). These efforts toward a greater recognition of cultural diversity in multicultural societies were certainly an improvement over prior social policies, curricula, and pedagogies that to that point had valorized the dominant majority cultural groups.

By the 1980s, professionals in psychology were also appealing for multicultural counseling competencies and standards (Sue, Arredondo, & McDavis, 1992). Thus, culturally skilled counselors were trained to be aware of their own cultural assumptions, values, and biases and to eliminate possible biases and discriminatory practices. They also needed to be respectful of differences in cultural beliefs (e.g., religious or spiritual worldviews about physical and mental functioning) and to value bilingualism in their counseling practices.

In 2002, the American Psychological Association (APA) approved as policy its core guidelines on multicultural education, training, research, practice, and organizational change for psychologists. Through these guidelines, psychologists were reminded of the need to be aware of their own cultural attitudes and beliefs that "can detrimentally influence their perceptions of and interactions with individuals who are ethnically and racially different from themselves" (p. 17); "encouraged to recognize the importance of multicultural sensitivity/responsiveness, knowledge, and understanding about ethnically and racially different individuals" (p. 25), and called on to "strive to apply culturally appropriate skills and other applied psychological practices" (p. 43). These guidelines are as applicable to educators and trainers as they are to psychotherapists.

Intercultural Communication

The more specific field called *intercultural communication* established that helping people to understand cultural differences in key dimensions such as communication context, physical space, nonverbal expressions, and negotiation styles is useful in preventing or reducing potential intercultural conflicts (Gudykunst & Mody, 2002). Likewise, scholars and managers of international education and study-abroad programs have highlighted their role in developing intercultural competencies, including, for example, understanding the worldviews of others, cultural self-awareness, capacity for self-assessment, skill at listening and observing, the ability to adapt to varying intercultural communication and learning styles, cross-cultural empathy, and understanding the value of cultural diversity (Deardorff, 2008, p. 34).

In the socially important field of health, increasing attention has been focused on an adequate response to the growing cultural diversity of societies due to immigration and globalization of the workforce. Research has shown that health professionals are often unable to meet the needs of ethnic minorities because of "a lack of understanding of cultural diversities, racism, racial stereotyping, lack of knowledge, exclusivity, and ethnocentrism" (Chevannes, 2002, p. 290). Language difficulties that have an impact on diagnosis and treatment, as well as the cultural lens of health care practitioners, also pose challenges for training in the delivery of effective health services in multicultural contexts (Royal Australian College of General Practitioners Curriculum for Australian General Practice, 2007).

The strategy of cultural competence has therefore been applied to address racial and ethnic disparities in health and health care by overcoming organizational, structural, and clinical barriers. As Bettancourt, Green, and Ananeh-Firempong (2003) suggested, key cultural competence interventions include "minority recruitment into the health professions, development of interpreter services and language-appropriate health educational materials, and provider education on cross-cultural issues" (p. 293).

Other health professionals have enriched the concept of cultural competence with terms such as *cultural proficiency*, which recognizes the positive role of culture in a person's health and well-being, and *cultural humility*, which "incorporates a health provider's commitment and active engagement in a lifelong practice of self-evaluation and self-critique within the context of the patient–provider (or health professional) relationship through patient-oriented interviewing and care" (Shaya & Gbarayor, 2006). Other specific cultural-competence intervention strategies include culturally diverse recruitment and retention policies, working with traditional healers, and use of community health workers.

More specifically, in the field of mental health training, considerable research and development efforts have been undertaken to design strategies for building multicultural competence. As compiled in Constantine and Sue's (2005) comprehensive collection of analyses, the APA's multicultural guidelines can be effectively implemented through several channels and processes. These include culturally sensitive assessment and diagnosis; using the APA's Multicultural Guidelines in individual, group, couple, and family counseling situations; career counseling for people of color; building multicultural competence around indigenous healing practices; and promoting multicultural competencies in clinic, hospital, school, and college settings.

Turning to the field of business education, it is now widely accepted that corporate organizations and business professionals need to understand the impact of cultural identity on business communication between people of different cultures (Jameson, 2007). With the globalization of business, as Chang (2008) wrote, "cultivating a global perspective toward the diversity and multiculturalism should start with an understanding of cultural values, perceptions, manners, demography, social structure, and decision-making practices of different regions" (p. 2). Otherwise, avoidable cultural misunderstandings can lead to embarrassment, conflicts, and costly blunders. Moreover, it is vital to be sensitive to paradigmatic differences between Western and Eastern business systems. A comprehensive report jointly prepared by the United Nations Alliance of Civilisations and the United Nations Global Compact Office (2009) highlighted both the challenges and opportunities of doing business in a multicultural world. By virtue of the rapid integration of peoples and communities worldwide, business can help to facilitate cooperation among diverse cultures and to overcome cultural, religious, and ethnic polarization through increased intercultural dialogue and understanding. Simultaneously, business organizations and professions need to manage intra- and intercultural diversity among their staff, clients, and other stakeholders through, for example, providing intercultural training for managers, creating an inclusive workplace, ensuring sensitivity to religious diversity (e.g., religious holidays, flexible prayer break times, prayer rooms), and responding to the needs of culturally diverse customers. As this report aptly emphasized, "in an interconnected world, in which we are increasingly aware of our differences, it could perhaps be said that *building cultures of understanding, respect and cooperation,* undermining the stereotypes that deepen patterns of hostility and mistrust among societies, is an *increasingly pressing aspect of the global sustainability challenge*" (United Nations Alliance of Civilisations and United Nations Global Compact Office, 2009, p. 21, italics in original). In sum, many business professionals need adequate training in intercultural communication skills and wider components of managing cultural diversity (Australian Multicultural Foundation and Robert Bean Consulting, 2010; McPherson & Szul, 2008).

Limitations of the 4Ds Approach

As we personally witnessed and experienced in our work as teacher educators after arriving, respectively, in North America and Australia, in practice, much of multicultural education tended to be limited to relatively superficial "celebrations" of different cultures. Teachers and schools focused primarily on what has been called the *4Ds approach* (dance, diet, dialogue, and dress; Zachariah, 1992), such as inclusion in annual school program festivals and representative cultural productions (e.g., literature, films) or leaders (e.g., heroes, heroines) of migrant or newcomer groups. As Banks (1989) put it, these contributions and additive approaches to multicultural education basically leave the mainstream-centric and Eurocentric curricula unchanged in terms of their goals, structure, and perspective. Most important, they "tend to gloss over important issues and concepts related to the victimization and oppression of ethnic groups such as racism, poverty and oppression" (p. 234). In contrast, Banks argued (pp. 237–239) for a transformation and, in turn, a social action approach, in which learners are enabled to understand the cultural fabric of a society from diverse ethnic or cultural perspectives and also to explore ways to overcome problems such as racism and discrimination.

Liberal Versus Critical Paradigms: Recognizing Power

Over the past 2 decades or so, there has been an increase in critiques of what may be identified as a *liberal* paradigm or worldview of multiculturalism and multicultural education. On the basis of a liberal theory of pluralism, which views Western societies as being based on multiple, competing centers of power in a free-market economy and democratic political system (Domhoff, 2005), the major deficiency of this dominant paradigm is to envisage societal harmony and equitable opportunity for all cultural groups as eventually resulting from improved intercultural understanding and respect. Importantly, it takes for granted the societal status quo and fails to recognize the structures and relationships of power (economic, political, social, cultural) that underpin the realities of racism and ethnic and cultural discrimination experienced by marginalized groups (Gordon & Newfield, 1996; James, 1999; May & Sleeter, 2010; McCarthy & Crichlow, 1993; McLaren, 1997; Nieto, 1996).

In contrast, the critical multiculturalism paradigm seeks to understand cultural diversity and intercultural relations in terms of the location of cultural, ethnic, or racialized groups within the power structures of a multicultural society and to engage learners in personal and social action to transform the society toward justice, equity, and mutual cultural and social enrichment. Similarly, Gorski (2007) argued for a "decolonizing intercultural education" (p. 1) in which the emphasis on interpersonal relationships and cultural awareness should not reinforce power hierarchies between the powerful and subordinated ethnic groups.

A number of advocates of critical multiculturalism have also suggested a critical race theory to challenge the perception of racism as being normal (Dei, 1996; Ladson-Billings, 2003). In this regard, as other "minority" professionals (e.g., Henry & Tator, 2009; Turner, Gonzalez, & Wood, 2008) in various contexts have also reported, we have both had experiences within academia that appear to have reflected prejudices and discriminatory conduct toward our non–Anglo-Saxon identity (although we also need to acknowledge with appreciation the support and solidarity given by other colleagues, including colleagues from majority cultures, to help us overcome those barriers). Beyond our campuses, we, too, like other minorities, have suffered from acts of discrimination, including racist name-calling, racist jokes directed at us, and unequal treatment on buses, subways, and restaurants. At the institutional level, apart from teaching our multicultural education programs with a critical orientation, we have also engaged in helping our faculties develop clear equity policies that eschew racist and ethnic discrimination and that provide affirmative and equitable guidelines for staff and students. We believe it is also vital to work with teachers and student teachers to promote critical literacy to overcome stereotyping in textbooks and on the Internet (Toh, 2004a). As Lewison, Leland, and Harste (2008) noted,

> critical literacy practices encourage students to use language to question the everyday world, to interrogate the relationships between language and power, to analyze popular culture and media, to understand how power relationships are socially constructed, and to consider actions that can be taken to promote social justice. (p. 3)

Identity and Global Education

Another central concept within a critical perspective on multiculturalism and multicultural education is *identity*. This concept needs careful exploration. The essence of this idea as it applies here is that members of the powerful and dominant groups in society see themselves as being without a culture, ethnicity, or racialized identity. With such an identity (or lack of one), "multiculturalism," "multicultural education," cultural "heritage," and other visible cultural signifiers (e.g., dress, foods, language) are viewed as being applicable to the minority or newcomer "others" and not to themselves. "Whiteness," then, is assumed to be a norm that does not need self-examination in terms of how it has led to positions of power and privilege while remaining silent about racism or ethnic discrimination (James, 1999; Roman, 1993). This tendency has been witnessed in the professional field of teacher education in which White student teachers and practicing teachers have resisted curricula and development programs trying to motivate them to recognize their "color-blindness," which in turn validates their perhaps unconsciously held discriminatory and racist attitudes and actions toward "others" who are different from the dominant cultural norms (Lawrence & Tatum, n.d.; Sleeter, 2001; Smith, 1998). However, such resistance can be overcome through patient, critical, dialogical, and transformative pedagogical strategies.

EM: The first graduate class in elementary social studies I taught consisted of 26 White students. At the start of the course, one student stood up and said, "I cannot take this class with a foreign professor" and was ready to leave. In response, I said that since the United States was the "leading" democratic country in the world, I would leave for 10 minutes while the class debated and voted on whether they would like to keep me as the professor. When I returned, the collective decision was that I should remain. The objecting student apologized to me at the end of the class, and by the end of the course we were relating well and with much intercultural respect. This happened at the City University of New York (CUNY)—Richmond College on Staten Island at the heart of *The Godfather* enclave. In another course, this one at the University of Cincinnati, one student strongly defended and academically supported his conservative and antimulti-culturalism views; he received a good grade in the course because I needed to role model my commitment to being nondoctrinaire.

TSH: In several classes for student teachers in a Canadian university, I sometimes received comments during class, in assignments, or anonymously in course evaluations to the effect that multi-culturalism and multicultural education were not relevant to the training. The view was expressed that if everyone in Canada would simply identify themselves as "Canadians" sharing common core values, it would lead to a harmonious and unified country, whereas emphasizing cultural identities and differences from other countries would only create divisions and conflicts. My approach has been to integrate dialogical and empowerment exercises in the courses that invite students to step into the shoes of the "others" and gently encourage them to critically interrogate their own perspectives for biases and, I hope, move toward solidarity with people who are marginalized and discriminated against.

Addressing Oppression

Simultaneously, critical multicultural education recognizes the impact of oppression due to racism on the identity of the discriminated "other" and hence seeks to modify curricula and institutional practices to transform consciousness and structures. Howard-Hamilton and Hinton (2011) noted:

> When faculty members (of higher education institutions) do not teach students how to create their own work and personal space from a multicultural lens they create a covert bias that limits students' growth and development. The classroom becomes a place in which specific material from the dominant culture is presented, giving a subtle message that this model fits everyone, that marginalized groups must accept the norm. . . . Moving into a transformation state requires that student affairs staff teach students how to analyze and assess the organizational structure that is covertly and overtly oppressive. . . . Implementing diversity workshops, creating committees to assess the campus and departmental climates, advocating workshops that support underrepresented groups, diversifying membership on key university committees that are part of retention efforts, and hiring staff members who are compatible with the demographic makeup of the institution all help to dismantle the hierarchical form of oppression that manifests itself in many college campuses. (pp. 23–24)

Addressing the Oppression of Indigenous People

Another critique of liberal multiculturalism that critical multicultural education needs to acknowledge in its theory and practice focuses on the identity and place of indigenous peoples in a culturally diverse society. For indigenous peoples in Canada, the United States, Australia, and New Zealand (First Nations, Native Americans, Australian Aboriginal people, Maoris, respectively), their historical relationships with their colonizers have been tragically marked by racism, inequalities, and human rights violations. Wars of conquest, displacement from their sacred lands, assimilationist schooling, and cultural domination have left painful legacies that are still hurtful today. Such legacies have also resulted in substantive economic, social, and educational inequalities for indigenous peoples while contemporary globalization and development activities (e.g., mining, logging) have compounded their marginalization (Bodley, 2008; Meyer & Alvarado, 2010). Hence, as Guerrero (1996) maintained, "there is a substantial case to be made for the necessity of decolonization before any genuine multiculturalism can take place" (p. 49), including compensatory reparations for educational restoration and preservation programs and a recognition of indigenous knowledge and wisdom. The growth of American Indian culture centers in the United States (Shotton, Yellowfish, & Cintron, 2010), advocacy for policies for integrating indigenous knowledge and pedagogy in First Nations education in Canada (Battiste, 2002), programs for Aboriginalization of schools in Australian Aboriginal communities, and indigenous studies in Australian teacher education programs (Hickling-Hudson, 2003) are all initiatives that a critical multicultural paradigm necessarily supports in solidarity with the rights of indigenous peoples. For one of us (TSH), these themes and issues were always included in multicultural or intercultural education courses in Canada and Australia, evoking a positive response from the First Nations and aboriginal students present. They challenged nonindigenous students to understand how the trauma of colonization can still remain, to support indigenous struggles for cultural survival and social justice, and to rethink the assumed superiority of Western knowledge and nurture openness to the value of indigenous knowledge.

Change and Identity

Whereas a festival or 4Ds approach to culture can directly or indirectly portray cultural identity as essential, fixed, and static, a person's expressed or preferred identity is not monodimensional but multidimensional and multi-layered, and it changes in response to interactions over time and space. Hence, as numerous analysts (e.g., Fried, 2011; James, 1999; McCarthy & Crichlow, 1993) have clarified, an individual's identity can encompass multiple facets or dimensions, including ethnicity, cultural tradition, "race" (or "racialized identity"), faith or religion, gender, sexual orientation, social class, and nationality. These multiple identities coexist and interact in complex and dynamic relationships. At the same time, critical multiculturalism allows for the possibility of a person or members of a community or group to highlight the centrality of one or more of these multiple identities in shaping their daily experiences in a particular societal context (e.g., being "Black" or being a "visible minority" living in multicultural society marked by racism or other culture-based discrimination). Our personal and professional experiences illustrate this perspective on multiple identities.

> EM: When I was teaching at CUNY, I made myself known not only as a Filipino American peace educator but also as a feminist and became an active member of the Feminist

Group of all CUNY Colleges. One great achievement of the group was a class action suit we filed against CUNY for equal pay and workload for women faculty. It took us more than 20 years to win the suit, and although each of us was recompensed only about $2,000, it was a significant victory for gender equality. Another multiple-identity issue I experienced was in the disagreement I had with another feminist, who questioned my credentials in terms of dress and sexuality. I responded by affirming my right both to be a feminist, and to choose my preferred lifestyle, and I pointed out that there are alternative frameworks of feminism.

TSH: Although I am a male and Chinese by cultural identity, my mother fortunately did not follow the usual Confucian patriarchal attitudes and relationships in my socialization. These social circumstances, together with my exposure to feminist ideas and practices, have led me to work for gender equality and women's human rights. Hence, all my multicultural education programs and courses have always mainstreamed gender perspectives, and as the next section of this chapter indicates, my social action for building a peaceful world included, for example, campaigning for the rights of women migrant workers in Canada. Another personal example of multiple identities for me lies with my Buddhist faith tradition, which continually intersects with my other identities in guiding my everyday life in a multicultural society.

EM and TSH: For both of us, our cultural identity cannot be said to have remained static over the years. Throughout our experiences living and working in diverse societies and countries, we have been guided by the value of being open to learning from other cultures, faiths, and civilizations. These intercultural and international relationships have certainly enriched us as members of a common humanity, even as we have retained a meaningful and assertive identification with our birthplace cultural identities. In this regard, the concept of hybridity (Werbner & Modood, 1997) has been a helpful analytical tool for clarifying how each person's identity has interacted with and been influenced by other cultures and identities. Hence, in critical multicultural education, we believe it is vital for educational processes and practices to help learners and teachers understand deeply and learn, when relevant, the philosophical and epistemological values and spiritualities of diverse cultures, rather than be limited to the superficial 4Ds or festivals approach often practiced in a the liberal multicultural paradigm.

LINKING THE GLOBAL WITH THE MULTICULTURAL: SYNERGIES WITH GLOBAL EDUCATION

In beginning this chapter, we recounted personal stories from World War II that alluded to the presence of one "global" dimension in our lives as we commenced our sojourn in the multicultural contexts of the United States and Australia. Again through examples drawn from our experiences as education professionals and as new residents or citizens, we next try to show how the field known as global education has integral links and synergies with multicultural education. As advocates of both multicultural education and global education, we believe that these fields of transformative education share many common values, principles, and conceptual understandings of complex human and people–planet relationships and can mutually enrich and sustain each other to build a more peaceful, just, compassionate, and sustainable world. Looking back, our respective entries into global education were inspired by a variety of influences and sources.

> EM: During 1971–1975, when I was an assistant professor at Richmond College and the Graduate School of CUNY, I was encouraged by the respected American pioneer of peace education Betty Reardon (1988) to join her and other academics as consultants to the Institute for World Order (Mendlovitz, 1975). There I met great scholars and friends, including Kenneth Boulding (1970), Elise Boulding (2000), Saul Mendlovitz (1975), Magnus Haavelsrud (1981), and James Oswald (Oswald & Matriano, 1974). The institute's programs contributed much to the understanding of global issues and problems such as disarmament and creating a just world order. At Richmond, I also established a Center for Global Education, which was affiliated with the United Nations as a nongovernmental organization. It was a good link for my growing commitment to global education (Reardon, Matriano, Carter, & Stanford, 1977) and to activities of the World Council for Curriculum and Instruction (WCCI; Matriano, 1980, 1988, 2000).

TSH: My catalysts for developing a commitment to global education (and peace education) came during my international student years. As an undergraduate in an Australian university, I became aware of the injustices and tragedy of war through the growing anti–Vietnam War protest movement. I recall marching with a million people in the huge moratorium event on the streets of Melbourne. Then, as a high school teacher in Malaysia, I participated with my students in a project to investigate pollution in the local river, which alerted us to the necessity of environmental sustainability. Later, as a graduate student in Canada, I joined the antiapartheid campaign in solidarity with the struggles of South African peoples for their rights and freedoms.

EM and TSH: From these early steps into the field of global education, besides developing and teaching courses in our respective faculties of education, we have always sought opportunities to connect with other educators worldwide to fulfill the field's values and vision. In Dr. Matriano's case, it has been through a lifelong commitment to WCCI, a transnational educational organization committed to "the promotion of equity, peace, and the universal realization of human rights" (WCCI, 1971, p. 1). Over 4 decades, WCCI conferences, workshops, research, and publication projects have enabled educators from diverse cultures and regions to share curricula and pedagogical ideas and best practices that can help to build a world based on nonviolence, justice, human rights, intercultural respect, and sustainability (Carson, 1988; Floresca-Cawagas, 1988; Matriano, 1980; Toh, 2000). For Dr. Toh, parallel to a similar involvement in international educators' networks such as WCCI, the International Institute of Peace Education and the Peace Education Commission of the International Peace Research Association, his journey in global education has taken him to diverse countries in both North (advanced industrialized) and South (less industrialized, low GNP) contexts. His contributions include peace education programs in the Philippines conflict zone of Mindanao; educational development partnerships with universities in Uganda, South Africa, Jamaica, and Nepal; and helping to establish the UNESCO-affiliated Asia-Pacific Centre of Education for International Understanding in South Korea (Toh, 2004b).

GLOBAL STUDIES AND EDUCATION: BEGINNINGS

It is always important, however, to acknowledge the scholars who first promoted the concept of global studies or global education. The community of U.S. educators and social scientists such as Robert Hanvey, Kenneth Tye, Willard Kniep, Lee Anderson, James Becker, Barbara Tye, and Merry Meeryfield deserves mentioning. Thus, in an early essay, Hanvey (1976) delineated a global perspective in education in terms of four elements: perspective consciousness—viewing the world from different perspectives; state-of-the-planet awareness, or understanding of global issues and events; system awareness, which recognizes the role of complex international systems reflecting the interdependence and dependence of state and nonstate actors; and participation opportunities, through which people develop capacities to participate in local, national, and international contexts. These elements are found in several publications, such as the 1991 *American Association for Supervision and Curriculum Development Yearbook* (Tye, 1991), Kniep (1985, 1987), and Merryfield (1995).

In applying such a global perspective to a curriculum, Becker (1991) provided many examples, including the study of histories of non-U.S. regions, to avoid the ethnocentric bias of an excessive focus on U.S. history, recognition that decisions at one place in the world can have an impact on other locations, understanding the problems of nuclear arms, unequal resource distribution, terrorism and refugees, rich–poor gaps, resource depletion, and interactions among peoples and nations. Anderson (1991) noted the need for the global education movement in the United States to encompass those seeking to expand

> the study of world history, world geography, world economic, world politics and world ecology . . . understanding of cultural diversity through the cross-cultural study of literature, art, music, dance, religion, . . . social customs, . . . foreign languages, . . . world problems such as the maintenance of national security, the control of warfare, the reduction of world poverty, the promotion of human rights, and the preservation of ecological well-being. (p. 13)

In our view, these scholarly and professional initiatives to develop a coherent field of global education have assisted in encouraging educators at all levels to move out of the hitherto primarily American-centric or Eurocentric perspective in social education.

THE LIBERAL-TECHNOCRATIC PARADIGM

As our mutual interests in global education deepened, we were also aware that in educational institutions and the wider society, there were programs and activities labeled *global studies* or *global education* with visions and purposes that were quite different from our own understanding of what global education should strive to accomplish. This *liberal-technocratic paradigm* (Toh, 1993) of global studies or education is, in our view, characterized by several themes. First, it tends to foster a superficial appreciation of culture, much like the 4Ds approach, in a liberal framework of multicultural education and views intercultural understanding as a major path to harmony and peace but without considering the relationships between "culture" and political and economic power structures. Second, it upholds a notion of "interdependence" that is assumed to be positive to all parties in the interdependent relationships, without questioning the history and quality of those interdependencies that in reality can benefit one or more sectors disproportionately, especially the more powerful ones. Third, there is a management ethos in dealing with problems arising from interdependence. The crises from global instabilities need to be safely controlled, albeit under the direction of elites and technocrats. Furthermore, an economic functionalist strategy in this approach stresses better knowledge of the "cultures" (e.g., language fluency) of potential trading partners to maintain a competitive advantage in business deals. But can this be a holistic intercultural understanding? Fourth, this liberal–technocratic paradigm of global studies or education upholds human and national "progress" in narrow terms defined by the yardstick of advanced industrial civilization based on unlimited economic growth and high mass consumerism. We have each witnessed the manifestation of this liberal-technocratic paradigm in different ways. Here are some examples.

> EM: A student preferred to opt out of my course in global education because she said all the people in her hometown in Kentucky were from monocultural, White Appalachian families, and hence they did not need a global curriculum. Two years later, it turned out that a Japanese car manufacturer had set up a plant in this town, whereupon the Board of Travelers' Aid International Office, of which I was a member, were receiving requests for short courses in Japanese to help local citizens communicate with the Japanese staff members. (This is just one example in which the drive to learn a language reflects economic self-interest.)

> TSH: The Alberta (Canada) Department of Education issued a policy statement called "Vision for the Nineties" in which being "global" stresses the enhancement of trading, commercial, and strategic interests of Alberta. Students were exhorted to learn more about Asian languages and cultures so that they could compete more successfully in the world economy.

CRITICAL PERSPECTIVES AND THEMES FOR EDUCATION AND TRANSFORMATION

In contrast to such liberal-technocratic goals, a considerable body of scholars and educators has been developing and advocating what has been called a *critical* paradigm of global education that clearly seeks to build a world for all peoples based on principles of nonviolence, justice, human rights, intercultural respect, and sustainability. The British world studies movement, for example, was a pioneer in catalyzing teachers to facilitate learners' critical thinking, analysis, and social action on diverse issues relating to world hunger, poverty, development inequalities, ecological imbalances, armaments, and discrimination (S. Fisher & Hicks, 1985; Richardson, 1976). Also influential was the work of Pike and Selby (1988), whose ideas paralleled American ideas in suggesting four dimensions of globality (spatial or local-global interdependence; temporal, which means exploring alternative futures; issues of critical global importance; and human potential that is nurtured through holistic learning) and five aims for global education (system consciousness, perspective consciousness, health-of-planet awareness, involvement consciousness, preparedness, and process mindedness). The environment, development (national, international), human rights, and peace constituted critical global issues in their framework.

Furthermore, as Hicks (2008) noted, global education in the United Kingdom developed in close synergy with development education, which questioned dominant paradigms of economic modernization and globalization for increasing rich–poor gaps; environmental education, which linked ecological balance with human survival; and peace education, which encompassed a wide range of conflicts and violence from wars and human rights violations to structural violence (injustices) and cultural or racial discrimination. Elsewhere, the growth of active movements of disarmament education, peace education, human rights education, multicultural education, futures education, and environmental education (now evolved as education for sustainable development) worldwide has also provided rich complementary ideas and strategies for global education programs (Burns & Aspeslagh, 1996; Fien, 2001; Haavelsrud, 1981; Huckle & Sterling, 2006; Hutchinson, 1996; Matriano, 1987; Reardon, 1988, 1995; Reardon & Cabezudo, 2002; Toh & Floresca-Cawagas, 1990). This holistic approach to global education has guided our work as educators since the 1980s.

> EM: In my courses, global education seeks to embrace our home—Planet Earth—and our human family. While facing the fast-changing processes of globalization and advances in technology and communication, the members of the world community need to be responsible

stewards of the environment, and the quality of life of the human family should be the priority. Everyone should be nurtured with the humane qualities of being, including kindness, compassion, justice, forgiveness, and respect, as well as the capacity for recognizing our differences and celebrating our similarities. Essentially, global education (and multicultural education) also means human rights education. All these fields converge in one vision and goal: to build a culture of peace for humanity and the planet. Many students have found their eyes opened to the wider world in a way that revealed the prevalence of injustice and human rights violations, as well as the possibilities for transformation toward a peaceful and just world.

TSH: In Canada, besides founding the global education courses at undergraduate and graduate levels, I also collaborated with the Global Education Network set up by the Alberta Teachers Association. Numerous workshops and conferences enabled teachers to integrate global education themes and creative pedagogies into their curriculum, and university youth visited South (or economically poorer) countries such as India, Mexico, and the Philippines for educational and social encounters with rural and urban poor communities, thus experiencing global education at the grassroots. Although a few students in classes or on these experiential trips expressed resistance (as is their right) to ideas that challenge the societal and global status quo, a majority felt moved to express their solidarity with the marginalized and to ask what they could do as active global citizens.

EM and TSH: For both of us, the various United Nations International Days (United Nations, n.d.) have also provided a meaningful space to involve students and faculty in commemorating and affirming global education values, responsibilities, and practices to promote human rights, women's equality, nonviolence, elimination of all forms of discrimination, and environmental sustainability.

Education for Disarmament and Conflict Resolution

More specifically, our experiences in global education have demonstrated the need to clarify individual themes of conflicts and violence in terms of root causes and then engaging learners to explore critical self-empowerment toward personal and social action for overcoming those conflicts. Also, in accord with the pedagogical principle of holism, the interconnections between different themes will always be explored to reveal complex causes and avoid partial or inappropriate solutions. For example, on the theme of educating for dismantling the culture of war or disarmament education, the challenge will be for learners to appreciate how wars and armed conflicts arise with their accompanying tragic suffering of civilians and refugees (Reardon & Cabezudo, 2002). A related question is, How can the deadly cycles of violence and counterviolence—such as the prevailing acts of "terrorism" and the "war on terrorism"—be transcended (Summy & Ram, 2008)? Will more militarization resolve the root causes? How can the continuing proliferation of weapons of mass destruction and conventional arms be stopped?

Also, at microlevels of life, the problems of domestic violence, school-based violence (e.g., bullying, shootings), community violence (e.g., gangs, violent crime), war toys, and violence in the media and information and communications technology all constitute key issues in global education. Education for dismantling this multifaceted culture of war therefore includes teaching values, knowledge, and skills in nonviolent resolution and transformation of armed conflicts and disputes; motivating and empowering citizens to engage in peace processes (mediation, negotiation) to complement official peace talks; abolishing the arms trade; promoting gun control laws; fostering trauma healing and reintegration of combatants, including child soldiers; supporting nonviolence and conflict resolution programs in schools (e.g., peer mediation); promoting campaigns worldwide to transform the production and distribution of cultural, leisure, and recreation products and services (e.g., media, toys, entertainment) toward peace-oriented items; encouraging media literacy to reject violence; and empowering women and changing males attitudes to stop domestic violence (e.g., Baker, Jaffe, Ashbourne, & Carter, 2002; Lantieri & Patti, 1996). Given its recent 10-year anniversary, the 9/11 attack on New York City is an especially challenging example of the need for global education. This act of violence led to a continuing spiral of militarization and counterviolence in many regions.

> EM: In Cincinnati, many Muslim students and faculty were subject to threats and harassment after 9/11 because of the stereotyping of Islam as a faith endorsing terrorism. "Go home!" was a frequent invective, to which one student responded, "I'm a White West Virginian woman; to where should I return?" By integrating open and sensitive discussion of 9/11 with human rights principles, many Muslim students felt empowered to challenge the post-9/11 atmosphere of Islamophobia, and other non-Muslims rallied in solidarity. The student teachers also worked on projects to teach about 9/11 in their practicum classes. In this regard, although they focused on an incident not related to 9/11, Japanese students

similarly revealed their painful awareness of how Japanese Americans or Canadians were wrongly interred during World War II as potential "enemies" or "spies."

TSH: After 9/11, I co-organized a learn-in on this act of violence with colleagues in the faculty of education and guest scholars. The discussions illuminated possible root causes and suggested non-violent alternatives to the aggressive tactic of militarized violence and wars in other countries. We also responded to teachers' requests for workshops to illustrate creative global education strategies that they could use in their schools to help students understand 9/11 more critically and heal from the trauma, instead of succumbing to fear, despair, and even enmity, which leaders in the United States, Canada, and allied nations often drew on to justify violent retaliation. Will the wars in Afghanistan and Iraq build peace in those countries or in the region and world?

It is also important to acknowledge that many of the issues raised under the theme of education for disarmament and conflict resolution, such as wars, 9/11, terrorism, and gun control, as well as issues in other themes of global education, are often controversial. Hence, when these issues are included in curricula, there is a need to adopt appropriate principles and pedagogical strategies for teaching controversial issues. In this regard, Shapiro (n.d.) provided several helpful guidelines, such as encouraging students to examine critically their own questions and possible biases in those providing answers or opinions; exposing students to multiple perspectives and viewpoints on the issues concerned; promoting dialogue among students and between teachers and students; encouraging independent and collaborative work; and providing opportunities for student action based on their conclusions. By following such guidelines, global education is clearly not promoting indoctrination. This does not imply, however, that global education is value free. Consistent with the values mentioned earlier (e.g., compassion, justice, respect, human rights, sustainability), global education assertively advocates the nonviolence, compassion, justice, sharing, respect, human rights, and sustainability that humane educational systems in democratic societies can be expected to foster.

Educating for Global and Local Justice

Another major dimension of global education relates to the theme of educating for global and local justice, or *development education*. This theme relates to educating learners on the root causes of the worsening hunger and poverty in the world today and analyzing and comparing alternative paradigms of "development" for meeting the basic needs of all human beings.

Can the dominant growth-maximizing, free-trade model based on foreign investment, transnational corporations (agribusiness, mining, factories), and control by international financial institutions (e.g., the International Monetary Fund, World Bank) serve the needs of the poor? In contrast, marginalized sectors (rural, urban poor, indigenous peoples, women) have criticized this dominant model for contributing to the growing gaps between rich and poor, especially in countries of the South (W. F. Fisher & Ponniah, 2003; Madeley, 2008; Shiva, 2005).

In summary, we argue that global education needs to address the root causes of such structural violence, and ultimately overcome it, by raising awareness, concern, and solidarity among North citizens to critique and transform the globalization policies of their own governments and powerful economic agencies (e.g., transnational corporations, international financial institutions) that perpetuate local and global injustices. Other approaches in support of this goal include catalyzing citizens of industrialized nations to support appropriate aid programs that benefit the marginalized in poor countries without creating dependencies, encouraging learners to initiate solidarity projects that ethically support the poor (e.g., boycotts of unethical firms, fair trade) both financially (e.g., fund-raising activities) and socially (e.g., volunteer work in marginalized communities), and empowering citizens in poor countries to understand the root causes of their marginalization and build people-centered development alternatives (Oxfam, 2006). In our global education classes and informal educational activities, this theme of global–local justice is exemplified by encouraging students to monitor official aid policies and to lobby for changes that prioritize programs that benefit the marginalized sectors rather than disproportionately benefitting the elite; we challenge them to rethink overconsumerist lifestyles. For example, in one case, students petitioned a large Canadian corporation and the Canadian government to acknowledge responsibility for a mining project that left a Philippine island ecologically and economically devastated.

Education for Human Rights and Responsibilities

A third dimension of a holistic global education framework focuses on the concept of human rights. Here we can draw valuable ideas from the many decades of work on human rights education, in which learners have gained a clear understanding of all forms of human rights (civil, political, economic, social, cultural) as embodied in successive and numerous declarations, covenants, conventions, and treaties (Claude & Weston, 2006). However, learners will also realize the continuing gap between theory and practice in many countries where human rights violations still occur, in part from political repression and armed conflicts.

Our model of global education also recognizes the tensions between the field of human rights and human rights education versus culture and cultural rights. How can cultural rights be upheld to the detriment of other rights (e.g., violence against women; An-Na'im, 1995; Peters & Wolper, 1995)? Finally, in education for international understanding, human rights must be accompanied by a sense of responsibility toward all others.

In summary, education for promoting human rights and responsibilities includes raising awareness and developing values and skills in participatory democracy and governance based on the rule of law. It also includes recognizing and promoting the vital field of women's human rights in diverse areas (education, health, employment, security from violence), which in turn also helps to enhance the well-being of other sectors of society (e.g., children). Such teaching opportunities can allow leaners to role-model and practice a culture of human rights within the school community, encouraging them to engage in human rights protection activities. Examples include petitions and clubs advocating for release of political prisoners; abolition of the death penalty; improved rights of marginalized or vulnerable sectors; ratification of human rights covenants, conventions, and treaties; and establishment of independent and effective national human rights commissions (e.g., Abdi & Schultz, 2008; Marks, 2010; Reardon, 1995).

In our global education programs, this dimension of human rights has been affirmed in various ways. Here are some examples.

EM: A group of Guatemalan refugees once settled in an Appalachian enclave of Cincinnati and were met with hostility from the local residents. The conflict was put on the agenda of the city's Multicultural Task Force, on which I served. When I raised this issue with a graduate class, the students wrote a petition letter to the task force appealing for friendly relations between the refugees and the locals. They also volunteered to conduct intercultural workshops for the newcomers and local inhabitants. In this way, the students felt empowered to help protect the rights of the refugees.

TSH: In Canada, my global education students learned about the case of a Filipina migrant "caregiver" worker who was charged by the immigration authorities with violating her work contract rules. However, the incident was actually her employer's fault. Hence, the students joined me and other concerned Canadians, including a local Catholic priest, to defend her human rights. The church provided the woman sanctuary for 6 months while we lobbied in the media and in Parliament for her fair treatment. In the end, the government compromised, allowed her to return to the Philippines briefly, and then accepted her back as a caregiver. Today, her family members have joined her in Canada, and all are now Canadian citizens.

Educating for Intercultural Understanding, Respect, and Reconciliation

Turning now to the theme of educating for intercultural understanding, respect, and reconciliation, global education is in clear synergy with the vision and goals of multicultural or intercultural education, as we clarified in the first half of our chapter (UNESCO, 2007, 2010). An additional insight is the importance of not immediately attributing conflicts between two or more cultural groups to cultural differences per se. Rather, although cultural factors can play a significant role, it is necessary to look for possible economic, social, and political root causes (e.g., displacement of indigenous peoples; Tauli-Corpuz, 2010).

> EM: I mention here an example of critical empowerment with regard to indigenous people's rights, as shown by two of my former graduate students, both from Taiwan. On their return to Taiwan from Cincinnati, these students, Vincent Hsieh and Angela Lo, who are currently professors at the National Kaohsiung Normal University, mobilized government and other funds to help rebuild an indigenous people's village that had been destroyed by a huge typhoon in 2009. Also, by engaging their own graduate students in such projects, Vincent and Angela are succeeding in fostering an intergenerational commitment to sustainable futures for marginalized indigenous peoples.

> TSH: In my case, the synergy between global education and multicultural education has been promoted through the theme of dialogue between faiths and between different civilizations (Little, 2007; Mays 2009). While serving as the inaugural director of a university-based Multi-Faith Centre in Australia, I conducted numerous interfaith dialogue activities to bring leaders and members of diverse faiths and spirituality traditions together to know and respect each other's beliefs and to find common ground in values and principles (Cawagas, Toh, & Garrone, 2007; Toh & Cawagas, 2006). These common values helped motivate people of diverse faiths to collaborate in building a culture of peace (e.g., to address climate change) and to dispel the myth of a clash of civilizations.

> EM and TSH: Over the decades, WCCI has certainly fostered, through its various activities, much sharing and commitment to the vision of unity in diversity, For example, recently the

13th International Conference of WCCI in Antayla, Turkey, highlighted the "dialogue of civilizations" theme, which motivated a special issue of the *International Journal of Curriculum & Instruction* (Toh, 2010).

Educating for Sustainable Futures

The growing field of education for sustainable development and a sustainable future is a vital dimension of global education (Kagawa & Selby, 2010). In understanding the impact and causes of environmental destruction worldwide, students are catalyzed to undertake personal and social transformation to overcome ecological crises. Unless human beings learn to live in peace with our planet, our survival is at stake (Kaza, 2008; Mische, 2006). The ecological crisis is rooted in unsustainable paradigms of development extolling unlimited growth, profit maximization, and fierce competition for natural resources. Education for building sustainable futures hence includes encouraging learners to assess their ecological footprint and to take personal and social measures to reduce its size; raising awareness among citizens of activities of local and external elites, agencies, and organizations, including corporations, of ecologically destructive activities and promoting solidarity for campaigns to enforce their environmentally responsible conduct; integrating education for sustainable development in formal, nonformal, and informal curricula and the institutional culture of schools and universities, thereby forming more sustainable behavior and lifestyles and eco-friendly institutions; and nurturing the principle of intergenerational responsibility so that citizens today consider the rights of future generations to survive with dignity and justice (Fien, 2001; Huckle & Sterling, 2006).

For both of us and for many colleagues, this "sustainable futures" theme in global education is becoming more institutionalized each year, as campuses adopt eco-friendly policies of recycling, reusing, and reducing. The link to multicultural education, however, needs to be more strongly articulated. One strategy we have found useful is to encourage students to look into their cultural and civilizational roots and discern values and principles that contribute to green visioning and practice. It is relevant to note also that the WCCI, in which we are both involved, has been promoting sustainable futures at many of its conferences and through its projects, such as the Green Medical Education initiative with Kaohsiung Medical University in Taiwan. While coordinating Griffith University's Multi-Faith Centre, Swee-Hin facilitated youth and leaders of diverse faith communities in workshops to catalyze their commitment and collaboration in building sustainable futures (Toh, 2009; Toh & Cawagas, 2006).

Educating for Inner Peace

Global education in our view also needs to encourage learners and educators alike to cultivate inner peace. This theme is regrettably not emphasized or even mentioned in many models for global education, in part because of a secular tendency among educators in industrialized societies of the North to stay away from ideas relating to spirituality and faith. But the symptoms of inner peacelessness are now increasingly evident, including alienation, despair, addictions, stress, anxiety, and related disease aggravated by the incessantly fast pace of work and living (Wilson, 2011). Thus, global educators are now returning to their traditional sources of knowledge and wisdom, combined with modern strategies, to focus on the inner peace dimension of life (Macy, 1998; Tisdell, 2003). Educating to cultivate a spirituality of inner peace includes encouraging learners to explore their levels of inner peace; understanding possible root causes for any inner peacelessness; engaging in healing and educational strategies that help cultivate inner peace; and integrating meditation and other contemplation practices into formal, nonformal, and informal educational programs. In addition, such education involves reminding and encouraging those practicing the cultivation of inner peace to engage simultaneously in building social or outer peace for nonviolence, justice, human rights, and sustainability, because inner and outer peace enrich each other dialogically (Whang & Nash, 2005). In both our experiences as global educators, the theme of inner peace has been indispensable.

> EM: Over the years, I have drawn, constantly and deeply, from my Catholic faith to maintain a sense of inner peace. This has helped me to sustain my spirit and focus in meeting the challenges of building a peaceful community, institution, and world. I know my colleagues, friends, and the many members of WCCI have their own ways of cultivating their inner peace. I respect their ways, for as the WCCI motto says, we need to live together in unity in diversity, which underpins both critical multicultural education and global education.

> TSH: As someone trying to learn and practice in the Buddhist tradition, I am mindful that cultivating inner peace is necessary in strengthening one's resolve to build outer peace. To talk about inner peace does not mean that it can be cultivated only via an organized faith or religion, although of course for many people, the source for spirituality is their faith. For others, a nonreligious commitment to spirituality will suffice. What is key in global education and multicultural education is that the cultivation of inner peace and the practice of outer peace are complementary and synergistic.

CONCLUSION

This chapter has been a journey through our theory and practice of multicultural education and global education. We hope we have clarified some of the key synergies between these two fields of transformative education. There remains, however, one key point of convergence between global education and multicultural education that deserves emphasis: the sharing of critical pedagogical principles and processes (Toh & Floresca-Cawagas, 1990). First, we have already mentioned holism, which accounts for the interdependence and interconnections between and among the constituent issues and themes. Second, a critical paradigm of either multicultural education or global education requires pedagogical strategies that do not promote a one-way, top-down transmission of knowledge that is passively absorbed by students, or what the Brazilian educator Paulo Freire (1998) called "banking education." Rather, critical multicultural education and global education promote dialogue—a collaborative process of teaching and learning so that critical thinking is catalyzed, and the minds, hearts, and spirits of learners can be sustained. Learners have knowledge, experiences, and realities to teach or share with each other and their teachers but are also humble enough to be open to learning from others. Hence, we include multiple creative, participatory, and dialogical teaching–learning strategies in our classrooms and other venues. At the same time, we ensure that different perspectives and worldviews are presented, because global issues are often controversial, and we are careful not to inadvertently take a stance of indoctrination (Shapiro, n.d.). A third common pedagogical principle in global education and multicultural education lies in the recognition that no education is free of values. For global educators and multicultural educators, these values (e.g., justice, nonviolence, respect, reconciliation, kindness, compassion) need to be brought to the surface and acknowledged because they provide one tool for critically assessing the validity of a policy or practice. Fourth, and most important, global education and multicultural education is based on the pedagogical principle of critical empowerment. Learners need not only understand the root causes of conflicts and barriers but must also be guided by this knowledge and be willing to engage in personal and social action to build a culture of peace.

There is a well-known ancient proverb that says a journey of 10,000 miles (or kilometers) starts with a single step. We hope this chapter has provided enough examples and a clear enough vision to indicate that our journeys in multicultural education and global education are a few steps along the way. However, we hope it is also clear that the journeys of the two fields of education are not divergent, but closely interconnected and synergistic.

REFERENCES

Abdi, A., & Schultz, L. (Eds.). (2008). *Educating for human rights and global citizenship education*. Albany: State University of New York at Albany.

American Psychological Association. (2002). *Guidelines on multicultural education, training, research, practice, and organizational change for psychologists*. Washington, DC: Author. Retrieved from http://www.apa.org/pi/oema/resources/policy/multicultural-guidelines.aspx

Anderson, L. (1991). A rationale for global education. In K. Tye (Ed.), *Global education—From thought to action. 1991 ASCS Yearbook* (pp. 13–34). Alexandria, VA: Association for Supervision and Curriculum Development.

An-Na'im, A. A. (Ed.). (1995). *Human rights in cross-cultural perspectives*. Philadelphia: University of Pennsylvania.

Australian Multicultural Foundation and Robert Bean Consulting. (2010). *Managing cultural diversity: Training program resource manual*. Melbourne: Australian Multicultural Foundation.

Baker, L. L., Jaffe, P. G., Ashbourne, L., & Carter, J. (2002). *Children exposed to domestic violence*. London, England: Centre for Children & Families in the Justice System.

Banks, J. A. (1989). Approaches to multicultural education reform. In J. A. Banks & C. A. M. Banks (Eds.), *Multicultural education. Issues and perspectives* (pp. 229–250). Needham Heights, MA: Allyn & Bacon.

Banks, J. A. (2008). *Teaching strategies for ethnic studies* (8th ed.). Boston, MA: Allyn & Bacon.

Battiste, M. (2002, October). *Indigenous knowledge and pedagogy in First Nations education. A literature review with recommendations* (A report prepared for the national Working Group on Education and the Minister of Indian Affairs, Indian and Northern Affairs Canada, Ottawa). Retrieved from http://www.usask.ca/education/people/battistem/ikp_e.pdf

Becker, J. (1991). Curriculum considerations in global studies. In K. Tye (Ed.), *Global education—From thought to action. 1991 ASCS Yearbook* (pp. 67–85). Alexandria, VA: Association of Supervision and Curriculum Development.

Betancourt J. R., Green A. R., Carrillo J. E., & Ananeh-Firempong, O. (2003). Defining cultural competence: a practical framework for addressing racial/ethnic disparities in health and health care. *Public Health Report, 118*, 293–302.

Bodley, H. (2008). *Victims of progress* (5th ed.). Lanham, MD: Altamira.

Boulding, E. (2000). *Cultures of peace: The hidden side of history*. Syracuse, NY: Syracuse University Press.

Boulding, K. E. (1970). *Peace and the war industry*. Piscataway, NJ: Transaction.

Burns, R. J., & Aspeslagh, R. (Eds.). (1996). *Three decades of peace education around the world: An anthology*. New York, NY: Routledge.

Carson, T. (Ed.). (1988). *Toward a renaissance of humanity: Rethinking and reorienting curriculum and instruction*. Edmonton, Alberta, Canada: University of Alberta.

Cawagas, V., Toh, S. H., & Garrone, B. (Eds.). (2007). *Many faiths one humanity. An educational resource for integrating interfaith perspectives in educating for a culture of peace*. Brisbane, Australia: Multi-Faith Centre, Griffith University & Edmund Rice Education.

Chang, S. J. (2008). When East and West meet: An essay on the importance of cultural understanding in global business practice and education. *Journal of International Business and Cultural Studies*, *2*, 1–13.

Chevannes, M. (2002). Issues in educating health professionals to meet the diverse needs of patients and other service users from ethnic minority groups. *Journal of Advanced Nursing*, *39*, 290–298. doi:10.1046/j.1365-2648.2002.02276.x

Claude, R. P., & Weston, B. H. (Eds.). (2006). *Human rights in the world community*. Philadelphia, PA: University of Pennsylvania.

Constantine, M. G., & Sue, D. W. (Eds.). (2005). *Strategies for building multicultural competence in mental health and educational settings*. Hoboken, NJ: Wiley.

Deardorff, D. K. (2008). Intercultural competence. A definition, model, and implications for education abroad. In V. Savicki (Ed.), *Developing intercultural competence and transformation* (pp. 32–52). Sterling, VA: Stylus.

Dei, G. J. S. (1996). *Anti-racism education: Theory and practice*. Halifax, Nova Scotia, Canada: Fernwood.

Domhoff, G. W. (2005). *Who rules America?* (5th ed.). New York, NY: McGraw-Hill.

Fien, J. (2001). *Teaching and learning for a sustainable future* [CD-ROM]. Paris, France: UNESCO.

Fisher, S., & Hicks, D. (1985). *World studies 8–13: A teacher's handbook*. Edinburgh, Scotland: Oliver & Boyd.

Fisher, W. F., & Ponniah, T. (Eds.). (2003). *Another world is possible*. London, England: Zed Books.

Floresca-Cawagas, V. (Ed.). (1988). Education for the twenty-first century. *WCCI Forum*, *2*(2), 1–158.

Freire, P. (1998). *Pedagogy of freedom. Ethics, democracy and civic courage*. Lanham, MD: Rowman & Littlefield.

Fried, J. (2011). Multicultural identities and shifting selves among college students. In M. J. Cuyjet, M. E. Howard-Hamilton, & D. L. Cooper (Eds.), *Multiculturalism on campus* (pp. 65–83). Sterling, VA: Stylus.

Gordon, A. F., & Newfield, C. (Eds.). (1996). *Mapping multiculturalism*. Minneapolis: University of Minnesota.

Gorski, P. C. (2007). *Good intentions are not enough: A decolonizing intercultural education*. Retrieved from http://www.everettcc.edu/uploadedFiles/Faculty_Staff/TLC/Diversity_Teaching_Lab/intercultural-education.pdf

Grant, C. A. (2006). *The evolution of multicultural education in the U.S.: A journey for human rights and social justice*. Retrieved from http://www.scribd.com/doc/33315164/The-Evolution-of-Multicultural-Education-in-the-U-S-A-Journey-for-Human-Rights-Social-Justice-CA-Grant

Grant, C. A., & Sleeter, C. E. (1989). Race, class, gender and disability in the classroom. In J. A. Banks & C. A. Banks (Eds.), *Multicultural education: Issues and perspectives* (pp. 61–83). Boston, MA: Allyn & Bacon.

Gudykunst, W. B., & Mody, B. (Eds.). (2002). *Handbook of international and intercultural communication*. Thousand Oaks, CA: Sage.

Guerrero, M. A. J. (1996). Academic apartheid: American Indian studies and "multiculturalism." In A. F. Gordon & C. Newfield (Eds.), *Mapping multiculturalism* (pp. 49–63). Minneapolis: University of Minnesota Press.

Haavelsrud, M. (1981). *Approaching disarmament education*. Guildford, England: Westbury House.

Hanvey, R. (1976). *An attainable global perspective*. Denver, CO: Center for Teaching International Relations.

Henry, F., & Tator, C. (Eds.). (2009). *Racism in the Canadian university. Demanding social justice, inclusion and equity*. Toronto, Ontario, Canada: University of Toronto Press.

Hickling-Hudson, A. (2003). Multicultural education and the post-colonial turn. *Policy Futures in Education, 1*, 381–401. doi:10.2304/pfie.2003.1.2.13

Hicks, D. (2008, July). *Ways of seeing: The origins of global education in the UK*. Paper presented at the United Kingdom ITE Network Inaugural Conference on Education for Sustainable Development/Global Citizenship, London, England. Retrieved from http://www.teaching4abetterworld.co.uk/docs/download2.pdf

Howard-Hamilton, M. F., & Hinton, K. G. (2011). Oppression and its effect on college student identity development. In M. J. Cuyjet, M. E. Howard-Hamilton, & D. L. Cooper (Eds.), *Multiculturalism on campus* (pp. 19–36). Sterling, VA: Stylus.

Huckle, J., & Sterling, S. (Eds.). (1996). *Education for sustainability*. London, England: Earthscan.

Hutchinson, F. (1996). *Educating beyond violent futures*. New York, NY: Routledge.

James, C. E. (1999). *Seeing ourselves* (2nd ed.). Toronto, Ontario, Canada: Thompson Educational.

Jameson, D. A. (2007). Reconceptualizing cultural identity and its role in intercultural business communication. *Journal of Business Communication, 44*, 199–235. doi:10.1177/0021943607301346

Kagawa, F., & Selby, D. (Eds.). (2010). *Education and climate change: Living and learning in interesting times*. New York, NY: Routledge.

Kaza, S. (2008). *Mindfully green*. Boston, MA: Shambhala.

Kivisto, P. (2002). *Multiculturalism in a global society*. Oxford, England: Blackwell. doi:10.1002/9780470694916

Kniep, W. M. (1985). *A critical review of the short history of global education: Preparing for new opportunities*. New York, NY: The American Forum for Global Education.

Kniep, W. M. (1987). *Next steps in global education: A handbook for curriculum development*. New York, NY: Global Perspectives in Education.

Ladson-Billings, G. (2003). New directions in multicultural education: complexities, boundaries, and critical race theory. In J. A. Banks & C. A. McGee Banks (Eds.), *Handbook of research on multicultural education* (2nd ed., pp. 50–65). San Francisco, CA: Jossey-Bass.

Lantieri, L., & Patti, J. (1996). *Waging peace in our schools.* Boston, MA: Beacon.

Lawrence, S. M., & Tatum, B. D. (n.d.). *White racial identity and anti-racist education: A catalyst for change.* Retrieved from http://teachingforchange.org/files/062-A.pdf

Lewison, K., Leland, C., & Harste, J. (2008). *Creating critical classrooms: K–8 reading and writing with an edge.* New York, NY: Erlbaum.

Little, D. (Ed.). (2007). *Peacemakers in action: Profiles of religion in conflict resolution* (pp. 3–24). Cambridge, England: Cambridge University Press.

Macy, J. (1998). *Coming back to life: Practices to reconnect our lives, our world.* Gabriola Island, British Columbia, Canada: New Society.

Madeley, J. (2008). *Big business, poor peoples.* London, England: Zed Books.

Marks, S. P. (2010). Human rights education in UN peace-building: From theory to practice. In PDHRE—The People's Movement for Human Rights Learning (Ed.), *Human rights learning: A peoples' report* (pp. 76–86). New York, NY: People's Movement for Human Rights Learning.

Matriano, E. C. (1980, December–January). *Lifelong learning for global development: Toward a humane quality of life.* Proceedings of the Third Triennial WCCI World Conference in Education, the Development Academy of the Philippines, Tagaytay City, Philippines. London, England: World Council for Curriculum & Instruction.

Matriano, E. C. (1987). Peace: A mission for world educators. In T. R. Carson & H. D. Gideonse (Eds.), *Peace education and the task for peace educators* (pp. 1–4). Edmonton, Alberta, Canada: World Council for Curriculum & Instruction.

Matriano, E. C. (1988). WCCI: A humanizing force in global curriculum building. In T. Carson (Ed.), *Toward a renaissance of humanity: rethinking and reorienting curriculum and instruction* (pp. 19–30). Edmonton, Alberta, Canada: University of Alberta Press.

Matriano, E. C. (2000). The impact of global changes on teacher education. Challenges, opportunities and a vision for a culture of peace. *International Journal of Curriculum and Instruction, 2,* 85–93.

May, S., & Sleeter, C. (Eds.). (2010). *Critical multiculturalism: Theory and practice.* London, England: Routledge.

Mays, R. K. (Ed.). (2009). *Interfaith dialogue at the grassroots.* Philadelphia, PA: Ecumenical Press.

McCarthy, C., & Crichlow, W. (Eds.). (1993). *Race, identity and representation in education.* New York, NY: Routledge.

McLaren, P. (1997). *Revolutionary multiculturalism.* Boulder, CO: Westview.

McPherson, B., & Szul, L. F. (2008). Business students must have cultural adaptability. *Journal of Organizational Culture, Communications and Conflict, 12*(2), 39–48.

Mendlovitz, S. (1975). *On the creation of a just world*. New York, NY: The Free Press.

Merryfield, M. (1995). *Teacher education in global and international education*. Retrieved from http://www.ericdigests.org/1996-1/global.htm

Meyer, L., & Alvarado, B. M. (Eds.). (2010). *New world of indigenous resistance*. San Francisco, CA: City Light Books.

Mische, P. (2006). The earth as commodity or community? In S. H. Toh & V. Cawagas (Eds.), *Cultivating wisdom, harvesting peace* (pp. 155–168). Brisbane, Australia: Multi-Faith Centre, Griffith University.

Nieto, S. (1996). *Affirming diversity*. White Plains, NY: Longman.

Oswald, J., & Matriano, E. C. (1974). *Earthship*. New York, NY: Institute for World Order.

Oxfam. (2006). *Education for global citizenship: A guide for schools*. Oxford, England: Oxfam.

Peters, J., & Wolper, A. (Eds.). (1995). *Women's rights, human rights*. London, England: Routledge.

Pike, G., & Selby, D. (1988). *Global teacher, global learner*. London, England: Hodder & Stoughton.

Reardon, B. A. (1988). *Comprehensive peace education: Educating for global responsibility*. New York, NY: Teachers College.

Reardon, B. A. (1995). *Educating for human dignity: Learning about rights and responsibilities*. Philadelphia: University of Pennsylvania.

Reardon, B. A., & Cabezudo, A. (2002). *Learning to abolish war. Teaching toward a culture of peace*. New York, NY: Hague Appeal for Peace.

Reardon, B. A., Matriano, E., Carter, M., & Stanford, B. (1977). *Discrimination: The cycle of injustice*. Toronto, Ontario, Canada: Holt, Rinehart & Winston.

Richardson, R. (1976). *Learning for change in world society*. London, England: World Studies Project.

Roman, L. G. (1993). White is a color! White defensiveness, postmodernism and anti-racist pedagogy. In C. McCarthy & W. Crichlow (Eds.). *Race, identity, and representation in education* (pp. 279–378). New York, NY: Routledge.

Royal Australian College of General Practitioners Curriculum for Australian General Practice. (2007). *Multicultural health*. Retrieved from http://www.racgp.org.au/scriptcontent/curriculum/pdf/multiculturalhealth.pdf

Shapiro, A. (n.d.). *Teaching on controversial issues. Guidelines for teachers*. Retrieved from http://www/teachablemoment.org/high/teachingcontroversy.html

Shaya, F. T., & Gbarayor, C. M. (2006). The case for cultural competence in health professions education. *American Journal of Pharmaceutical Education, 70*, 1–6. doi:10.5688/aj7006124

Shiva, V. (2005). *Earth democracy*. Cambridge, MA: South End.

Shotton, H. J., Yellowfish, S., & Cintron, R. (2010). Island of sanctuary: The role of an American Indian culture center. In L. D. Patton (Ed.), *Culture centers in higher education* (pp. 49–60). Sterling, VA: Stylus.

Sleeter, C. E. (2001). Preparing teachers for culturally diverse schools: Research and the overwhelming presence of whiteness. *Journal of Teacher Education, 52,* 94–106. doi:10.1177/0022487101052002002

Smith, R. (1998). Challenging privilege. In R. C. Chavez & J. O'Donnell (Eds.), *Speaking the unpleasant* (pp. 197–210). Albany, NY: State University of New York at Albany.

Sue, D. W., Arredondo, P., & McDavis, R. J. (1992). Multicultural counseling competencies and standards: A call to the profession. *Journal of Counseling and Development, 70,* 477–486. doi:10.1002/j.1556-6676.1992.tb01642.x

Summy, R., & Ram, S. (Eds.). (2008). *Nonviolence: An alternative for defeating global terror(ism).* New York, NY: Nova Science.

Tauli-Corpuz, V. (2005, May). *Indigenous peoples and the Millennium Development Goals.* Paper submitted to the fourth Session of the UN Permanent Forum on Indigenous Issues, New York. Retrieved from http://www.tanzaniagateway.org/docs/indigenous_peoples_and_the_MDGs.pdf

Tisdell, E. J. (2003). *Exploring spirituality and culture in adult and higher education.* San Francisco, CA: Jossey-Bass.

Toh, S. H. (1993). Bringing the world into the classroom. Global literacy and a question of paradigms. *Global Education, 1,* 9–17.

Toh, S. H. (Ed.). (2000). Educating for a culture of peace [Special issue]. *International Journal of Curriculum & Instruction, 2*(1).

Toh, S. H. (2004a). Learning to live together: Fighting stereotypes from textbooks to the Internet. In *Proceedings of the Universal Forum of Cultures—Barcelona 2004* (pp. 147–159). Paris, France: UNESCO.

Toh, S. H. (2004b). *Uprooting violence, cultivating peace: Education for an engaged spirituality* (2004 Professorial Lecture). Brisbane, Australia: Griffith University.

Toh, S. H. (2009). Dialogue among and within faiths for the weaving of a culture of peace. In M. S. Michael & F. Petito (Eds.), *Civilizational dialogue and world order* (pp. 69–92). London, England: Palgrave McMillan.

Toh, S. H. (Ed.). (2010). Dialogue among civilizations [Special issue]. *International Journal of Curriculum & Instruction, 7*(1).

Toh, S. H., & Cawagas, V. F. (Eds.). (2006). *Cultivating wisdom, harvesting peace: Educating for a culture of peace through values, virtues and spirituality of diverse cultures, faiths and civilizations.* Brisbane, Australia: Multi-Faith Centre, Griffith University.

Toh, S. H., & Cawagas, V. F. (2009). Transforming the ecological crisis: Challenges for faiths and interfaith education in interesting times. In D. Selby & F. Kagawa (Eds.), *Education and climate change: Living and learning in interesting times* (pp. 175–196). London, England: Routledge.

Toh, S. H., & Floresca-Cawagas, V. (1990). *Peaceful theory and practice in values education.* Quezon City, Philippines: Phoenix.

Toh, S. H., & Floresca-Cawagas, V. (2000). Educating towards a culture of peace. In T. Goldstein & D. Selby (Eds.), *Weaving connections: Educating for peace, social and environmental justice* (pp. 365–388). Toronto, Ontario, Canada: Sumach.

Turner, C. S. V., Gonzalez, J. C., & Wood, J. L. (2008). Faculty of color in academe: What 20 years of literature tells us. *Journal of Diversity in Higher Education, 1,* 139–168. doi:10.1037/a0012837

Tye, K. (Ed.). (1991). *Global education: From thought to action. 1991 ASCD Yearbook.* Alexandria, VA: Association for Supervision and Curriculum Development.

United Nations. (n.d.). *United Nations observances. International days.* Retrieved from http://http.un.org/en/events/observaces/days.html

United Nations Alliance of Civilisations and United Nations Global Compact Office. (2009). *Doing business in a multicultural world: Challenges and opportunities.* New York, NY: Author.

United Nations Educational, Scientific, and Cultural Organization. (2007). *UNESCO guidelines on intercultural education* (pp. 12–30). Paris, France: Author. Retrieved from http://unesdoc.unesco.org/images/0014/001478/147878e.pdf

United Nations Educational, Scientific, and Cultural Organization. (2010). Investing in cultural diversity and intercultural dialogue. *UNESCO World Report.* Paris, France: Author.

Werbner, P., & Modood, T. (Eds.). (1997). *Debating cultural hybridity.* London, England: Zed Books.

Whang, P. A., & Nash, C. P. (2005). Reclaiming compassion: Getting to the heart and soul of teacher education. *Journal of Peace Education, 2,* 79–92. doi:10.1080/1740020042000334118

Wilson, G. B. (2011). The search for inner peace: Considering the spiritual movement in tourism. *The Journal for Tourism and Peace Research, 1*(3), 16–26.

World Council for Curriculum and Instruction. (1971). *Constitution of the World Council for Curriculum and Instruction.* Retrieved from http://www.wcci-international.org/constitution

Zachariah, M. (1992). Linking multicultural education and development education to promote respect for persons and cultures: A Canadian perspective. In J. Lynch, C. Modgil, & S. Modgil (Eds.), *Human rights, education and global responsibilities* (Vol. 3, pp. 273–288). London, England: Routledge.

11

IMPROVING INTERNATIONAL MULTICULTURAL COMPETENCE BY WORKING AND STUDYING ABROAD

DANNY WEDDING

The various countries of the world are linked economically, intellectually, culturally, and politically in ways heretofore unimagined. Smartphones, tablet computers, and the Internet keep us connected with family, friends, and work, domestically and internationally, so that one can work from one's hotel room in almost any country in the world. Indeed, I have spent extensive time in some of the most interesting cities in the world (e.g., Hong Kong, Beijing) sitting alone in my room, answering e-mail, writing articles and book chapters, and pausing now and then to chat with friends on Skype or Gmail. These friends, as often as not, are half a world away.

Perhaps nothing symbolizes the explosive growth of telecommunications more than the cell phone and the Internet. It is estimated that in 2010 there were 5.3 billion cell phones (i.e., almost as many cell phones as people on the planet) and 2.1 billion people who used the Internet (Central

DOI: 10.1037/14044-011
Internationalizing Multiculturalism: Expanding Professional Competencies in a Globalized World,
R. L. Lowman (Editor)

Intelligence Agency, 2011). Of course, these numbers have only increased since 2010, and it is now likely that the number of cell phones actually exceeds the total global population.

The linkage between the countries of the world, as well as the subcultures within each country, has been in part the result of a profound knowledge explosion, and we are increasingly linked by our mutual need to access and use these new data, information, and knowledge. One salient symbol of this seismic shift occurred in 2002 when a tipping point was reached and, for the first time, the worldwide digital storage capacity overtook total analog capacity, and electronic media became more prevalent than printed media (University of Southern California, 2011).

Internationalization has resulted in an ever-increasing number of global opportunities for students who now routinely build international activities into undergraduate and graduate curricula. The skills these students will need when traveling and studying abroad are in many ways the same skills they will need to work effectively and harmoniously with people in their own country who have different cultures, habits, traditions, and languages. For example, knowledge of Spanish will facilitate travel, business, and education in Spain or most countries in Latin America or South America, but it can be equally useful in Southern California or Texas; respect for Buddhist traditions and values can help one negotiate the rules and rituals associated with visiting a temple in Thailand, but it can also help you build a more harmonious relationship with a Cambodian neighbor or colleague.

In short, there is marked overlap between international competencies and multicultural competencies, despite the fact that these two intellectual spheres have been characterized by relative intellectual isolation with little crossover or communication between practitioners and researchers who work, write, and publish independently in these two obviously linked but seemingly disparate arenas. This history of isolation is changing, and scholars in each camp are coming to realize just how much they have to learn from one another.

Some universities in the United States are especially committed to providing international opportunities for students and have staked their future on international education. For example, Webster University, a small liberal arts university in St. Louis, made a serious commitment to internationalizing its curriculum and now offers a "Global MBA" and a "Global MA in International Relations," with campuses in Australia, China, England, Japan, Mexico, the Netherlands, Switzerland, and Thailand. Other universities, including elite ones, have established international campuses where they train both their own students and international students. For example, in 2008, New York University established a campus in Abu Dhabi.

There are also abundant new opportunities for professionals willing to work outside the United States. Management professionals from the United

States are increasingly posted abroad, frequently joining a large expatriate community but also developing the language and cultural skills necessary to fully experience the pleasures associated with international living. Academics also take advantage of free summers or sabbaticals to teach abroad, and these experiences can dramatically enrich their university research, teaching, and service. Some federal programs explicitly support educational exchanges; Fulbright fellowships, for example, have been awarded since 1946. More than 310,000 "Fulbrighters" have participated in the Fulbright Scholar Program (U.S. Department of State, 2011), and I personally have completed Fulbright fellowships in Thailand and Korea. International education flows in both directions, and more than a half million international students are currently studying in the United States (Wedding, McCartney, & Currey, 2009). Frequent interaction with international students studying in the United States is one step toward acquiring the knowledge, skills, and attitudes necessary for living abroad successfully.

This chapter highlights the commonalities in, and differences between, multicultural and international competencies, with particular emphasis on the skills necessary to function effectively in a rapidly shrinking world. The chapter includes examples of efforts to train multiculturally and internationally sensitive professionals for work in other cultures (or to work with individuals from other cultures who are immigrants and refugees) as well as examples of insensitive behavior. It overviews what we now know about how to enhance multicultural and international competencies needed by professional practitioners and describes the knowledge and skills—and, more important, the attitudes—necessary for professionals to function effectively in a dynamic world that is increasingly complex, international, and multicultural.

OVERLAP OF MULTICULTURAL AND INTERNATIONAL COMPETENCIES

Despite the obvious overlap in concerns and challenges, a significant gap exists between researchers and practitioners concerned with multicultural issues and those researchers and practitioners focused on the skills necessary for successful adaptation to international living. This gap is to some extent rooted in profound and disturbing economic realities. Writing about elementary education, Ian Hill (2007) noted:

> These two disciplines [international education and multicultural education] have grown independently and from two quite different angles. Multicultural education is anchored in state systems of education and seeks to respond to the needs of migrant children, generally representing a lower socio-economic section of the community. International

education is historically linked to the international school movement catering principally for the children of diplomats, UN personnel, and employees of international companies as they move around the world; for this reason, international education has often been described as elitist. (p. 246)

In short, those researchers and educators concerned with multicultural issues have often worked with marginalized groups, whereas those of us fortunate enough to work preparing students to participate fully in international programs have often worked with privileged students who had the financial resources required to take advantage of supplemental educational opportunities such as semester- or year-abroad programs. These differences in foci and priorities may in part account for the relative indifference in academia to the overlapping interests of multicultural and international researchers and scholars. (However, this may be changing. For example, in 2011, the American Council of Education implemented its "At Home in the World Initiative." This program, initially piloted in eight colleges and universities in the United States, is explicitly designed to support higher education institutions in their efforts to fulfill their service mission in a globalized society by linking their diversity and multicultural programs with their international education initiatives.)

Chapman and Hobbel (2005) developed a typology for multicultural education that shows the progression from assimilation (a model widely promoted before 1960) to pluralism (the current dominant model of multiculturalism). The five steps of this model involve, in increasing order of sophistication, *monoculturalism* (in which one national culture is assumed to be appropriate for all students), *tolerance* (characterized by the inclusion of limited information about other cultures), *acceptance* (in which cultures are acknowledged as separate entities), *respect* (characterized by bicultural education), and *affirmation and solidarity*.

Despite growing globalization, there has been relatively little discussion of the core competencies necessary for successful international life and work. This in part results from the fact that many of these competencies are often country-, culture-, or region-specific. For example, the skills necessary to be successful as an expatriate living in Paris may be very different from those necessary for coping with the cultural differences one would find working in Dhaka, the capital city of Bangladesh. In fact, when thinking about core international competencies, one immediately beings to think about differences rather than commonalities, and a healthy respect for cultural differences ensures that one does not glibly suppose that the skill set that made one a successful Peace Corps volunteer, for example, will make one a successful corporate manager living abroad. The differences between countries, cultures, and roles are simply too great and the cultural divides too wide.

However, there are some commonalities between multicultural and international competencies, and this chapter describes the overlap between the competencies associated with successful international experiences and those competencies that accompany multicultural expertise in one's home country.

Language Competencies

Approximately 6% of the world's population speaks English as a first language, and about 11% of the population speaks English reasonably well as a first, second, or third language. However, in both science and business, English is rapidly becoming a lingua franca for the world; more than 80% of scientific publications are in English, and approximately 15 million people work with scientific English, two thirds of them in countries where English is not the first language (Montgomery, 2011). At international conferences and professional meetings, professional papers are commonly presented in English, and when four business executives from Japan, Thailand, China, and Vietnam get together to make a deal, both the discourse and the documents are likely to be in English.

Although an expatriate's knowledge of the language of his or her host country may not be absolutely necessary, almost everyone who has lived internationally will agree that one's experience is far richer if one takes time to learn the local language. In some countries, polyglots are the norm (e.g., Singapore and Switzerland each has four official languages, Canada has two), and scholars are often surprised to discover how common it is for even highly educated U.S. citizens to speak only one language. (This point is captured in a joke: What do you call someone who speaks three languages? *Trilingual*. What do you call someone who speaks two languages? *Bilingual*. What do you call someone who speaks one language? *An American!*)

Second-language skills are increasingly important multicultural tools necessary to support one's work in the United States. For example, the United States is home to more than 45 million Hispanics, and Spanish is the primary language spoken in the home by over 34 million people living in the United States. This makes the United States one of the world's largest Spanish-speaking countries (the population of Mexico, the country with the largest Spanish-speaking population, is about 111 million). Some graduate school programs in psychology (like that at the University of Texas–El Paso) now require that students be facile in Spanish before they can graduate.

Even if one never becomes fluent in a second language, learning a few hundred words and a few dozen key phrases will significantly enhance one's international experience. In addition, learning at least the rudiments of another language is a way of showing respect and paying homage to one's hosts and their country. Exchanging a few sentences when meeting an international colleague helps one quickly establish a bond of friendship, and it provides the colleague an opportunity to demonstrate his or her personal language skills in a comfortable and nonchallenging way. If one also uses these opportunities to learn a few new words, one quickly acquires the working vocabulary needed to "get by" in a host country. In addition, one quickly discovers that it is relatively easy to communicate some basic information (such as the fact that you are a divorced professor with two children). Any number of free or low-cost online language programs make it easy to acquire these basic language skills before beginning an international experience.

Knowing and Understanding Your Own Culture

You will often be surprised by how much your international friends will know about U.S. culture. My oldest son once sat around a campfire in the Russian steppe and described himself as being from "St. Louis, a city south of Chicago," assuming his new friends would not be familiar with St. Louis. He was surprised when his friend remarked (correctly), "Yes, just yesterday I was telling someone that Chuck Berry still often played gigs in St. Louis."

I write about the portrayal of psychopathology in contemporary films, and I have been surprised—and delighted—to discover that university students and educated professionals around the world routinely watch U.S. films and are conversant with the names of actors and recent releases. Likewise, people around the world follow U.S. politics and typically know dramatically more about our country's politics than we know about their politics and politicians—and sometimes more than we know about our own. For example, it is sometimes said that U.S. citizens are blithely and benevolently unaware of Canadian politics, whereas Canadians are malevolently well informed about what is happening in the United States.

One necessarily has to be sensitive to political topics when traveling, but discussing politics can also enrich your own perspectives. I was in Mexico and Greece shortly after George W. Bush was elected for a second term, and my hosts in both countries were genuinely perplexed about how we could have elected this man for a second 4-year term. (I shared their bewilderment.)

Your own culture has profoundly shaped your values and beliefs every bit as much as it has those of your international friends, and it is important that you take time to think about how these values and beliefs will influence your perceptions as you travel and the quality of the overall international experience. Female colleagues have experienced considerable discomfort in meetings with Muslim men who expected them to have their head covered or who would not shake a proffered (female) hand. I personally traveled and lectured in South Africa during the time of apartheid, and it seemed repugnant to me to hear my psychology host addressed as "Master" by his female

African housekeeper, although this seemed perfectly natural to my friend, who had grown up being addressed this way.

Two overall points are important: (a) You need to appreciate how your own experiences have shaped your values and beliefs and (b) knowing just a little about U.S. politics, sports, movies, and culture will make it far easier for you to make friends and engage in conversation with your international friends. In contrast, not knowing who won the most recent World Series, for example, leaves you appearing to be woefully ignorant about your own culture and its values.

Understanding Culture

Language is a critical component of culture, but the concept encompasses much more. *Culture* refers to the shared attitudes, practices, and values that characterize an organization, group, or institution, and it includes the ways in which people express themselves through art and science; the ways in which they perceive, understand, and interpret the world; spiritual beliefs and values; the ways in which members of a group socialize; and the day-to-day realities of socialization, negotiation, and interaction (Roshan Cultural Heritage Institute, n.d.). Knowing something about these attitudes, practices, and values is essential to success in a multicultural world.

I have seen—and cringed at—multiple examples of stupidity, and (sometimes well-intended) faux pas, in my international travels. Some of the more salient examples include the woman in a revealing tank top in a Thai temple, a tourist having his photo taken with a Buddha statue after placing his baseball cap on the Buddha's head, and a brilliant college professor showing slides of meditating women with bare arms and legs at a psychology conference in Tehran. Simply taking time to read about the values of your host country (Thailand, Cambodia, and Iran, in these examples) would have made it easy to avoid these egregious errors. One can also discuss culture values and issues with colleagues or friends from the country one will be visiting or working in, and it is possible to learn a great deal about the culture of other countries from reading novels (e.g., *Little Bee* by Chris Cleave or *Snow* (2002) by Turkish Nobel Laureate Orhan Pamuk) or viewing films (e.g., *Monsoon Wedding, The Gods Must Be Crazy, El Norte*).

The offensive and demeaning behaviors of some Americans may be tolerated because of economic necessity, and multiculturally and internationally competent professionals need to be sensitive to these fiscal realities and the disparities that often exist between our hosts and ourselves. It is not unusual for the money spent on even a short vacation to be equal to or exceed annual income for someone in the developing country that is visited. However, ethical people do not abuse others simply because they can, and sensitive professionals remain alert to the possibility that economic realities can profoundly influence their interactions with the people they meet abroad. The image of the "Ugly American" has persisted since the 1958 publication of a novel by that same name, and this stereotype has been reinforced by loud, boorish, and ethnocentric behavior or by ethically questionable behavior such as the 2012 Secret Service involvement with prostitutes in Colombia. Rotabi, Gammonley, and Gamble (2006) presented a conceptual model for international learning based on core ethical principles and values (social justice and human rights, community capacity, dignity and worth of the person, self-determination, boundaries, competence, facilitated learning in a safe environment, integrity) that offers tangible suggestions for avoiding the ostentatious display of power and privilege.

Knowledge, Attitudes, and Values

The United Nations Educational, Scientific and Cultural Organization (UNESCO) outlined seven Guiding Principles of Educational Policy that underscore the knowledge, attitudes and values that support multicultural understanding in an international world (UNESCO, 2011). They are as follows:

1. An international dimension and a global perspective in education at all levels and in all its forms
2. Understanding and respect for all peoples, their cultures, civilizations, values and ways of life, including domestic ethnic cultures and cultures of other nations
3. Awareness of the increasing global interdependence between peoples and nations
4. Abilities to communicate with others
5. Awareness not only of the rights but also of the duties incumbent upon individuals, social groups, and nations towards each other
6. Understanding of the necessity for international solidarity and cooperation
7. Readiness on the part of the individual to participate in solving the problems of his community, his country and the world at large. (p. 2)

A second typology listing the attitudes and values necessary for success in an international setting presents those developed by the International and Multicultural Education, Research, Intervention, and Training (I-MERIT) program at Alliant International University, my current employer. I-MERIT (see also Chapter 1, this volume) is the home of the university's diversity initiatives, which are aimed at institutionalizing multicultural and international values and perspectives in all of Alliant's education and training programs and in its organizational culture. The I-MERIT values, beliefs, and guiding principles are listed in Exhibit 11.1; they serve as a framework for understanding the values that facilitate international exchange.

The simple value of respect will greatly enhance one's international experience and minimize the likelihood of negative encounters or exchanges. In addition, it is critical to appreciate the wide individual differences that may exist within cultural groups. One example is found in the Hispanic–Latino population in the United States; although grouped under a single rubric, primarily on the basis of language, individuals from Cuba, Venezuela, the Dominican Republic, Mexico, and Spain have very different cultural experiences and expectations.

In my experience, cultural curiosity is another trait found in almost everyone who reports a positive international experience, and those people who are intrigued by maps, *National Geographic*, and travel documentaries make good travelers and expatriates. The world is intrinsically fascinating, and travel offers us a rich opportunity to sample the splendor of our diverse and multicultural world.

The Importance of Homework

It is axiomatic that anyone visiting, living in, or working in another country will benefit from spending some time preparing for the experience, and the rewards of travel and international living are likely to be directly proportional to the time and energy invested in preparing for the experience. The Internet

---

EXHIBIT 11.1.
I-MERIT Values, Beliefs, and Guiding Principles

Respect. We respect and value diverse ways of learning, knowing, and accomplishing goals.

Dialogue and engagement. We can foster individual and collective growth and adaptation by listening to many voices, reexamining assumptions, and working through conflict.

Partnership. We can generate better solutions and increase our chances of success by collaborating across differences.

Continuous learning. A major component of effectiveness is the extent to which we can continuously expand our knowledge and awareness both individually and collectively.

Responsibility. Each of us benefits when we take responsibility, personally and collectively, for building a more inclusive community.

Humility. No one person or perspective has the whole answer.

Commitment. Building inclusion is a long-term process and requires ongoing commitment.

Note. I-MERIT = International-Multicultural Educational Research Intervention and Training (a program at Alliant International University). Used with permission of Alliant International University.

has made learning about other languages and cultures much easier than at any other time in history, and the sheer amount of information available is staggering. The U.S. Department of State (http://www.state.gov/countries), the World Bank (http://data.worldbank.org/country), and the Central Intelligence Agency (CIA) *World Factbook* (http://www.cia.gov/library/publications/the-world-factbook) all provide credible and useful information about other countries, and these are recommended places to start as you prepare for international travel or living. Psychologists specifically interested in learning more about the profession and practice of psychology in other countries can visit the International Union of Psychological Sciences' "Psychology Resources Around the World" at http://www.iupsys.net/index.php/praw.

The admonition to do one's homework before visiting another country applies equally to the need to read about and learn about other cultural groups in the United States, especially if one presumes to offer professional services to individuals from these groups. The Internet has made it easy to enhance one's sensitivity to the values, beliefs, and attitudes found in diverse cultural groups.

Appreciation for the Commonalities in the Human Experience

Although we often stress the differences between groups and individuals when writing about multiculturalism and international living, the reality is that members of our species are remarkably alike. The Taj Mahal is universally recognized as beautiful, play is a natural and worldwide practice of children, parents love and protect their children everywhere in the world, and travel underscores the fundamental premise of Buddhism: We all suffer, grow old, and die. Taking some time to contemplate these basic truths (e.g., watching children playing in any playground in the world) will enrich your international experience.

Know Where to Go If You Get in Trouble

International travelers expect their trips abroad to go smoothly, and usually they do. However, life can sometimes unexpectedly become extraordinarily complicated, and a few simple precautions can help tremendously in these situations. At the very least, when traveling abroad, one should have the address and phone number of the relevant U.S. consulate or embassy, and it is useful to have a copy of your passport in your luggage and perhaps in another location. Having a list of all your credit cards and other essential travel documents you carry in your wallet stored along with relevant phone numbers for reporting loss will simplify things tremendously if your wallet is ever stolen. A simple list of frequent flyer and frequent guest programs for various airlines and hotels can also be useful. Keeping the contact information for local colleagues or friends with you at all times also is advisable. Finally, knowing the local words for *sick, hospital, doctor, emergency,* and *police* can be tremendously helpful during a crisis.

Specific Recommendations for Academics

Being a college professor is a high-status occupation in almost all parts of the world, and frequently academics are more highly regarded in other countries than in the United States. This has certainly been my experience throughout Asia. Your time abroad can be enriched if you take time to visit some of the world's great universities (e.g., the Sorbonne in Paris, the University of Heidelberg in Germany, Sophia University in Tokyo). It is also useful to drop by your discipline's home department. You most likely will be surprised by how welcome your hosts will make you feel. I personally travel with a flash drive whenever I am abroad, and I am prepared to present on a moment's notice if the opportunity arises. These impromptu presentations to colleagues and graduate students have been some of my favorite travel memories.

You may also want to volunteer to lead discussion groups with graduate students in which you describe life as a professional in the United States. Many of the students who come to your talk will be interested in studying in the United States.

If you are visiting a large city, you may want to explore the option of staying with a colleague or a graduate student or his or her family during your visit. Your host family is likely to reject payment for their hospitality, but gifts for your new friends are always welcome.

SUMMARY

The world is a fascinating place, and telecommunications, advances in transportation technology, and the Internet have opened up unparalleled opportunities for interaction with friends, colleagues, and business partners around the globe. Taking time to learn about the language and the culture of your host country will greatly facilitate your time abroad, whether you are a visitor or an expatriate. Learning the local language is invaluable if you truly want to understand your host country and its citizens. Being open to new experiences, curious about the world, and sensitive to cultural differences will significantly enhance your international experience, as will some appreciation for the universal experiences that bind us all together as members of the same species, confronting many of the same struggles. The same set of knowledge, attitudes, and values will also enhance your ability to work with diverse cultural groups in the United States, and you will find that both international experience and multicultural outreach have the potential to make your life and your work significantly more enjoyable and meaningful.

REFERENCES

American Council on Education. (2011). *At Home in the World Initiative*. Retrieved from http://www.acenet.edu/Content/NavigationMenu/ProgramsServices/cii/current/gap/index.htm

Central Intelligence Agency. (2011). *The world factbook*. Retrieved from https://www.cia.gov/library/publications/the-world-factbook/geos/xx.html

Chapman, T., & Hobbel, N. (2005). Multicultural education and its typologies. In S. Farenga & D. Ness (Eds.), *Encyclopedia of education and human development* (Vol. 1, pp. 296–301). New York, NY: Sharpe.

Hill, I. (2007). Multicultural and international education: Never the twain shall meet? *International Review of Education, 53*, 245–264. doi:10.1007/s11159-007-9048-x

Montgomery, S. L. (2011). English and science: Realities and issues for translation in the age of an expanding *lingua franca*. *JoSTrans: The Journal of Specialized Translation*. Retrieved from http://www.jostrans.org/issue11/art_montgomery.php

Roshan Cultural Heritage Institute. (n.d.). *Definition of culture*. Retrieved from http://www.roshan-institute.org/474552

Rotabi, K. S., Gammonley, D., & Gamble, D. N. (2006). Ethical guidelines for study abroad: Can we transform ugly Americans into engaged global citizens? *British Journal of Social Work, 36*, 451–465. doi:10.1093/bjsw/bcl010

United Nations Educational, Scientific and Cultural Organization. (2011). *Recommendation concerning education for international understanding, co-operation and peace and education relating to human rights and fundamental freedoms*. Retrieved from http://www.unesco.org/education/nfsunesco/pdf/Peace_e.pdf

University of Southern California. (2011, February 11). How much information is there in the world? *ScienceDaily*. Retrieved from http://www.sciencedaily.com/releases/2011/02/110210141219.htm

U.S. Department of State. (2011). *The Fulbright program*. Retrieved from http://fulbright.state.gov/about.html

Wedding, D., McCartney, J. L., & Currey, D. E. (2009). Lessons relevant to psychologists who serve as mentors for international students. *Professional Psychology: Research and Practice, 40*, 189–193. doi:10.1037/a0012249

III

CONCLUSION

12

INTERNATIONALIZING MULTICULTURALISM: MAJOR THEMES AND WRAPPING UP

RODNEY L. LOWMAN

This book is about internationalizing multiculturalism. It has raised and attempted to answer the following question: What do professionals need to know to be both multiculturally and internationally competent? Perhaps the major theme of the chapters in this book could be summarized by saying, "a lot." As each chapter has demonstrated, in today's world, the professional needs to understand that both multicultural and international considerations affect many, if not most, diversity issues in all parts of the world.

Of course, no single book can comprehensively address every aspect of "what every professional must know" in every profession and in all multicultural and international situations. This book was not intended to be a comprehensive textbook but rather an invitation to help open professionals' eyes, minds, and hearts to possibilities and to understand why a broadened definition of *multiculturalism* both matters and, we have argued, has become essential. If their authors have achieved their intended purpose, these chapters ask

DOI: 10.1037/14044-012
Internationalizing Multiculturalism: Expanding Professional Competencies in a Globalized World,
R. L. Lowman (Editor)

readers to see the need, the possibility, and the opportunity to think of multi-cultural and international perspectives as mutually beneficial and synergistic.

MAJOR THEMES

A number of integrative themes worth summarizing here transverse the chapters of this book.

1. **Multiculturalism–internationalism partly concerns righting wrongs and protecting those who hold less power to help reduce oppression and promote basic rights.** There are few traditional areas of multiculturalism that do not reflect a long history of battles on scales large and small to reverse or contain discrimination and oppression. This is true in the vast majority of world cultures, and in some there is much work to do to achieve basic worldwide human rights standards, such as those promulgated by the United Nations in its *Universal Declaration of Human Rights* (see, e.g., United Nations, n.d.).

   In some areas of multicultural concern (e.g., gender; see Cawagas, Chapter 3, this volume; racial equality, see Taylor, Chapter 2, this volume), there have been major advances, including legislation mandating equality in many countries and in the professions (see, e.g., American Psychological Association, 2003). Legal bans on discrimination in a number of countries exist, but there can be no doubt that considerable work remains to remove barriers to equality and to end prejudice, violence, and pay differentials based on extraneous factors (see, e.g., Bahun-Radunovic & Rajan, 2008; "Racial Discrimination and the Global Economic Downturn," 2011; Taborga, 2008). In other areas (e.g., lesbian, gay, bisexual, and transgender [LGBT] issues: Chan, 2010; Fellmeth, 2008; see also Kuba, Chapter 5, this volume), minor progress has been made in destigmatization, yet substantial barriers to equality and freedom from fear, oppression, or worse remain.

   Why, after decades and in some cases centuries, do basic rights for those who are "different" from the norm by virtue of characteristics not under their control remain elusive? Among other reasons, human beings appear to be predisposed to categorical thinking (Quinn, Macrae, & Bodenhausen, 2007) that too often translates into stereotypes (Wright & Taylor, 2007) and prejudice (Devine, 1989; see also Lowman, Chapter 1, this volume). Power issues (e.g., Fiske, & Molm, 2010; Subacchi, 2008) preserving the status and differential distribution of resources of the "haves" (including those related to skin color; see Gaertner & Dovidio, 2003; Gaertner et al., 2003) also serve to keep differences in place. Human aggression (Anderson & Huesmann, 2007), although apparently decreasing worldwide (Pinker, 2011; Zakaria, 2011), remains a factor in the continuity of prejudice in many parts of the world.

There are no simple ways to remove these adverse conditions once and for all. Increasing awareness of the unfairness of discriminatory beliefs and behavior may work in some contexts (e.g., Gaertner & Dovidio, 2005), but enforced laws and regulations are often also needed to protect those vulnerable to discrimination and harassment. Recognizing the near-universality of some of these issues (e.g., prejudice, racism, tribalism, genderism, religious superiority) can serve to advance understanding of the phenomena and integrate findings across locations to develop more integrated and coordinated strategies to advance multicultural–international agendas

2. **Multiculturalism–internationalism is partly about creating a vision of a fully integrated society.** Multiculturalism–internationalism may be seen by some, particularly the privileged, as being about protectionism and treating some groups differentially, but at its best, it is about creating a new world vision and a new world order in which there can be true equality of opportunity and the ability to live quiet lives free of oppression and discrimination. The integrated world economy (see Lopez & Ensari, Chapter 7, this volume; Kelly & Chung, Chapter 8, this volume) leads the way in showing the positive advantages—and the inevitability—of the integration of multiculturalism and internationalism in commerce. The business world is perhaps the one application area of multiculturalism–internationalism that has advanced rapidly and more or less willingly to embrace international perspectives because not to have done so would have meant conceding much commerce to those who have. In this case, there has been compelling economic incentive to internationalize. However, in most other areas of internationalizing, the issues have been framed more in terms of costs than of opportunities.

The reality, of course, is that a world without the boundaries as they once existed is already here, seemingly to stay, and increasingly the world will have to move beyond nations as sovereign deciders on these issues. We have seen the positive (and also some negative; see, e.g., Wolf, 2011) consequences of the changes in worldwide communications and travel that have in large part resulted, among other outcomes, in the overturning of historically intractable regimes (e.g., the Arab Spring with the incipient democratization of countries such as Egypt and Libya and the major reforms engendered in Jordan, Saudi Arabia, and others). National boundaries reflect issues of national origin (see Leach, Leong, Inman, & Ciftçi, Chapter 4, this volume) and are already rapidly changing their meaning and impact when billions of people around the world can no longer be kept in isolation or in ignorance of what is happening elsewhere.

We also have already seen the beginnings of the delivery of professional services in distant locations, sometimes with the professional not leaving the office. As the technology develops further, services will be delivered worldwide in a number of professions. This is the ultimate vision of multiculturalism–internationalism: a world that is united more than it is divided, where commonalities more than differences are accentuated, and where professional access is not limited to the "haves." With the economic explosion of India and China, we have seen a glimpse of a new world order (Subacchi, 2008).

3. **As with most things, advanced ("North") countries are largely "privileged" on issues of multiculturalism–internationalism compared with non-Western ("South") nations.** Whichever issues of discrimination and oppression there have been, and whichever remain, have largely affected developing ("South"; see Cawagas, Chapter 3, this volume; Matriano & Toh, Chapter 10, this volume) nations. The "advanced" nations are more likely to have laws and other protections and enforcement mechanisms built in to help lessen discrimination on the basis of gender, race, national origin, and even sexual orientation and identity. Nonetheless, in any advanced nation, there will be those, often the ones who have borne the brunt of discrimination on nonrelevant factors, who will look to their nation and local or regional government to find the laws they need for protection and too often find them lacking. Even when there are legal protections, attitudinal issues can make lives miserable. As Kuba (Chapter 5, this volume) shows, however, in many

countries, being LGBT, to name just one type of diversity, is in no way a protected condition. Being identified in some countries as LGBT can result not only in discrimination but also in incarceration or even death. The struggles of those in nations where positive change has occurred are no less difficult simply in knowing that advances in civil rights in their countries may be much greater than in "developing" nations. It should, however, help contextualize the progress that has been made and encourage people to reach out and help those in less advanced countries promote their causes.

4. **For areas of diversity in which internationalism is more about addressing oppression than about necessity (e.g., the necessity of internationalism in business settings), understanding the experience of oppression in other cultures helps to contextualize and broaden the ability to work professionally with people in one's own country.** Internationalism in many ways is about searching for the universal across varied, more localized manifestations. For example, it can be argued that in certain areas of nontolerance and diversity concerns, oppression has been slower to change than in others. It is useful to consider why.

As an example, Kuba's treatment of LGBT issues in this volume shows a large chasm between "tolerant" and "intolerant" nations. She identifies some of the factors that have resulted in greater and lesser tolerance but notes that the degree of oppression of LGBT persons is widespread even where other areas of diversity have advanced. It is useful to ask, for example, why LGBT issues are so charged and generally seen negatively throughout the world.

Or again, broadening the perspective, why is women's second-class citizenship so common throughout the world? Despite major changes and advances, there are few places in the world where women's rights are recognized and disparities eliminated.

For professionals, it is useful to consider how changes in status and country affect health and mental health, world orientation, and whatever other issues are likely to affect the particular area of practice. For educators, thinking about how students can be taught universal topics through the lenses of the particular that they wear is also important. For all, the question of how oppression and discrimination against those perceived to be of lesser power or importance must be considered.

Furthermore, for all who care about multicultural matters, it is enriching to learn from the experiences of others in distinct cultures and find commonalities of cause and potentially of effect (change strategies). Also important, when professionals understand the universalism of the struggle for equality among women, those of minority race, and other diverse populations, greater understanding of the cultural envelope (Plant, 1958) in which their clients live becomes possible.

5. **Both individual (idiographic) and group or country (nomothetic) issues need to be considered in integrating multicultural and international perspectives.** There are always issues that require careful attention in moving from the individual to the group and from the group to the individual in the context of a specific culture, a challenge that increases in the context of multiple cultures. Leach et al. (Chapter 4, this volume), for example, describe ways that aspects of modal characteristics associated with national origin can be described and measured. Yet these authors urge caution in moving too quickly from such generalizations to assumptions about individuals. The same can be said about every topic in this book. Although for many, membership in certain identity groups has resulted in oppression, others in the same group have been raised in privilege or used their own abilities, skills, and personality to resist efforts at control. The latter individuals may identify with the issues of their group but may not have experienced them personally in an adverse way. The professional therefore must be ready to understand the experiences and perspectives of those who have been treated badly as the result of their identity groups (Alderfer, 2011), but he or she must not force those perspectives onto individuals when they do not fit or are irrelevant.

6. **Sensitivity to multicultural and international diversity is the first step in being able to work effectively with individuals across diverse backgrounds. Understanding the diversity issues of others starts with understanding one's own issues.** Recognizing that the delivery of professional services always takes place in a cultural context, one is likely to be sensitive and understanding of why these issues matter. In this volume, Hurley and Gerstein (Chapter 9) provide examples of these issues in mental health; Matriano and Toh (Chapter 10) in education; and Lopez and Ensari (Chapter 7) and Kelly and Chung (Chapter 8) in the world of business. By continually extending his or her knowledge of how well-established diver-

sity constructs may be affected, even in one's own setting and culture, by international constructs, the professional will be ready to change approaches or context to work effectively with such issues when they matter. These issues do not occur in isolation, however. Most professionals need to understand their own issues and reactions to others if they are to be effective in multicultural and international contexts.

7. **There is no reasonable way that most professionals can ever know all there is to know about every culture they may encounter over the course of their practice.** Because of the multitude of variations of the dimensions discussed in his book, no professional can be equally expert in all multicultural and international issues. It helps to know a lot about the major international issues facing the professional's clients in a particular geographic area(s) and to have a methodology through which new issues can be studied and mastered as they arise. It is therefore important to have templates that enable one to do the necessary research when working with unfamiliar multicultural or international issues (see Leach et al., Chapter 4, and Limberg, Chapter 6, this volume). Awareness of the areas of knowledge or other deficiencies is the first step; motivation to change ignorance to knowledge is the second.

8. **It is rarely wise to make a priori assumptions about what matters to particular clients at a particular point in their lives.** For example, those who have obtained asylum in a more benevolent country may have escaped torture or even death in their homeland, but this does not mean their feelings about the countries they left behind or for their new country of residence are not conflicted (in this volume, the compelling examples of Kuba's [Chapter 5], Matriano and Toh's [Chapter 10], and Taylor's [Chapter 2] help the reader understand the kind of extreme conditions people can experience in an oppressive regime). Often, those for whom multicultural and international issues matter greatly may also be disappointed when moving to an environment that endorses but does not deliver a more supportive multicultural or internal context. There may have been an idealization of the new environment and a (temporary at least) de-idealization of the former culture that need to be understood and sorted out as expectations are confronted with reality. Similarly, clients who experience depression rather than elation at the new context are not unusual (see Hurley & Gerstein, Chapter 9, this volume). Even a few minutes with clients to try to

understand their reality, emotions, and ambivalences is time
well spent.

9. **Contextualizing clients' issues in a cultural context is generally desirable, even when the issues seem tangential.** In health care, for example, the focus is likely on the medical problems or issues at hand, and the consultation with a medical professional is likely focused on addressing those issues. However, assumptions about the patient–medical professional relationship in the context of gender (Cawagas, Chapter 3, this volume), the role and presence of family members, issues with significant others in the case of LGBT clients (Kuba, Chapter 5, this volume), for example, may all be contextual issues that, if addressed, will go far in building a good patient–helper relationship. The role of educators is to enhance learning but to do so, students need to feel affirmed. Sensitivity of the teacher to stereotyping and verbal or other abuse of students perceived as "different" by their peers can help to counter teasing, bullying, and nonacceptance. Sensitivity to the power dynamics in issues at work (e.g., those identified by Lopez & Ensari, Chapter 7, this volume) helps in communicating a message that this work team (or organization) takes cultural issues seriously.

10. **Few who are privileged necessarily see themselves that way or are sensitive to the power that is implicit in their roles.** Professionals are, almost by definition, privileged in the culture in which they work. They have heavy responsibilities but also are given autonomy and typically are highly rewarded. Professionals may therefore need to push themselves to understand their clients' lives when it comes to their cultural and international backgrounds and to empathize with their clients' plights as they affect the issues for which professional help was sought. The chapters by Cawagas (Chapter 3), Taylor (Chapter 2), Kuba (Chapter 5), and Matriano and Toh (Chapter 10) are all eye-opening accounts of what some others in the world—and in our own communities—struggle with every day.

11. **Exposure to new cultures and populations, both in one's own and other countries, helps.** Traveling to other countries (as Wedding advocates in Chapter 11, this volume), is a powerful way to help people better understand the realities of other cultures and test the generality of one's own. Going not just to wealthy and "safe" countries but also to ones where

the issues of diversity and oppression remain major concerns broadens one's empathy and engagement when working in one's own culture.

CONCLUSION

The integration of international with multicultural can be conceptualized as an advance in understanding cultural issues in professional practice. Evolutionary, not revolutionary, steps are probably needed—a difference more of degree than kind. The book has attempted to show that the traditional categories of multiculturalism can be enhanced by internationalism without sacrificing what matters to multicultural advances that people have worked so hard to achieve.

There is substantial learning to be had in any area of diversity practice by expanding the focus from domestic concerns to include international ones. Most who have made that transition have found that their understanding of multicultural issues in the domestic context has been enhanced. Ultimately, with the rapid internationalization of the world, such concerns are not just nice things to do; instead, they increasingly describe the minimal competencies necessary to be a successful professional.

REFERENCES

Alderfer, C.P. (2011). *The practice of organizational diagnosis: Theory and methods*. New York, NY: Oxford University Press.

American Psychological Association. (2003). Guidelines for multicultural education, training, research, practice, and organizational change for psychologists. *American Psychologist, 58*, 377–402. doi:10.1037/0003-066X.58.5.377

Anderson, C.A., & Huesmann, L.R. (2007). Human aggression: A social cognitive view. In M.A. Hogg & J. Cooper (Eds.), *The Sage handbook of social psychology* (concise student ed., pp. 259–288). Thousand Oaks, CA: Sage.

Bahun-Radunovic, S., & Rajan, V.G.J. (Eds.), *Violence and gender in the globalized world: the intimate and the extimate*. Surrey, England: Ashgate.

Central Intelligence Agency. (2011). *World factbook*. Washington, DC: Author. Retrieved from https://www.cia.gov/library/publications/the-world-factbook

Chan, P. (Ed.). (2010). *Protection of sexual minorities since Stonewall: Progress and stalemate in developed and developing countries*. New York, NY: Routledge/Taylor & Francis.

Devine, P. G. (1989). Prejudice and out-group perception. In A. Tesser (Ed.) *Advanced social psychology* (pp. 467–524). Boston, MA: McGraw-Hill.

Fellmeth, A. (2008). State regulation of sexuality in international human rights law and theory. *William and Mary Law Review, 50,* 797–936.

Fiske, S. T., & Molm, L. D. (2010). Bridging inequality from both sides now. *Social Psychology Quarterly, 73,* 341–346. doi:10.1177/0190272510389007

Gaertner, S. L., & Dovidio, J. F. (2005). Understanding and addressing contemporary racism: From aversive racism to the common ingroup identity model. *Journal of Social Issues, 61,* 615–639. doi:10.1111/j.1540-4560.2005.00424.x

Gaertner, S. L., Dovidio, J. F., Banker, B. S., Rust, M. C., Nier, J. A., Mottola, G. R., & Ward, C. M. (2003). The challenge of aversive racism: Combating pro-White bias. In S. Plous & S. Plous (Eds.), *Understanding prejudice and discrimination* (pp. 491–499). New York, NY: McGraw-Hill.

Pinker, S. (2011). *The better angels of our nature: Why violence has declined.* New York, NY: Viking.

Plant, J. S. (1958). *The envelope: A study of the impact of the world upon the child.* Cambridge, MA: Harvard University Press.

Quinn, K., Macrae, C. N., & Bodenhausen, G. V. (2007). Stereotyping and impression formation: How categorical thinking shapes person perception. In M. A. Hogg & J. Cooper (Eds.), *The Sage handbook of social psychology* (concise student ed., pp. 68–92). Thousand Oaks, CA: Sage.

Racial discrimination and the global economic downturn. (2011). *World of Work, 72,* 9–12.

Subacchi, P. (2008). New power centres and new power brokers: are they shaping a new economic order? *International Affairs, 84,* 485–498. doi:10.1111/j.1468-2346.2008.00719.x

Taborga, C. (2008). Women's economic empowerment: Realities and challenges for the future. *International Social Science Journal, 59,* 27–34. doi:10.1111/j.1468-2451.2009.00675.x

United Nations. (n.d.). *Universal declaration of human rights.* Retrieved from http://www.un.org/en/documents/udhr

Wolf, N. (2011). *The viral storm: The dawn of a new pandemic age.* New York, NY: Times/Henry Holt.

World Bank. (2011). *Data by country. The Philippines.* Washington, DC: Author. Retrieved from http://data.worldbank.org/country/philippines

Wright, S. C., & Taylor, D. M. (2007). The social psychology of cultural diversity: Social stereotyping, prejudice and discrimination. In M. A. Hogg & J. Cooper (Eds.), *The Sage handbook of social psychology* (concise student ed.; pp. 361–387). Thousand Oaks, CA: Sage.

Zakaria, F. (2011). *The post-American world* (2nd ed.). New York, NY: Norton.

INDEX

313

Asian Americans
  cultural congruence of methods
    for, 101
  leadership styles of, 218
  use of community health care
    services by, 231
Asian culture, restraint in, 95
Asian Indians
  cultural values of U.S. migrants and,
    91
  individualism and affluence for, 97
Asian Institute of Management
  (AIM), 174
Asians, use of health care services by
  Asian-Americans vs., 231
Assimilation model, 292
Assumptions
  about clients' values, 309
  in organizational culture, 210
Asylum seekers. See also Refugees
  feelings about home countries, 309
  importance of national identity, 135
  LGBT individuals as, 112, 115, 125
  in New Zealand, 125
  PTSD in, 7
  in South Africa, 125
Aten, J. D., 154, 161
Atheism, 147, 150
"At Home in the World" program, 292
Attitudes
  for competence with LGBT
    individuals, 112–113
  of global team leaders, 192
  for multicultural and international
    competence, 185–189
  for success in study abroad programs,
    296–297
Australia
  diversity in national identity of, 122
  multicultural education in, 259
  oppression of indigenous people,
    265–266
Australian Aboriginal people, 265–266
Authentic global culture, 211–212
Authentic leadership, 209–210
Automatic cognitive–affective
  processes, 9
Autonomy, 99, 211
Avoidance, tolerance through, 151

Awareness. See also Self-awareness
  in MAKS model, 238–239
  state-of-the-planet, 270
  system, 270

Baker, W. E., 95
Banking education, 281
Banks, J. A., 262
Banksy (graffiti artist), 53
BBC (British Broadcasting
  Corporation), 37–38
Becker, James, 270
Behavior
  criminalization of sexual, 116,
    129, 135
  in cross-cultural studies of values, 87
  and identity for LGBT individuals,
    110–111
Behavioral cultural intelligence, 189–190
Beijing Platform of Action, 59
Belief history, client's, 156–158
Beliefs
  in clients' reality, 152–155
  conflicts of, 160
  and gender roles, 145
  organizational, 155–156
  of organizations, 155–156
  as pathology, 154
  resistance to changes in, 163
  treatment of religious experiences
    as, 154
Benefits, for global employees, 184–185
Berkel, L. A., 231
Best-fit practices model for alliances, 206
Betancourt, J. R., 260
Biases
  class, 117–118
  in LGBT-supportive countries, 111
Bilingualism, 293–294
Binder, J., 9
Bisexual individuals. See Lesbian,
  gay, bisexual, and transgender
  (LGBT) individuals
Black men, same-sex behavior by White
  vs., 116
Bond, Michael, 94
Bosnians, gender violence against, 62–63
Bottom of the pyramid (BoP) business
  strategies, 205

Held, D., 11
Hendry, C., 206
Heppner, P. P., 87, 237–238, 245, 246
Heternormativity, 113n1, 121
Heterogeneous cultures, 96–97
Hicks, D., 272
Hierarchy vs. egalitarianism dimension, 99–100
Highly religious clients, working with, 161–162
Hill, Ian, 291–292
Hindrances, assessing clients', 159–160
Hinduism, 153, 163
Hinton, K. G., 265
Historical frameworks
    for LGBT clients' home nation, 134–135
    for positions on race, 42–45
HIV/AIDS crisis
    in Jamaica, 128
    in South Africa, 125–126
    and treatment LGBT individuals, 120, 125–126, 128–130
    in Zimbabwe, 129–130
Hobbel, N., 292
Hofstede, G., 87, 90, 92–95, 183
Hofstede's model of cultural values, 90, 92–95
Holistic approach to global education, 272–273, 281
Holland, John, 102
Holmberg, I., 204
Homogeneous cultures, 96–97
Homogenization, 207
Homosexuality, criminality of, 127–128.
    See also Lesbian, gay, bisexual, and transgender (LGBT) individuals
Honor crimes, 70–71
Hopelessness, Muslim views of, 157–158
Horvath, L., 192
House, R., 204, 206, 207
Hovland, Kevin, 42, 53
Howard, John, 122
Howard-Hamilton, M. F., 265
Hseih, Vincent, 278
Hui, C. H., 93
Human experience, commonalities in, 298
Humanistic spirituality, 149

Human nature, in Kluckhohn and Strodtbeck's model of cultural values, 89
Human rights
    confronting violations of, 235
    cultural vs., 277
    and female genital mutilation, 69–70
    in global education, 276–277
    and "honor" crimes, 70–71
    in internationalism and multiculturalism, 304–305
    for LGBT individuals, 113–116
Human Rights First, 115, 123
Human Rights Watch, 131
Human trafficking, 64–65
Humility, cultural, 260–261
Hurley, E., 243, 308
Hussein, Saddam, 41
Hypodescent, 50

IASSW (International Association of Schools of Social Work), 236
Idealization, of less oppressive environments, 309
Identity(-ies). See also Multiple identities
    and behavior, 110–111
    common ingroup identity model, 181–182
    gender and sexual, 116–118
    in global education, 263–265
    in global teams, 192
    intersectionality of, 193
    of LGBT individuals, 110–111, 116–119, 122
    in multicultural education, 263–268
    in multiculturalism, 10–11
    national, 50–51, 122, 135
    of organizational members, 217
    race in construction of, 47–49
    religious, 118–119, 144
    social identity theory, 182–183
    superordinate, 181–182
Ideology, secularism in, 147
Idiocentrism–allocentrism model, 96
Idiographic issues, in internationalism and multiculturalism, 308
IFSW (International Federation of Social Workers), 236
"If We Must Die" (Claude McKay), 47

Japanese military
    gender violence by, 61–62
    occupation of Malaysia and
        Philippines, 256, 257
Jefferson, J. L., 157
Jeffreys, E., 116
Jim Crow laws, 51
Johnson, Colin R., 112
Johnson, P., 204
Josephson, A. M., 156
Jubilee Debt Campaign, 75
Judaism, 158. See also Ultra-orthodox
    Jews
Justice
    in critical internationalism, 52
    global, 275–276
    local, 275–276
    social, 73–76
    and unjust discrimination, 19
Justice (General Principle D), 19

Kalibatseva, Z., 101
Kaplan, M., 117
Karabacakoglu, F., 203
Karakas, F., 162
Karau, S. J., 183
Kawahara, D. M., 218
Kelly, Louise, 200, 308
Kenya, male sex workers in, 120
King, A., 60
King, Rodney (beating of), 43
Kirmayer, L. J., 232
Kluckhohn, F. R., 89–92, 183
Kluckhohn and Strodtbeck's model of
    cultural values, 89–92
Knapp, S., 245
Knowledge
    in MAKS model, 238–239
    of mental health professionals
        working with LGBT
        individuals, 112–113
    for multicultural and international
        competence, 185–189
    for success in study abroad programs,
        296–297
Kollman, K., 122
Korea, short-term orientation in, 94
Kosovo, international mental health
    assistance in, 232–233
Kraft Foods, 205

Kuba, Sue A., 306, 307
Kuwait, gender roles in, 145

Labor, feminization of, 74
Language competencies
    as international competencies, 16
    for international/global teams, 191
    from study abroad programs, 293–294
Languages, research on, 297, 298
Laos, medical care during gender
    transition in, 118
Law of Registration of Rectification of
    Sex, 121
Laws
    on discrimination, 5, 304
    Jim Crow, 51
    LGBT-supportive, 123
    miscegenation, 117
    Morality, 114, 127–128
    rape, 131–132
    religious influences on, 145–146
    sodomy, 128–130
Leach, M. M., 20
Leader–follower relationships, 179
Leaders, of global teams, 192
Leadership. See also Global leadership
    effectiveness of Mexican managers,
        218
    as team-level competency, 188
Leadership Worth Following, xiii, xiv
Learning, 190, 281
Lee, Benjamin, 52
Leland, C., 263
Leong, F. T. L., 87, 101, 237–238,
        242, 243
Lesbian, gay, bisexual, and transgender
        (LGBT) individuals, 109–137
    civil rights for, 111–112
    discrimination against, 306–307
    experiences of prejudice for, 120
    family relationships of, 120–121
    identity and behavior for, 110–111
    international human rights for,
        113–116
    knowledge and attitudes for practice
        with, 112–113
    national identity of, 122
    professional practice competencies
        with, 134–136
    religious identities of, 118–119

Men having sex with men (MSM).
    See Lesbian, gay, bisexual, and
    transgender (LGBT) individuals
Mental Health Facilitator Program
    (MHF), 233
Mental health professionals, 227–247
    advocacy for LGBT rights by, 132
    challenges with competencies for,
        246–247
    cultural congruence model for,
        101–102
    cultural issues for American, 7
    DSP model of competencies for,
        240–241
    interactions of clients and, 238
    international assistance from, 232–233
    international competencies for, 87–88
    international movement for, 230–237,
        246–247
    international multiculturalism for, 6
    multicultural competencies for, 261
    multicultural counseling movement
        for, 228–230, 246–247
    multicultural education for, 259
    practice with LGBT individuals,
        112–113, 132–136
    self-awareness of religion, spirituality,
        and secularism for, 150–156
    training for, 241–246
Mestizaje, 54
Metacognitive cultural intelligence, 189
Mexican-Americans, 121, 231
Mexicans
    civil rights for LGBT, 110
    leadership styles and effectiveness,
        218
    per capita income of, 12
    use of community health care
        services by, 231
MHF (Mental Health Facilitator
    Program), 233
Middle East, mistrust of Americans in,
    41–42. See also specific countries
Midlife organizations, global culture for,
    216–217
Migrant workers
    competencies for professionals
        dealing with, 76–77
    female, 74–76
    human rights issues for, 277

Migration
    by LGBT individuals, 112, 135
    and multicultural education, 259
Militarization, direct violence and,
    60–66
Military personnel
    gender violence by, 60–63
    multiculturalism training for, 18
Mindfulness techniques, 163
Minorities
    multicultural education as concern
        for, 263
    protection of, 125
    use of mental health services, 229
Miovic, M., 154
Miscegenation laws, 117
Miscellaneous Offences Act
    (Zimbabwe), 130
Missions, of teams, 182
MNEs (multinational enterprises),
    205–206
Model Rules of Professional Conduct
    (American Bar Association), 20
Modernization, 65, 73
Money boys, 136
Monge, P. R., 202
Monoculturalism, 292
Moral compassion, in spirituality, 149
Morality Laws, 114, 127–128
Moral values, religious/spiritual
    community and, 159–160
Motivation, awareness, knowledge, and
    skills (MAKS) model, 238–239
MSM (men having sex with men).
    See Lesbian, gay, bisexual, and
    transgender (LGBT) individuals
Multicultural competencies, 22
    for business professionals, 261–262
    case example, 176–185
    commonalities in, 292–293
    definition of multiculturalism,
        175–176
    domestic vs. international, 13
    future research in, 193–194
    for individuals, 176, 187, 189
    international vs. domestic, 13
    interpersonal-level, 176, 187, 189–190
    for mental health professionals, 261
    in modern business environment,
        173–175

National Organization for Women, 66
National origin, contextualization of, 84–85
National values, 83–103
  case example, 88–89
  and contextualization of national origin, 84–85
  cultural congruence model for, 100–103
  cultural values as, 86–88
  Hofstede's model, 92–95
  Kluckhohn and Strodtbeck's model, 89–92
  Schwartz's national cultural value theory, 99–100
  studies of, 85–86
  Triandis's cross-cultural model, 95–98
Native Americans, 265–266
Naturalism, 150, 154
Nature spirituality, 149
NBCC-I (National Board of Certified Counselors International), 233
NCADV (National Coalition Against Domestic Violence), 66
Nelson, S. D., 229
Net-in migrators, 13
Net-out migrators, 13
Nevada, immigrant population in, 14
New Jersey, immigrant population in, 14
Newly-formed organizations, global culture for, 216
New Orleans, Louisiana, xii–xiii
New York, immigrant population in, 14
New York University, 290
New Zealand
  as LGBT-supportive nation, 118, 124–125
  oppression of indigenous people in, 265–266
  religious identity of, 118
New Zealand Status Refugee Status Appeal Authority, 124
NGOs. See Nongovernmental organizations
Nilsson, J. E., 231
Nomothetic issues, in internationalism and multiculturalism, 308
Nongovernmental organizations (NGOs)
  alliances of corporations and, 204–206

services from, after Southeast Asian tsunami, 233
Non-Western nations, multiculturalism–internationalism in, 306–307. See also specific countries
North, The
  defined, 60
  inner peace in global education for, 280
  multiculturalism–internationalism in "South" vs., 306–307
  social justice in, 73
North American Free Trade Agreement (NAFTA), 44
Norton, R., 114

Ogbonna, E., 91
Okal, J., 120
Okin, S. M., 68, 69
Oklahoma, diversity in, xi, xii
One-drop rule, 50
Ontario Consultants on Religious Tolerance, 70
Openness to experience, 185, 188
Oppression
  confrontation of, 235
  in developing nations, 306
  of indigenous people, 265–266
  in internationalism, 304–305, 307–308
  international vs. multicultural movement on, 234
  in multicultural education, 262, 265–266
  in multiculturalism, 304–305
  in Palestine, 52
Organizational beliefs, 155–156
Organizational culture. See Culture (organizational)
Organizational diversity, 204–206
Organizational structure, of religions, 158
Organizations, 199–220
  cultural challenges in global organizations, 206–207
  developmental stages of, 216–217
  facilitating global culture at, 208–212
  globalization for, 173, 200–201

Resilience, 134
Resolution on Culture and Gender
 Awareness in International
 Psychology (APA), 236
Respect
 in global education, 278–279
 in RRICC guide, 163
 and success in working and studying
 abroad, 297
RESPECT (Rights, Equality, Solidarity,
 Power, Europe, Co-operation
 Today), 75
Respect, in pluralism model, 292
Respect for People's Rights and Dignity
 (General Principle E, APA Ethics
 Code), 19
Responsibility, in RRICC guide, 163
Responsible corporate citizenship, 219
Responsible global leadership, 208
Rest and recreation (R&R) centers, 63
Restraint, 95
RFA (Rain Forest Alliance), 205–206
Richmond, V. P., 206, 207
Rights, Equality, Solidarity, Power,
 Europe, Co-operation Today
 (RESPECT), 75
Rokeach Value Survey, 94
Role congruity theory of prejudice, 183
Rowlands, J., 77
R&R (rest and recreation) centers, 63
RRICC guide for religious sensitivity, 163
Rural areas, experiences of LGBT
 individuals in, 112, 133

The sacred, in spirituality, 148–149
Sa'id, Edward, 48–49
Saldivar, Vanessa, 54
Same-sex marriage
 in Canada, 124
 in South Africa, 126
 in Spain, 118
 and working in LGBT-supportive
 countries, 114
San Diego County, California, 3–4
Saunders, S. M., 160
Schein, E., 209, 211, 218
Schmidt, P. L., 202
Schmidt, W. V., 207
Schrimshaw, E. W., 120
Schwartz, Shalom, 90, 99–100

Scientific medical model, 152–153
Second Intifada, 36
Secularism
 in attainment of client goals, 162–164
 and collaboration with clients'
 friends and family, 164–165
 defined, 149–150
 in development of professional
 relationships, 156–162
 influences of, 146–147
 professionals' self-awareness of,
 150–156
Selby, D., 272
Selective approach to international
 competency training, 242
Self-actualization, 164
Self-awareness
 cultural, 189
 global, 191
 as individual competency, 185
 of religion, spirituality, or secularism,
 150–156
Self-esteem, 182–183
Self-expression, for LGBT individuals,
 137
Self-fulfilling prophecy phenomenon, 179
Self-management, 185
Self-reflection, 164
Self-reflexivity, 202
Self-sufficiency, in secularism, 150
Sensitivity, to diversity, 308–309
September 11 terrorist attacks, 258,
 274–275
Sequential interdependence, 181
Servant leadership, 212
Sex, defined, 58
Sex industry, 65, 120, 128
Sex tourism, 63–64, 67
Sexual acts, venue for, 120
Sexual identities, of LGBT individuals,
 116–118
Sexual orientation. See Lesbian,
 gay, bisexual, and transgender
 (LGBT) individuals
Sexual satisfaction, relationship factors
 and, 133–134
Sexual violence, 67
Shapiro, A., 275
Shome, R., 6–7
Short-term orientation, 94–95

Siegel, K., 120
Silent March, 46–47
Simpson, O. J. (trial of), 43–44
Singer, M. C., 117
Singh, A. K., 111
Singhal, M., 155
Skills
    in MAKS model, 238–239
    for multicultural and international
        competence, 185–189
Small- to medium-sized enterprises
        (SMEs), 206
Social contact hypothesis, 9
Social identity theory, 182–183
Social issues, comparative aspects in,
        52–53
Social justice, 73–76
Social norms, 96–97
Social relations, 91
Social services, 67, 75
Social work, 234, 236, 244
Society, integrated, 305–306
Sociocultural systems, of international
        clients, 238, 245
Sociopolitics, secular influences in, 147
Sodomy, definitions of, 126, 131
Sodomy laws, 128–130
Soft universalism, 245
Solidarity, in pluralism model, 292
Song, Sarah, 69
South, The
    access to education in, 76
    defined, 60
    gap between rich and poor in, 276
    multiculturalism–internationalism in
        the North vs., 306–307
    social justice in, 73
South Africa
    civil rights for LGBT individuals in,
        109–110
    discrimination and harassment of
        LGBT individuals in, 119, 120
    as LGBT-supportive nation, 125–126
    race and view of same-sex behavior
        in, 116
    welfare of children in, 120–121
Southeast Asia, gender transition in, 118
Southeast Asian tsunami (2004), 233
Soviet Union (former), trafficking in
        women and girls from, 64–65

Spain
    civil marriages in, 118
    family relationships in, 121
    religious identity in, 118
    rights for LGBT individuals in, 110,
        121
Spanish language, prevalence of, 293
Sparrow, P. R., 206
Spiritual communities, benefits of,
        159–160
Spiritual experiences, dimensions of, 149
Spirituality
    in attainment of client goals, 162–164
    and collaboration with clients'
        friends and family, 164–165
    defined, 148–149
    in development of professional
        relationships, 156–162
    humanistic, 149
    influence of, 144–146
    nature, 149
    in organizational beliefs, 155
    and organized religion, 154
    professionals' self-awareness of,
        150–156
    religious, 149
Spiritual leaders, collaboration with,
        164–165
Sri Lanka, religious and secular law in,
        146
Stage, C. W., 211
Starbucks, 84, 205
State-of-the-planet awareness, 270
Stereotypes
    based on national origin, 84
    and country-level operationalization
        of culture, 87
    in multicultural teams, 183
    of Muslim women, 68
    and prejudice, 8, 304–305
Stoddard, E. W., 45
Strauss, A. L., 132
Strodtbeck, F. L., 89–92, 183
Structural partnerships, for global
        integration, 192
Structural violence
    competencies for challenging
        gender-based, 76–78
    gender-based, 73
    in global education, 276

Turkey
    civil rights and family values in, 121
    cultural values in, 91
    feminine culture of, 94
Turner-Essel, L., 243
"Two-spirited" people, 124

"Ugly American" image, 296
Ultra-orthodox Jews
    collaboration with, 164–165
    gender-match issues for, 163
ultra-orthodox Jews
    views of illness and health by, 153
U.N. See United Nations
Uncertainty avoidance, 94
Underdevelopment, social justice
        and, 73
Understanding
    of culture from study abroad
            programs, 294–296
    in global education, 278–279
    in global teams, 192
    and interpersonal intelligence, 188
UNESCO (United Nations
        Educational, Scientific and
        Cultural Organization), 296
United Arab Emirates, immigration
        in, 13
United Kingdom. See also Great Britain
    civil rights and family values in, 121
    global education in, 272
    multicultural education in, 259
    short-term orientation in, 94
United Nations (U.N.), 236, 304
United Nations Alliance of
        Civilisations, 261–262
United Nations Educational, Scientific
        and Cultural Organization
        (UNESCO), 296
United Nations General Assembly joint
        statement on LGBT rights, 115,
        123, 125
United Nations Global Compact Office,
        261–262
United Nations International Days, 273
United Nations International Research
        and Training Institute for the
        Advancement of Women
        (INSTRAW), 58–59

United States
    approaches to diversity in, 53–54
    civil rights for LGBT individuals
            in, 110
    cultural complexity of, 96
    cultural congruence model in, 100
    cultural issues for LGBT individuals,
            117
    cultural values of, 91
    diversity in, 53–54
    domestic multiculturalism in, 44–45
    effectiveness of leaders in, 212
    family and civil rights for LGBT
            individuals in, 135
    foreign-born clients of mental health
            services in, 227–228
    foreign citizens' knowledge of,
            294–295
    foreign policy vs. ideals of, 40–41
    gender violence by military personnel
            of, 63
    immigration in, 13–14
    internationalism in, 12
    international movement in, 230–237
    international training opportunities
            in, 242–244
    migrant communities in, 112
    multicultural counseling movement
            in, 228–230
    multicultural education in, 259
    multiculturalism in, 5–6
    national identity of, 122
    oppression of indigenous people in,
            265–266
    racial issues in, 42–44
    religion and spirituality in, 144, 146
    tolerance through avoidance in,
            151–152
    uncertainty avoidance in, 94
    well-being and religiosity in, 160
    working with internationals in,
            13–17
Universal Declaration of Human Rights
        (United Nations), 304
Universities
    guidelines on multiculturalism from,
            20–22
    use of counseling services by
            international students, 231
Unjust discrimination, 19

Urban areas, experiences of LGBT
   individuals, 112, 133
Utopian perspective, on globalization,
   201–202

Values
   assumptions about clients', 309
   cultural, 86–88, 295
   moral, 159–160
   national. See National values
   in organizational culture, 210
   pluralistic frame for, 190
   for success in study abroad programs,
      296–297
   Western, 20, 45–46, 208–209
VandeCreek, L., 245
Vasconcelos, A. F., 155
VEA Technologies, 215–216
Verma, R., 111
Victorian morality, treatment of LGBT
   individuals and, 129–131
Vietnam war, gender violence during, 63
Violence
   direct, 60–66
   domestic, 66, 67, 133
   gender-based, 60–67, 76–78
   and militarization, 60–66
   physical, 66–67
   sexual, 67
   structural, 73, 76–78, 276
Virtual collaborations, 177–179, 184
Volpp, L., 71

Waehler, C., 243
Walby, S., 133
Walmart, 84
Wang, Ping, 213–215
War
   culture of, 60–61, 274
   gender violence during, 61–63
WCCI. See World Council for
   Curriculum and Instruction
Webster University, 290
Well-being, religiosity and, 160
Wessells, M. G., 232

West Bank, barrier along, 37–38, 53
Western societies
   in liberal paradigm of multicultural
      education, 262–263
   multiculturalism in, 256
   restraint in, 95
Western values
   exporting, 45–46, 208–209
   and global leadership, 208–209
   in multicultural guidelines of
      professional organizations, 20
West Indian immigrants, 232
West Pakistan, gender violence in, 62
White men, same-sex behavior vs. by
   Black men., 116
Whiteness, in multicultural education,
   263
White rule, in Zimbabwe, 130
Whitley, J. E., 118–119
Whitley, R., 232
Willox, L., 151
Wittes, Tamara Coffman, 41
Witztum, E., 162
Woldu, H., 91
Women. See also Gender
   marginalization of, 58
   stereotypes about, 183
Women's rights, 307
Working abroad, 17–18, 232–233,
   290–291
World Council for Curriculum and
   Instruction (WCCI), 256, 268,
   269, 278–279
World War II, 61–62, 256–258
Worthington, E. L., 149, 154

Yeganeh, H., 91
Yogyakarta Principles, 115
Yoruba people, views of health and
   illness by, 153
Yugoslavia, gender violence in, 62–63

Zimbabwe, LGBT-opposing policies in,
   129–130

ABOUT THE EDITOR

Rodney L. Lowman, PhD, is currently a distinguished professor in the California School of Professional Psychology and is past dean, provost/ vice president of academic affairs and acting president of Alliant International University. His ancestry mirrors the theme of this book, as his paternal grandmother moved to Indian Territory in a covered wagon and his maternal grandparents were from Canada and Spanish Honduras, Central America.

The author or editor of nine books and monographs, Dr. Lowman has published more than 100 scholarly publications and made hundreds of professional presentations all over the world. Besides the present book, his works include *Handbook of Organizational Consulting Psychology*; *The Ethical Practice of Psychology in Organizations* (2nd ed.); *The Clinical Practice of Career Assessment: Interests, Abilities, and Personality*; *Counseling and Psychotherapy of Work Dysfunctions*; and *Pre-Employment Screening: A Guide to Professional Practice*. He currently serves as editor of *Consulting Psychology Journal: Practice and Research*, the flagship journal in the field of consulting psychology, and was founding editor of *The Psychologist-Manager Journal*. He has also served on the editorial boards of other journals and has lectured widely both in the United States and abroad on professional ethics, consulting psychology, and counseling and psychotherapy of work dysfunctions.

Dr. Lowman is a Fellow of the American Psychological Association (APA), Divisions 12 (Clinical Psychology), 13 (Consulting Psychology), and 14 (Industrial and Organizational Psychology), and he is a Diplomate of the American Board of Assessment Psychology. He also serves on the Advisory Board and heads the Scientific Advisory Board of Leadership Worth Following, a Dallas-based consulting firm. He is past president of the Society for Consulting Psychology and for the Society for Psychologists in Management and has held many leadership roles in the American Psychological Association. Currently Dr. Lowman serves as research domain leader and has served as elected APA council representative for the Society of Consulting Psychology, and, beginning in 2013, for the Society of Industrial and Organizational Psychology. Dr. Lowman has received many honors and recognitions for his professional work, including the Kilburg Service Award from the Society of Psychologists in Management, the Service Award from the Society for Consulting Psychology, and the International-Multicultural Provost's Pillar Award from Alliant International University.

Dr. Lowman is president of Lowman and Richardson/Consulting Psychologists, PC and is licensed as a psychologist in California. He currently resides in San Diego, with his spouse, a clinical psychologist and mental health administrator. Their daughter is a writer and entrepreneur who lives in Boston.